THE ART OF

PLAY PRODUCTION

PLAYS AND PLAYWRIGHTS SERIES

Edited by Arthur Hobson Quinn

A complete survey of the English Drama, with books of selected plays to accompany the compact but authoritative accounts of the drama.

ELIZABETHAN PLAYWRIGHTS
Felix E. Schelling
TYPICAL ELIZABETHAN PLAYS
Felix E. Schelling

MODERN ENGLISH PLAYWRIGHTS
John W. Cunliffe

THE ART OF PLAY PRODUCTION
John Dolman, Jr.

The following volumes are in preparation:

ENGLISH PLAYWRIGHTS, 1660-1820
Arthur E. Morgan
TYPICAL ENGLISH PLAYS, 1660-1820
Arthur E. Morgan

MODERN ENGLISH PLAYS
John W. Cunliffe

MODERN CONTINENTAL PLAYWRIGHTS
Frank W. Chandler
MODERN CONTINENTAL PLAYS
S. M. Tucker

THE ART OF PLAYWRITING
Walter Prichard Eaton

(Other volumes to be arranged for)

Harper & Brothers, Publishers

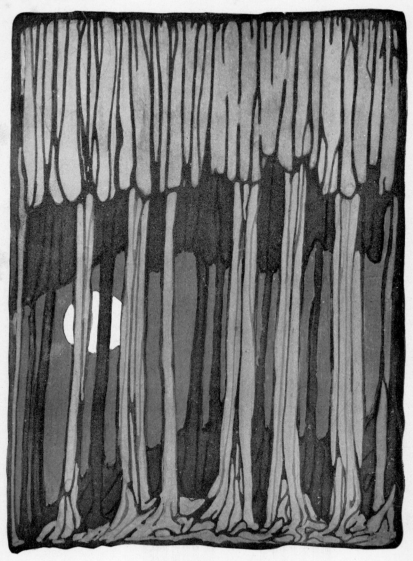

DECORATIVE SYMBOLISM

Design by the late Mr. Guernsey Moore for a woodland setting consisting of draperies and a back drop. The sky is dark blue; the tree trunks are in two shades of olive gray, and the foliage above in two shades of dark green. (See Chapter XVIII.)

THE ART OF
PLAY PRODUCTION

BY

JOHN DOLMAN, Jr.

Professor of English in the University of Pennsylvania

HARPER & BROTHERS PUBLISHERS
New York and London

THE ART OF PLAY PRODUCTION
COPYRIGHT, 1928, BY HARPER & BROTHERS
PRINTED IN THE UNITED STATES
FOURTH PRINTING
F-E

▼

TO MY MOTHER

WHO WAS BORN TO THE THEATRE,
AND WHOSE KNOWLEDGE OF STAGE
TRADITION AND STAGE TECHNIQUE
WAS THE FIRST SOURCE OF THIS
BOOK

CONTENTS

CONTENTS

viii

CONTENTS

ILLUSTRATIONS

ILLUSTRATIONS

PREFACE

THIS book is for the beginner, but not for the dabbler. It does not presuppose any previous experience in play production, but it does presuppose a realization on the part of the reader that the art of play production is not to be learned in a day—that it is, in fact, a lifetime study, to be approached with humility and patience.

There is a notion abroad that whenever two or three are gathered together for any purpose, it is appropriate to produce a play; and that anybody can produce one if only somebody else will tell him briefly and in words of one syllable exactly how to do it. With this universal dramatic urge I have the deepest sympathy, but those who would begin the study in a hurried and casual way have already been supplied with the kind of predigested information they need. So many books exist for that purpose that another would be inexcusable.

This book is addressed, rather, to the ambitious amateur who is seeking to build up a permanent and artistic producing group; to the student with professional aims who wishes to make a broad practical approach to the study of the theatre before plunging into specialization; to the student in the liberal arts who wishes to balance his study of dramatic literature and playwriting by an additional approach from the standpoint of the director; and to the teacher in college, secondary, or primary school, who is called upon to produce plays. It is addressed to the amateur, not the professional, because the professional presumably knows his business already; but there is no implication that amateur production is properly inferior to, or essentially different from, professional production.

It has been my aim to offer a great deal of practical information, and I believe that as much will be found in the following pages as in any book on the subject. But I have tried also to interpret the information in terms of artistic principles—to give reasons as well as advice. In order that the principles and reasons may be made clear in relation to the practice I have found it necessary to outline them first, and for that reason the introductory chapters will seem a trifle abstract. The reader who is seeking condensed information rather than understanding will find Chapters V, VII, VIII, XII, XIII, XVI, and XIX of most immediate interest; but the more abstract chapters will have equal practical usefulness for the reader who wishes to know how to think and do for himself.

Most books on play production give the major portion of their space to the problems of play mounting and stagecraft. It seems to me that those of acting and directing are rather more important, and have been unduly neglected, and so I have given them greater space. I have confined the discussion of scenic art and stagecraft to the last three chapters, beginning with a brief survey of the most fundamental motives to be found in the history of scenic art, continuing with an evaluation of modern movements in scenic art in terms of those motives, and ending with an attempt to suggest the best methods in stagecraft for amateurs, again in terms of artistic motives.

It is a pleasure to acknowledge the many helpful criticisms and suggestions contributed by my friends and colleagues. My thanks are due especially to Professor Reese James for a detailed criticism of the first fourteen chapters; to Professor Percy Van Dyke Shelly for a thorough overhauling

CHAPTER I

INTRODUCTION

THE theatre of today embraces so many forms of activity that an exact definition of the director's problem is hardly possible. There are many different kinds of plays and many different methods of producing them; there are operas, pantomimes, musical comedies, revues, ballets, and minstrel shows, all of which belong to the theatre in its broadest sense, and all of which involve direction of some sort; and then there is that wonderful new art of the theatre—the "theatre of tomorrow"—which is to throw off the shackles of literature and of outworn stage tradition, to liberate the soul of the theatre, shame the realist, abolish the actor, and perhaps the play, and leave the artist of the theatre free to express himself in the abstractions of line, mass, color, movement, light, rhythm, and übermarionettes; appealing directly to the soul of the observer through the senses and emotions without interference from that baser organ, the brain! In this theatre the director will of course be supreme, being the only person of importance left.

THE DIRECTOR AS ARTIST

In the art of the drama proper it is the author who supplies the principal idea, determines the purpose, and functions in general as the original creative artist. But it is very generally agreed that a play is not a play until it is realized upon the stage, however important it may be as pure literature. From the standpoint of the theatre the written or

1

printed text is merely a set of instructions telling the director, the actors, and the technical staff how to go about the task of giving life to the play. The art of the theatre is not an individual art; it is essentially a group art, in which the author, the director, the scenic artist, the actors, the musicians, the stage crew, and even the audience all contribute to a common creative effort. It is the director, therefore, rather than the author, who is responsible for the finished product. The author, even when he is his own director, can hardly foresee all the conditions and problems that may arise in the course of production. What he does as author is suggestive, but not necessarily conclusive, and it remains for the whole group, working under the director's guidance, to carry the creative effort to its full realization.

In this sense, then, the director is as much a creative artist as the author himself, and must share the author's creative attitude. No amount of technical knowledge or facile craftsmanship will take the place of a true grasp of the author's purpose. Not infrequently a new play is half re-written at rehearsals, and even though the director may do none of the actual re-writing it is often his feeling for the play as a whole that serves to bring out the need of revision and to suggest the manner. No director can be expected to make a good play out of an idea that is in its inception hopelessly bad, but he can be, and often is, expected to make a finished play out of a very rough and unfinished text. Often, too, he is expected to take a play that was written for other times and conditions, and adapt it for a new type of production and a new audience. If not a dramatist he must at least be a competent "play doctor."

From the creative point of view it becomes evident that the first business of the stage director is to understand the nature and purpose of the drama as an art; and to understand this clearly he must know something of the fine arts in general —especially of their purpose.

THE NATURE OF THE FINE ARTS

The fine arts may be described as those activities which exist primarily for the purpose of giving æsthetic pleasure— that is, pleasure dependent upon the appreciation of beauty. There are, of course, many different notions as to what constitutes beauty; one person may find his conception of it in a vivid sunset, another in a tragic poem, and another in a particularly smooth-running gasoline engine. Some enjoy beauty only in connection with utility; others prefer it alone and for its own sake. But the power to appreciate some sort of beauty is almost universal; hence the wide appeal of the fine arts, and the wide variety of different arts to satisfy different natures.

For a proper understanding of the fine arts, then, one must keep in mind their common æsthetic purpose. But that alone is not enough. One must also be able to discern, through all the variations of subject matter, method, and technique, a single common principle governing the relationship of art to life: the principle of conventionalization. The fine arts, despite their differences, are all alike in that they offer us, not life itself, but a representation of life in terms of artistic conventions. Perhaps representation is too narrow a word; some artists insist that art should be a presentation rather than a representation; others that it should be a reading or interpretation of life, or a criticism of life, or a direct expression of the artist's thought or feeling. It is not necessary to settle this question, nor to insist upon an exact definition of the term convention. Obviously the conventions are different for different arts, both in kind and degree. It is,

3

however, the principle of conventionalization that distinguishes art from reality.

Thus the fine art of painting aims to give æsthetic pleasure by representing or expressing life through the convention of line, mass, and color on a flat surface; there is no actual movement, and no actual depth, though both, of course, are suggested. The fine art of sculpture leaves out color, or reduces it to a conventional monotone, and leaves out movement also, but retains depth. Photography ordinarily leaves out color, depth and movement, but is so accurate in other respects that the artistic photographer usually finds it necessary to use some screening or de-focussing process to eliminate unessential detail. With brush or crayon it is hard to imitate nature accurately, but with the camera the difficulty is to avoid being *too* natural. It is significant that whenever artistic representation becomes too natural it ceases to be artistic. Thus we find that natural color photography has not proved popular as a fine art. It is very useful for giving us a truer vision of unfamiliar beautiful things, as in the *National Geographic Magazine* or the scenic motion picture, but it is not in itself an effective means of creating beauty artistically. It is too much like life. So, as a rule, is colored statuary, especially when the coloring is natural and the statue life size. In the imitation of reality there must always be some element of *un*reality—not untruth, but unworldliness or unfamiliarity—or the result, no matter how beautiful as life, does not appeal to us as art.

It will be noted that all of the arts mentioned conventionalize by retaining some of the elements of life as naturally as possible and boldly rejecting others as unessential. Their technique is based upon the simple principle of *selection*. The art of literature in general, and the art of the drama as generally understood, belong in the same class.

4

INTRODUCTION

ABSTRACTION IN THE FINE ARTS

Some arts, however, go farther in the direction of conventionalization; they reject all of the concrete elements of life itself, and translate the thought or feeling into a language of abstractions—of pure form. Music, the most popular and universal of all the arts, is one of these. It expresses moods or feelings in terms of musical tones and rhythms, abstract things that have no specific or rational meaning in themselves but gain their effects directly through their power to stir up emotions. We accept and enjoy this convention because our senses tell us that it is a beautiful one; because it enables us to assume an æsthetic attitude; and the more accustomed we become to such abstraction the more we resent any attempt to re-rationalize music by injecting elements of the concrete. So-called "descriptive music" is quite generally displeasing to persons of cultivated taste, except perhaps when it is frankly humorous, or associated with child's play, as in the case of the *Children's Symphony* of Haydn. We are slow to accept a new form of abstraction in art, but when we have grown used to one and found it beautiful and satisfying we do not care to have it violated.

Of late years there has been a marked tendency in some quarters toward a greater degree of abstraction in all the fine arts. Cubism in painting, futurism in music and poetry, and expressionism in the theatre are theoretically examples of this—though in all these, as in other radical reforms, the principles involved have been much beclouded by opportunists seeking easy notoriety and by insane adherents seeking to satisfy their craving for the abnormal. An exhaustive discussion of abstraction in art would be out of place in this book; but the existence of the tendency cannot be ignored by anyone who would understand modern stage directing. There

5

is a great deal to be said for the enrichment of our opportunities to enjoy beauty in its more abstract forms; but one can have little sympathy with those extremists who would abolish all art not highly abstract. It is true that many of our finest æsthetic feelings spring from such arts as music and the dance; but there is no need on that account to abolish representational painting, or the classic realistic novel, or the drama. These things give pleasure too. If new and beautiful abstractions can be found in connection with the art of the theatre through which real messages of the spirit can be artistically conveyed, let us have them by all means. But let us also cherish the art of the drama proper—an art that is in some respects more concrete than any other because it retains actual life, speech and movement, as well as color and form; but that is second only to music in the permanency and universality of its appeal.

THE NATURE OF THE SENSE OF BEAUTY

The sense of beauty, universal as it is, has long been a puzzle to mankind, and after two or three thousand years of discussion we do not seem able to agree upon an explanation.

The ancients thought of beauty almost exclusively in connection with the fine arts, making very little mention of the beauties of nature as such. Yet with apparent inconsistency many of them emphasized the element of imitation in the fine arts, alleging that beauty lay in the subject matter imitated, and that the measure of the artist's achievement was his ability to reproduce beautiful subject matter accurately. Some even went so far as to maintain that there could be no beauty, no æsthetic pleasure, in the artistic representation of what was not in itself beautiful.

Plato and Aristotle were among the first to modify this

6

idea, Aristotle recognizing that under some conditions the representation of actual ugliness might give æsthetic pleasure. Neither, however, was fully able to explain the phenomenon. Aristotle seemed to think that admiration of the skill with which the imitation was accomplished was the source of the pleasure, a theory that has found much support in modern times among certain schools of realists. He also developed the well known "theory of catharsis," the theory of beauty in tragedy based upon the idea of a cleansing or purging of the spirit of the observer. Plato tried to explain beauty by emphasizing the pleasure to be drawn from unity in variety. This became, and still is, one of the leading thoughts in æsthetic philosophy, but it explains the method of the fine arts rather than the æsthetic purpose; it will be considered in that connection in a later chapter. The Greeks thought the pleasure of unity a sensuous one, and their insistence upon the idea is partly responsible not only for the widespread exaltation of the unities in later times, especially in France, but also for the common notion that all art is sensuous.

Modern writers in general have ridiculed the idea that imitation or representation is the key to beauty. They have pointed out that if this were so there would be no excuse for art at all, since the beautiful object in nature would always be more beautiful than any possible imitation of it; whereas it is well known that we often take more pleasure in the representation than in the reality. They have pointed out also, following Aristotle, that we often take the very greatest pleasure in the representation of the tragic—of that which, in the reality, would give us the greatest pain. In other words they have denied that æsthetic pleasure in the fine arts is based *either* upon the intrinsic beauty of the object imitated or upon the fidelity of the imitation.

But that is about all they agree upon. When it comes to offering a substitute explanation they differ widely. One says that beauty lies in the symbolism of the imitation; another that it lies in the revelation of the artist's own soul in his interpretation of what he sees; another that it lies in the extent to which the creative impulse is exercised by the observer through his imagination. Some confuse their æsthetic with their ethical theories, and assert that beauty is truth, and truth beauty, or that beauty is approach to goodness or perfection; others adopt a religious point of view, and say that beauty lies in the approach to God. But possibly the largest number, following the Greek idea, believe that the sense of beauty rests on a more or less sensuous appreciation of form.

IS BEAUTY SENSUOUS?

The latter view finds considerable support in the teachings of modern psychology, and appeals especially to those who have started with a philosophical concept and are seeking to justify it on psychological grounds. But it raises a difficulty: If appreciation of beauty is purely a matter of the effect of form on our senses, what about the thought content of so many fine arts—literature and the drama, for instance? Is that merely incidental, and of no consequence? Or if we find pleasure in thought, must we regard that pleasure as non-æsthetic?

There are some who do not hesitate to go so far. Ethel Puffer,[1] for instance, seems to take such a position with respect to the fine arts in general, freely admitting the value of intellectual pleasure, but denying that it is æsthetic. Gordon Craig certainly takes it with respect to the theatre, demand-

[1] *The Psychology of Beauty.*

8

ing such unity of sensuous appeal as the Greeks themselves hardly dreamed of, and lamenting bitterly the intellectual distractions that are always getting in the way.

To complain that this theory would exclude from æsthetic consideration such plays as those of Shaw or Galsworthy would be to invite the criticism that Galsworthy is a moralist anyhow, and Shaw a propagandist. Let us consider, then, not Shaw or Galsworthy, but Shakespeare. Although there is some sensuous appeal in the poetry of Shakespeare, it is not so much beauty of form or sound as beauty of thought that has made him the world's greatest poet; and it is not so much the appeal to the senses through sound and spectacle as the appeal to the understanding through revelation of human character and motive that has made him the world's greatest dramatist. Yet surely the pleasure he gives us is æsthetic in the highest sense. If not, then æsthetic pleasure is too narrow and trivial to bother about, and is not the sole or principal aim of the fine arts—as, indeed, certain critics are now asserting. Some of us prefer to keep the term and make the interpretation broad enough to cover the kinds of pleasure we really do take in the fine arts.

What then is æsthetic pleasure in the broad sense? To formulate any sort of helpful answer we must take into consideration certain elements which play no direct part in ancient philosophy. A few recent writers, combining philosophical thought with scientific investigation, have clarified the problem considerably, and have given us some principles of æsthetic appreciation that are not only of great interest, but of great practical value to the stage director. The most notable contribution of this sort in English has been made by Herbert Sidney Langfeld in his book *The Æsthetic Attitude*, a book which every stage director should read.

THE ART OF PLAY PRODUCTION

THE PSYCHOLOGY OF APPRECIATION

It is quite usual for artists and æsthetes to scoff at psychology—except, perhaps, abnormal psychology—and to insist that art is on a higher plane than science and altogether independent of it. To some extent one must share this view, for too much science breeds self-consciousness and self-consciousness destroys ease and naturalness in art. But there is no profit in ignoring facts, and there are some facts about human behavior which so vitally affect our concept of beauty and our reaction to it that the creative artist cannot escape them. He may ignore them, or he may conform with them unconsciously; he may succeed in his art through blind inspiration. But play production, being a group art, is of necessity a more conscious art than some others. The director's task, being largely that of criticizing and harmonizing the work of others, must be more consciously performed than those of some other artists, and he must thoroughly understand what he is doing.

Psychology is still, of course, an experimental science, and psychologists differ widely in their fundamental explanations of human behavior. Most of them, however, concede the importance of what is called motor response in relation to our emotional sensibilities, including our reaction to beauty. Motor response may be explained very simply in terms made familiar through elementary physiology as taught in the schools. Everybody knows that the human organism is controlled through a nervous system, of which the brain itself is the apex, and that the main portion of the system consists of two sets of nerves: sensory nerves, which report the experiences of the sense organs, and motor nerves, which control the movements of the muscles. Nearly everybody is familiar with what is commonly called "reflex action," whereby certain

10

sense impressions are received and corresponding motor impulses discharged without conscious realization.[1] Some school books assert that this function is carried on by the spinal cord, and some appear to treat it as exceptional. In point of fact it is quite normal; indeed it takes care of most of the impressions we receive. Only a few of the most striking impressions ever reach the brain—or at any rate the consciousness.

It has been suggested that in the matter of location the whole system is relative; that the motor response to a sense impression may originate at any nerve center between the receiving point and the brain itself, depending upon the degree of reaction demanded by the particular impression. If the impression is a trifling one, as when we feel a little dust on the eyelash, the sensory report may travel no farther than the nearest nerve center before finding its natural path of motor discharge—in this case a "wink reflex." There is no demand upon the conscious attention, and only a small part of the organism is involved. If the impression is equally routine, but larger in scope, as when we are crossing a street and see a curb before us, the impression may have to travel a little farther before it can discharge into appropriate motor action, since more distant portions of the body are involved in stepping up a curb than in winking the eye; but unless there is something a little striking or unusual in the experience it is still quite likely to be unconscious and automatic. In walking through a mile of familiar streets one may step up and down a score of curbs, turn corners, and avoid obstructions, without ever being conscious of the sense

---

[1] Some modern psychologists define a reflex as an inherited response, but as the whole question of heredity is still in dispute the definition is of no use to us. I am using the term in the popular meaning of *unconscious* response, though, to be sure, no one has yet successfully defined consciousness.

11

impressions that have made him do these things, or of the motor activities involved in them. Only when an impression is unusual, contrasting, or vivid, does enough of it reach the brain to engage attention; and perhaps even then a part of it finds its way into motor response automatically and in advance of the resulting thought process.

There is nothing new in the mere observation of motor response, nor in the fact that some of it is unconscious. Long before the nervous system itself was discovered men had observed that certain perceptions caused certain muscular reactions; and even the ancients knew that some of these reactions had something to do with the appreciation of beauty. What is comparatively new is the scientific recognition of a general law—simple, but universal—governing the relation of motor response to sense impression.

THE LAW OF MOTOR RESPONSE

The law is this: For every stimulus impressed upon the human organism there is a direct motor response, the nature of which depends upon two factors, (1) the nature of the stimulus, and (2) the nature of the past experience of the organism.

By a stimulus is meant primarily an impression received through one of the senses and conveyed to the brain, or toward the brain, by the sensory nerves; but it may be added that an imagined stimulus is also capable of inducing a motor response.

By a motor response is meant an impulse to activity, carried to the muscles of the body through the motor nerves. When the impulse is strong enough and is not inhibited or suppressed in any way it results in a clearly defined muscular action, and we are all familiar enough with such manifestations. But many of our motor impulses are too feeble to

12

result in any outwardly visible action, and many more are inhibited either consciously or unconsciously by reason of the restraints imposed upon us by civilization and education. That is why the operation of the law so often escapes notice, and why we get into the habit of supposing that perceptions sometimes result merely in thought or feeling, and not in action. What really happens is that every time we see, hear, touch, taste, or smell something we experience almost instantly a corresponding motor response, even though it be limited to a mere "action pattern" or "motor set," imperceptible to the eye. The existence of such a concealed response, when no outward response is discernible, can be proved in the laboratory through the use of delicate instruments which record changes in blood pressure, muscle tensions, and the chemical reactions in the body. It has been claimed that a witness may be detected in a lie by this method; that no matter how skilful he may be in concealing his inner reactions from an ordinary observer he is helpless to prevent the occurrence of automatic responses easily recorded by the proper instruments.

MOTOR ATTITUDES IN ÆSTHETIC APPRECIATION

The observation of a work of art takes place through the senses, particularly those of sight and hearing. According to the law, there must be certain motor responses induced by such observation, and it seems reasonable to suppose that the nature of these responses may have something to do with whether or not we derive pleasure from the observation. As a matter of fact it can be shown that our æsthetic enjoyment is chiefly dependent upon our motor attitudes—is actually felt in terms of those attitudes.

This is a strong statement, and at first glance may seem inconsistent with my previous contention that there is an intellectual as well as a sensuous element in beauty. But it must be remembered that the motor attitudes are dependent upon two factors: the observer's previous preparation and the stimulus itself. It is in the observer's previous preparation that the intellectual element is to be found. Into that preparation enter not only all the sights and sounds that have ever fallen upon his senses, but also all the thoughts and emotions that have resulted from them, either directly or indirectly. Sense stimuli are in themselves meaningless; it is only as they take on meaning in terms of the individual's experience that they become significant. A new-born infant, though his senses function, fails to notice even very obvious sights and sounds. It is not until the child has grown familiar with certain impressions and begun to make associations and draw inferences that he begins to show appreciative response. If beauty were a matter of pure form, without meaning, and appreciation nothing but an automatic effect of form on sense, the youngest infant not blind or deaf would have as keen an appreciation of the fine arts as the most experienced connoisseur. Perhaps he has, but the evidence does not seem to show it. It seems to show rather that the highest æsthetic appreciation must be learned through experience; or in other words that one's power to assume a pleasurable motor attitude toward a work of art must be acquired through familiarity with the stimuli involved, and understanding of their significance in relation to the whole experience of life.

The artist's problem, then, is largely the problem of producing the right motor attitudes in his audience. To do so he must take into consideration both of the governing factors —the nature of the stimuli, and the previous experience of his audience. Since the stimuli with which he is to make his appeal are themselves intelligible to his audience only in terms of previous experience, the two factors cannot be separated, but must be studied together.

For the stage director such a study is especially important, because he cannot escape the responsibility of appealing to his audience as a whole, regardless of their individual differences. A painter or a poet can express himself on canvas or paper with the feeling that the public can take his work or leave it; he expects appreciation from some and not from others, and he knows that the unappreciative ones will not interfere with the others. But the stage director cannot afford to neglect any of his audience, for if he fails to reach some of them their indifference or hostility will soon affect the rest. The painter may concern himself with expression, leaving the matter of *im*pression to accident; the stage director must think in terms of *im*pression. To do so he must understand this matter of response as well as it can be understood.

An exhaustive study of the psychology of response would be impossible here. There are, however, two major principles on the æsthetic side of the study which are of such direct importance to the stage director as to call for special consideration. The first of these is the principle of imitative or "empathic" response as an element of appreciation.

CHAPTER II

THE IMITATIVE IMPULSE

A VERY large number of our motor responses are in some way imitative. Of that we can be sure, though the exact part played by imitation in our behavior, and especially in our learning processes, is another subject of dispute among the psychologists. Children certainly employ imitation in learning, if only to strengthen impressions already received, and most of their play is imitative. If older people seem less imitative than children it is partly because their behavior is more complex and therefore less easily analyzed, and partly because they have learned to suppress many of their motor responses as a matter of good manners. But the impulses are there, and those which are not outwardly visible are often of great importance in relation to artistic appreciation.

If a man with a very peculiar walk passes a group of children at play they are very likely to fall in behind and follow him, imitating his walk and exaggerating it. Perhaps this impulse is not so very far from the basic impulse of acting. But we do not always recognize the fact that older people feel the impulse just as strongly as children, and that they suppress it only because civilization has taught them to do so. They may be unconscious of the impulse, but that is because the lesson of inhibition has been so well learned that it operates instantly, and suppresses the impulse before it gets started.

THE IMITATIVE IMPULSE

THE PRINCIPLE OF EMPATHY

In contemplating an object of beauty we commonly assume an imitative attitude toward it, feeling out the lines of the object in our own bodies. Thus when we behold the ocean or the mountains we involuntarily throw back our shoulders and expand our lungs, seeming to feel in ourselves the vastness and grandeur of the scene. When we watch a ballet dancer in motion we follow out in imagination her every movement, feeling the grace and lightness as if it were our own. When we listen to music we instinctively seek out the rhythm and follow it with bodily pulsations of some sort, even beating time with feet or hands. And when we see a human being in a dangerous or painful position—a steeplejack about to fall from a high building, for instance—we experience much of the sensation of pain or danger in ourselves. When the stimuli are strong and the restraints weak we show these imitative responses in visible action; more often we feel and conceal them; and more often still we experience them only as motor sets, or patterns, and are not even conscious of their nature.

The importance of these imitative motor responses in relation to the sense of beauty has been pointed out by numerous writers,[1] but the most helpful discussion from the standpoint of stage direction is to be found in Langfeld's book, *The Æsthetic Attitude*. Following Titchener he calls such responses "empathic," and the term "empathy," already widely used, seems likely to become the accepted one in English.

Not all empathic response—not even all pleasant empathic response—is æsthetic, but it is probable that all æsthetic

[1] Lipps, Groos, Puffer, Bosanquet, Santayana, and others. The idea is well known in Germany as the *"Einfühlungstheorie"* of Lipps.

17

pleasure is empathic. Obviously we can experience pleasant empathy only in what is itself pleasant; the empathic response to pain cannot be pleasant, since it consists in feeling the pain in our own attitude. This suggests an important limitation of the fine arts which some extreme realists disregard. However, a painful empathy with respect to a part of something may not be inconsistent with a keen enjoyment of the whole—as, for instance, when dissonances are properly employed in music, or when sorrow plays a part in drama. In such cases the unpleasant empathies may serve to season the pleasant ones by contrast, provided, of course, that the pleasant ones dominate; and this has led some philosophers to believe that the highest form of æsthetic enjoyment lies in a balance or harmony of varied empathies. This may be nothing more than a restatement in modern terms of the old Greek theory of unity in variety, but it is a little more concrete, and more susceptible to laboratory test.

One interesting version of the theory [1] is that complete æsthetic pleasure is to be found only in perfect repose; and that such repose is to be found only in a perfect balance of empathic responses, a balance equivalent to neutralization. This theory has the advantage of seeming to explain the well known principles of balance and proportion in design, and is not inconsistent with the rules of harmony in music and the principle of poetic justice in literature. Moreover, it seems to fit in perfectly with another principle of extreme importance, the principle of æsthetic distance—of which more later.

EMPATHY IN THE THEATRE

Empathic responses play an equally vital part in all of the fine arts, but in some arts they are obscure and difficult

[1] See Puffer, *The Psychology of Beauty.*

to study. Just how, for example, does one empathize in a Gothic cathedral? Unquestionably there is an imitative impulse of some sort, possibly a stretching upward in imitation of the vertical lines, but there can be no exact imitation because living muscles cannot take the form of a stone building. The very impossibility of exact imitation limits the response to a motor pattern, even if there are no inhibiting influences. Similarly, in contemplating a landscape, or a piece of furniture, or any inanimate object of beauty, one can but feel the lines, in a rough sort of way; he cannot counterfeit the object as a whole.

But the art of the theatre is in terms of human beings— live ones, moving and speaking and showing emotions; and in these one can empathize more vividly and completely than in any other conceivable medium. Herein, I believe, lies the deep and universal appeal of the theatre: deep, because we can go so much farther in our empathic responses; universal, because all kinds of people can respond to it. To empathize properly in an etching, a beautiful building, or a symphonic poem, one must have had some artistic experience, some training, some cultivation; but anybody can feel an imitative response to a human being, and anybody can take pleasure in it.

Nearly everybody likes to share the experiences of other human beings. That is the gregarious nature of man. Also, nearly everybody nurses certain suppressed longings for human experiences that he has not himself had, and never expects to have, and perhaps in his better judgment does not really want to have. In the theatre he is enabled to satisfy these longings vicariously, without entangling himself in the obligations and embarrassments that may be incidental to the real experience—just as the spectator at a football game feels in his own muscle tensions the thrill of heroic endeavor without actually suffering the hard knocks. This is a large part of the appeal of sport; it is also a large part of the appeal of fiction in literature, and the theatre is the most vivid form of fiction.

This being so, the director can ill afford to ignore or neglect the principle of empathy, and its specific application to the art of the theatre. Bearing in mind the two factors that govern every response—the nature of the stimulus and the nature of the observer's previous preparation—he must ask himself what imitative responses each character, each scene, each piece of action will evoke, and whether they will be pleasant. There are other considerations, of course, but if he can cultivate the ability to foresee empathic effects he will find that many of the most serious problems of play production become easier of solution.

EMPATHY IN CASTING

Many a play has been spoiled by errors in casting, quite apart from the abilities of the actors as actors. The leading lady may be a beautiful and capable actress, yet fail to win the kind of sympathetic interest that is essential to the play. The critics will say that she lacks "personality," or that her personality is not suited to the part. But "personality" is a vague word. It is more accurate to say that she lacks the power of inducing the proper empathic responses in the audience.

Generally speaking the women in the audience empathize most strongly in the heroine, while the men empathize most strongly in the hero. Nothing could be more whole-hearted than the response the women give to an actress who can make them feel the experiences of the heroine imaginatively in their own bodies. This is the secret of Ethel Barrymore's power to attract and move large audiences of women. "When Ethel

Barrymore speaks," a woman once said to me, "all the heart throbs I have ever felt come back to me." Her deep chest tones, her heaving bosom, and her eloquent little gestures seem to grip the women and make them one with the character —no matter how bad the play. I recall seeing the men in the audience convulsed with laughter some years ago at the absurdities of her death scene in a play called *Déclassée*, by Zoë Akins, while the women wept and suffered with an æsthetic exaltation that Bernhardt at her best could hardly have given them. On the other hand the reader will no doubt recall many actresses—beautiful, accomplished, and perhaps pleasing to the men—who have seemed always to leave the women in the audience cold and unresponsive.

Conversely, there are actors who antagonize the men in the audience for no apparent reason; actors who seem capable enough and look their parts, who are popular, perhaps, with the women, but who produce only savage disgust in the men. The photodrama is particularly afflicted with such actors. There is the actor with deep dark eyes and curly hair and the build of a Greek god; the women say: "How handsome he is! What soulful eyes! How well his sport flannels fit him!" But the men are very likely saying: "Good Lord! look how he holds a tennis racket! If I held one that way I'd feel like a fool or a sissy." The trouble is, they *are* feeling it —empathically—and the sensation is painful.

In choosing a cast, therefore, the director should consider two things: the direct effect of each player upon those who are to empathize most strongly in the character he represents, and the indirect effect upon those who are to empathize in some other character set off against him. The actress who is to play a sympathetic part must be able to appeal to the women by making them feel the experiences of the character in their own bodies, and she must be able to fit in properly with the empathic responses which the men are giving to the male characters. In other words, if she is to play the heroine she must be capable of making every woman feel like the heroine herself, and of making every man in the audience fall in love with her vicariously. Every man must feel that it would be no hardship to embrace her; else when the hero does so there will be a revulsion of feeling.

On the other hand, if the actress is to play an unsympathetic part it is just as necessary that she should be capable of inducing an opposite effect. Many will remember Jane Grey's playing of the unfortunate daughter-in-law in Galsworthy's *The Skin Game*. It was a beautiful and moving interpretation, but it almost ruined the play by upsetting its balance; Miss Grey induced a degree of sympathy the character should not have had, and many people missed the message of the play in consequence. It was not her fault; it was a plain case of miscasting through failure to foresee empathic response. On the other hand Eva LeGallienne, ordinarily a sympathetic actress, was able in Molnar's *The Swan* to create just the right atmosphere of coldness,[1] while her leading man, Basil Rathbone, succeeded perfectly in creating the repulsive empathies intended by the author.

The physical characteristics of actors are important empathically, and must be considered in casting—beauty, grace, stature, voice, and the rest. But the imagination is even more important, for it is the actor with a lively and flexible imagination who is most apt to create the proper empathic effects. Of the physical characteristics, voice seems most closely associated with imagination, at least when adequately controlled. Mrs. Fiske insists upon voice as the most important

[1] I have heard several women condemn the play because she was so cold!

concern of the actor, a vehicle of the imagination, but to be considered before it because more susceptible to training and more generally in need of it. It is precisely because of its great empathic power that voice is so significant; and it is not only a vehicle of the imagination but to some extent an index of it. The director choosing a cast must look both for imagination and for the physical means of inducing empathic response, and the voice will tell him much about both.

NATURALISM AND EMPATHY

Despite the attacks of the expressionists most actors strive, by countless little tricks of stage business or pantomime, to create an impression of naturalness. It is largely through empathy that they succeed. When Uncle Josh, in *The Old Homestead*, washes his face in a basin of soapy water and then goes groping blindly for a towel he induces an instantaneous response in those of us who have done likewise. When Abraham Lincoln, in Drinkwater's play, wakes up after sleeping in a chair at Grant's headquarters, the stiffness he feels in his legs is felt empathically by the audience. When a character in a play develops a cold in the head we laugh, but we laugh with a lively sense of the reality of that discomfort. Whenever a little touch of naturalness heightens the illusion it is the empathic response that is at work; we are feeling the reality of the character because he is doing things that, in terms of our past experience, we can easily imagine ourselves as doing.

The function of stage business in general is largely empathic. There are those, of course, who would do away with stage business, especially in poetic drama, on the ground that it is cheapening, and that great beauty of emotion can best be revealed through the play of voice and imagination in speech. Perhaps it can, if the artist is equal to the task—pure reading being undoubtedly a higher and more difficult art than acting. But we are considering acting, and not reading. Too much stage business is, of course, distracting, even in the most realistic drama, and stage business for its own sake is never justifiable. But as a means of creating the proper empathies stage business is not only justifiable but is sometimes more effective than the voice itself, for the reason that it is less difficult to manage. The voice is subtle, even treacherous, and but few actors have it under perfect control; while stage business can be invented by the director and performed by the actor with a certain assurance of accuracy and stability.

The dramatist sometimes feels this, and so plans to have important or significant scenes played in pantomime; and the director can often point up or intensify scenes in this way. Many of Bernhardt's most telling scenes were silent ones, turning perhaps upon a single expressive gesture, rightly chosen to begin with, and then played with absolute precision at every performance—this despite her possession of a truly great voice.

Humorous scenes are often most amusing in pantomime. In *The Professor's Love Story* the whole situation at the beginning of the play is conveyed clearly and entertainingly to the audience, before a single word is spoken, by the professor's behavior as he sits at his desk trying to write. In *The Boomerang*, Arthur Byron, as Dr. Sumner, pictured the difference between a man not in love and a man in love by a difference in pantomime. He did it largely with his feet. In the later scene he walked about with the curious bewildered footsteps of one strongly moved yet highly perplexed by his own emotions; without a line of explanation the audience

24

caught his state of mind perfectly, and laughed at the turn of affairs.

Sometimes it is the significant silence that conveys the big moment of a play, as in the final scene of Tchekoff's *The Cherry Orchard*, when the old servant who has been forgotten and left behind dies all alone; or in the similar (but earlier) scene in Herne's *Shore Acres*. Sometimes silence is more eloquent than voice. To say this is not to deny the power of voice; but if in a silent scene there is no vibrant sympathetic voice to stir the proper emotions, at least there is no poorly controlled, disillusioning voice to interfere with them and make them hollow; and if the director has planned the movements and business effectively and the actor has imagination the empathic response will be strong. It is an unfortunate fact that not one actress in twenty can weep vocally, and be convincing, and that not one in a hundred can laugh convincingly. Yet a false cry or a false laugh is empathically one of the most unpleasant experiences anybody can have in the theatre. Very few directors seem to realize this, or if they do they are at a loss how to correct the trouble. Sometimes it cannot be corrected at all so far as the voice is concerned, but pantomime can often be effectively substituted. An actress whose audible cry would make one's blood run cold can achieve a very satisfactory suggestion of grief by simply turning away from the audience, covering her face, and jerking her shoulder as if she were sobbing.

In general, if the dramatist has done his work well the big scene of a play will have been prepared for, and the empathies of the audience will carry it with but the simplest suggestions from the actors.

It has often been remarked that some actors act only with their voices, or with their faces and hands, while others act with their whole bodies. As a general rule the latter are immeasurably more effective, because they evoke more empathic response. As the pirate in *Captain Applejack*, Wallace Eddinger conveyed the somewhat hollow bravado of the dream more by his walk than by his words; he walked just as you or I would walk if we dreamed ourselves a little braver than we are. As Marie in *Liliom*, Hortense Alden achieved an exit that was a masterpiece; ordered away by the "carrousel woman" she had to go clear across the stage with never a word to say (thus violating the ordinary rules of stage procedure), but she did it with such an impudent expression and such a baffling mixture of shamble and skip that she left the audience literally tingling with her mood. Lenore Ulric, in *Kiki*, was Kiki from the tips of her fingers to the tips of her toes.

There are possibly more actresses than actors who can "act all over"—Mrs. Fiske, Blanche Bates, Ruth Chatterton, Pauline Lord, Katherine Cornell, Winifred Lenihan, Eva LeGallienne, Mary Nash, Jeanne Eagels, and Patricia Collinge, to mention only a few other contemporary ones. The actress has perhaps more need of this faculty than the actor, women being commonly less reserved in movement than men. But there are many stage people of both sexes who fall short of the ideal in coördination of bodily movement, who fail to stir up adequate emphatic response because they do not seem to be feeling things down to their toes; and there are some who, failing to use their extremities expressively, use them distractingly—make all sorts of meaningless and irrelevant movements that stir up no empathies except those of amateur uncertainty and self-consciousness. It should be the aim of every actor to make his whole body responsive to his imagination, and it should be the director's aim to choose actors and actresses who have succeeded in doing so.

THE EMPATHY OF THRILLS

With an understanding of empathic response we are in a position to appreciate the tremendous effect of thrilling situations in the theatre.

The drama is built out of contrasts and conflicts, out of obstacles and dangers and their overcoming. The greater the danger or obstacle, the greater the empathic satisfaction in seeing it overcome. It is the director's business, therefore, to see that the dangers are so presented that the audience will feel them keenly in their own imaginative experiences.

In recent years we have had a deluge of thrilling mystery plays, and the phenomenal popularity of many of these, especially of *The Bat*, has been largely due to the skill with which empathic effects have been handled. Mysterious banging of doors and rattling of chains, hairy arms reaching in through windows or out through panels in the walls, lights going out suddenly, trap doors opening in the floor, threats of vivisection or sudden death—by such means are the audiences made to feel danger through identifying themselves with the imperilled character. In *The Ghost Breaker*, one of the earliest of this series of plays, there was a scene in which the hero, after a fruitless search for the disturbers in a haunted house, stood near a huge suit of armor. Suddenly the latter came to life, and raising a prodigious sword prepared to bring it down on the hero's unsuspecting head. Audience after audience screamed in horror at the scene; they felt that sword descending on their own heads.

It is remarkable what nonsense audiences will accept if the thrill is only made strong enough. Most of the popular thrillers make no pretense of being anything but claptrap, but they play to packed houses, and the audiences scream with expectancy when the lights go out, even before the rise of the curtain. However, equally thrilling effects can be obtained in melodrama of a higher type and greater dramatic sincerity; in William Archer's *The Green Goddess*, for example, the empathies were as powerful as in *The Bat*.

In the photoplay abundant use is made of the empathic thrill, particularly in comedy; in fact the film comedy is largely based upon it, with wild rides on motorcycles, trains, or automobiles, with runaway baby-carriages, narrowly avoided collisions, and dare-devil stunts of all kinds. In Harold Lloyd's early film *High and Dizzy* one experienced with the principal character all the perils of slipping and falling on a narrow ledge some ten stories above the street; and when the window moulding to which he was clinging suddenly gave way one's stomach seemed literally to turn over. It was almost too harrowing as a theatrical experience, but audiences seem to like such things, and there have since been many imitations. The photoplay director has a peculiar opportunity to intensify the empathic sensations by first showing you the character in a precarious position, and then moving the camera to that position and showing you the danger just exactly as the character sees it. This is the strongest possible aid to complete empathy.

All these are extreme cases. Fortunately, not all empathic thrills are quite so harrowing, or theatre-goers would soon become a race of neurotics. There are gentler thrills that are still thrills. One could hardly have watched Holbrook Blinn in *The Bad Man* consuming unbelievable quantities of tobasco sauce without feeling one's own hair stand on end; but the effect was amusing rather than disturbing. When a large gob of ice cream slips down a lady's back in a Charlie Chaplin film one easily shivers, but laughs at the same time.

A favorite situation in comedy is that of embarrassment. Nearly everybody has imagined—or dreamed—how it would feel to be caught out in public inadequately clothed, or to be called upon for a speech when unprepared, or to forget one's lines in an amateur play; and when a character in a story or play gets into a similar situation one feels his experiences keenly. The predicament of the young man in *To The Ladies* who finds his memorized speech preëmpted by another speaker strikes a response in almost everyone; and that of the man who innocently loses his trousers is so universally horrifying that it has been worked to death, especially in the motion pictures.

EMPATHY IN POETIC JUSTICE

One of the most intense empathic effects in the theatre, and one of the most truly dramatic, is that which one feels in the satisfaction of poetic justice. The concept of poetic justice may be an intellectual one, depending upon a nice balance of æsthetic and ethical ideals; but the actual sensation in seeing the concept realized is as physical as that of scratching a mosquito bite, or—better—of killing the mosquito.

When, to take a very simple and obvious case, the villain in a melodrama takes mean advantage of a defenseless female, and for a time goes unpunished, there is gradually built up in the audience an intense itch to see that villain get what is coming to him. That itch much be satisfied, or the play is no play. When it is satisfied—when in the last scene the hero, his patience exhausted, rises in just wrath and smites the villain—the empathic ecstasy is so keen that only a child with his freedom from inhibitions can do justice to it. Pick out a melodramatic photoplay—one with a child hero, if possible, like Jackie Coogan's *Little Robinson Crusoe*— and go to the matinee when the house is full of children. See how quickly and instinctively they identify themselves with the hero, how they hiss and hate the villain, how they groan each time he escapes, how they fall into dismayed silence as he captures the heroine; and then how they burst into frantic cheering as the hero rides to the rescue, and scream with delight as poetic justice is finally achieved. Here is empathy in its simplest but most vigorous form. One may laugh at it for its childish crudity, but no one is likely to make a good stage director who does not realize that the most culti-vated artistic appreciation is a development and refinement of the same thing.

The desire to see the villain vanquished can hardly be separated from the equally cogent desire to see the hero win out. The latter desire is particularly strong when the hero is not merely the protagonist but a heroic or admirable character as well. Hero worship is a powerful element in drama as it is in life, and we all recognize its claim upon us; but we do not always realize that it is largely empathic.

When Sherlock Holmes, in Gillette's play, walks calmly into danger with a quiet reassuring mastery of the situation we enjoy feeling that we are like that ourselves. We are not, of course—most of us, at any rate—but the very fact that he makes us feel a bravery and an efficiency greater than our own accounts for the pleasure he gives us. The small boy perhaps prefers a hero like Tom Mix or Bill Hart (the name of the character does not matter to the small boy), a big, rough, two-fisted, quick-shooting, hard-riding hero who can make the boy feel like a stronger and braver animal. The small girl perhaps prefers Pollyanna. It is the older man with a somewhat studious turn of mind, believing in the mastery of intellect over brute strength, who empathizes best in Sherlock Holmes; and it is the calmness and the masterful intelligence even more than the bravery of the great detective that give such a man his greatest thrill.

There was a remarkably satisfying effect of poetic justice

in a photoplay released some years ago called *One Glorious Day*—one of the best feature comedy films ever turned out, and one that ought to be revived. The story is that of a particularly vigorous and bellicose spirit named Ek, who, escaping from the land of unborn souls, visits the earth ahead of time. Seeking a ready-made body to inhabit he finds that of a certain professor of psychology; it is not just what he is looking for, but it is the only one he can find unoccupied, the professor being just then engaged in a psychic demonstration which requires the presence of his disengaged spirit at a seance some distance away. Ek occupies the body and spends "one glorious day" on earth. The point is that the professor (delightfully played by Will Rogers) is an honest, inoffensive soul, much imposed upon by his neighbors, including a set of grafting politicians who are making him their innocent tool. We are just itching to see the scoundrels get what they deserve—but with little hope because of the professor's mildness and innocence—when Ek takes possession of the body. The transformation is electrifying; the professor (with the soul of Ek) tears into his enemies like the god of wrath. We have been wanting action, and we get it, with a rapidity and thoroughness that make us whoop for joy.

BEAUTY IN THE THEATRE

The empathies of the theatre are varied in the extreme, because the art of the theatre is complex. Many of them are not pleasurable or suggestive of beauty in themselves; the beauty in such cases lies in the effect of the whole, in the harmony and balance of empathies as the conclusion of the drama is reached. But normally it is the pleasant empathic effects which we expect in the theatre, and which give us our sensation of beauty. There is room in the theatre for all the beauties of pure form that belong to painting, sculpture, music, literature, and the dance. The director must study and apply all these. In addition there are empathic effects of great beauty belonging to the theatre in its own right—like the thrill of Bernhardt's acting voice, or the rhythm of the ant scene in *The World We Live In*, or the crescendo of light and music at the end of Act One of *The Miracle*. The best thing about the modern movement in the theatre is that through it we are finding more and larger opportunities for such effects—opportunities to enjoy beauty in the means as well as the end of play production. The danger is only that the means will eclipse the end; that in our enjoyment of form we shall forget all about purpose or meaning.

DETRIMENTAL EMPATHY

Not all empathic responses are helpful to the æsthetic purpose of a play. At the same time that the director is striving to build up the pleasing ones he must be on his guard against unnecessarily displeasing ones, that hinder, or distract, or annoy.

When Romeo climbs a rickety lattice-work in the balcony scene, threatening to pull Juliet and the balcony down on top of him, there is a strong empathic effect, but it is unpleasant, distracting, and ruinous to the play. A few modern producers are to be thanked for sparing their audiences that customary agony. Every piece of flimsy scenery or rickety stage furniture is a possible source of detrimental empathy, especially if an actor must risk his weight on it in some way.

When Hamlet jumps into Ophelia's open grave the effect is nearly always bad. It is traditional for him to do so, and of course one can explain away the difficulty by supposing that there is room enough in the grave for him to stand beside her, but it always looks as if he had jumped right on her stomach! The more one empathizes in Hamlet the more revolting the sensation. Yet actors and directors go right on perpetuating that unpleasant bit of business.

In the Warfield-Belasco production of *The Merchant of Venice* there was a final scene in the moonlit garden at Belmont in which Portia dropped property flowers upon the heads of Lorenzo and Jessica, who lay oblivious to their surroundings in a fond embrace. The flowers fell on Jessica's face with an impact audible all over the house; Jessica, well rehearsed, did not seem to feel them, but the audience did—empathically—and the sensation was anything but pleasing.

A situation that often occurs, especially in stock or amateur production, is that of the hero who is called upon to carry another character on or off stage and is hardly equal to the task. So great is the distracting empathy that some gallery wit is sure to shout "Oof!" and put the house in an uproar. The director should try to choose his cast with foresight in such matters, and to train his actors to simulate ease even when they do not feel it. There is a knack about carrying people, and even a strong actor will seem to labor heavily in carrying a lightly built girl unless the scene has been carefully rehearsed. It may be said in passing that quite as much depends upon the skill of the person carried as upon that of the carrier.

Unpleasant and detrimental empathies may be stirred up by badly placed furniture, unnecessary business, clumsy movements, ill-fitting costumes, excessive make-up, and a thousand and one little things that escape the notice of many directors. If David Belasco knew how to avoid unpleasant empathies as well as he knows how to create dramatic ones his productions would be among the greatest of our time. If D.

W. Griffith and others could realize how many detrimental empathies are evoked by the "close-up" in the photoplay—especially when excessive make-up is employed—they would revise their methods considerably. It is in avoiding detrimental empathies that the director's skill is put to the severest test. The dramatist may foresee and suggest the positive empathic effects that are needed in order to carry the meaning of the play; but he cannot foresee the distracting influences that may arise in the course of rehearsals. Neither can the director foresee them; he must be on the spot during rehearsals in order to check them as they arise.

Examples of empathy, good and bad, could be multiplied indefinitely; but perhaps I have already given more than enough to illustrate the principle. It is the director's problem to apply it. He may learn much about empathic motor responses by observing people and their reactions, by analyzing the most common dreams—for they reveal the experiences, motives and desires of men, their fears and inhibitions—and especially by studying the behavior of children. But in noting these things and in trying to apply them in such manner as to strengthen the pleasurable empathies he must be constantly on his guard lest he destroy another factor essential to æsthetic appreciation—the factor of artistic detachment or, as Langfeld calls it, "æsthetic distance."

CHAPTER III

ARTISTIC DETACHMENT IN THE THEATRE

MOTOR impulses may be roughly classified in two groups, those which are participative, and those which are non-participative. An impulse to dodge an approaching automobile is participative, or an impulse to ward off a blow, or to greet a friend, or to catch a ball, or to hiss the villain in a play, or to shout a warning to the heroine. In a response of this type one feels himself involved with the subject-matter, not merely in imagination but in reality; he is himself a part of the situation to which he is responding. But an impulse to feel out the lines of a painting imitatively, or to beat time to the music of a band, or to applaud good acting, is quite different; the observer experiences a certain attitude of detachment, participating in imagination perhaps, but not in actuality.

It is this attitude of detachment which Langfeld calls "æsthetic distance," and which seems to him essential to the appreciation of beauty. He points out, for example, that one may stand on the deck of a ship enjoying the beauty of a stormy sea just as long as he can feel that it does not concern him personally; but the moment an extra large wave threatens to sweep the deck and engulf him he loses his detachment and with it his æsthetic appreciation. Similarly one may take keen pleasure in watching the beauty of an electrical storm—until the lightning strikes too close. In the contemplation of the fine arts a detached attitude is normal

35

and essential, and every conceivable device is employed by the artist to maintain it. The painter encloses his picture in a frame, that it may be set apart from the reality of its surroundings; the sculptor places his statue on a pedestal for the same reason. Each strives to preserve whatever suggestion of reality is necessary to the truth of his message and to the production of the proper empathic response, but no more. All superfluous elements of reality he tries to eliminate, lest they remind the observer too forcibly of his own affairs, and thus destroy his sense of detachment. For the same reason the illustrator uses a soft pencil or a pen instead of a camera; the dramatic poet makes his characters speak in blank verse; the musician employs abstract sounds. Each, in other words, conventionalizes life in some way, and it seems clear that at least one of the functions of such conventionalization is the preservation of a detached attitude.

In the first chapter it was pointed out that naturally colored photographs and statues are not æsthetically satisfying in the highest sense. This is because, by bringing reality too close, they destroy æsthetic distance. They may give us pleasure of a kind—we may like them for what they represent, or for the skill displayed in their making—but they do not appeal to a cultivated sense of beauty, and sometimes they give positive displeasure. Nothing could be more painful, for example, than the hideously "lifelike" wax figures which are so often used for the display of clothing and millinery in our shop windows. For the most part they are characterless in attitude and feature, yet so natural in physical detail as to suggest nothing less than remarkably well preserved corpses. The best undertakers discovered long ago that a lifelike make-up on a corpse only makes it look more deathlike; but some window-decorators have not yet profited by their experience. Fortunately, however, there are signs of improvement, and quite recently some of the shops have been displaying millinery upon grotesquely comic heads, with sharp angular lines, and crude, though soft, colors—caricatures, of course, but interesting and amusing, and much more artistic than the old wax figures because capable of being viewed with detachment.

THE PLAY INSTINCT

The significance of the detached attitude may be a little clearer, and the conditions under which it is most likely to break down may be better understood, if we think of it in terms of the difference between work and play, between necessity and pleasure.

Two basic traits are universally essential to the survival of any species in any environment: the instinct of self-preservation and the instinct of perpetuation of the species. It happens that the great majority of living creatures are so constituted in relation to their environments that the business of satisfying these two instincts occupies all their time and energy. Even such comparatively high orders of animals as cows and chickens spend most of their waking hours eking out a living, and if they seem at times to do nothing it is probably only because their bodies are fatigued and need rest. They cannot be said to have an actual surplus of time in which to play or to develop their social or spiritual interests.

The luxury of surplus time is given only to a few species, and only in the highest of these does it seem to have resulted in the development of a well marked play instinct. The goldfish has plenty of time on his hands, but he does not appear to do much with it. The dog, on the other hand, learns to play—to romp and gambol, to do all sorts of unnecessary things, and to experience a very obvious pleasure in doing them. His play is no doubt indirectly beneficial—certainly it is not unfavorable to survival, or playful dogs would long since have become extinct—and in that sense it may be only a particularly unconscious manifestation of the instinct to survive. But the point is that the play instinct, from its earliest inception, is based upon leisure time, and upon freedom from any immediate conscious concern about self-preservation.

In its simplest form play is but a pleasant exercise of the body—exercise not inconsistent with bodily health, yet not consciously related to it. But as intellect increases and life grows more complex, there is need for mental exercise as well as physical. At the same time it becomes increasingly difficult to preserve the play attitude, to escape the bitter necessities of existence, because the memory and imagination have been developed, and even though there is plenty of surplus time the worries of life linger in the thoughts. In order to play, man, like any other animal, must have surplus time; but he must also have some means of escaping the pursuing sense of reality. With bodily play this is easy, for the shock of concrete sense impressions demands his attention; and doubtless this is one reason for the great popularity of athletic games. But with mental play man must have something more than an assurance that his life is not immediately at stake; he must have sufficient detachment to take him out of the maze of associated thoughts which are always trying to drag him back into reality. In the most abstract kind of mental play that we know—the fine arts—he must have the highest and most effective sense of detachment possible. In other words he must have a sense of æsthetic distance.

It may well be asked why the term "distance" is used. The meaning is figurative, of course, referring more to an idea than to a physical measurement; yet physical distance, or the suggestion of it, is not infrequently the means of maintaining an attitude of detachment. We often back off from an object in order to view it æsthetically, and sometimes we squint at it and try to see it through a kind of haze. We seldom appreciate the full beauty of a valley until we can view it from a distant hilltop, and we are proverbially indifferent to the beauty that may be found at home. Almost anything beautiful is spoiled for us if we get too close to it, much more so than if we get too far away. There is, of course, no exact distance that is always right; a painting might seem too distant at twenty feet and a mountain too close at a mile. The question is purely relative, the point being that for æsthetic appreciation the distance must be sufficient for the maintenance of a detached attitude.

In one sense, of course, the whole matter of a detached attitude is relative. The attitude of a football player is highly detached by comparison with that of a soldier in battle; but that of a spectator at a football game is detached by comparison with that of the player. The fine arts call for more detachment than any other form of play—for such detachment as is only possible to a highly developed imagination. They call, in other words, for the highest type of play attitude. But because, in attitude, they still belong to play rather than to the business of living, less violence is done to the æsthetic attitude when it slips to a lower form of play than when it slips out of the play attitude altogether and into actuality. That point is worth remembering, for it sometimes marks the difference between crude art and a morbid realism that is not art at all.

ÆSTHETIC DISTANCE IN THE THEATRE

In the modern theatre the sense of æsthetic distance is very strong and very definite. The elevated stage serves not only to enhance visibility but also to set the play apart from the audience as a statue is set apart on its pedestal. The proscenium arch, or "picture frame," serves the same function. Usually the stage is brightly lighted while the auditorium is darkened, and there is a curtain which is raised or drawn aside only during the actual performance of a scene. All these things put together tend to offset the effect of reality created by the use of living actors, and to maintain a sense of detachment on the part of the audience.

At the present time the art of acting is very sharply distinguished from the art of oral reading. The distinction is not a matter of form or method, of costume, make-up, or scenery, or the lack of them, or of the presence or absence of supporting actors: it is altogether a matter of æsthetic distance.

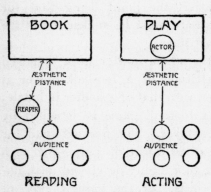

FIG. 1.—DISTINCTION BETWEEN ACTING AND READING

In reading, the audience and reader are one, enjoying the book together. There is æsthetic distance, but the reader and the audience are on the same end of it; the book is on the other. The reader is really one of the audience, in constant communication with the rest and sharing his enjoyment of the reading with them. Being in possession of the book— or of the memorized text—he is in a situation of leadership, but he is in no sense a part of the book himself; there is no pretense or illusion about his identity, and no detachment in his audience's attitude toward him. He may go very far in enlivening his reading by play of voice, gesture, and facial expression, so long as what he does is clearly suggestion; but he must avoid an attitude of exhibition.

The actor on the other hand is part of the play, and very much on exhibition—not in his own identity, but in that of the character he represents. His own personality is suppressed or discarded; there is no sense of communication between him and his audience, for they are in the world of reality and he is in the world of imagination. The æsthetic distance is between the audience and the play; and the actor, unlike the reader, is on the play end of it. For the actor to "step out of the picture" in any way, or to establish any sort of direct communication with his audience, is to break down the basic convention of modern acting.

It is true that these distinctions were not always as absolute as they are today. In the public theatre of Elizabethan times, for example, there was no proscenium arch, and there were no footlights to throw a glamour of unreality about the actor. In the private theatres the actors did not have the stage all to themselves, for young men of wealth and fashion insisted upon platform seats.[1] Elizabethan audiences, especially in the public theatres, were boisterous and unruly, voicing disapproval as readily as approval, and laughing loudly at the obscenities and the buffoonery. They did not hesitate to exchange remarks with the actors, and to break up a play if they did not like it. Under such circumstances it is doubtful whether the sense of illusion was very highly developed. What there was must have been the result of good drama and powerful individual acting.

Conditions in the seventeenth and eighteenth centuries were even less conducive to a sincere æsthetic attitude in the theatre. The custom of seating the young gallants on the stage persisted even in the public theatres and when women began to

[1] For the distinction between public and private theatres see Chapter XVII.

be employed to play the female parts the behavior of the audiences grew even more disorderly. The plays were as licentious as the times; few of the actresses were of good repute, and they flirted openly with the gallants on the stage and in the boxes. Interruptions were frequent, and riotous disturbances in the audience not at all uncommon.

Of course the behavior was not all disorderly. There were good plays, and there was good acting, and there was plenty of hearty appreciation of both. But few people seemed to have such a sense of obligation to artistic sincerity and consistency as is taken for granted in our better theatres today. One of the first to feel it was Thomas Betterton; but he was ahead of his time. Not until David Garrick became a power in the English theatre did things begin to change.

It was Garrick who first succeeded in driving the London audience off the stage—inspired, perhaps, by Voltaire, who had instituted a similar reform in France. In so doing he re-created that psychological barrier between actor and audience that is the basis of modern theatrical convention. Like Betterton he abandoned the Elizabethan custom of entering out of character and only beginning to act at the center of the stage, and of dropping out of character between speeches. He forbade his actors and actresses to carry on flirtations or conversations with members of the audience, or to establish communication with them in any way. He insisted that they know their parts perfectly. He even required them to dress in such a way as to suggest the characters they portrayed, instead of to display their own charms to advantage—although he made no attempt at historical accuracy in costuming, and himself played Macbeth in the contemporary uniform of a British general. His technique of production was not modern, but he was almost the first to set consistency and sincerity of imagination above mere histrionics, and to approximate a modern sense of æsthetic distance in the theatre.

Most people who love the theatre today—the "legitimate" theatre at any rate—value the artistic sincerity that dates from Garrick. Those who go to the theatre for rough animal play can get all they want in cheap vaudeville and in certain classes of motion pictures. Those who go to draw æsthetic pleasure from an artistic representation or presentation of life appreciate a sincere, consistent, imaginative effort on the part of the artists, and an orderly, sympathetic attitude on the part of the audience. Yet there are many who are ruthlessly condemning the modern theatre for its illusion, its "peep-hole" realism, its "picture-frame" stage, and who are clamoring for a return to the greater freedom and spontaneity, the greater intimacy, the more direct theatricalism of the Elizabethan platform or the eighteenth century forestage. It might be well for them to ask themselves whether they would be willing to accept also the loss of æsthetic distance, the coarse jests of unruly audiences, the private flirtations of the actresses, the bombardments of eggs and fruit, the general lack of a sense of obligation to artistic truth and consistency. I seriously doubt the possibility of restoring the one thing without the other.

The modern theatre undoubtedly needs reform and improvement. Everybody admits that it is too commercial. Sometimes it is too realistic; there is too much attempt at illusion. Sometimes there is too much space, too much convention, too little human appeal. But there can be no real progress in throwing overboard the whole technique by which we have gained a sense of sincerity and consistency in the theatre. The difficulty is not to be overcome by establishing personal intimacy between the actor and the audience. Anybody who likes that can satisfy his tastes by attending one of our musical revues in which half-clothed chorus girls come down the aisles and fraternize with the audience. That is intimacy—the same kind that so annoyed David Garrick. It does not represent progress in the art of the theatre; it represents reversion to a cruder and coarser age.

THE PROSCENIUM AND THE FOURTH WALL

There is one phase of the modern anti-realistic movement in the theatre which is so essentially a problem in æsthetic distance that it demands consideration here. This is the attack on the proscenium or "picture-frame" stage on the ground that it represents a room with the fourth wall removed, an accidental "peep-hole" view of life pictured with photographic accuracy. Such representation, the critics say, is too realistic, too concrete, too artificial, too flat, too distant. Let us abolish the proscenium arch, therefore, and substitute an apron or platform stage; let us bring the actor out of his frame and restore the plastic, three-dimensional art of older times. Let us abandon the attempt to create illusion, to deceive by pretense; let us make the actor frankly an actor; let us have abstract theatricalism instead of concrete representation. They do not say, let us abolish acting in favor of reading or declamation, but sometimes that is what they appear to mean.

On the whole such propaganda reveals an annoying inconsistency and confusion of thought. That the criticism is the result of severe provocation is evident; in their unfavorable reaction to specific abuses the complainants are quite generally right. It is in their analysis of causes, their interpretation of conventions, that they seem to go astray.

The proscenium arch is not, and never has been, conventionally representative of a fourth wall removed. The producer who attempts to make it so is guilty of false reasoning and ignorance of theatrical history and psychology, to say

44

nothing of very bad taste, and he deserves everything the modernists say about him. Fortunately he is rare, but unfortunately we sometimes find him in high places. When the Moscow Art Theatre, in Act Three of *The Three Sisters*, attempted to suggest the invisible fourth wall by arranging the furniture against the curtain line as if it were backed up against that wall, the device was positively and seriously wrong. The effect was unreal, distracting, and inartistic. A still worse effect was produced several years ago in this country in a play called *Dog Love*, written and acted by William Hodge; a cottage interior was shown with broken walls on both sides, a broken ceiling, and bits of exterior setting all around the edges, including the exterior of the roof above. One expected something to happen on that roof, and was disappointed when nothing did; while the broken walls, with their painful details of torn and mangled bricks, constantly obtruded themselves upon the attention and made one wonder how the dreadful catastrophe had occurred. In *The Judge's Husband*, a later play by the same author, there was one interior scene showing elaborate roof trusses cut off in mid-air, leaving the roof apparently unsupported and likely to fall down at any minute! In Eugene O'Neill's *Desire Under the Elms*, no less a person than Robert Edmund Jones lent himself to a similar enormity by putting a whole house on the stage, and then removing various parts of the front wall to expose first one room and then another, and sometimes two or three at a time; as a result some members of the audience gave much of their attention to wondering which section would come out next, and how they were fastened on, and whether the frail-looking house would be able to stand the strain. There was, of course, a real need for a divided setting in that play to convey the essential irony of certain scenes; but it need not have been so obtrusive.

Something of the same distracting effect occurs, however, every time a two-room scene is shown on the stage with the edge of a division wall staring the audience in the face— no matter how necessary to the action of the play. In the first act of *Anna Christie*, as produced by Arthur Hopkins, there was a particularly bad arrangement of this kind. The division wall was not brought forward to the curtain line; it was stopped half way, doubtless for visibility at the sides of the house. But it was evident that the actors on one side could see those on the other, and that when they passed from one room to the other through the door in the partition they were taking the longest route. One worried a little about that, and about the missing portion of the wall, and wondered whether it had gone with the fourth wall wherever the latter had gone. In one scene of a Harvard prize play called *Nancy Ann* there was a similarly abbreviated division wall, with an actress posted at the very edge, supposedly on one side of it; but all through the scene she was continually allowing her elbow or the edge of her skirt to lap over the space where the imaginary part of the wall was supposed to be, much to the annoyance of any one with a consistent imagination. The director had evidently realized that the division wall was bad, for in a subsequent scene in which it was not needed he had it removed, expanding one of the two rooms to fill the entire stage—thereby, unfortunately, creating a new distraction, and doing more harm than good. Divided settings are not uncommon, for they lend themselves to many humorous effects, and some dramatic ones, but it is doubtful if they can ever be artistically satisfying.

In good theatrical technique there is simply no suggestion of a fourth wall. The fact that indoor and outdoor scenes are shown through the same proscenium arch should be enough to allay the myth; if the proscenium represents a missing wall in a room scene, what does it represent in a woodland setting? Some critics have been strangely troubled by the fact that in the interior setting we see only three sides of the room. But who ever saw more, at one time? A human being does not have eyes in the back of his head; his field of vision is always limited to some three-fourths of a circumference. The convention of the proscenium arch is not the convention of an imaginary fourth wall, but that of a very real limitation of the field of vision, made definite for the sake of avoiding distraction; the raising of the curtain is not the lifting of a wall, but the beginning of a chapter of fiction—a measure of time rather than space.

The function of the proscenium arch is merely to frame the picture, to set it off by separating the fiction of the play from the reality of its surroundings, to prevent the eye from wandering to irrelevant things—in short, to maintain æsthetic distance. A painting is framed for the same reason. To say that a picture is too flat, or that the perspective is bad, or that the frame is too large, or too ornate, or too conspicuous, is legitimate criticism in either art. But to say that the proscenium arch should be abolished for any of those reasons is just as silly as to say that we should hang our pictures without frames; to demand that it be replaced by a platform stage is just as ridiculous as to insist that all painting be replaced by sculpture.

There is a place for sculpture, and there is a place for the platform stage. The latter existed before the proscenium arch, and gave way to it only because the arch was more convenient, lent itself to more varied effects, and strengthened æsthetic distance. It is still possible to perform some types of plays effectively and without loss of æsthetic distance on platform stages; Shakespearean plays are well adapted to such a technique, as are most poetic or symbolic plays. But it is wise to remember that the greatest plastic theatre in history—the theatre of Attic tragedy—lent itself readily to burlesque, and was much ridiculed in its own time; the comedies of Aristophanes are full of gibes at the unconvincing methods of contemporary tragedy.

When the modernists talk about "freeing the actor from his cage" or "bringing him out of his picture frame" I am always reminded of an exploit in one of the old Hanlon Brothers' pantomimes by which an actor really was brought out of the picture. He was suddenly projected some fifty feet out into the auditorium on the end of a long wooden beam. It was good circus, and fetched a lively scream from the ladies sitting down front, but it was not æsthetically pleasing, and would have been fatal to any consistent imaginative concept in a real play. The effect is only slightly less destructive when an actor comes too close to the footlights or too far out on the apron of the stage. The spell of a photoplay is often broken when an actor approaches too close to the camera, as if he were about to jump off the screen. In a recent experiment with three-dimensional motion pictures water from a hose appeared to come right out into the audience; the result was an attitude much more nearly hysterical than æsthetic.

The fact is that we do not want the actor to come out of the picture. We want him above everything else to stay in. At present we find it easier for him to do so when the picture is framed. The frame is not part of the picture, but it defines the limits of the composition and establishes the proper æsthetic distance. A statement by James McNeill Whistler, cited by Arthur Symons and by Langfeld, is apropos: "The one aim of the unsuspecting painter is to make his man 'stand out' from the frame—never doubting that, on the contrary, he should, and in truth absolutely does, stand *within* the frame—and at a depth behind it equal to the distance at which the painter sees his model. The frame is, indeed, the window through which the painter looks at his model, and nothing could be more offensively inartistic than this brutal attempt to thrust the model on the hither-side of this window!"

ÆSTHETIC DISTANCE AND THE SENSE OF COMMUNICATION

The arrangements of the stage and setting are after all only incidental elements in the establishment and maintenance of æsthetic distance. The chief element is psychological, and depends upon the actor. To maintain the proper attitude on the part of the audience the actor must consistently and rigidly refrain from a sense of communication with them.

To be sure, this principle does not apply to all theatrical entertainment. It seldom applies to the comic scenes of vaudeville and musical extravaganza, or to the humorous monologue. But these types of entertainment are not properly classified as acting, no matter how worthy or well done. By acting is meant the attempt to present a play with imaginative consistency.

An actor must, of course, convey the author's meaning to his audience. He must do more: he must convey a very subtle suggestion of appreciation of that meaning; that is his service as an interpretative artist. He must not appear visibly to enjoy the play as a spectator, yet he must somehow suggest an attitude of enjoyment to the observer. At the same time he must seem to be, not himself, but the character he represents, and as such he must seem to belong to another world, the world of fiction, of imagination. The instant he allows a bond of communication to become established between him and his audience the imaginative spell is broken.

I once sat very far from the stage at a production of *The Devil's Disciple*. When Dick Dudgeon swaggered in and dominated the scene I found it very delightful. It was as if he were saying, "Here am I, folks of the play, Dick Dudgeon, a whale of a character." But certain friends of mine who sat near the stage told me later that the effect was spoiled for them by the actor's habit of looking directly into the eyes of the audience with a communicative expression. To them it had seemed as if he were saying, "Here am I, ladies and gentlemen of the audience, a whale of an actor." For them æsthetic distance had been destroyed.

In Basil Dean's production of *The Skin Game* which toured this country in 1921-22 the auction scene was played with the auctioneer facing the audience and pretending to offer them a chance to buy real estate. The actor was a good comedian and the scene was amusing, but the artistic sincerity of the production was badly weakened. The auctioneer was in actual communication with the audience and apparently anxious to get a real response from them, and one found himself wondering why some irreverent spirit did not take him at face value and offer a bid. And then, just at the end of the scene, some one did so; a confederate in the audience shouted an offer and the sale was closed, while the audience, instead of paying attention to the play, were looking around and craning their necks to see who had created the disturbance. Nothing could have been more destructive of æsthetic distance. It may be argued, of course, that the artist should have freedom to alter the conventions, and to attain pleasing and entertaining effects in any way he sees fit. But was the effect pleasing, in this case? I sent a group of students from a class in play production to see *The Skin Game*, and to criticize the stage direction; they had heard no advance comment and had not yet studied æsthetic distance, but nearly all of them condemned the auction scene severely, on the ground that it broke the artistic illusion. "When I go to the theatre," one of them wrote, "I go to sit in the audience; I do not care to be mixed up in the play."

A similarly unpleasant effect was accomplished in the Morosco production of a Chautauqua comedy called *Across the Street*. In one scene of that play the real audience was made part of an imaginary political meeting, some of the actors occupying seats in the parquet, heckling the speakers, passing to and from the stage, and finally starting a small riot. In the Chautauqua performance of the same play, with an amateur cast and very inadequate scenery, the scene in question was made infinitely more convincing and more pleasing because directed at an imaginary audience off stage right.

Advocates of the plastic stage have pointed triumphantly to the achievements of Max Reinhardt in his "Theatre of the Five Thousand" in Berlin, in which he has staged vast tumult scenes with the stage in the center of the auditorium and with actors and supernumeraries mingling with the audience and coming and going in all directions. I have not had the pleasure of seeing these productions; but in Reinhardt's New York production of *The Miracle* æsthetic distance was perfectly maintained. There were seven hundred actors, and many of them came and went through the aisles, but they ignored the audience completely and established no sense of communication with them. Because of the mystic character of the play and the remarkable atmosphere of the theatre— remodeled to create the illusion of a cathedral—one could feel that he was present in spirit only, or that he was dreaming the whole thing. It was the atmosphere that served the purpose ordinarily served by the picture frame.

ILLUSION IN THE THEATRE

The question of illusion in the theatre seems to be a very confusing one. The expressionists are constantly berating the realists for attempting to create an illusion of real life on the stage, yet they seem to approve of a production like *The Miracle*, in which there is a more powerful illusion than in most realistic plays.

The truth is that the word illusion is ambiguous: there are really two kinds of illusion. There is the illusion of deception, and there is the illusion of art, and the difference between them is precisely that between the liar and the actor. The illusion of deception is inartistic and has no place in the theatre, but the illusion of art is the life of the theatre.

The illusion of art is a thing of the imagination. In it there is pretense, but no deception. The child expresses it perfectly when he says, "Let's pretend." He has no intention of deceiving anybody, not even himself. It is all a game, with nobody really fooled; but for good sport one must play the game consistently and whole-heartedly, allowing no interference with the imaginative concept. So in the theatre. Nothing is real; nothing is supposed to be. Children of a larger growth are pretending, that is all, but the more completely and sincerely they carry out the pretense—short of actual deception—the more pleasure they get out of it.

Langfeld, as usual, sees the matter clearly. "The question of realism in art," he says, "has caused much difficulty because it involves ideas that have appeared hard to reconcile. The dramatic critic asks for 'real' situations and 'real' incidents. He objects to a play that seems artificial, that does not correspond to life, yet we have said that a truly æsthetic enjoyment demands a sense of unreality. The seeming contradiction is readily explained by the fact that the object may be as real, in the sense of true to life, as is consistent with the intent of the artist, but the attitude of the observer should be different from that generally assumed toward the world. If we are able to maintain an æsthetic attitude, the most stirringly real play will continue to be a play for us, and the most ultra-realistic picture will continue to be a work of art, and the most lifelike statue will remain for us a series of graceful lines in marble; that is, we shall have maintained our distance, and the object will have remained an object of beauty."

In other words, what is bad in art is not illusion—or the lack of it—*per se,* but loss of æsthetic attitude on the part of the observer. Such illusion as is consistent with æsthetic distance is generally desirable. At the same time it must be borne in mind that imaginative illusion can be very powerfully induced by other means than realism of detail.

HOW MUCH ILLUSION?

An æsthetic attitude in the theatre can be destroyed either by too much or by too little illusion. When the scenery is tawdry and unconvincing, when the costumes are too palpably makeshifts, when the acting is feeble, or when somebody steps out of the picture or establishes communication with his audience, there is too little illusion, and one finds it impossible to maintain an æsthetic attitude. When, on the other hand, the scenery is so unnecessarily realistic as to distract attention from the play itself, or when the acting is so vividly real that one forgets it is acting and takes it for truth, there is too much illusion; the illusion of art has been replaced by deception, and the effect is again unæsthetic.

Actors, directors, and scenic artists not infrequently overdo the attempt to create illusion. Since the only measure of success in the theatre is the response of the audience they very naturally and properly play for such response; but sometimes they forget that not all response is æsthetic. It may, for example, seem like a triumph of art when some member of the audience is so carried away that he forgets himself and laughs or cries aloud, or cheers the hero, or warns him of the villain's approach with a cry: "Look out! Here he comes!"—or otherwise feels himself a participant in the play. As a matter of fact it is not a triumph of art, but a triumph of hollow deception at the expense of art, for art stops short when the observer loses his sense of detachment.

There is a story that one of the famous actresses of England—Mrs. Kendal, if I remember correctly—in playing a scene very like that of the death of her own child, so gave way to emotion herself that the audience could not stand the realism of it, and a woman stood up and cried, "No more! No more!" Highly emotional scenes always involve some risk of thus destroying distance and creating an undesirable sense of reality. So do scenes of terror. The armor scene in *The Ghost Breaker* was a case in point; for some people it was too strong in its empathies, and spoiled the æsthetic attitude. People like to be thrilled, even to the point of pretending to be scared, but they do not like to be *really* scared. It is to forestall such losses of distance that most terror plays are provided with comic relief. The tremendous success of *The Bat* was partly—though not wholly—due to the fact that time and again the terror was just saved from unendurable reality by the absurdities of Lizzie, the low-comedy serving-woman.

The more abstract or the more conventional the type of artistic presentation, the greater the sense of unreality; and the easier it is to maintain æsthetic distance. Sometimes there seems to be actual pleasure in an illusion of unreality about something one knows to be real. The Parade of the Wooden Soldiers in the *Chauve Souris,* for example, seemed to please people of all ages and all degrees of culture. One knew, of course, that the soldiers were real men, but the illusion of woodenness was so perfect that one became a child again, with a child's delight in a toy. Personally I recall a very distinct loss of æsthetic distance and a very palpable displeasure upon one occasion when a member of the wooden army lost his balance slightly, and for the instant became quite human in the effort to regain it; for me the illusion was spoiled, and I felt an unpleasant shock in being suddenly reminded that the soldier was not really unreal.

The highest form of art is in its essence very close to child's play; the difference lies in its being carried out with a skill and consistency sufficient to satisfy the more critical imaginations of adults. The *Chauve Souris* was largely child's play, performed with great skill and good taste, and it delighted the most cultivated and artistic audience of England, France and America, as well as Russia. *The Yellow Jacket,* by Hazleton and Benrimo, makes use of the highly naïve, "let's pretend" attitude of the Chinese theatre, and, in spite of the distractions created by the Property Man, gives keen æsthetic pleasure even to a sophisticated American audience. It is a fact often lost sight of by modern producers that a simple technique not only proves more stimulating to the imagination and more productive of illusion than an elaborate one, but renders the task of maintaining æsthetic distance vastly easier.

Illusion is after all a relative matter, and no definite technique can be specified for maintaining it in all cases. But it may safely be said that whatever tends to distract the attention from the main idea or to disrupt the imaginative concept, tends to destroy illusion, and to spoil the æsthetic attitude. It is remarkable how much the imagination can do with the barest suggestion, provided only that there is no distracting influence to recall reality or otherwise disturb the attitude of detachment. It may even be said that the stimulation of the imagination is the easy part of play production, while the hard part is the suppression of the many distracting influences that are potential enemies of æsthetic distance.

THE ACTOR AS A SOURCE OF DISTRACTION

One of the worst sources of distraction in the theatre is too much emphasis on the identity of the individual actor. When the audience recognizes an actor not as the character he represents, not even as *an* actor, but as *the* actor—David Warfield, Ethel Barrymore, or George Arliss—there is an obvious interference with the illusion. Up to a certain point this may be beneficial, as a defense of æsthetic distance against too much illusion of reality. But in the modern commercial theatre it is often carried so far that it interferes seriously with the imaginative concept. The star system leads one to think of Ethel Barrymore as Ethel Barrymore rather than as Lady Colladine or Mrs. Tanqueray. In discussing a play one finds himself using the actor's name instead of the character's name; often he cannot even recall the latter. The greater the emphasis upon the star and the more unchanging his or her personality in different parts, the greater the strain on the illusion.

The screen is even worse than the stage in exploiting actors instead of characters. Mary Pickford is a hard-working and versatile actress, but she is always Mary Pickford to her admirers; nobody remembers her as Jean, or Tess, or Dorothy. Tom Mix is Tom Mix to every small boy; why bother one's head with his various fictitious names? Bill Hart is

always Bill Hart and Douglas Fairbanks is always "Doug."
Perhaps it does not matter so much in comedy, especially low
comedy; perhaps it is right that Charlie Chaplin should
always be Charlie Chaplin. After all it is the *character*
Charlie Chaplin, not the actor Charlie Chaplin, that we
remember. But in a serious play it does matter that the
audience should be utterly unable to think of a character as
such. Recently some of the more artistic producers have
been realizing this and have been taking measures against it;
many photoplays are being released with no stars featured,
and with no mention of the actors except in the list at the
beginning; and in some instances—as in Griffith's *America*
—the names of the actors are omitted altogether, in order to
concentrate attention on the characters. The latter plan
seems a bit extreme, for a reasonable interest in knowing who
did the good work is not inconsistent with an æsthetic attitude; a better plan would be to give the cast at the end of
the film, or to provide the audience with printed programs,
or to post the cast in the lobby of the theatre. The worst
possible plan is to display the actor's name with that of the
character when the latter first appears, and in type four or
five times as large. No actor can overcome such an obstacle
to illusion.

Bad as the star system is, it is no more destructive of illusion than the stock company, especially the neighborhood
stock company with each actor a local favorite. In a stock
production the action is usually suspended ten or twelve times
in the first act while each member of the company in turn
steps out of the picture to acknowledge his "reception." The
greater his disguise, the more hilarious the shout of recognition from his admirers. Illusion is almost impossible under
such circumstances, and if there are moments when the audience is profoundly moved by the play it is because of

unusually good acting or because of the more rugged imaginations of the unsophisticated. The ordinary cheap stock company thrives, of course, only where a higher form of art would starve to death; it furnishes relatively uncultivated audiences with a healthy form of play, but the attitude it induces is not, as a rule, highly æsthetic. Sometimes the convincingness of even the most popular type of play is jeopardized by the stock company sort of intimacy.

On one occasion *The Bat* was performed by a stock company in Philadelphia. When the mysterious shrouded figure skulked across the darkened stage in the last act, and the whole point of the play rested upon his identity remaining undiscovered, a naïve enthusiast in the audience recognizing some familiar mannerism, shouted out: "That's John Lott!"—mentioning, significantly enough, the actor and not the character, and of course giving the plot away completely.

In amateur production there is something of the same difficulty—intensified perhaps by the fact that the actors are personal acquaintances of the audience. On the other hand, most amateur groups choose more serious and more artistic plays than the stock companies, and at least aim at a higher level of æsthetic accomplishment. The result, provided always that the acting is reasonably good, is apt to be a better suppression of personality, and a more consistent imaginative illusion.

The repertory system, whether amateur or professional, is always open to the objection that the oftener one sees and recognizes an actor in different rôles, the harder it becomes to accept the illusion in each new rôle; what the star system does to destroy illusion with respect to one actor the repertory system tends to do with respect to all. Perhaps it is to overcome this tendency that the Moscow Art Theatre company takes such pains with make-up, costume, and all details of characterization, and refuses to tolerate applause or curtain calls during the play, or anything else likely to destroy illusion. The fine work of this organization proves that the repertory system can with proper care be made consistent with the highest degree of æsthetic distance; neverthless, the use of the same actors in successive plays, or in two or more parts in the same play, is essentially a disadvantage, and must be compensated for in other ways if the proper illusion is to be maintained.

EXTERNAL AIDS AND HINDRANCES TO ILLUSION

The vogue of the Moscow Art Theatre strengthened a movement already begun in this country to discourage receptions, curtain calls, interrupting applause, and such sources of distraction. Within reason the movement is a wise one, but when it results in applause from one half of the audience and indignant cries of "Hush! hush!" from the other, it is probable that there is more loss than gain. In planning a reform it is always well to consider the alternative. Confusion and ill feeling may be more detrimental to the æsthetic attitude than old fashioned honest applause, and when we remember that the latter has some real value in stimulating the actor it would seem unwise to abolish it altogether. Personally I should like to see the reception abolished, and applause somewhat restrained except at the ends of acts. There is no serious loss of distance when real curtain calls are spontaneously given and gracefully received, provided they are taken *in character*—as they are by most sincere actors and actresses today. Curtain speeches in character may even add to the effectiveness of the play, especially in comedy; Frank Bacon's delightful little speech in *Lightnin'*, telling how he (Lightnin' Bill Jones) and General Grant won a certain battle, was a case in point. But there is a very distinct loss when an actor steps out of character to deliver a curtain speech before the end of the play. The effect is not so serious in light comedy, and perhaps not in classic repertory, where one knows the play by heart anyway; but in a serious realistic play, given for the first time, it is in very bad taste. Some of our best actors still do it, perhaps because they are old timers and cling to the traditions of an earlier generation.

There is one thing that may be said in favor of curtain speeches and of many other elements of intimacy, and that is that they do make for a warmer relationship between actor and audience, a greater human sympathy. This in itself is good, provided the distraction is not too great. The older dramatists used to solve the problem by means of a prologue or induction of some sort. An actor came before the curtain not as an actor but as a speaker, a sort of master of ceremonies, to put the audience in a proper mood and adjust them to the requisite point of view. Modern counterparts have often been successful. The one-man "Chorus" in *The Yellow Jacket* plays a very important part in establishing and maintaining æsthetic distance; while pretending to be the manager of the play he is in reality the leader of the audience, teaching them step by step how to appreciate the play, and appreciating it with them. A very similar function is performed by Balieff, director of the *Chauve Souris*, and no small part of the pleasure given by that entertainment is due to his ability to put the audience in a mood of delighted anticipation before the first act begins. In none of these instances, however, does the person who addresses the audience have to step out of the picture to do so, as in the case of an ordinary curtain speech.

A great many producers today have abolished the orchestra music between the acts, on the ground that it interferes with the atmosphere of a serious play; but of course this is a very thin disguise for a doubtful form of economy. It may be true that a bad orchestra playing cheap trashy music is detrimental to the atmosphere of a beautiful play; but the obvious remedy is a good orchestra playing appropriate music. Even the worst music is preferable to dull, cheerless silence, broken only by chatter and small talk and the horrid cries of chocolate vendors; for at least it preserves a suggestion of the play attitude, and distinguishes the theatre from the railway station. Moreover, there is a definite function of relief— mental and physical—performed by the theatre orchestra; it checks the destruction of æsthetic distance through too much and too powerful illusion, and the more serious the play the more important this function. In Russia, where a highly pessimistic people take their art with a ghastly seriousness, the elimination of the orchestra may aid the æsthetic attitude; but in this country it most certainly weakens it. If the managers could but realize how many former theatre-goers have been driven away by the dismal intermissions they might not marvel so much at the spectacle of people paying high prices to see trashy movies—supported by symphony orchestras.

THE ARTISTIC BALANCE

Hardly anything is to be gained in art by going to extremes, for art is essentially a matter of balance. It has often been observed that we take the greatest pleasure in a combination of the real and the imaginary, the familiar and the strange, the true to life and the true to art. That which is totally unfamiliar is uninteresting because it is meaningless; it gives us no basis of comparison. That which is totally familiar is uninteresting because it is monotonous and humdrum. Interest lies always in a balance of the extremes. It may be that such a balance is pleasurable because it permits us to empathize without losing æsthetic distance. The familiar element, besides giving us the thrill of recognition, stirs our empathic responses; while the unfamiliar preserves the consciousness of detachment.

I do not insist that empathy and æsthetic distance offer a complete explanation of our pleasure in the fine arts, but it seems probable that they are essential elements of such pleasure. Certainly they strike a balance. In the theatre it is the director's business to see that this balance is maintained, and that neither element is allowed to exclude the other.

CHAPTER IV

PLAY PRODUCTION AS DESIGN

SO FAR we have been considering, somewhat abstractly, the nature of the æsthetic appeal in the theatre, and the artistic ideals and purposes in play production. We have now to consider the matter of translating these into actuality through plan and execution.

Creative planning or composition in the fine arts is generally spoken of as Design, and in the schools of fine arts it is treated as a separate study with its own body of principles and precepts. These principles and precepts hold good for every fine art, no matter what the medium; and one of the most valuable lessons an artist can learn is that good design is good design, whether the object be a poem, a temple, or a woman's hat.

In the theatre the problem of design is especially complex, because of the composite nature of the art and the large number of elements that have to be considered and put in order. The black and white artist designs in line and mass; the painter in line, mass, and color; the musician in melody, harmony, and rhythm; the poet in words and meter; the dancer in bodily movement and gesture. But the stage director must often design in all of these elements at once. It is inconceivable—and unnecessary—that he should be so expert in all arts as to compete with the specialists, but it would seem particularly essential that he know the underlying principles of good design common to all of them. Without such knowledge

63

he can hardly hope to achieve a consistently unified and pleasing effect.

Curiously, however, the principles of design as such are seldom taught in the schools of dramatic art, and seldom treated in the books on play production. The best courses in design are to be found in the schools of industrial art and particularly in the schools of architecture; and most of the good books on design have been written by persons trained in architecture, painting, or sculpture rather than in poetry, drama, or the theatre. Organized principles of design seem to play very little part in theatrical discussion, even in relation to the professional theatre, and one is led to wonder how many of our directors, actors, and critics have ever read a book on design or taken a course in design. Perhaps it is because they have not done so that so many theatre-trained directors are now finding themselves overshadowed by their scenic artists, and in a fair way to become dependent upon them for their major effects.

THE ORIGINS OF DESIGN

The best way to study the principles of design is to consider the origin and growth of primitive art. It is a matter of common observation that primitive art is nearly always good art. Bad art is generally a product of insincerity, and insincerity flourishes best in a sophisticated civilization. There is, for example, almost no parallel in the art of primitive peoples for the meaningless ginger-bread architecture of 1850 to 1890.

If the reader doubt this, let him spend an afternoon in some good museum of archeology, one containing a large collection of implements, pottery, clothing and the like, representing the culture of a comparatively simple race—the American Indian, for example. He will observe that while many of the implements are crude, judged by modern standards of manufacture, they are well and effectively made to serve their original purpose; also that they are ornamented in a simple but attractive way, suggesting that their makers took real pleasure in the work and in the product, aiming to satisfy their sense of beauty as well as their sense of utility. But he will seldom, if ever, find an instance in which the primitive designer allowed his sense of ornament to run away with his sense of utility, or allowed himself to indulge in orgies of meaningless elaboration. Grotesqueries he will find, of course, wild flights of imagination and fancy, but almost invariably subordinated to the purpose for which the object was intended, or to the ideas of magic potency associated with that purpose.

When primitive man made a bow and arrow, for instance, he wanted first of all a bow and arrow that would work, for he knew that his life might depend upon it. He chose the kind of wood that gave the strongest spring; but if there were several kinds equally good he chose the kind which also looked best and pleased him most. If he needed something to keep the dampness out he looked about him for some resinous substance that would serve as a varnish, the best he could find for the purpose. But if there were several substances equally effective he chose the kind that best lent itself to ornamentation—the most highly colored kind, for instance; or perhaps he used several kinds of different colors, working them out into a design. Finding that his bow could be improved by wrapping certain parts of it with rawhide or reeds, he chose the best materials for the purpose, but when several colors would do equally well he alternated them or interwove them into a design. The purpose of the design might be to give pleasure or to invoke the powers of magic; doubtless the latter purpose came first. The more dependent the craftsman was upon his bow as a weapon the more affection he lavished upon its construction, and the more pains he took to give it magic power and beauty. The small boy today does very similar things to his hockey stick or tennis racquet, and from about the same motives.

While the warrior was engaged in making his bow the woman was busy, perhaps, in making baskets or pottery. She also aimed first at utility, and only secondarily at beauty. She also used the materials at hand—reeds for the basket, clay for the pottery—and she developed the ornament out of the same materials. The earliest potters in all parts of the world worked their designs out of different colored clays; it was only in a later, more sophisticated, and less honest age that they learned to paint imitations of those designs on the surface.

In the development of ornament primitive peoples drew naturally on their observation of things about them, and particularly upon nature. Human life furnished some of the motifs, but most of them were drawn from flowers, birds, animals, trees, mountains, rivers, the sun, the moon, or the stars. It is noteworthy, however, that these motifs were conventionalized almost from the first. Since the ornamentation was usually associated with magic there was no serious attempt at pictorial realism. When primitive men sought to portray actuality it was usually to convey a message of some kind; in their arts they were content with the crudest suggestion, and concerned chiefly with fitting the ornament into some general scheme. If they wanted to decorate a bow with the figure of an alligator they did not distort the bow to portray the alligator correctly; they distorted the alligator to decorate the bow. It is possible that this is the origin of conventionalization in the arts; certainly it is the origin of many conventional motifs familiar in historic ornament.

PLAY PRODUCTION AS DESIGN

The subject of primitive art is a fascinating one and will repay a great deal of study. The more one sees of the work done by the earliest designers in all parts of the world, the more respect he feels for their simplicity, sincerity, and good taste, and the more he begins to realize that the problem of good design today is how to achieve a similar quality in the face of the complexities and perplexities of modern life.

Two facts about primitive design stand out above all others: First, the artist's fidelity to his utilitarian purpose, and secondly, his fidelity to his materials. The opinion appears to be unanimous among writers on design that these two elements are natural and basic in the history and psychology of art, and that no sound achievement in design is possible without them.

THE UTILITARIAN BASIS

To say that all good design is founded upon a basis of utility is seemingly to contradict the opinion previously maintained concerning artistic detachment and the purely æsthetic purpose of the fine arts. The assertion, however, will stand analysis.

It must be remembered that design did not begin with the fine arts. It began long before the fine arts, in the days when men were still too preöccupied with the struggle for existence to indulge in art for art's sake. There was a strong play impulse among primitive men, but it existed for a long time as applied to the useful arts before it resulted in the development of separate arts entirely given to the purposes of æsthetic pleasure. The early artists whose work we so much admire were thus not artists at all in the narrower sense of that word; they were craftsmen, men who worked with their hands to produce useful articles and to satisfy their actual needs, but who took pleasure in doing their work well and beautifully.

We still have the craftsmen; we still make useful articles and endeavor to beautify them at the same time. Good design in the crafts still means, above all, fidelity to the structural purpose of the object, whether a building, a piece of furniture, or an evening gown. Refinement and enrichment we expect, but they must be kept subordinate to utility.

At the same time we have given freer rein to our play impulses by establishing certain special arts such as music, painting, and the drama, which have no other purpose than to give pleasure. All of them began as useful arts with some ulterior application—a religious one in many cases—but by a process of evolution they have become independent and purely æsthetic. All of them, however, still make use of design, and good design in the fine arts is identical in principle with good design in the useful arts. Fidelity to the utilitarian purpose means, in the fine arts, fidelity to the *purpose*, whatever that happens to be—to the central idea or emotion which it is the aim of the artist to convey. It is just as essential for the fine artist to know what he is trying to do as it is for the craftsman; and it is just as essential that he subordinate his love of elaboration and ornament to the main or fundamental idea.

This, then, is the first lesson that the stage director can learn from the primitive craftsman. How often does one find in a theatrical performance anything like the rugged simplicity and directness, the sheer beauty of form, the sincerity of method, which are so easy to find in the glass cases of any good archeological museum? How often can he feel that at no point in the play has the director or the actor forgotten the chief message of the play? There can be no question that many stage directors, amateur and professional, are seriously in need of just this simple lesson.

In the theatre the utilitarian purpose is simply the purpose of the play; the telling of a given story, or the expounding of a given theme. Good design in play production is design in which the director shows the same regard for his main business that the primitive man showed in making his bow, and the same unwillingness to sacrifice the main business to ornament in even the slightest degree.

FIDELITY TO MATERIALS

The second lesson which the stage director may learn from the primitive craftsman is that of fidelity to the natural limitations of means, methods, and materials; and it is a lesson even more urgently needed in our theatres than the first one.

The primitive craftsman used the materials that were at hand, the kinds of wood, clay, or stone that were natural to the soil he lived upon. He used them not only for the structural elements but also for ornamentation, because he built his ornamentation out of the structural elements.

In modern art the ornamentation is too often but a vestigial remnant of the more organic ornament of earlier times, and sometimes it is not even that. Sometimes it is purely extraneous decoration plastered on from the outside and composed of cheap and unrelated materials. Almost everything today is an imitation of something else; even the most substantial looking stone buildings are built first of steel and the stone hung on afterwards. Some years ago we began imitating stone with terra cotta and plaster; now we imitate even the plaster with sheet iron or copper. The point is not that we *use* sheet iron or copper, but that in using a new material we try to pretend that it is something else; and instead of developing a structural and ornamental design appropriate to the new material we borrow lamely from the design belonging to the old.

Of course it will never be possible to return completely to the rigid simplicity of primitive times, nor is it, perhaps, desirable. It is not necessary to confine ourselves to materials accidentally at hand when better materials may be obtained. Indeed, with improved methods of transportation everything is, in a sense, at hand. It is not necessary, and not possible, to reject the suggestions that come to us from other arts, or other races, or other ages, in order to build up an honest and sincere art of our own. We need not, and cannot, follow the methods of primitive craftsmen with literal accuracy.

What we can do is realize that there are natural limitations connected with every art, and that the sincere artist recognizes these limitations, whatever they are, and abides by them. He does not struggle uselessly to transcend them, but seeks rather to turn them to account, to make conventions of them, and to find actual beauty in them.

This is a lesson that some would-be artists never learn. They sputter and storm at all limitations and conventions, and strive ceaselessly for some sort of "new freedom"—which means, more often than not, freedom from the obligation to hard work and painstaking study. In their efforts to attain the new freedom they often give us merely incoherence, tawdry imitation, and bad craftsmanship, and call it—quite accurately, perhaps—self expression. They seem to miss the obvious fact that the greatest artists have never needed much of that sort of freedom; that they have always found true freedom, not in servile unoriginality, but in a sane and honest recognition of natural limitations. It would not be too much to say that the limitations make the freedom, for they relieve the artist of the necessity to attempt the impossible.

The true artist, like the true craftsman, first considers his purpose; secondly he considers the medium in which he is to work, choosing it in accordance with his purpose; and lastly he considers the possibilities and limitations of the medium. If his medium is the pencil he does not try to make it do what only the brush can do; if it is the brush, he does not try to make it imitate the work of the camera. If his medium is the motion picture he does not make it a clumsy imitation of the stage play; he develops it according to its own capabilities, recognizing that though it may lack some elements of appeal to be found in the stage play, it can do many things that the stage can not.

The stage director, working in an art that is a combination of many others, is constantly tempted to borrow indiscriminately from those others—to use beautiful settings, beautiful costumes, beautiful lighting effects, beautiful music, simply because they are beautiful, and without regard to their effect on the development of the central idea. He, almost more than any other artist, is in need of the lessons to be drawn from a study of primitive design. Fidelity to the main thought or purpose, and fidelity to the natural limitations of material— those are the fundamentals upon which he must build if he is to achieve an art that is honest.

But there is much more to the study of design than these fundamentals. The experience of several thousand years has naturally enabled those engaged in creative art to observe some of the possibilities and limitations of the human mind, and some of the peculiarities of human response, and as a result of such observation to formulate certain working principles of composition. Among the best known and most universal are those of Unity, Emphasis, Rhythm, Balance,

Proportion, Harmony, and Grace. All of these are broad enough to find equal application in all the arts, and psychologically sound enough to be beyond question. It goes without saying that the stage director should understand them.

UNITY

The principle of unity, as the name indicates, is the principle of one-ness or singleness of thought; it is perhaps the most widely recognized of the principles of composition.

That the mind naturally seeks unity doubtless everyone will agree; the ancients observed the fact and modern psychologists have re-discovered it and proved it by laboratory tests. It would seem that singleness of effect is, if not essential, at least conducive to understanding, to interest, and to æsthetic pleasure.

In the matter of understanding it is evident that, all other things being equal, the mind can more readily grasp a single idea than several ideas at the same time. Many people, while admitting this, still neglect the principle because the observance of it involves some effort, and because it seems to them that after all one can think of several things at once if necessity demands it.

Laboratory tests do not seem fully to support this theory. They seem rather to show that the mind is extraordinarily limited in the perception of even the simplest sort of multiplicity—the multiplicity of elementary units in a group, for instance. Most people can distinguish between a two-spot and a three-spot at cards or dice by what seems to be a single act of perception; but few, if any, can distinguish a nine from a ten except by some analytical or associative process—by counting, or by mental division into two fours and a one, or by recognition of a familiar pattern. The Braille system of reading for the blind is based upon the belief that direct perception is limited to groups of four or five elements, or six at the outside limit. In other words, in the effort to grasp several things at once, the mind finds itself limited to very small groups of the simplest units.

As for more complex ideas, it has been pretty clearly shown that the mind can give attention to but one at a time, and that whenever it appears to carry two simultaneously it is really alternating between them, very rapidly perhaps, but none the less completely. It is obvious that the result of such alternation must be some loss of efficiency, however slight, accompanied by some mental strain. For clarity of understanding, therefore, unity is desirable.

For interest it is equally desirable, because interest depends upon attention, and lack of unity represents diffusion of attention. The greatest enemy of attention is distraction, and lack of unity is distracting because it is constantly calling the attention away from one thing to consider another. The mind quickly tires of this and loses interest.

But while a lack of unity is injurious to interest, a unity which is too simple and obvious is no less injurious in another way. We all know the effect of monotony: any attempt to give constant attention to that which does not change results either in mind-wandering or in sleep. Singleness in itself, though an aid to clarity, is not conducive to sustained interest. Sustained interest lies rather in the discovery of singleness in multiplicity, of unity in variety. This is the reason why a symphony is more permanently interesting than a popular song. The latter may seem more interesting on first hearing, but we soon master all there is of it and it ceases to give us fresh stimuli. The symphony, however, contains many elements, and after frequent hearings we still find our interest engaged by the problem of discerning the unity in the variety. Of course the unity must be there, but it must not be too simple or obvious. It is commonly said that one's interest in a composite idea is proportional to the number and variety of elements that are disciplined into a single effect.

There is still another way in which the need of unity is felt in the fine arts, and that is with respect to æsthetic pleasure as we have tried to define it. If our sense of beauty is largely dependent upon empathic response it will be apparent that a lack of unity is likely to be unpleasant in that it will provoke responses that are not in harmony. It has been demonstrated in the laboratory that conflicting empathies create physical shocks and strains. Langfeld reports an experiment in which an observer was asked to admire a picture, which after a time was suddenly removed and replaced by another just like it but diametrically reversed. The result was a distinct physical shock. We all know the empathic effect of a discord in tone or color. Whenever there is lack of unity there is danger of unpleasant empathy, and unpleasant empathy is what, in the fine arts, we are for the most part striving to avoid.

It is not necessary to accept the Greek notion that all æsthetic pleasure is based upon the discovery of unity in variety in order to appreciate the fact that unity of effect does play a considerable part in enabling us to enjoy the fine arts, including the art of the theatre.

EMPHASIS

The principle of emphasis is most often met with, by name at least, in the study of rhetoric; but it is really quite as universal in the arts as any other. It is the principle of appeal to attention through intensification of sense impressions. Important elements of composition are to be given conspicuous positions to appeal to the eye, or conspicuous inflections to appeal to the ear; they are to be "pointed up" that they may not escape attention.

In written discourse emphasis is largely attained through the placing of important words at the beginning or the end of each sentence or paragraph, those being the positions most likely to catch the eye. The dramatist, assisted by the director, is carrying out the same principle when he tries to provide an interesting first scene and a strong "curtain" for each act of a play. The painter finds his points of emphasis in the high lights, the contrasts, or the effects of converging lines—the spots that naturally claim the attention of the observer—and into those spots he puts the important elements of the pictorial idea. The emphatic position in any type of composition is the position that makes the greatest claim upon the senses, and provides the strongest stimulus to renewed attention.

In the theatre well balanced emphasis is a constant need, and a difficult problem. Here a story is told briefly—much more so than in a novel, for instance—under conditions that are not always favorable to steady attention. If the play is to convey its message in the short time allotted, the important elements of the story must be so pointed up that nobody can possibly miss them, and in this the dramatist needs every bit of help the director can give him.

The dramatist, as a rule, employs the methods of the writer to gain emphasis, including such rhetorical devices as the exclamation, the periodic sentence, the suspended climax, and the leading question. He likewise provides, or suggests, most of the major dramatic emphasis by his arrangement of situations, character contrasts, and conflicts of motive.

The actor points up important lines or scenes by means

of vocal emphasis, gesture, pause, and all the devices of the orator, as well as by action and stage business, and the importance of his work in this respect can hardly be exaggerated.

But the director must oversee and coördinate all these, and at the same time provide other means of emphasis when these fail. There are endless possibilities of emphasis in the theatre through control of line, mass, color, light, force, tempo, movement, and music; and many of these escape the attention of the dramatist because he cannot visualize everything in advance, and of the actor because his attention is too deeply concentrated on his own part. It is in the adjustment of emphasis that the director performs one of his most valuable functions, and one that can only be performed in actual rehearsal.

RHYTHM

A third principle of composition is that of rhythm. Rhythm is usually defined as periodicity or pulsation, or the more or less regular recurrence of emphasis.[1] Whenever stress or accent recurs periodically, or whenever there is a discernible alternation of strong and weak, or high and low, or positive and negative, or light and dark, or fast and slow, or of any other contrasting elements, we have a form of rhythm.

The appeal of rhythm is easily explained by the fact that we ourselves are rhythmic creatures. The pulsations of the blood are rhythmic, respiration is rhythmic, and most of our bodily activities such as walking, running, swimming, rowing,

---

[1] Many artists nowadays use the word rhythm so loosely as to include mood, atmosphere, character, motive, tempo, and what not. They use it, in short, as a summation of all qualities in art. This is partly mysticism and partly vagueness. Rhythm does not imply the exactness of meter, but it does imply some sort of pattern in recurrence; and any vaguer usage impoverishes the language.

hammering, sawing, sweeping, and so on tend to be rhythmic. In other words our habitual motor activities are trained, tuned, and accustomed to rhythm.

When we contemplate an object of beauty we experience imitatively the motor responses suggested by it. If those responses are rhythmic they tend to fit in with the natural experience of the body, and it is not difficult to see that they are more likely to be pleasing than if they fail to fit in. Everyone is familiar with the manifestation of this principle in our ready appreciation of music, especially martial music or dance music. The more obvious the rhythm the better we like it on first hearing; less obvious rhythms are baffling at first because we have difficulty in adjusting our bodily responses to them, though once mastered they may give us quite as much pleasure as the simpler ones with the added delight of unity discovered in variety. But nothing is more distressing from an æsthetic point of view than a rhythm that is so imperfect or so difficult as ultimately to defy adjustment—a point that some ultra-modern composers seem to have missed.

Many people, though quite accustomed to the idea of rhythm in music and dancing, seem unaware that the same principle is involved in every sort of composition, in every arrangement of line, mass, and color, in every inflection of pitch, force, and tempo, in every variation of movement or position. The empathic responses to painting or sculpture are, as we have already seen, less conscious than those to music or dancing, and we are less aware of any rhythmic element in them. But the effect is there, and is no less important because it happens to be subconscious.

In highly conventional art, like music or cubistic painting, the rhythms may be very obvious and direct, and similar elements may be repeated frequently in the same medium.

In representative art, however, they must be in some measure concealed, else they tend to distract attention from the subject-matter. The painter achieves this concealment by avoiding direct repetition of line or mass in the same medium, and by contriving instead to echo a line of one medium by a line of another—similar, but not the same. The line of a woman's arm may be echoed, not by another arm, but by a fold of drapery or a portion of the sky line; a mass of red may be echoed by a mass of pink or orange, or a dark shade of one color may be echoed by a dark shade of another. On the stage a group of characters may be so arranged that the lines of the setting echo the lines of the group. In plot-building a lesser plot may be made to echo a greater one, as the love of Gratiano and Nerissa echoes that of Bassanio and Portia in Shakespeare's play.

The art of the theatre, being so highly complex, affords a greater multiplicity of possible varied rhythms than almost any other; at the same time it is so concretely representative that it will not bear rhythms which are too obvious. This spells opportunity for the director who would achieve good design, but it also spells danger, for the temptation to play with rhythms at the expense of meaning is great. In this, as in other matters of design, surprisingly good things may be accomplished by purely negative methods—by avoiding bad rhythms, and by so arranging the different elements that their natural rhythms may not clash with each other or with our bodily rhythms—in other words by not doing the wrong things as much as by doing the right.

Much of the experimental drama of recent years provides opportunity for more pronounced rhythms than the older drama without sacrifice of meaning. In Eugene O'Neill's play *The Emperor Jones*, for instance, there is a persistent rhythm furnished by the beating of a tom-tom, a rhythm

White

"THE BEGGAR ON HORSEBACK"

A scene from the Winthrop Ames production suggesting the jazz rhythms that pervade the dream. Neil McRae (Roland Young) dreams that he has married the heiress he does not love, and is oppressed by the exaggerated magnificence of her family and home. When the butler is summoned he pops into view from behind a marble column. The next time he is summoned two butlers appear simultaneously. The third time four appear; and the fourth time no less than eleven appear, one from behind each column. A combination of regularity and exaggeration is carried through the whole dream.

that functions, one might almost say, as the nemesis of the play. In *The Hairy Ape* one or two scenes are boldly rhythmic, especially the Fifth Avenue scene with the masked chorus. In Max Reinhardt's spectacle *The Miracle* there is much rhythm of light and movement in addition to that of the music. In *Johannes Kreisler*, the German expressionistic play, and in the photoplay *The Cabinet of Dr. Caligari*, there are good examples of the jagged angular rhythms of line suggestive of an insane frenzy. In *The Beggar on Horseback*, the entertaining dream-play by Kauffman and Connolly, there is a remarkable suggestion of the way in which the rhythms of life may enter into a dream. The hero of this play, a young composer, is given an opiate by his physician, and falls asleep to the rhythm of a café orchestra across the street—a rhythm that is anathema to him. There follows a lengthy and fantastic dream through which the same rhythm, heightened and exaggerated, runs on and on until one feels that the whole world has been "jazzed up." The effect here is not distracting in the least; rather it carries the point of the play, and so represents good design. The rhythmic effects, obvious as they are, belong intrinsically to the author's message, and the thoughts and sensations of the audience are swept along together.

Perhaps the most stirring use of bold rhythm for truly dramatic effect which it has ever been my good fortune to witness was that in the Ant Scene of the Czecho-Slovakian morality play, *The World We Live In*, the play in which the Kapek brothers satirized all human life by representing human beings as insects. In that scene the spirit of modern industrialism and imperialism was epitomized in the movement of countless busy creatures with a restless, relentless, ceaseless rhythm that got under the skin and carried one to a pitch of excitement not often equalled in the theatre.

Even in the simplest and most direct art there are infinite possibilities of rhythmic effect, but with corresponding possibilities of disaster. If the rhythm is made too obvious it distracts attention from the main thought to be conveyed, and the technique of the art becomes unpleasantly mechanical. On the other hand if there is not enough rhythm, or if the rhythms are too complex, our motor responses are baffled and we experience a sense of restless futility and dissatisfaction.

BALANCE

Balance, Proportion, and Harmony are all closely associated with each other and with the principle of Unity, because all involve the same problem of empathic adjustment. The principle of balance has to do, of course, with the maintenance of stability through equalization of contending forces.

The simplest form of balance is the form we call symmetry, which consists of exactly equal grouping on both sides of a central line or plane, each side the reverse of the other (*A, B,* Figure 2). It is chiefly useful in conventional design, the freer forms requiring balance of a more subtle kind.

In the theatre symmetry is often employed in the designing of formal settings for operas, spectacles, and symbolic plays, and in the grouping of characters and choruses in such productions. In the seventeenth and eighteenth centuries it was much more generally employed than it is today, even for comparatively realistic plays; the normal stage group was triangular, with the important character up stage center as the apex of the triangle, and the minor characters equidistant down right and down left. The modern tendency, however, is away from pure symmetry, even in opera and musical comedy—so much so that when *The Beggar's Opera* was revived a few years ago and played in the eighteenth century manner it seemed very stiff and strange to us.

A more subtle form of balance than the symmetrical is achieved in design by a modification of the leverage principle.

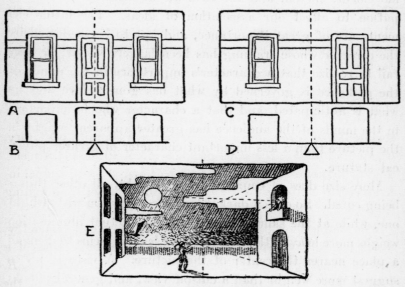

FIG. 2.—FORMS OF BALANCE

A and *B* are symmetrical, *C, D,* and *E* unsymmetrical but balanced on the center line. In *E* the triangle connecting the two figures and the moon forms one balanced element; the two buildings with their lines of perspective form another. But note that after a moment the triangular balance becomes less satisfactory because the figures hold interest longer than the moon, and begin to outweigh it.

It is well known that a light weight may be made to balance a heavy one if placed proportionately farther from the fulcrum of a lever. Assuming that the center of a picture represents the fulcrum, the various elements may be grouped according to their apparent or suggested weight in such a way as to satisfy the sense of balance without even approximating exact symmetry (*C, D, E,* Figure 2).

Apparent weight in a picture is governed by such qualities as light and shade, color intensity, size, and suggested movement, as well as by association of ideas. In the theatre all of these must be considered, and in addition we have real movement, speech, and the elements of memory and anticipation to affect our association of ideas. The latter elements are of great importance, and apt to be neglected by the director whose training has been largely visual; he may fail to realize that a character's importance in the minds of the audience is governed by what has gone before and by what is anticipated, and that a character who is important in the minds of the audience has greater apparent weight in the picture than a less important character of greater physical stature.

Mere size does of course, suggest weight, all other things being equal. So does a dark color by comparison with a light one, while at the same time we find that actual illumination weighs more heavily than shadow—at least it seems to demand a place nearer the center of the picture. A vista seems to suggest more weight than a cut-off view, and generally looks better near the center. Movement toward the center appears to outweigh movement away from the center. A group of characters ordinarily outweighs a single character; but this may be reversed when the single character is of great dramatic importance. Generally speaking, when the physical elements are equal, apparent weight is governed by intrinsic interest; hence our traditional custom of giving the dominating character the center of the stage.

The matter of balanced weight in design is psychological rather than physical, and the key to it is to be found in the relative strength of our empathic responses. Herein also lies the reason why balance is so very important æsthetically.

We must balance our empathies for the same reason that we must unify them—that is, to avoid actual displeasure. The physical sensation of losing balance is unpleasant, even painful, to all normal people; and a picture that lacks balance makes us feel that sensation empathically.

The nature of the sense of balance itself is somewhat of a mystery. The semicircular canals of the inner ear are supposed to have something to do with it, but however that may be there is no doubt that it exists as a very real thing, even in early childhood. The fear of falling is one of the earliest fears, and whenever one feels a loss of balance that fear seems to come upon him, even though there be no actual danger. In childhood the sense of balance is crude and imperfect, or at any rate the muscular response is crude and imperfect; but as one grows older he becomes more sensitive and more skilful through practice, and those who are most sensitive and most skilful develop the keenest and most delicate sense of balance. From the standpoint of æsthetics it is not necessary to understand the nature of this sense, but it is quite necessary to realize its existence, its relation to pain and pleasure, and its effect upon our empathies.

PROPORTION

Closely associated with the problem of balance is that of proportion, which involves all questions of quantitative relationship.

The first thing to learn about proportion is that it is everywhere—that all things are relative, and therefore proportional. At the same time there is no such thing as an absolute basis for proportion; even the basis is relative. You may draw a picture of a man and then put a hat on him, raising the question of whether the hat is too large or too small for the man. Or you may draw the hat first, and then draw a man to fit the hat, as a small boy often does. Which method is the better depends upon circumstances; if you are making a poster for the window of a hat store the boy's method

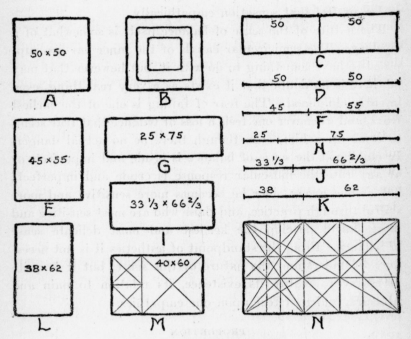

FIG. 3.—STUDIES IN PROPORTION

M represents the proportion of the "rhythmic half." *K* is (approximately) the "golden section," and *L* and *N* are golden rectangles. Note the repeated, or rhythmic, relationships in the subdivisions of *M* and *N*.

may be the more logical one. The safest starting point for any problem in proportion would seem to be that which is most closely associated with the dominant thought or purpose of the work under consideration.

The psychology of proportion is a little more obscure than that of balance, and on one point seems a bit inconsistent with it. Balance implies equality, yet equality is a relatively uninteresting proportion. Balance is a matter of pivoting weights—or apparent weights—on a center, but if we make the center of balance the exact center of a picture (as in E, Figure 2) the effect is not entirely pleasing. We do not seem to like an equal division; it may be that our empathic responses in such a case are too evenly balanced, creating an impasse or dilemma which baffles the mind more than it rests the senses. The mind demands unity, and there can be no unity where there is division without subordination (as in C and D, Figure 3). The effect is too much like walking a tight rope; the balance is good, but too critical.

In respect to the proportion of length and breadth the same rule seems to hold; a square is generally less interesting than an oblong, especially when its squareness is emphasized in some way (as in B, Figure 3). The square is a very useful element in combination with others, but as an independent form it has the same baffling quality as the bisected line. One never knows whether it is right side up.

However, mere inequality is not in itself a sign of good proportion. A rectangle forty-five by fifty-five (E, Figure 3) looks a bit "dumpy" by itself, while one twenty-five by seventy-five looks too long and narrow (G, Figure 3); though again it must be said that both are useful enough elements in composite design. A proportion of thirty-three and a third to sixty-six and two thirds, or one to two, is much better than either of these, and may be contemplated separately without great violence to the æsthetic sense. The rectangle of one to two is not particularly interesting (I, Figure 3), but in the division of lengths a proportion of one to two is generally fairly pleasing (J, Figure 3).

It is this proportion that governs the length of the rectangle shown at M, the famous rectangle of the "rhythmic half," which many designers consider the most useful, if not

the most beautiful, basic form. A square is extended by half
a square, so that the length is one and one-half times the
breadth; the rectangle thus consists of one large square and
two small ones, which seem to echo it rhythmically. There
is no doubt that the eye finds this proportion beautiful, and
the fact that the diametric ratio is simple—two to three—
makes it easy to use.

But there is one other proportion which for pure abstract
beauty has been long regarded as the finest of all: the proportion of the so-called "golden section." It is expressed in
the formula,

$$x : y :: y : x + y$$

Mathematically this is a difficult formula to handle, for the
relationships involved are not perfectly commensurate, but
for all practical purposes in design the ratio may be regarded
as that of thirty-eight to sixty-two. The "golden section"
is illustrated at K in Figure 3, and the golden rectangle at
L and N. The internal relationships of the golden rectangle
are most interesting. Take a square from one end, and you
have a smaller golden rectangle left; take a square from that
and you have a still smaller one. Draw the diagonals of the
squares and rectangles as at N, and you have a perfect deluge
of little squares and rectangles, most of the latter showing
the golden ratio. If there is rhythm in the discovery of the
repeated squares in the "rhythmic half" there must be much
more in the discovery of all these subtleties of repetition.
Whether our appreciation of these forms really is rhythmic
would be hard to say. The relationships are all so abstract
that one wonders whether the mind can grasp them without
conscious effort, and of course it is the unconscious response
rather than the conscious that we must consider. Certainly

there is general agreement that these two proportions are pleasing.

It must not be thought, however, that all the elements in a composite design should display the golden ratio, or even an approximation of it. That would be monotonous in the extreme. There is plenty of use for the less beautiful forms provided they are worked together harmoniously, counter-balancing each other's faults, and producing a total effect of good proportion. A poorly proportioned actor may fit in with other actors to make a well proportioned group; or a poorly proportioned group may join with furniture and setting to make a well proportioned stage picture. When we hang a long narrow picture over a mantel-piece we do so because that element, badly proportioned in itself, is just what is needed to complete an effect of good proportion for the whole scheme of decoration. The west front of Notre Dame Cathedral shows several long narrow rectangles, and several short squatty ones, and the central element is a square, enclosing a circle. Yet the proportion of the whole, and the interrelations of the parts, are excellent beyond description.

In the composite art of the theatre there are problems of proportion as between the theme and the plot, the ascending and descending action, the climax and sub-climaxes, the play and its acts, the main character and subordinate characters, the lines and the business, the actors and the setting, the words and the music, the thought and the feeling; and there are problems of internal proportion in most of these elements, including those of visual proportion in the composition of the stage pictures.

The director cannot solve these problems by slide-rule methods. He cannot say for instance that in a play lasting one hundred minutes the main climax should occur at the end of the sixty-second minute; or that the proscenium arch should always measure exactly thirty-eight by sixty-two feet; or that the performance should consist of three parts words and two parts music. What he can do is to cultivate his own sensibilities in the matter of proportion by first making an intelligent study of the principles involved, and then forming a habit of observing proportions—not only in objects of art but in everything about him. After a time he will find that a bad proportion in any phase of his work will be as painful to him as a bad note is to a musician.

HARMONY

After what has been said about unity and empathy, and their relationship, the principle of harmony may be easily understood. Each element in a composition provokes a corresponding empathic response, and in order that these responses may blend agreeably the elements themselves must be in physical harmony.

The laws underlying the principle are those of physics and physiology. Harmony of pitch, in music, for example, is a question of the frequency or rate of vibration of the sound waves. The audible frequencies range from about sixteen cycles per second to several thousand. Each octave in the ascending scale represents a doubling of the frequency. The frequency ratio between a note and its octave is thus one to two, a very simple ratio; every second beat of the higher note coincides with a beat of the lower (A, Figure 4), and the result is a harmonious blending of sound, empathically pleasant. Other combinations of notes, like the first and third or first and fifth, have frequency ratios only a little less simple, and produce almost equally pleasant harmonies. But some notes have frequencies that do not bear a simple relation to each other, and such notes in combination produce dissonances because the beats almost never coincide (*D*, Figure 4).

In a similar way the slower rhythms of the tempo in music and dancing show problems of harmony which have a simple

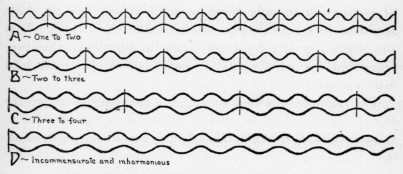

A ~ One To Two

B ~ Two to three

C ~ Three to four

D ~ Incommensurate and inharmonious

FIG. 4.—HARMONIOUS AND INHARMONIOUS FREQUENCIES

mathematical basis. A movement in two-four time, for example, blends readily with one in four-four or common time, while a movement in three-four or waltz time does not. Within reasonable limits we enjoy the effort to harmonize slightly different movements, just as we enjoy the effort of finding unity when it is not too obvious; and it is to give just such pleasure that some composers make use of displaced accent, triplets, grace-notes, syncopation, and cadenzas. In general, however, the more easily the rhythms blend the greater the sense of harmony and the greater our empathic enjoyment.

The problem of color harmony is much more abstruse. Differences in color theoretically represent differences in the rate of vibration of light, but as the frequencies of light run to trillions of cycles per second it is hopeless to look for any mathematical basis of empathic effect. Moreover, the visual sensation of color does not seem to bear an absolute relation to the mechanical theory of color, the physiological laws being quite distinct from the physical ones. Theoretically there are vast numbers of pure colors between the lowest red and the highest violet of the spectrum, each having its own definite frequency. Actually the normal eye is capable of distinguishing only three primary colors, and all color sensation is but a varying combination of these three. It is the physiology of color rather than the physics of the spectrum that the artist needs to know—but of that more in a later chapter.

The point here is that there are underlying laws governing the relationships of all natural elements, and that when these laws clash the empathic effect is essentially unpleasant.

GRACE

Herbert Spencer defined graceful motion as "motion that is effected with economy of force." A graceful line, figure, or picture is one that suggests, empathically, a similar economy of force.

Grace does not mean weakness or passivity. A graceful motion may be forceful, swift, and impetuous, if the result achieved is in proportion and there is no sense of futility or waste. It is in the suggestion of misapplied effort, or of effort impeded by hopeless incapacity or unsuitability that we experience a sense of ungracefulness. To feel that a motion is graceful we must feel that there is no easier or pleasanter way of accomplishing the desired result.

Grace is pleasing for the obvious reason that normal human nature dislikes unnecessary effort, or the empathic suggestion thereof. It is not that we are all hopelessly lazy; indeed, most of us enjoy a sense of bodily activity, and gladly expend energy in a good cause. But we do not like to waste it in mere friction, and we do not like the baffling

sense of futility when the results seem inadequate in proportion to the effort expended. We like to get the largest
and freest sense of action from the least possible effort. This
undoubtedly accounts—at least partially—for the great
popularity of such sports as skating, tobogganing, and motor-
ing. It also accounts for the fact that we prefer a smooth
sweet-running eight-cylinder car to a rattling wheezy "one-
lunger." We feel the labor and strain of the latter in our
bodily responses, and the sensation is distressing. The man
who regularly drives his own car becomes extraordinarily
sensitive to the slightest change or irregularity in its rhythms,
and suffers bodily distress at any indication of loss of power.
Objects in nature affect us in the same way. It is pleasant
to watch the seemingly effortless flight of a sea gull, soaring
into the wind on motionless wings; but a waddling duck is
not so pleasing an object, especially to a fat man. The mere
sight of a dachshund is painful—or would be but for the
saving relief of humor. From the standpoint of unsatisfying
effort nothing, probably, is more distressing than the sensation we sometimes experience in a dream when our feet seem
weighted with lead, and the slightest movement seems to
require almost superhuman effort.

When we empathize in the suggested movement of a picture
or statue, or the real movement of a character on the stage,
we normally prefer that movement to be graceful—that is,
easy and economical of effort. There are exceptions, of course
—movements and situations in which the meaning demands
awkwardness. But gratuitous awkwardness we resent, because
we cannot help feeling it in ourselves. I have mentioned the
effect when one actor has to carry another and seems to have
great difficulty in doing so. Similarly when an actor stands
or moves awkwardly, or when the setting displays ungraceful

lines, we are bound to feel uncomfortable because our induced motor patterns are ungraceful.

But what lines are, as a matter of fact, ungraceful? What classes of lines suggest economy of force, and what classes do not?

Off hand one might suppose that a straight line, being the shortest distance between two points, would represent the greatest possible economy of force in motion, and consequently the finest grace. This, however, is not the case. What is gained by economy in distance is more than lost by the sense of effort in keeping the line straight. If one tries to walk a chalk line for fifty or a hundred feet he is quite conscious of the effort required, and if he tries to draw a straight line on paper he finds it much more difficult than to draw certain types of curves. The effort suggested by the straight line is the effort of self-conscious rigidity, of intentional resistance to contending forces, of artificial and precarious balance. This does not mean that the straight line is never useful in design, but it does mean that its usefulness is generally to be found in the achievement of effects other than grace.

So for the perfect circle. It is useful, but not primarily graceful, at least with respect to the motion that it suggests. An arc of a circle is, like a straight line, artificially regular and self-conscious; its motion is maintained against the insistent pull of centrifugal force, and therefore implies considerable effort. The circle is most pleasing when used whole, with the emphasis upon its unity and centrality; it is least pleasing when the eye is led around its circumference.

Somewhat more grace may be found in the other conic section curves: ellipse, parabola, and hyperbola (*B, C, D,* Figure 5). They are not all perfectly graceful, especially if considered in their entirety, but they do show some variation of curvature at different points and a portion of one side taken near the focus is sometimes fairly pleasing.

Still more graceful curves are to be found among the so-

FIG. 5.—STUDIES IN GRACE OF LINE

Conic section curves: *A*, circle; *B*, ellipse; *C*, parabola; *D*, hyperbola. Higher degree curves: *E*, spiral of Archimedes; *F*, reciprocal or hyperbolic spiral; *G*, lituus; *H*, logarithmic spiral; *J*, catenary curve. Double curves: *K*, two circular arcs; *L*, a lituus and a spiral of Archimedes; *M*, an arithmetic spiral and a lituus.

called "higher plane" curves—that is, curves whose mathematical formulas involve trigonometric functions or coefficients higher than the square. Most of the spirals belong to this class (*E*, *F*, *G*, *H*, Figure 5). Another curve, by some artists considered the most graceful of all, is the catenary curve, or festoon curve—the curve made by a perfectly flexible cable or chain supported at two points (*J*, Figure 5). This is often seen nowadays, slightly modified for engineering reasons, in suspension bridges, and is, of course, very common in draperies and decorations.

The trouble with straight lines and circles is that they imply a perfect balance of forces not often found in nature.

Natural forces are unequal, and the confluence of unequal forces results in curves of more varied type and more complex formula. Such curves are more graceful for the very reason that they seem more natural, less studied, less suggestive of conscious effort. It is precisely because the catenary curve is the natural position of flexible draperies that it suggests absence of effort.

These are all single curves, but with other things equal a double curve is ordinarily more graceful and more interesting than a single one. Its superior grace is doubtless due to the compensating effect suggested; the centrifugal force developed in the first part is absorbed or neutralized by the opposite force in the second part. Even in double curves, however, an exact equality between the two parts is not pleasant; we prefer curves in which we can discern no studied ratio. It is economy of mental as well as physical effort that constitutes grace.

Perhaps that will do to suggest the principle. The application of this and other principles of design in the art of the theatre is obvious enough in a general way if one remembers the strength of empathic effects in the theatre; and of course it is obvious in relation to scenic art. No stage director can possibly know too much of the principles of design, or have his tastes and sensibilities too highly trained.

CHAPTER V

PREPARATION OF THE PLAY

WE TURN now to the more practical problems of play production; and for the sake of order and completeness I shall begin with some elementary matters that will seem to have little relation to the technical principles so far discussed. The usefulness of the latter will, however, become gradually clearer as we proceed.

Most books on play production for amateurs devote considerable space to the problem of choosing a play, but this is so largely a matter of local conditions that no specific recipe appears to be very helpful. The professional producer chooses a play that he thinks will bring in a large profit; the amateur chooses one that be thinks is within the capabilities of his actors and his equipment, and that promises to please the particular audience to which he must appeal.

In the latter particular the amateur producer sometimes runs unwisely to extremes. When the audience is a popular one, not especially intellectual, he selects entertaining comedies and farces, and for a time all goes well. The audience enjoys an occasional evening of harmless laughter and the players have a good time. But neither the players nor the audience make very much intellectual or artistic progress; the work of staging and rehearsing seems more and more futile and irksome, the older members grow tired of doing all the hard work, and withdraw; very young people take their places, and the dramatic purpose gradually gives way to a social one. When, on the other hand, the audience is a bit "arty," the producer is apt to select more or less unpleasant plays of the ultra-realistic, or expressionistic, or psychopathic type, with the result that after a time the company degenerates into a class in abnormal psychology, and the audience dwindles until only the neurotics remain.

As a matter of general policy it would seem best to choose plays sufficiently varied in their appeal to keep the interest of the normal human animal, but at the same time sufficiently good in a literary and artistic way to make the work spent on them worth while. The real test of a play is its effect upon the players. If they grow to like it better and better as they work with it—to see new meaning, new humor, new beauty in each repetition, even after five or six public performances— the play is a good play, and is worth doing, both for its own sake and for its influence on the morale of the organization. But if after a half dozen rehearsals it seems to grow wearisome, the sentiments begin to seem tawdry and the jokes stale, the ultimate effect will be bad.

THE ONE ACT PLAY

It is a matter of frequent dispute whether an amateur organization should give most of its time to the production of one act plays rather than plays of full length. It is quite properly pointed out that the one act plays at present available for amateur production are more numerous, more varied, more fanciful, and generally more original than the longer plays equally available; that they are simpler to produce, offer a better distribution of parts, and require fewer rehearsals. Moreover, they are undoubtedly cheaper. Few carry a royalty higher than ten dollars a performance, many are to be had at five, and some are free of royalty; whereas modern plays of three or four acts at all comparable in literary merit are held at fifty or one hundred dollars a performance. These are all good arguments for the use of the one act play, and because of them the one act play is very popular with amateurs, especially with those worthy groups of amateurs who are trying to raise the artistic and literary standards of the drama.

But the one act play has certain serious limitations, one of which is that the modern audience unquestionably prefers the unity of the longer play. This has been demonstrated again and again. With the same group of players, the same direction, and the same potential audience, the bill of one act plays draws a small attendance and the full length play a large one. Quite apart from the financial advantage it is clearly better for the players and for the organization to have the largest and most eager audiences possible. Another limitation is that the great majority of modern one act plays, though high in artistic aim, are amateurish in execution; they are, as a matter of fact, largely the work of amateur dramatists. To conceal this quality in the production requires the most expert direction and the highest skill of the professional actor, especially in the reading of the lines. It is the ambition of most amateurs to approach a professional standard of ease and smoothness, but their best chance of doing so is to start with a play that is not in itself amateurish, and the one act play seldom gives them this opportunity. Finally, the one act play is not nearly so good a training school for the actor as is generally supposed. It is true that three or four one act plays offer more leading parts than one long play, but on the other hand the one act play is much less exacting in its demands for teamwork—the most important and the most difficult part of acting—and it is generally episodic in structure with very little suggestion of growth or development. One may learn to play isolated scenes and do character bits, to portray single traits or moods, and still have no conception of the larger problems involved in acting —problems of emphasis, balance, proportion, development, and coördination. On the whole, the earnest amateur will learn more by playing a small part in a big play, under good direction and in company with more experienced players, than he could learn by playing more important parts in several one act plays.

As to the choice of particular plays there is little to be said. It is altogether a matter of what is wanted and what is available. In the bibliographical appendix of this book will be found some suggestions as to where to look for the best list of plays; no actual lists are included for the reason that their usefulness would be merely temporary.

The matter of royalties is a serious one for amateurs. Authors cannot be blamed for wanting to be paid for their labors, and amateurs should regard the payment of royalty, when due, as their first obligation. But the prevailing royalties for good modern plays are undoubtedly too high, and amateur groups in very small theatres cannot afford to pay them. They must either forego the use of desirable plays, or steal them; and many, unfortunately, are dishonest enough to do the latter. Authors and agents take the position that good plays are valuable property, and should not be rented for production at a low price; but the actual effect of high flat royalties is injury to the authors' interests. Honest, responsible amateurs in the little theatres, who would gladly pay a modest royalty for a good play, refrain from using that play if the royalty is too high; while the dishonest ones give it surreptitiously, often under a false title, and without crediting the author.

The system of flat royalties is all wrong. Fifty dollars is not an excessive royalty for a recent popular success when it is to be given to an audience of a thousand people at one dollar a ticket; but when a little theatre group is playing two or three times a month to a subscription audience of one hundred and fifty at ten dollars a season, a fifty dollar royalty is prohibitive. The willingness of many authors and a few agents to reduce royalties in a good cause does not solve the problem; it puts the whole thing on a charity basis, and favors those whose lack of self-respect will permit them to beg for special consideration. Several attempts have been made by the Drama League and the various little theatre organizations to secure a better working agreement with authors and publishers, but with little progress. The only system that ever will be, or can be, equitable, is an honest percentage system.

STUDYING THE PLAY

It would seem natural after selecting a play—if not before—to study it carefully in order to discover the author's aim and purpose. Yet many directors, amateur and professional, are content to omit this step, and to plunge right into rehearsals with the idea of learning the play in the process. In a professional production the skill of the actors and their ability to coöperate quickly with the last-minute inspirations of the director sometimes save him from the consequence of this procedure; but the amateur director can count upon no such luck. If there is one supreme shortcoming of the inexperienced actor it is his inability to unlearn something which he has once learned wrong, and if rehearsals are begun before the director knows what he is about, some things certainly will be learned wrong, and will have to be unlearned. Moreover it is well to remember that the director who shows a thorough knowledge of the play at the first rehearsal commands the respect of his actors and gets better work out of them.

The wise director will, therefore, seek first to know the play, to understand its construction, its plot, theme, and characters, and to grasp the full significance of the author's message.

In construction, every play is basically a conflict between two main forces, one of which is more universal, abstract and extensive than the other. The fortunes of the protagonist, his aims, ambitions, and desires, ordinarily constitute the more particular force; while the more universal consists of the law of God or man, the doctrine of chance, the established conventions, prejudices, and inhibitions of society, or the larger influences of heredity or environment. Another way of saying the same thing is to say that every play represents the struggle of a protagonist against forces greater than himself—or, as some put it, against Fate.

A play in which the protagonist triumphs over the universal forces is technically a comedy, and one in which the universal forces triumph over the protagonist is technically a tragedy. These designations do not always correspond, of course, to the popular ones, or the ones stated in the playbills. Most of Barrie's plays, for example, are known and billed as comedies, but are in reality tragedies in that the characters fail to rise above their obstacles. Some of the broadest farces are technically tragedies for the same reason. On the other hand many of the most intense dramas, like *The Merchant of Venice*, or *The Two Orphans*, are technically comedies, because they end triumphantly, with the obstacles overcome.

If a director is to produce a play intelligently he must know the nature of the conflict involved; he must know which is the universal and which the particular force, and whether the play is a comedy or tragedy. He must know what subordinate plots or counter plots there are, and what relation they bear to the main plot. He must know the nature and position of the climax—the high point of action, the point at which the main plot turns and begins to resolve itself in the final direction. Without such knowledge he cannot hope to work up the proper dramatic foreshadowing, to point up the important scenes, and to maintain the proper balance and proportion.

But plot is not all. In nearly every play there is also a theme, an abstract idea of some sort, often more important than the plot. It is generally the theme, rather than the plot, that determines the spirit of the play and the mood in which it is to be played. In a satirical play, for example, the plot may be quite serious, and a group of actors who grasp the plot but miss the theme may perform the play as a romantic comedy or heroic tragedy, failing completely to carry the point. In Shaw's *Saint Joan* the plot is the tragic story of the life and death of Joan of Arc, but the theme is the cynically humorous one that although the saints are good souls who mean well, they are hard to get along with in real life, and are much to be preferred in the dead and canonized state. The whole flavor of any play depends upon the director's recognition of the theme.

One can always find the plot—if there is one—by reading the play, but the theme and spirit and mood are sometimes so subtle and elusive that they can only be sensed after considerable study. A knowledge of the author and of his other work is here very helpful; likewise a knowledge of dramatic history and the kinds and types of plays current in each period. When it is possible for the director to confer with the living author the advantage gained is great. The ideal situation is of course that in which the director is himself the author. In the latter case he will not only be familiar with the text of the play, but will—presumably—know the author's intention throughout, and will have visualized the scenes and characters in his imagination. When the director is not the author his first task is to put himself imaginatively in the author's place.

The question of whether the director has the right to consider himself the author and to change or falsify the author's meaning is interesting, but it is a moral or legal question rather than an artistic one, and so a little out of our province. It is well within our province, however, to consider how he may best modify or alter or adapt the written text in order to convey the author's message with the greatest artistic fidelity.

EDITING THE TEXT

When a new play is staged under the direction of the author, or in consultation with him, it ordinarily undergoes considerable last minute alteration. Only a very egotistical author regards his text as final and inviolable, or supposes himself infallible in the matter of foresight. In the case of an older play, however, many directors consider the text too sacred for alteration. With respect to plays of high literary or poetic merit there is some justification for this feeling; yet it is almost inconceivable that any play could be revived after a lapse of time and played by a different company, in a different theatre, with different costumes, settings, and properties, and to an audience of different training and environment, without at least some modification of text. It may well be that the greatest service the director can render the author is to adapt the text to the new situation in such a way that the message of the play may not be lost.

This does not necessarily mean a great deal of re-writing or addition to the text—the dangers of which are fairly obvious. It means, as a rule, intelligent cutting, judicious re-arrangement of scenes, excision or alteration of passages that may have lost their original meaning through changes in language or through loss of allusive reference; alteration of phraseology to meet the unavoidable limitations of the actors; and modification of the action as necessitated by limitations of equipment.

The recognition and acceptance of limitations are among the director's first concerns, and their importance from an æsthetic point of view has already been emphasized. When the limitations are such as to make adequate production of a given play impossible, the only honest procedure is to choose another play. When they are such as not to interfere with the main thought of the play it is far better not to struggle uselessly against them, but to accept them frankly and adapt the play to fit them.

For example, if the text calls for hearty laughter on the part of the heroine, and the leading lady, otherwise satisfactory, is unable to laugh convincingly on the stage, the question then arises: Is the laughter essential to the thought of the play? If so, there are only two possible solutions, a new leading lady or a new play. If not, why ruin the play by an unconvincing laugh? Would it not be better to revise the text, eliminating the laugh?

Or suppose that the text specifies a practical staircase for entrances and exits in full view of the audience, and the limitations of the stage make such a thing impossible. Again the question: Is it essential to the meaning of the play? If so— another play, or another theatre. If not, the best plan is to do without the staircase and alter the text to suit. It is generally more satisfactory to eliminate the impracticable feature entirely, even at the cost of considerable change in the text, than to adopt a pretentious compromise. One group that I knew of went to a great deal of trouble to solve just such a staircase problem on a very restricted stage by having an archway built out from the wall, with one or two steps leading up into it and a platform on which the actor might stand concealed after having supposedly gone up stairs. But the members of the audience—all regular subscribers—knew that there was a solid wall behind that archway and that the actor must be hiding just out of sight, and their attention was distracted accordingly; they were busy watching to catch a glimpse of his elbow or coat-tails instead of paying attention to the play. It would have been possible to have used an ordinary exit, right or left, with an imaginary stairway off stage, and to have suggested it by a line in the text and by having the actor look upwards at the proper angle when making his exit. The simpler solution will almost invariably prove the better, for the very good reason that the imagination requires only a little assistance in a constructive way, whereas it is very easily distracted by any sort of unnecessary complication.

The amateur director has, of course, a great many more limitations to contend with than the professional. The latter usually works in a regular theatre with standard equipment, and almost anything called for in the text can be supplied in some fashion. In reviving an old play he can use the stage directions of the original production, placing entrances and exits as called for in the text, and depending upon the stage manager and stage crew to reproduce the original effects with reasonable accuracy. He cannot always choose an ideal cast, especially in stock company work, but at least he can rely upon some experience and adaptability on the part of his actors, and he can expect steady attendance at rehearsals and earnest work. The amateur director, on the other hand, must often put up with the most distressing obstacles in limitation of stage space and equipment, in lack of time and assistance, in inadequacy of financial resources, and in the inexperience of his actors. Under these circumstances he will more often find himself under the necessity of modifying the text.

It would be impossible to catalogue all the types of alteration and modification that are most apt to prove necessary, but the mention of one or two of the most common may suggest the sort of thing a trained director must be prepared to do.

CUTTING

The most common of all is, of course, cutting. Most long plays, especially five act plays, are, in the original text, too long for modern production, especially by amateurs, and must be considerably abridged. Even a modern comedy arranged for professional production in two hours and a half will often require further cutting when produced by amateurs, partly because the waits are apt to be longer, and partly because the amateurs are apt to be slower in getting through the dialogue. Accurate timing of a play cannot, of course, be done until rehearsals are going smoothly, but the intelligent director can do the bulk of the necessary cutting in advance if he gives his mind to it, and in so doing he can combine cutting for length with abridgement for clarity and consistency.

Most amateur directors, and a good many professional ones, put altogether too much confidence in the so-called standard "acting editions," especially of Shakespeare's plays. Many of these represent stage precedent dating back to the eighteenth century—a period when Shakespeare was generally misunderstood and misinterpreted—and in some instances they represent very radical revisions of Shakespeare by eighteenth century authors determined to make him conform to the spirit of their own time. Even the best acting editions are, as a rule, taken from the prompt books of eminent actors who made their cuttings primarily for the display of their own talents rather than for the unity of the play.

The modern director, amateur or professional, should make his own acting edition. In the case of Shakespeare he should start with a good standard edition based on the First Folio of 1623. By cutting out the portions least helpful in conveying the meaning to his particular audience, and by rearranging and adapting the remainder, he will get something more honest and more effective than he could get by following the prompt book of Garrick or Forrest or Booth—based originally, perhaps, on a revision by Colley Cibber.

In the preparation of an English play for production in America it must be borne in mind that there are some language differences, that some words and phrases which are merely commonplace in England are unintelligible or misleading to an American audience. Where such elements are necessary to the English flavor, and the English flavor is necessary to the play, they should of course be left in, even at the expense of a footnote in the program explaining them. More often it will be found that an omission or substitution can be made with a gain in clearness and without loss of truth or spirit.

In the same way obscurities of meaning caused by lapse of time are best ironed out, unless there is some definite gain in archaic flavor to be had by leaving them in. A play twenty or twenty-five years old is not generally old enough to be worth treating as archaic; costumes, settings, properties, and dialogue may best be brought up to date, and the time specified as "the present." But a play seventy-five or one hundred years old is usually beyond this process, and so better played in the spirit of its time. Even in the latter case there will be some passages in the text that because of obsolete words or lost allusions will do more to destroy clearness than to bear out the archaic flavor. The author intended them to be clear; if they are not, it may be falsifying his meaning more to leave them as they are than to change them.

But the most troublesome modifications of text are those made necessary by the limitations of the actors. For example, many dramatists make a habit of leaving lines of dialogue unfinished for the sake of naturalness, allowing the characters to interrupt each other as people do in real life. Professional actors are sometimes able to carry this out in a natural way, but inexperienced amateurs have great difficulty with it; either they interrupt too soon, destroying the meaning, or they interrupt too late, leaving an awkward pause. What is worse, the actor who is to be interrupted anticipates it in his tone, and stops with a suggestive coaxing inflection as if to say, "Come on now, interrupt me; that's the end of my line." In another chapter I shall try to suggest ways of combatting these tendencies when the meaning requires that the broken dialogue be retained. But when it does not, the director will often find it more expedient to complete or curtail the interrupted lines, and to rely upon other means of achieving naturalness. There is no use in retaining a device which the author intended for naturalness if the effect with a particular actor is greater *un*naturalness.

The language of many plays is literary rather than conversational, and only actors of some ability and experience can deliver such language convincingly and without artificiality. When the play is of high literary merit it is of course better to put up with the artificiality for the sake of the beauty; but when the only effect of the artificiality is stiltedness—as in the case of many nineteenth century plays —and when the actors are inexperienced, a certain amount of re-writing for naturalness will be found expedient. An actor who cannot say, "The carriage waits," without appearing a stick may be able to say "The carriage is waiting, sir," with reasonable naturalness.

In the preparation of the text the director should always make sure that his scholarship is equal to the task, and that he is not merely working upon ignorance and guesswork. If he feels the need of revision and is not competent to do it himself he should seek help of some one who is.

THE PROMPT BOOK

All cuts and revisions should be carefully marked in the prompt book and in the individual parts to be given the actors, and care should be taken to see that all subsequent corrections are entered in both places.

If the play is in printed form and on small pages, the best way to prepare the prompt book is to cut up two copies and paste the pages on larger sheets of heavy paper with margins, so that all corrections, stage directions, calls and warnings can be clearly entered. The whole can then be roughly rebound. If the play is type-written it will usually have plenty of marginal space for this purpose. If it is rented and must be returned without disfiguration it may be interleaved with blank sheets clipped to the pages, and the notes entered on these.

It is an evident advantage for the director to have his prompt copy ready for annotation when he begins his study of the play, so that he can enter all his notes and comments as he goes. This sometimes results in so much marking up that a new and simpler copy has to be prepared for the prompter to use at actual performances; but aside from the cost of the additional copy this is not a disadvantage. In my own case I prefer to work this way, and to keep possession of the original copy myself. This leaves me free to include many detailed directions with which I should not want to burden the prompter, and to omit from my copy the various calls, warnings, and back-stage cues that should always appear in the actual prompt copy.

PLANNING THE SETTINGS

Having mastered the play and made the necessary cuts the director can set about planning the settings. The actual designing of settings to complete the beauty of the production is a special problem, and will be more appropriately considered in a later chapter. Moreover, it is often delegated to some one other than the director. But it is the director's own work to determine how many settings are needed, what their general arrangement is to be, what the dominating note of each is to be in order to establish the mood of the scene, and how the entrances and exits are to be placed—the latter being a very important advance consideration.

There are three different ways in which the problem of setting may present itself to the director. It may be a question of how to design a new setting appropriate and adequate to the play. Or it may be a question of how to modify and rearrange a stock setting so as to approximate the arrangement called for in the text. Or—and with most amateur directors this is the usual experience—it may be a question of how to make shift with the only setting available. Many a professional director who could solve the first problem easily would find his ingenuity seriously taxed by the last.

ENTRANCES AND EXITS

Insofar as there is any option in the matter the director should exercise the greatest care in the placing of entrances and exits, for they have much to do with the effectiveness of stage pictures and bits of action. What might be called the stock arrangement for interior settings provides three entrances, right, left, and center (*A*, Figure 6), the center door being often a double one or a large open doorway. The

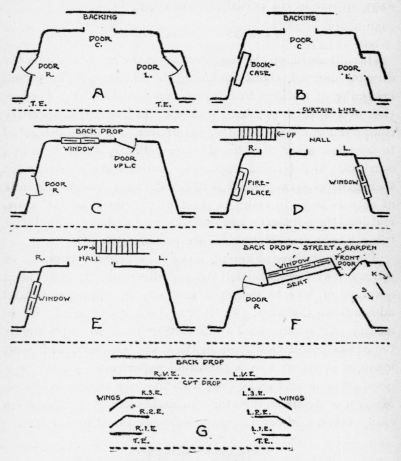

FIG. 6.—ARRANGEMENTS OF ENTRANCES AND EXITS

A, B, and *C* are common arrangements in cottage interiors. *D* and *E* suggest city houses, and *F* a suburban house. *G* is the conventional wing-and-drop exterior setting, with old-fashioned numbered entrances.

constant repetition of this same arrangement in a succession of plays is of course monotonous, yet the plan is a good one, flexible, and adaptable to almost any play. It is certainly better to use the stock entrances than to be obliged to do without them when they are needed. One of the worst possible handicaps in the arrangement of stage pictures and movements is to be denied the use of an entrance where one ought to be placed for best effect.

In general the following suggestions will be found helpful in the planning of entrances and exits:

1. Have enough of them to account for all comings and goings and to tell the story intelligibly.

2. Do not have more than are needed. An unused exit, visible to the audience, is a source of constant distraction; people are busy wondering where it leads to or who is to come in by it when they should be paying attention to the play. If a stock set is used having an extra door not needed in the play it is better to make a window of it, or an alcove, or to conceal it with draperies or a piece of furniture (*B*, Figure 6). The number of exits should be as small as is consistent with clarity and convincingness. Ordinarily two or three will be enough; some plays, especially farces and melodramas, require more.

3. Let each exit mean some particular place mentioned or implied in the text, and then see to it that it is always used by an actor supposed to be going to that place, or coming from it. Audiences are very quick to notice a discrepancy in this. It is sometimes possible, of course, to use one exit as indicating several places. For example, an upstairs sitting-room may have only one doorway leading to the hall, used alike by persons going to another room or to the street. An open doorway may be made to suggest two exits, one right and the other left, according to which way the actor turns. In the setting shown at *D*, Figure 6, two archways give on a hall; the street door is imagined in the hall off stage left,

and the rest of the house off right. At *E*, Figure 6, there is only one doorway to the room itself, but it shows three exits: a street exit off right, a back hall off left, and a stairway leading up.

4. Let the arrangement be a conceivable one, possible in a real house—not necessarily an exact imitation of reality built to scale, but something bearing at least a slight resemblance to the arrangements familiar in real life, so that the audience is not unduly puzzled and distracted. The settings shown at *A* and *B*, in Figure 6, are possible, though not particularly suggestive of reality. That at *C* is sufficiently convincing as suggesting a small cottage. Those at *D* and *E* suggest real city houses, and have been effectively used in many plays. The setting at *F*, representing a country house, is an elaborate attempt to be convincing; it shows a hallway and front door at stage left, with an exit to the kitchen at κ and one to the stairway at s; and the situation is further clarified by a broad window showing the outdoor approach through a front garden. So far the arrangement is successful enough as suggesting a real house, but it is very one-sided, and would tend to throw the action too constantly to the left; and in a feeble attempt to correct this the director has added a most unconvincing door at the right, the effect of which is to puzzle the audience as to the construction of the house, and so distract them. After all, the problem is not so much how to create a positive illusion of reality as how to avoid destroying illusion by distracting attention. The trouble with a setting which is too unreal is that it does just that.

5. Let the entrances be so placed as to be easily seen by all the members of the audience. Nothing is more annoying to the spectator than an arrangement like that at *A*, Figure 7, which represents the stage of a certain club-house. The walls are solid and immovable, and the proscenium arch is narrower

than the stage itself, so that the right door is always invisible to nearly half the audience, and the left door to the other half. Every actor entering right or left must walk about six feet in view of some of the audience before he is visible to all of them; and whenever during the action he goes near either side of the stage some of the audience are left in doubt as to whether he has gone off or not. In arranging entrances and exits the director should have in mind the shape of the auditorium as well as that of the stage, and should take pity on those who are unfortunate enough to occupy the stage boxes and the sides of the balcony.

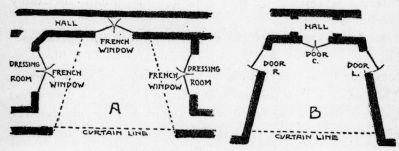

FIG. 7.—TYPICAL CLUB-HOUSE STAGES

6. Let some of the entrances be placed down stage. This is especially important in a long act with much coming and going. An arrangement like that at *B*, Figure 7, representing another stupidly designed club-house, grows fearfully monotonous after a time. If the action is to be kept down stage each entering character must walk straight toward the audience before he seems to be part of the play, and straight away from it before making his exit. The result of such an arrangement is either an arbitrary awkwardness, or an irresistible tendency for the actors to hang back up stage. In a formal play the artificial parade to the footlights is some-

times acceptable, especially if it be made a frank convention throughout; but in a realistic modern comedy it is destructive of illusion. Only the most skilful director can arrange natural stage movements for such a setting.

7. Let the doors be hung to swing down stage, as at *A* and *C*, Figure 6. The arrangement at *A*, with the doors swinging down stage and opening off stage, is the usual one; but that at *C* is fairly common, and is very useful when a character is to peep in and be seen doing so. Only very exceptional circumstances would justify a door placed to swing up stage, for the fairly obvious reason that the movement of an actor entering or leaving by such a door would almost inevitably be clumsy.

8. Avoid the use of the so-called "tormentor entrances," i.e., the spaces between the proscenium arch and the "tormentors," or false proscenium, as at T.E. in *A*, or *G*, Figure 6. The audience does not naturally think of them as doorways; they are part of the frame whose purpose is the maintenance of æsthetic distance, and their use for entrance or exit is destructive of illusion, especially in realistic plays.

9. In exterior scenes with wing settings, as at *G* in Figure 6, avoid indiscriminate use of the entrances and exits between the wings. Establish the meaning of each exit used, and stick to that exit for that meaning. If it seems confusing to leave some of them constantly unused it may be possible to block them up from the stage by means of set pieces—trees, rocks, benches, bushes, or fences, or perhaps projecting bits of buildings. Never block up an entrance off stage, however, when it looks open as seen from the stage. To do so is to invite some nervous or forgetful actor into a most embarrassing trap.

10. Let the most important entrances—those that are to figure most vividly in the essential action of the play—be so

placed as to catch the eye easily; and if possible have them so designed as to create a sense of expectation. When an actor enters through an inconspicuous doorway the effect is one of surprise; when he enters through a conspicuous or seemingly significant doorway it is rather one of inevitability satisfied. Usually the latter is the more desirable effect.

WINDOWS

The placing of windows may be part of the problem in design and decoration, or it may be a matter of the essential action of the play. When the dramatist requires a character to look in or out of a window, open or close one, speak or signal from one, or when there is some significance in the light coming through a window or in the view seen through it, the placing of that window is just as fundamental to the action of the play as the placing of entrances and exits.

A window through which the audience is expected to see something should normally be placed up stage, either in the rear flat or in a sharply slanting wall, and not in a side wall visible to only half of the audience. A large window is best for this purpose, so that the backing to be seen by the audience can be placed at a reasonable distance behind the window and still be visible in all parts of the house. If the view is to include anything supposed to be below the level of the stage the window must be set low; otherwise the people on the orchestra floor will be too conscious of looking up hill and seeing down hill.

When a character on the stage is to look out of a window and to show some important reaction to what he sees outside, and it is not necessary for the audience to see for itself, the window is best placed in the side wall, fairly well down stage. This enables the actor, as he looks out of the window, to show at least his profile, and perhaps a three-quarter view of his face.

Important entrances can often be pointed up very effectively by the judicious placing of windows. A character seen passing a window before he enters takes on a heightened interest, and makes as deep an impression on the audience as if he had paused in tableau; at the same time there is no suspension of the action of the play, and no sense of self-conscious artificiality. The device is so good that it has been somewhat overworked by professional producers; but even this has not destroyed its usefulness. Sometimes the dramatist prescribes it; Barrie, for instance, makes skilful use of it in his charming little semi-pantomime, *Pantaloon*.

When a window figures significantly in the action the whole setting must be designed about that window. It is just as important as any entrance or exit. Conversely, it must not be forgotten that a window is a natural point of interest, so that the placing of one in a too conspicuous position when it has little or no real significance in the play is sure to cause more or less distraction.

LIGHTING

Since the advent of electricity, stage lighting has come to be an important part of scenic art. As a problem in design there will be more to say of it later. But even in the rough planning of his settings the director must take into consideration the major sources of light, and their relation to the action of the play. Without knowing the sources from which the light is to come he cannot know which are the conspicuous places on the stage, and how his groups are to be placed for emphasis.

In interior scenes representing daytime the windows are thought of as the natural sources of light, and whenever possible the audience should be allowed to feel that the light actually comes from them. Of course it is very seldom that a stage can be adequately lighted from this source alone; something must be sacrificed to keep the actors' faces out of constant shadow. A little gentle assistance may be had from the footlights and borders, and perhaps from a concealed floodlight or two. So long as this extra light is not obtrusive no harm is done; but it is singularly disturbing to watch a midday scene indoors when it is obviously ten times brighter indoors than out. One is depressed by the feebleness of the supposed sun, and annoyed by the artificial glare of the footlights.

In evening scenes indoors the windows will, of course, be dark, or a dull blue, and the sources of effective light will be internal and frankly artificial. Care should be taken to place table lamps, floor lamps, and fireplaces so that the actual light from them may fall upon points of emphasis in the stage groupings. A visible chandelier ought never to be used, for the reason that it blinds the audience; a concealed floodlight behind the teaser will give general illumination from the ceiling in a natural way, and the audience will not worry much about the source. Footlights and borders may be used in moderation, the former to brighten the faces of the actors and remove the triangular shadows from under their noses, the latter to kill unwanted shadows on the walls. In general, audiences will be much less curious about the sources of artificial light in an evening scene than they will about the sources of supposed daylight.

Symbolic scenes, or scenes intended to convey a single larger mood, can often be played in bold relief with a single source of light at one side or above, and with simple plastic effect. The posture of the character, the composition of the picture, the poetry of the lines, and the emotional effect of the light itself serve to convey the mood. But in scenes depicting subtleties of character, humor, dialogue, or repartee, or revelation of inner thought and feeling, the action must gen-

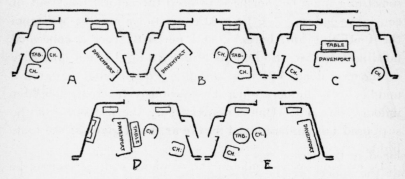

FIG. 8.—ARRANGEMENTS OF FURNITURE ON A SMALL STAGE

erally be placed in more general illumination and the lighting of the actors' faces considered before either naturalism or abstract beauty.

FURNITURE

As a rule it is best to fix the positions of the furniture as carefully in advance as those of the doors and windows, especially of those articles of furniture that are to be used by the actors—tables, chairs, sofas, and the like. Last minute changes are of course more easily made than in the case of the doors and windows; but last minute changes are to be avoided as far as possible.

The amateur is often at a great disadvantage in the arrangement of furniture by reason of the small size of the stage on which he is obliged to work. The small stage is crowded to the limit with a davenport, a table, and two chairs, and perhaps one or two wall pieces. Practically speaking, there is only one arrangement of these, with the davenport on one side and the table and chairs on the other (as at *A*,

Figure 8). This can be reversed (as at *B*), but the variation is slight, and after one has seen the two arrangements a few dozen times he begins to tire of them. If the davenport is

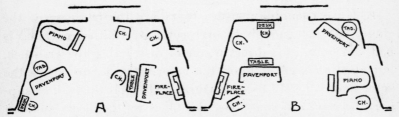

FIG. 9.—ARRANGEMENTS OF FURNITURE ON A LARGE STAGE

placed in the center (as at *C*) there is a freshness of effect, but the spaces at the sides are too limited for freedom of action, and the general feeling is one of stiffness and formality. If it is placed approximately at right angles facing a fireplace (as at *D*), it looks out of scale, and tends to split the room in two. If it is placed against the side wall (as at *E*), one side of the audience does not get a full view, and as soon as you move it out a little you get back to the arrangement at *A*. If the davenport is left out and one or two chairs substituted there is a slight variation of effect, but the stage is apt to look spotty and disunified. Unless the character of the play is such as to admit of some very unusual arrangement, the director finds himself, therefore, constantly baffled in the attempt to get variety.

A great deal has been said and written about the superior intimacy of the small stage and the cold artificiality of the large one, but the large stage has a distinct advantage when it comes to arranging furniture. It holds more furniture without overcrowding and it permits of an infinite variety of different arrangements without detriment to the playing space and without unnaturalness. The arrangements shown in Figure 9 merely suggest what utterly different effects may be obtained on a moderately large stage by rearrangement of the same furniture.

In the placing of stage furniture the most important considerations are the following:

1. Have enough furniture to relieve the bareness of the stage, but not enough to overcrowd it. Either extreme is bad, not only in its direct power of distracting the audience, but also in its effect upon the actor. On a bare stage the actor finds it hard to seem natural. He feels the lack of support, becomes self-conscious, and takes refuge in declamation instead of acting; in a declamatory play this may do no harm, but in a realistic play it is bad. On an overcrowded stage he feels his movements hampered, and is unable to develop the freedom necessary to dramatic contrasts. Of course some plays, and some scenes, call naturally for more furniture than others. A blank verse tragedy calls for less than a prose comedy, simply because the poetic play permits of a more declamatory style of acting, and is less dependent for its effects upon naturalism in business. A brief street scene may require no furniture at all, and a scene in a poor man's cottage may be appropriately played with very little; while a scene in the living room of a great mansion in which a number of guests are to be served with tea may require a great deal. But the best rule is always one of moderation.

2. Except when there is some point in a stylistic production, avoid startling or conspicuous furniture. Furniture which is too interesting, either in its design or in its placing, is a common source of distraction.

3. Avoid a dead level of furniture. If too many chairs, tables, and sofas are the same height there is a persistent horizontal line across the stage which catches the eye and creates a distraction.

4. Specify chairs and sofas at least seventeen inches high;

eighteen if possible. Lower chairs may suggest ease and comfort when the actors are sitting down, but when it comes time for them to get up there is trouble. It is a real effort to rise from a low, soft chair, and it is impossible to rise from one with freedom, eagerness, and force. This fact is most amusingly brought out in A. A. Milne's play *The Dover Road*, in which the crafty Latimer completely disarms the indignant outbursts of his unwilling visitor by getting him to sit in a particularly low, deep chair. It is distressing to see the action of a play temporarily suspended while several members of the cast assist the elderly matron to rise from a sofa—or, worse, while she attempts to do so unassisted.

5. Have the furniture so arranged as to suggest reality, though not necessarily to represent it. It is natural, for example, to place chairs near a table, and a lamp on the table, and to have a davenport near a fireplace. There is no need to imitate the conventional arrangements illustrated in the advertisements of the August furniture sales; but it is best to avoid any arrangement that is queer or outlandish, or that provokes a housewife in the audience to murmur, "If that was my room I'd move that davenport where a body could sit on it and feel like one of the family."

6. At the same time it is essential to remember that the stage is not life, but a conventionalization of life in terms of certain accepted limitations. If the furniture were arranged exactly as in an ordinary living room too many of the actors would have to sit with their backs to the audience, and the latter would feel a sense of exclusion. The stage is not a room with one wall removed. It is a room, or other place, subjected to a peculiar convention, a kind of warping, or better, an opening out toward the audience like the unfolding of a flower. One can only acquire a keen sense of this relationship through the study of many stage settings. The

setting must give the observer fifty or a hundred feet away as comprehensive a view of its essential features as one gets of a real room by standing just within it; and this can only be done by some sort of distortion. The thing is to keep the distortion to a minimum; yet a surprising amount is permissible when it is carried out in accordance with the accepted conventions to which audiences are accustomed.

7. Do not place pieces of furniture in position to block the entrances and exits. A clear sweep for characters entering or leaving adds much to the effectiveness of the dramatic action.

8. Be sure that adequate playing space remains for the actors who are not sitting down—space especially for them to cross from right to left or left to right, or diagonally up or down stage. A reasonable amount of freedom in arranging diagonal crosses is a great help to the director who is trying to break up a "talky" scene, or to maneuver his characters into the positions necessary for some later bit of action.

9. In a long scene, and especially in a long play with only one setting, plan to have some of the chairs moved by the actors at appropriate points in the dialogue. In this way it is possible to get some variety of grouping with comparatively little furniture. But be careful not to have an actor move a chair, sit down on it, pop up again, and put the chair back, all in such a brief time as to make the device seem obvious and unconvincing. Even professional directors sin frequently in this respect. When a chair is moved there should be some apparent reason, as when two people draw their chairs closer together for secrecy in conversation, or when a gentleman places a more comfortable chair for a lady. A chair that has been moved out of place can often be replaced quite naturally a little later by a servant.

What has been said of regular furniture applies also to other large stage properties. Small properties need not be considered here; some of them have to do with the designing of the setting, and some of them, especially the "hand props," have to do with the action of the play and the business of the characters. The placing of the latter is part of the problem of planning the action itself.

CHAPTER VI

PLANNING THE ACTION

HOW much of the action of the play, including stage movements and positions, and stage "business," should be planned in advance of rehearsals?

This is a subject of perpetual controversy. Most experienced directors believe in careful pre-planning in the matter of stage directions. They believe in fixing every movement, every stage position, every piece of stage business, as early as possible, and making only such changes as may be dictated by unforeseen necessity or discovery of error. At the same time there are a few eminent men of the theatre who hold the opposite view, maintaining that to fix the details of stage movement and business in advance of rehearsals is to stifle the actor's freedom of interpretation and make the performance a soulless piece of mechanism.

Mr. Granville-Barker, for example, insists that "the physical action of the play must not be defined while the thought and feeling that should prompt it are still unsure," [1] and he has the support not only of those careless and lazy people who cannot bring themselves to the labor of thinking things out in advance, and of those supreme egoists who think their unguided inspirations inevitably more truthful than the accumulated experience of others, but also of many thoughtful, conscientious workers in the theatre who believe that true art is unpremeditated, spontaneous, and free of conscious mechanism.

[1] *The Exemplary Theatre*, p. 218.

PLANNING THE ACTION

There is, of course, no real disagreement in the major premise: Whatever tends to destroy the actor's freedom of interpretation in such a way as to make his performance coldly mechanical ought certainly to be condemned. Whether or not the actor can be conscious of his technique without loss of art, the audience ought *not* to be conscious of it; ought not to feel the mechanism dominating the thought and emotion. The question at issue is whether adherence to specific stage directions helps or hinders the actor in the attainment of that sort of freedom which we all agree is desirable. Since our whole procedure in the planning of a production will depend upon how we answer this question its importance is obvious.

UNPREMEDITATED ART

There are those who go so far as to maintain that the action of a play should never be specifically defined, either before or after rehearsals have begun; that the actor should be free to come and go according to his inspiration and to invent his own business under pressure of emotion, and to do it differently at every performance. No one, to be sure, claims that a mere tyro can act well by this method; the theory presupposes at least an experienced actor, if not a great one. No one whose opinion is worth serious consideration denies that there are limitations imposed by the facts of the play and by the necessity of some slight coöperation with the other players. There are, of course, advocates of a return to the primitive drama of improvisation—but that is another matter. Granted that the actor ought to know his lines and speak them accurately, that he ought to give the proper cues to his colleagues, that he ought to make his entrances and exits on time and according to the meaning of the play, and that he ought to take his assigned part in the action essential to the plot of the play, the advocates of freedom demand that the actor shall not be required to speak a given line from the same spot at every performance, or to light his cigarette on the same line, or to illustrate his emotions with the same piece of business. They demand more. They demand that he shall have as much freedom to reinterpret his part at each performance, and to express his interpretation spontaneously in action, as is possible without actually disrupting the play.

The motive back of this opinion is sound and praiseworthy. It is the feeling that what matters in a play is the content of thought and emotion, and not the technique of expressing it. This is the fundamental basis of good design—what I have called the utilitarian basis. Yet the opinion itself is unmistakably posited upon the notion that good art is necessarily unpremeditated.

A more absurd notion would be hard to find. The very phrase, "unpremeditated art," is a contradiction in terms. If art were unpremeditated the greatest artists would all be babies, for babies are the only people who can be entirely guiltless of premeditation. The very fact that the greatest artists are people of mature experience in art, and that they grow greater through experience, is sufficient proof that premeditation of some sort is not inconsistent with the highest art. True art is sincere art, but a thing can be wholly sincere without being in the least unpremeditated.

ACTING IN THE PALMY DAYS

Advocates of interpretative freedom are constantly referring to the methods of the last century, when great actors travelled about the country playing with resident stock companies, often without rehearsal and usually with only one or two rehearsals in each place. We have no such acting nowadays, they tell us, and no such giants of the stage as

Booth, or Barrett, or Forrest, or Charlotte Cushman, or Macready; or their predecessors, Kean, Mrs. Siddons, or Charles Kemble. These people could act anywhere, with anybody, and could dominate the stage and the audience by sheer force of passion and eloquence. No humdrum mechanical repetition in those days. Each performance was different; you could see the same actor in the same part a dozen times and never twice alike.

They neglect to add that of the dozen performances two might be stirringly good, four acceptable, two more dull and lifeless, one a complete artistic failure, and the other three broken up altogether by some disaster to the scenery, or the illness of the star, or a riot in the audience. Variety is the spice of life, and the palmy days were spicy.

As a matter of fact, a little reading in the biographical literature of those times—there is plenty of it available, for almost every actor or actress of any prominence leaves at least one volume of biography—will quickly reveal a vast amount of discontent with conditions on the part of the actors themselves. The sincere, painstaking actor of two, three, or four generations ago, complained bitterly of the slipshod methods of his time, of the lack of reliable support from the companies he visited, and the lack of time for adequate rehearsal; of the nerve-racking uncertainties of production, and the fact that success in a performance was so dependent upon chance and the inspiration of the moment. Macready tells us that he was thought very eccentric and amateurish because he insisted upon ten or twelve days of study before performing a new rôle, and that he was much ridiculed for acting at rehearsals. "It was the custom of the London actors," he says, "to do little more at rehearsals than to read or repeat the words of their parts, marking in their entrances and exits, as settled by the stage manager, and their respective places on the stage." [1] Of Charlotte Cushman it is said that "Beyond the due expression and feeling given to the words, which she could never quite wholly omit even in study or at rehearsal, the acting was left to the inspiration of the time and place." [2] The inference seems to be that she *tried* to omit "the due expression and feeling," or that her contemporaries expected her to. Whether Miss Cushman approved of the system does not appear, but under it she shone at the expense of the play. Surely Juliet is the most interesting figure in *Romeo and Juliet,* but when Miss Cushman played Romeo the critics praised her for two or three columns without mentioning Juliet. When she played Lady Macbeth they seldom mentioned Macbeth. The whole system was one that meant inevitably the exaltation of the exceptional actor with the temperament and the emotional power to thrive under it; but it meant also the degradation of the lesser actor, and the emphasis of parts rather than plays, which is perhaps the chief reason why the giants of day before yesterday stood out so prominently.

Even so, it is well to realize that the giants did not have quite the freedom they are sometimes supposed to have had. In the first place their activities, especially on tour, were for the most part confined to a standard repertory of well known plays, and for these plays the essential movements and business were already established by tradition, and familiar to experienced actors everywhere. But for this the travelling star system could never have existed at all. The star had, of course, the privilege of making changes, and the chief purpose of rehearsals was to let the supporting actors know what changes were to be made. In the second place even the London actors, as we see by Macready's remark just

[1] Macready's *Reminiscences,* p. 109.
[2] Emma Stebbins' *Life and Letters of Charlotte Cushman.*

quoted, acknowledged the authority of the stage manager to settle their exits and entrances and their respective places on the stage, as all but the most childishly temperamental actors always have done.

The chief reason why the matter so established was less elaborate and more sketchy than it is in most modern plays was the fact that the standard drama, especially the poetic drama, was less dependent for its effects upon stage movements and business, and more upon the declamation of the lines. The taste of the time was for a style of acting that many of us today would not call acting at all, a passionate, oratorical style that focused attention upon the actor rather than the play, and compelled acceptance of certain artificial conventions which may or may not have been more artistic than our present conventions but were unquestionably different. It may be doubted whether very many serious critics of the stage today really want to see a return to the conditions of the last century, or would if they understood them.

THE PRICE OF FREEDOM

But we have not yet disposed of the contention that for freedom of interpretation the actor must be unhampered by specific stage directions, a contention still made by numerous modern directors quite out of sympathy with the hasty, slipshod methods so common a century ago. To quote again from Mr. Granville-Barker's stimulating book: [1] "In nearly all plays (except, of course, those of pure mime) the physical action is extraordinarily unimportant, the mental and emotional action all in all. Delay, then, in entering the physical phase should not trouble the experienced actor. He has no business to be agitating his mind at rehearsals (much less at a performance) over physical movements, unless they are

[1] *The Exemplary Theatre*, p. 212.

such matters of gymnastics as fighting, dancing, or the rough and tumble of farce. His training should so have equipped him that all such things come without thought; come one way or another, with one way as right as the other. His thought he needs to match with the plays' thought, and it is not so often he'll have any to spare." And he adds the astounding footnote: "For all that, though, I have known an experienced actor to worry himself almost to death about how he should get out of a stage room when, after all, the only way was through the door."

It is precisely because I agree with Mr. Granville-Barker's premise that I disagree with his conclusions. I agree that the actor "has no business to be agitating his mind at rehearsals (much less at a performance) over physical movements." But if the actor is any good at all he most certainly will agitate his mind about them, unless the director does that work for him in advance; and the footnote cites a case to prove it. There is positively only one way in which a good actor, in anything but a highly declamatory play, can avoid agitating his mind about physical movements at an actual performance, and that is by having them so well learned in advance that he can perform them without agitation; only thus can he purchase the freedom of mind necessary to real freedom of interpretation. If the actor mentioned in Mr. Granville-Barker's footnote had been told by a competent director which door to go out and how to go out, and had learned the movement at the first rehearsal, he might not have been obliged to agitate his mind about it at later rehearsals—much less at a performance.

The assertion that the physical action will "come one way or another, with one way as right as the other," seems incredible as coming from an experienced man of the theatre. He cannot mean literally that one way is as right as another.

He cannot mean that he has never been annoyed in the theatre by an awkward, ugly, or distracting movement, or has never seen an ineffective entrance or exit. He must mean simply that such annoyances are due to the actor's inexperience, and that to the well trained actor—as indeed he says—such things come without thought. Yet he instantly assails his own position by citing, in the footnote, the case of "an experienced actor" to whom such things did *not* come without thought, and who was obliged to agitate his mind about them. He could have cited many others. Most sincere, painstaking actors are quite willing to admit that the business of a play does not come to them without thought; that on the contrary they must pay for their apparent freedom and spontaneity by weeks of intensive labor, by working out every detail of action, by articulating it with the lines, and by memorizing both lines and action so perfectly as to render them almost subconscious.

ARE STAGE DIRECTIONS INHIBITORY?

Much of the opposition to specific stage directions lies in the notion that they inhibit the actor, render his performance mechanical, and check his creative impulses.

As a matter of fact they do nothing of the kind—not if they are good stage directions. On the contrary they leave the actor perfectly free to interpret the part in his own way. Of course I refer to directions covering movement and business, and not to coaching or instruction in the meaning of the part. The two things are quite separate. Now and then, it is true, a single specific action planned by the director may prove inconsistent with some later development of the actor's interpretation; in that case we have a legitimate and proper reason for a change. But the vast majority of stage directions have surprisingly little to do with the individual actor's interpretation of his part.

In illustration I may cite a production of Barrie's *The Admirable Crichton* which I staged some years ago for a college dramatic club. Partly to employ as many members as possible and partly to guard against disaster in case of illness we used two separate casts, giving them identical stage directions and shifting them about at rehearsals until every player was accustomed to playing with every other. This play calls for some very intricate movements and a good deal of business; there are many properties, and in some of the scenes there are many people on the stage at once, all taking part in the action. Our stage was laid out to scale at rehearsals, and all the furniture placed exactly; and every movement was planned down to the most minute detail. There had to be some changes, of course, but all matters of doubt were settled early, and the play was rehearsed almost without change for about six weeks. The action was articulated with the lines, and each player knew exactly the position and attitude in which he was to deliver each word of his part; he knew exactly when to flick the ashes off his cigarette, when and from whom to receive a cup of tea, which hand to take it with, where to sit down and when to get up. Because of the inexperience of the players and our special desire for a smooth performance we went to extremes, and indulged in much more exacting drill than is at all usual with amateurs or at all necessary with professionals.

Yet a surprising thing happened—surprising at least to those who could not see the use of so much precision, and who were afraid of a mechanical effect. We gave eight performances with the two casts alternating, and half way through the second performance it became evident that we had two different plays! One cast gave us a romantic comedy, the other a cynical, ironical satire. When one cast played the other was always in the audience. There was keen rivalry, and each cast, largely because it did not have to agitate its mind over entrances or exits or stage business, was free to seek new shades of meaning through comparison. Not a single important stage direction was changed during the week, but new inner meanings were brought out at every performance, and the difference between the two versions grew greater as the week progressed.

When *The Bat* was at the height of its popularity there were companies playing in a number of cities, with identical scenery and properties, and identical stage directions, but although the play was one that depended in maximum degree upon the action there was a great difference between companies. The Chicago company, for instance, played it apathetically, as a commonplace melodrama, with a little rather forced comic relief. The Philadelphia company played it as a hilarious farce, with just enough mock seriousness to keep the cold chills chasing the laughter. The one production was mechanical, with the movements and business too obviously a mere part of the day's work; but the other, prepared from exactly the same stage directions, was as spirited and natural as is possible with that type of play.

With identical stage directions you can have a good or a bad performance, according to the spirit and ability of the actors; or you can have two entirely different interpretations. You can even have two different interpretations by the same company, for there are many cases on record in which the mood or tone of a scene, or even of a whole play, has been changed, without any change in the words or action. It is said that Lemaître created the comic part of Robert Macaire by rehearsing it as the serious melodramatic part it was supposed to be, and then suddenly turning it into burlesque at the opening performance, while the other actors (with the exception of Firmin, who was in the secret) played on with perfect seriousness.

On the whole, it seems quite as absurd to demand that the action of the play be left to the inspiration of the moment, as to demand that the words be improvised differently at each performance. To the talented and experienced actor the one thing is as likely to come naturally as the other; within certain limitations both are possible, but the result is not very apt to be the highest order of art.

THE JAMES-LANGE THEORY

The idea that "the physical action of the play should not be defined while the thought and feeling that should prompt it are still unsure" makes a strong appeal on the ground of common sense and sincerity; but is it in accordance with scientific fact? It seems to me to run afoul of the so-called "James-Lange Theory," now pretty generally accepted by students of human psychology. According to this theory, feeling, or emotion, is not the cause but the result of action. To go back to the law of motor response: For every stimulus received by the organism there is an immediate and direct motor response, the nature of which depends partly upon the nature of the stimulus, and partly upon the previous experience of the organism. Whether a given stimulus will produce a given action, or a given motor set, depends upon the thoughts and feelings in the subject's past experience, perhaps, but not upon an intermediate emotion in the given case. It is the motor response that is the primary reaction. What we call feeling or emotion is secondary; it is the realization in consciousness of the motor state.

Thus when we see an automobile bearing down upon us, or hear a warning signal, we do not jump out of the way because we are frightened; we jump out of the way because our experience has taught us to do so automatically, and if we are frightened it is because we have had to jump out of the way. Whether we do jump out of the way depends altogether upon our previous training. City-bred people, accustomed to dodging traffic, jump promptly and in the right direction; or perhaps it would be more accurate to say that only those whose responses are lively on this point have survived. What is often called "presence of mind" is not presence of mind at all, but rather absence of mind; it is neither intellectual nor emotional, but is purely a matter of automatic response properly prepared for by previous training and sufficiently quick and accurate to function before there is time for thought.

Whether the James-Lange theory is sound or not is of course debatable, and the question is too abstruse for discussion here. But in view of its wide acceptance it would seem a little dangerous for a stage director to assume that the action of a play is necessarily or merely the result of the actor's emotions. It may, as a matter of fact, be the cause. At any rate the theory gives some hint of the importance of action in relation to emotion, and suggests the danger of hastily devised and inappropriate action, whether planned early by the director or later by the actor.

It also suggests that the right actions, thoroughly rehearsed to recur automatically, may have some effect in calling up the desired emotions in the actor, and empathically in the audience.

TECHNIQUE AND TRICKERY

There is another sort of opposition to the careful planning of stage movement and business; a sort that comes less frequently from actors and directors than from critics, authors, and professors of literature. It is based on an exalted worship of sincerity, and takes the form of denunciation of all conscious technique as a kind of trickery.

One of the best teachers of dramatic literature in the country takes somewhat this view. Whenever one mentions to him the manner in which certain effects are achieved in the theatre through control of attention, creation of suspense and anticipation, invention of business to naturalize movements, and the like, he throws up his hands in deprecation. "Trickery! Trickery!" he says; "All trickery!"

He is right, of course. It is trickery. But so in a sense is all art. The only perfect absence of trickery is to be found in pure accident, and pure accident is not art. Life itself may or may not be pure accident, but art is design—the antithesis of accident.

One of the most eminent representatives of the "No Trickery" party is Mr. John Galsworthy. His position in the matter is amusingly stated by Mr. William Archer, as follows:[1] "Even the most innocent tricks of emphasis are to him snares of the Evil One. He would sooner die than drop his curtain on a particularly effective line. It is his chief ambition that you should never discern any arrangement, any intention, in his work. As a rule, the only reason you can see for his doing thus or thus is his desire that you should see no reason for it." And Mr. Archer adds: "He does not carry this tendency, as some do, to the point of eccentricity, but he certainly goes as far as any one should be advised to follow. A little further, and you incur the danger of becoming affectedly unaffected, artificially inartificial."

Exactly. If you do not drop your curtain on an effective line you must drop it on an ineffective one; but why in the world should you? What artistic end is achieved by choosing the greater of two evils? By Mr. Galsworthy's own standard,

[1] *Playmaking*, p. 328.

a curtain on an ineffective line is a greater evil than the usual curtain, because it calls attention more insistently to the author's technique. The audience expects an effective curtain, and takes such a curtain as a matter of course, without undue attention to the why and the wherefore. But when the curtain descends on a commonplace line the audience is left wondering whether the stage manager blundered, or if not, why the author chose such a peculiar ending—wondering, in short, what particularly subtle and elusive brand of trickery he had in mind.

It is a characteristic of enthusiasts that they seldom examine alternatives; they consider the frying pan but not the fire. When sincere artists revolt against the pettiness and crudity and obtrusiveness of much modern stage technique they are abundantly justified by the facts; but they are not right in concluding that all stage technique is bad, nor are they right in substituting an obtrusive and distracting absence of technique—a technique of ostentatious inartificiality.

With respect to the movement and grouping of characters on the stage it is well to remember that the alternative is not between an effective grouping and no grouping. It is between an effective grouping and an ineffective one. If the characters are on the stage at all they are making some kind of an impression on the audience, and if the director does not see to it that the impression is helpful to the purpose of the play it is pretty sure to be detrimental. A bad group or movement is just as distracting, just as inimical to sincerity, as a good one, and it is unpleasant in its own right besides. If the director does not control the empathic responses of his audience the audience will empathize anyhow, and in all probability they will empathize in the wrong things. That is exactly what happens when an actor makes an awkward or amateurish movement or gesture, or stands in an awkward posture, or does not know what to do with his hands. Well planned movement or business has at least this virtue, that it keeps the actor's body occupied and prevents him from doing all sorts of wrong things and so stirring up unwanted effects.

One cannot too strongly insist upon this negative side of stage technique. Good stage technique lies quite as much in knowing what to avoid as in knowing what to do, and one of the best reasons for trying consciously to do an effective thing is to guard against the likelihood of doing an ineffective or positively distracting thing unconsciously. It may seem illogical to emphasize the negative side of a creative art, but the point is that the artist must keep the imagination of the audience working on his side. So long as he can avoid doing the wrong thing he need offer little more than suggestion, and the imagination of the audience will do the rest; but the moment he does something obtrusively ineffective the imaginative concept is shattered.

MONARCHY OR COMMUNISM?

Whether much or little of the action is to be planned in advance, the question still remains: Who is to plan it? Shall the director work it out in advance of rehearsals and then dictate it ready-made to the actors; or shall the actors be allowed to work it out for themselves in rehearsal, with the director serving merely as critic?

Upon this question, also, expert opinion differs. Some directors, thinking first of the importance of unity in the production, insist upon the autocratic method. Gordon Craig, with his idea of the actors as "übermarionettes" and the director supreme, exemplifies this view. Others, moved by a love of sincerity in realism, feel that action evolved "naturally" in rehearsal, with comparatively little interference from the director, is more likely to be right.

PLANNING THE ACTION

The history of Stanislavsky and the Moscow Art Theatre affords an interesting exposition of both points of view. At one time, as Stanislavsky himself tells us in his autobiography, it was his custom to plan every detail of the action before calling a rehearsal, and to require rigid adherence to it on the part of his actors. More recently he has gone to the other extreme, and his present method is to begin with round-table discussion of the play, followed by informal rehearsal, at which the actors try out various movements, offer suggestions, and continue the discussions until the finished play gradually evolves.

How much of the fine ensemble playing of the Moscow group is due to the method now employed, and how much to the rigorous training which they received under the older method, is a matter of speculation. In my own judgment most of it is not primarily due to either. I believe that the greatness of the Moscow Art Theatre is to be attributed chiefly to the high character of the artists, to their painstaking sincerity, to the solidarity of the group, and to the long period of study and rehearsal given to each play before its first performance. Under such conditions either method might give good results.

The advantage of what may be called the communistic method lies in the greater opportunity for creative work on the part of the individual artist, and the greater stimulus to group imagination. But this advantage cannot be fully realized unless there is abundant time for careful study and rehearsal, and unless the players are experienced, and able to lose themselves imaginatively in the parts. The Moscow players, men and women of education and character, associated through long years of sincere creative effort, are able to realize it as few others could.

But even the Moscow players cannot escape all the faults

of the communistic method. The system makes for good naturalism, but good naturalism is not necessarily good theatre. Real life is full of meaningless accident, of planless and unbeautiful distraction; but a play ought not to be. In the Moscow production of *The Three Sisters*—in some respects the finest piece of play production I have ever seen— there are some remarkable ensemble scenes, in which family and friends come and go, servants answer the door-bell, dinner is served, there is laughter, music and movement, and all is carried off with sincerity and conviction, not to say dash. But there are some awkward stage pictures; there are clumsy movements; actors get in each other's way, blanket each other's lines, and play important bits from unemphatic positions; in short there are theatrical imperfections which no competent American stage director would tolerate. They are natural enough, in the sense that they might happen in real life, but in the theatre they are distracting; they take attention from more important things, and they are displeasing in themselves.[1]

The obvious answer to this criticism is that it is better to have some technical imperfections coupled with great artistic power and sincerity than to have technical perfection without the sincerity, and in this I heartily concur. But I do not believe the alternative is inevitable. Certainly there is no inevitable alternative between monarchy and communism. There is a middle course, analogous perhaps to government by responsible ministry, recognizing neither the divine right of autocracy nor the divine right of do-as-you-please. In a permanent theatre it may be wise to provide some form of appeal from arbitrary rulings of the stage director, but it is

---

[1] I had the pleasure of talking this matter over with a former member of Stanislavsky's company. He sustained my criticism of *The Three Sisters*, and told me that the imperfections I have mentioned were well known to the players.

not wise to leave those matters that are largely matters of team work either to pure accident or to the whims of a dozen divers and changeable temperaments.

After all, the real test is the test of results. With the possible exception of one or two Belasco plays I think I have never seen a production the faults of which could be in any way attributed to too much dictation of movement and position by the director; but I have seen scores of productions, amateur and professional, that were ragged and restless for the very obvious reason that the actors were moving pretty much as they pleased and very much at cross purposes. Rare indeed is the amateur production that could not be improved by more detailed, more skilful, and more unified direction of movement.

CHAPTER VII

STAGE MOVEMENT

ASSUMING that stage movement,[1] stage groupings, and stage pictures are to be carefully planned, what principles and methods should govern the planning?

The problem is a problem in design, and the principles that apply are the principles of design as we have already considered them. . But they must be translated into the concrete terms of stage technique.

In plotting stage movements one must remember that the movements, and even the characters themselves, are but parts of a composite design, of which the central element is the thought of the play; and that success will depend not only upon the director's grasp of the thought but upon his ability to visualize his characters against a background of setting and furnishing, of line, mass, and color; and upon his power to coördinate speech, action, and sometimes music, into a single harmonious composition.

To assist him in visualizing the movements he will sometimes find it expedient to employ some sort of mechanical aid —something to stimulate the imagination. Of course he will lay out the stage setting of each scene in the form of a plan on paper, and mark on the plan the positions of the entrances and of the furniture. Often he will find it helpful to mount the plan on a soft drawing board and use push pins to repre-

---

[1] The distinction between stage movement and stage business is not an exact one, and there are many overlappings, but in general the term movement refers to changes in the location of the characters on the stage, the term business to bits of individual illustrative action.

sent the characters, moving them about as a means of studying the groupings. Bits of colored sealing wax molded over
discarded phonograph needles make excellent push pins for
the purpose—this being, I believe, the only known use for
discarded phonograph needles. Some directors construct
cardboard models of the settings, and even of the properties,
and use little paper-doll figures to represent the characters.
For decorative or symbolic plays, in which stage pictures,
lighting effects, and color harmonies are of first importance,
the latter method has special advantages. For ordinary
plays, and especially for those involving many characters in
rapid motion, the horizontal plan is probably more helpful.

METHODS OF NOTATION

For setting down stage movements in the prompt-book some
method of notation is necessary. The terms Right (R.), Left
(L.), and Center (C.) are almost universally employed in this
country to designate stage positions—right meaning the
actor's right as he faces the audience. Most directors also
use the terms Right Center (R.C.) and Left Center (L.C.) for
the intermediate positions. "Down," or "down stage," means
toward the audience, and "up," or "up stage" away from the
audience. The direction to proceed from one side to the other
is usually indicated by the word "cross" or the sign X. In
most professional prompt-books these are about the only
terms used, and directions are given only in a very rough
way. The experienced actor is supposed to perfect the details himself. Thus when he is told to "cross down R." he is
supposed to know instinctively which way and how far to go.

It sometimes happens, however, that a single direction may
mean any one of a half dozen things. In *A*, Figure 10, for
example, an actor up left (U.L.), told to "cross down R.",
might follow any one of the paths indicated. When, because

of the inexperience of the actors, or for any other reason, it becomes desirable to specify movements in more detail, some more accurate system must be found. The zoning system illus-

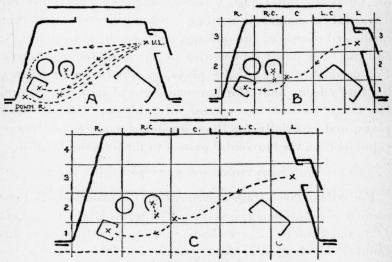

FIG. 10.—METHODS OF PLOTTING STAGE MOVEMENTS

trated in *B* and *C*, Figure 10, serves the purpose very effectively. It has the merit of retaining the usual designations of R., R.C., C., L.C., and L., and the lateral zones may correspond roughly with the old wing entrances, L. 1. E, L. 2. E, and so on (*G*, Figure 6, page 110).

In laying out a zoning plan it is important to know the exact dimensions of the set, and consequently of the zones, and to place all articles of furniture accurately to scale. A davenport, for example, is usually about seven feet long by three feet wide; the largest chair is about three feet square. In *B*, Figure 10, the proscenium opening is twenty-five feet, the depth fifteen feet, and the zones five feet each way. In *C* the proscenium opening is forty feet, the depth twenty feet, and the zones eight feet one way and five feet the other.

Such a system as this makes it possible to record stage directions with reasonable precision. When an actor at L. 3 in *B* or *C* is told to cross to R.C. 2, shake hands with Mr. Jones, and at his invitation sit down R. 1, he knows exactly what is meant.

The commercial director and the inspirational director may laugh at a scheme so mechanical; but when one is dealing with inexperienced players and a fairly intricate play it may mean just the difference between a reasonably finished performance and a hopelessly crude and amateurish one.

NO MOVEMENT WITHOUT A PURPOSE

The first and most important principle in the designing of stage movements is to avoid all purposeless movement.

The soundness of this principle is apparent, yet it is constantly being violated by inexperienced actors and directors, and sometimes by experienced ones. Nothing is more difficult to achieve than unaffected repose; the untrained actor fidgets and wanders whenever he is on the stage, unable to keep his hands or his feet still, yet having no conscious purpose in moving them. The director must teach him to suppress this tendency, or to divert it into purposeful movement.

To say that there should be no movement without a purpose is not to say that a play should be all talk, with the actors sitting or standing about like statues. There are plenty of legitimate reasons for stage movement, and whenever one of them is present and not inconsistent with the larger purpose of the scene, or of the play, it is possible to design an appropriate movement. But purposeless movement is never good design, because movement attracts attention, and purposeless movement *dis*tracts it from the thought of the play. Every movement should have a purpose, and the purpose should be associated, or at least consistent, with the main purpose of the scene and of the play. That is the fundamental principle of all design, the principle of the utilitarian basis.

Among the many types of stage movement, classified according to purpose, the following are most important:

1. Movement dictated by the plot itself, or prescribed by the dramatist as essential action. Such movement is, as a rule, the easiest to follow, and the least likely to create distraction, being naturally part of the main interest of the play. The entrances and exits of characters ordinarily belong to this class; also such movements as are involved in fighting, dancing, hiding behind screens, serving stage meals, telephoning, and the like. While this type of movement is not fool-proof, it is less likely to be overlooked by the director or to lead him into difficulty than some of the other types.

2. Movement for delineation of character, or state of mind. For this purpose stage business is more often useful than stage movement, but movement serves to convey some of the broader effects. A restless or excited character, for example, should be moved about the stage frequently, and may sit down and jump up a half dozen times in a short scene; a calm or phlegmatic character must do nothing of the kind. A firm character may be given straightforward, decisive movements; a weak or bewildered character should be given little aimless, abortive ones.

Since character is likely to be closely associated with the purpose of the play, this type of movement, like the first, is fairly easy to handle and to keep within the bounds of unity. The chief danger is that of over-emphasis on unimportant but interesting minor characters.

3. Movement for emphasis. This is a little less obvious and

not so generally understood. Some directors seem to think that emphasis is just a matter of having important lines spoken forcefully, and that it is largely the business of the individual actor. However, the audience is watching, not an actor, but a play—a complex thing spread over a large stage, with many actors, and with the center of interest constantly shifting. Out of this complexity it is the director's task to pick those elements which the dramatist would wish to have emphasized, and make them stand out. The actor must, of course, "point up" the important line; but before he can do so the director must maneuver him into an effective position —often the center of the stage, but not always so—and must do it in such a way as to focus attention upon him at the right moment.

Moreover, there is a kind of emphasis in movement itself, and certain types of movement are more emphatic than others. A quick movement, for example, is normally more emphatic than a slow one; the emphasis, however, is in the contrast, and on a stage where everybody else is moving the one character who remains motionless may seem most emphatic. A movement toward stage center is ordinarily more emphatic than one toward the wings, and a movement toward the audience more emphatic than one away from the audience. When a movement accompanies a line, there is a gain in emphasis if the movement is started a little ahead of the line; a loss if it is started later. One may work out a whole system of normal contrasts in emphasis based in this way upon types of movement.

4. Movement for control of attention. This, of course, includes movement for emphasis; but the general problem of controlling attention in the theatre is so important and so little understood by most amateurs as to demand separate consideration in a later chapter. Movement is only one means

to such control, but skilfully handled it is a legitimate means.

5. Movement for suspense and anticipation. Half the force of a dramatic episode lies in the proper preparation for it, the proper creation of suspense and anticipation in the minds of the audience. The dramatist knows this, and provides for it by what is called "dramatic foreshadowing," by "planting" certain ideas in advance, and by anticipatory lines of dialogue. But at least a part of the problem still rests with the director, and proper control of stage movement may be one factor in the solution. The entrance of an important character, for example, may be made more effective if the characters already on the stage are so moved as to create a gap in the stage picture at the point where the character is to appear. In Act One of Drinkwater's *Abraham Lincoln,* as staged by Lester Lonergan, the first entrance of Lincoln was skilfully anticipated. The scene was in Lincoln's home. Two of his neighbors, who had come to congratulate him on his nomination, were conversing by the fireplace at stage right, and waiting for him to appear, while the entire left side of the stage was vacant. The only door was at stage left. The unbalanced picture at once created an expectation of Lincoln's entrance. After a moment the door opened, and in came—not Lincoln, but a pert serving maid, who bustled about for a moment, more than filling the gap, and then went out, leaving, by contrast, a greater sense of emptiness than before. The emptiness was sustained for two or three minutes, during which one's desire to see Lincoln grew more and more insistent; then the door opened, and in came—again not Lincoln, but Mrs. Lincoln. She also filled the gap pictorially, yet one felt a restless impatience to have her out of the way, and a sense of relief when, after giving a hint that her husband would soon appear, she also went out.

148

"Now," we thought, "we shall see Lincoln," and our anticipation had reached its highest pitch. A little too much
delay at this point and the whole effect would have been
spoiled; our impatience would have turned to annoyance and
disgust. But the timing was perfect, and in just a few
seconds more the door opened a third time and Lincoln appeared, becoming instantly the focus of attention. Perhaps
the chief gain through the use of this device was the fact that
it permitted the quietest and most repressed sort of acting
on the part of the actor playing Lincoln, without loss of
emphasis; had there been no preparation he would have had
to "act up" a little in order to dominate the scene.

6. Movement for pictorial effect. The desirability of good
stage pictures is well known, and generally appreciated by the
amateur. Movement for the purpose of maneuvering characters into good pictorial groups, and out of bad ones, is clearly
justified, and if not performed too suddenly or too pointedly
it is ordinarily quite satisfying to the audience.

The principles of composition in design we have already
considered, and stage pictures should be good in composition.
Some directors, however, fail to realize the extent to which
good composition in stage pictures may differ from good composition in painting or sculpture. In painting there are but
two dimensions, with a suggestion of the third. In sculpture
there are three, and in stage pictures there are four.

The fourth dimension is time. Stage life is not still life;
it is moving, dynamic, and the composition of every picture,
like that of every chord in music, is affected by memory of
what preceded and anticipation of what is to follow. In
music it is possible to use some very inharmonious chords
by way of transition to better ones; and in the same way it
is possible to use some bad stage pictures in the course of a
rapidly moving scene, provided only that the action is not

allowed to rest on the bad ones. Whenever there is anything in the nature of a tableau on the stage the picture should be good in composition.

In a painting, each element affects the composition almost at its face value; but in a stage picture—even a tableau lasting several minutes—each element has a value dependent upon association of ideas through other pictures in the series. Thus a very good stage picture might seem a very poor pictorial composition to a newcomer just entering the theatre; and a single exposure from a well directed photoplay might make a very poor "still" picture of the scene. Indeed, the photoplay director usually has a number of specially posed "stills" taken for advertising purposes, because pictures clipped from the film are not good enough as separate pictures, and do not tell enough of the story. As parts of a moving composition they may be good, but as separate compositions they are often dead and meaningless.

7. Movement for rhythm. The place of rhythm in the movement of ballet, opera, and musical comedy is obvious enough, but it is only in recent years that we have begun to realize the tremendous possibilities of rhythm in serious drama. The rhythm of poetic verse has long been established as an element of drama (although it is now the fashion of some actors to obliterate it, even in Shakespeare), and various forms of prose rhythm have been effectively used by such dramatists as Synge, Masefield and O'Neill. But rhythm of movement is to the modern producer of serious plays largely a new toy—or rather an old one re-discovered, since it was common enough in the festival drama of primitive times. Just as the poet and musician have used rhythm of sound for direct expression of mood, the modern producer is learning to use rhythm of movement. A little study of such plays as *The Yellow Jacket*, *The Emperor Jones*, *The Hairy Ape*, *The*

World We Live In, R. U. R., The Gods of the Mountains,
Liliom, and *The Beggar on Horseback* will reveal some of the
opportunities. There is almost as much room for development
here as in the matter of setting and lighting—and just about
as much danger of over-emphasis.

8. Movement for Tempo. Most plays call for variations
of pace, partly as a means of avoiding monotony and partly
as a means of expressing variations of mood and emphasis.
Some scenes should proceed more rapidly than others—or
seem to do so. The most obvious changes of tempo are of
course those in the utterance of the lines, but these may be
supplemented by variations in the rate and character of the
movements.

9. Movement for position. Movements not in themselves
clearly motivated are often necessary as a preliminary means
of getting characters into position for other movements, or
for business. Naturally, such preliminary movements should
be as unobtrusive as possible; in the hands of an unskilled
director they are very apt to seem arbitrary and mechanical.

10. Movement for compensation. When, for good reasons,
a character must be moved from one place to another, it
often happens that the balance of the group is upset, and
to restore it some sort of compensating movement on the part
of another character becomes necessary. A good actor with
years of training should make such compensating movements
naturally and almost unconsciously; but some otherwise good
actors are temperamentally insensitive to the stage picture,
and would not learn to "give" in fifty years of experience.
It is worth remembering that many of the best compensating
movements actually precede the movements they are designed
to balance (See *B*, Figure 12, page 160).

11. Movement for illustrating changes of thought or relationship. The grouping of characters on the stage should

suggest their relationship; and changes of relationship should be symbolized by changes of grouping. When this is skilfully done one can follow the meaning much more easily, and the occasional loss of a word or line is much less likely to put him at sea.

12. Movement for relief. In almost every play there are moments of monotony, of "talkiness," or of too sustained emotional strain, and the wise director will seek to provide some sort of relief from them, by movement or otherwise. It should be remembered, however, that movement for relief means movement for the relief of the audience—not the actor. The most awkward and fidgety movements of the rankest amateur are in the nature of relief for the actor—but hardly for the audience.

Other legitimate purposes of movement might be mentioned, but these are the most important and will serve to suggest the possibilities. A skilful director will contrive to design the movements in such a way as to accomplish the various purposes harmoniously and with the greatest economy of means; that is, he will make one movement serve several purposes at the same time. He will also take pains to articulate the movements with the lines and with the individual "business" of the actors.

TRADITIONAL RULES OF STAGE MOVEMENT

The professional stage abounds in traditions, technical as well as personal. Many of them have to do with particular plays, but there are some general rules of stage movement, business, and acting technique that have been passed along for generations, and regarded, especially by those to the theatre born, as more or less sacred. The tendency in the "art" theatres, nowadays, is to discard such rules along with the footlights and the proscenium arch and other moss-backed traditions, on the ground that they hamper the artist's freedom of expression. But it seems to me just as stupid to cast them aside without analysis as to obey them blindly. The best way for the intelligent actor or director to treat them is to study them with a view to understanding the æsthetic or psychological principles involved, and then to apply the principles rather than the rules.

Among the traditional rules that may affect the designing of stage movement, the most important are the following:

1. The actor should always face the audience when speaking. This is a blanket rule inherited from the days when acting was declamation; under modern conditions it must often be modified. The principle is reasonable enough— namely, that the play is for the audience and should as a whole be played toward them.

2. Humorous or telling lines should be spoken straight front, with a sort of round-eyed frankness, and with a slight lift toward the balcony. This rule, of course, can be overworked, but the psychology is sound and audiences are accustomed to the convention without realizing it. Many a good line is thrown away through needless disregard of the principle involved, which is simply that the actor must signal the author's intention to the audience without establishing direct communication with them. When he can think of a better way of doing so, no harm is done. The device is especially useful in conveying "dry" humor, which is apt, otherwise, to miss its laugh.

3. All important scenes should be played down stage. This is an inheritance from the apron stage of the eighteenth century and the platform stage of the sixteenth, and may be modified considerably in the modern theatre. In the main, however, it is still sound.

4. Movements should follow straight lines. This obviously

admits of exceptions, and even the principle is open to dispute on the score of grace. The intention is to make the movements seem decisive and purposeful, and this in itself is good.

5. An entering character should come well on stage and not linger in the entrance. This is an excellent rule except when the action of the play calls for unmistakable exceptions.

6. When two characters enter in conversation, the one speaking should come last. The idea is that otherwise the speaker would have to turn and address the person following, thereby blocking his entrance. Numerous exceptions suggest themselves at once, as, for instance, when the speaker is a master or mistress and the other a servant.

7. An exit should always be made on a line; that is, a character should not go out while another is talking. If necessary the line should be broken by a pause, so that the last few words may be spoken from the doorway as the character goes out. The reason underlying this rule is that a character going out when others are speaking distracts attention from them and at the same time renders his own exit ineffective; on the other hand if he finishes speaking some distance from the exit and the others withhold their speeches until he is gone there is an awkward stage wait. Of course, even the latter is sometimes justified by the meaning, as it was in the memorable exit of Marie, in *Liliom*, mentioned in an earlier chapter.

8. When two characters in conversation are to sit on a sofa or davenport, the one who is to talk most, or whose words are most important, should be placed at the up-stage end. This, of course, is merely a device to enable that character to face the audience.

9. When a character stands at stage right his weight should rest on his right (or down-stage) foot, and his left (or up-

stage) foot should be slightly advanced (*A* and *B*, Figure 11). For a character at stage left the directions should be reversed.

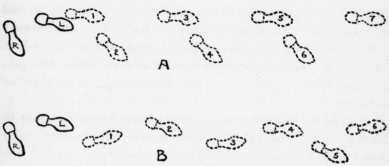

FIG. 11.—FOOT POSITIONS IN TRADITIONAL STAGE TECHNIQUE

10. When a character at stage right starts to walk toward the left, he should start by taking a half step with his left (or up-stage) foot, and then a full step with his right (or down-stage) foot. If he is to speak as he moves, or if the movement is to be leisurely, he should advance his left foot farther than his right to keep him facing partly toward the audience (*A*, Figure 11).

These two rules, if applied with literal precision, carry acting back to the artificial declamatory technique of the last century. Yet they cannot be entirely ignored, for nothing is uglier than the movement by which a character partly facing the audience at stage right starts to walk left with the *right* foot, crossing it over the left (*B*, Figure 11). It makes him look bow-legged and pigeon-toed, and at the same time swings him away from the audience in an awkward manner.

11. When a character in a similar position at stage right is to retire (step backward) a pace or two, he should first shift his weight slightly to his left foot and then take a half

step backward with his right; then (if necessary) a full step with his left.

12. All turns should be executed toward the audience, not away from it; that is, an actor walking to stage left and back should turn to his right, not to his left. This is an old rule that has been so rigidly applied by professionals (even in the moving pictures) as to result in occasional absurdity. I have seen an actor execute a veritable pirouette through 270 degrees to avoid turning 90 degrees with his back to the audience.

13. When a character is to kneel on one knee, it should be the down-stage knee; that is, if he is kneeling at stage center facing left, his right knee should be down and his left up.

14. When a man and woman embrace, the man's down-stage arm should be below the woman's, his up-stage arm above. The object, of course, is to let the woman's face, rather than the man's, swing toward the audience as they relax.

Some of these rules may seem very old-fashioned and arbitrary, yet there is a good deal of wisdom and experience packed into them. The director who will consider each of them in its relation to empathy, æsthetic distance, and the principles of design, can hardly fail to learn something of value; at least he may learn when the rule can be safely violated.

SUGGESTIONS AND WARNINGS

In designing stage movements one must constantly remind himself that the stage is not real life, but a conventionalized representation of life; hence the warping of the stage setting, the opening out of the stage picture, the suppression of un-necessary detail—including all accidental or meaningless movements—the selection and emphasis of essentials. It is for the latter purpose that stage movements should ordinarily be free, bold, and decisive, as well as meaningful, like the lines of a crayon sketch or the color masses of a poster picture. They are to register on the audience suggestively, with a minimum of distraction. The pest of amateur dramatics is the "stage wanderer"—the actor who edges and sidles about the stage, fidgets constantly, and is never still. His movements may be "natural", but there are so many of them and they are so indecisive and characterless that they mean nothing. Good movements do not complicate; they simplify and clarify.

Many directors think of stage movement entirely in terms of the grouping of characters. This is important, pictorially and psychologically, but less important than the main business of conveying the thought of the play. Movements designed for the sake of the picture alone are subject to more or less alteration in rehearsal, since the full effect cannot be accurately determined until costumes, scenery and lights have been tried out together. Inexperienced directors must be warned against:

1. Grouping characters for pictorial effect at the expense of meaning.

2. Designing an excellent stage picture in line and mass, only to have it turn out an atrocity in color.

3. "Dressing the stage" too carefully—as with too much symmetry, or too even a distribution of characters. The latter makes for spottiness and against unity, besides obscuring the meaning.

In regard to the psychology of grouping, it should be remembered that proximity of characters ordinarily suggests relationship, while distance suggests isolation; and that a down-stage position, or a central position, denotes importance, at least with respect to the thought of the moment.

ASIDES AND SOLILOQUIES

One of the most troublesome problems in stage movement is the provision for "asides" and "soliloquies". When a character in soliloquy has the stage to himself he may of course take the center; but when a character speaks apart, other characters being on the stage, it is ordinarily best to give him the extreme position down right or down left. When two groups are to hold separate conversations, each unheard by the other, it is obviously well to separate them as far as possible right and left. Nothing could be more stupidly unconvincing than the arrangement used some years ago in the restaurant scene in *Déclassée*, in which persons at a table way up stage conducted an aside conversation (for the benefit of the audience) by shouting it over the heads of other characters at a down-stage table who were not supposed to hear it —though it must have nearly deafened them. The same principle was involved in the closet scene of the Barrymore *Hamlet*, when Hamlet spoke his asides over the head of the praying King, who was between him and the audience. Ordinary intelligence should enable a director to avoid such mistakes as this. But the problem of maneuvering the characters into suitable positions is sometimes very difficult; often the dramatist prescribes several aside conversations of different groups of characters within a very few moments, as Barrie does in the tea scene of *The Admirable Crichton*, and it taxes the director's ingenuity to make all of these convincing and at the same time to make the movements leading up to them seem natural.

In the eighteenth century it was the custom for an actor having an aside speech to advance a step or two and speak it directly to the audience. This brings him completely out of the picture, and to a modern audience is distinctly painful, though some of the older actors still cling to the tradition. Unless the director is trying to suggest the flavor of eighteenth century technique (as was done in George C. Tyler's sesquicentennial revival of *The School for Scandal*), or unless there is some peculiar dramatic value in the asides, as in O'Neill's *Strange Interlude,* he should eliminate as many asides as possible; and when an aside is unavoidable he should have the actor ready in position down right or left to deliver it with a minimum of ostentation. If the actor looks slightly upward as he speaks, with his eyes focussed at infinity, the suggestion is that he is talking to himself rather than to the audience, or that the dramatist is speaking through him personally; and there is very little loss of illusion.

GRACE IN STAGE MOVEMENT

As far as possible, stage movement should be designed to be graceful in plan, this being especially important to those of the audience who sit in the balcony or gallery. In other words, the path taken by the actor should be graceful as seen from above.

This may seem inconsistent with the traditional rule about moving in straight lines. A slightly curved line, especially a double curve, is more graceful and less studied than the straight line; and if there is much furniture on the stage it is often more practical. On the other hand, too much curve in the actor's path suggests too much concern about the movement itself and too little about the objective. A fair rule is to use straight movements for short distances and strong objectives, such as eager approach, determination, or haste (*A*, Figure 12); and to use slightly curved movements over longer distances, or for less urgent objectives (*B*, Figure 12), or for avoiding the furniture (*C*, Figure 12). In any case, where a movement must necessarily be curved it is obviously better that a graceful rather than an ungraceful curve should be used. When a single movement cannot be made graceful in plan it can often be broken into two shorter and more

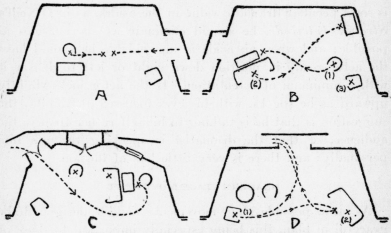

FIG. 12.—GRACE OF PLAN IN STAGE MOVEMENT

In *A* an entering character rushes eagerly to greet one already on, and the movement is a straight line. In *B* the movement (2), understood to be necessary, is anticipated and compensated for by the movement (1). In *C* a character enters breezily up R., and goes to the table at L.C., avoiding the furniture in an easy double curve. In *D*, movement (1) is not very graceful, but if the character can appropriately shake hands with another on the davenport before leaving, the movement can be broken into two graceful ones as at (2).

graceful movements, with a line or a piece of business between them (*D*, Figure 12).

Grace of plan is especially desirable in movements designed for a platform stage, because the third dimension plays a more important part on such a stage. The platform stage creates many special problems for the director in that movements and groupings must be so designed as to be effective as seen from three different directions, and in the case of the central or "circus" stage from all four directions. No matter which way the actor faces on a central stage some members of his audience are always behind him. That is one reason why the central stage is suitable only for a very limited number of plays—plays depending for their effects upon mass movement and pageantry rather than individual acting. Deep apron and platform stages suffer in a lesser degree from the same limitation. In designing movements for three-dimensional stages, the director must achieve great variety in the grouping, but he must not permit his actors to pivot constantly as they speak in a futile effort to reach all parts of the audience at all times. That is a trick of the orator, and goes with the direct sense of communication. In the actor it kills illusion.

The director must, of course, have considerable experience before he can expect to design movements on paper and have them work out on the stage satisfactorily. He should study closely the way in which they do work out at each new attempt, and should not be too loath, at first, to make changes in rehearsal. The very best directors make plenty of mistakes and plenty of corrections. But if the beginner will digest the underlying principles here suggested, and especially the various purposes of stage movement, and will analyze carefully the movements in as many professional productions as possible, he will soon cultivate at least a little of the right sort of sensitivity.

CHAPTER VIII

STAGE BUSINESS

WITH stage business, as with stage movement, the most important principle to observe is: None without a purpose.

TYPES OF STAGE BUSINESS

Classifying stage business according to purpose, we find that many of the purposes are similar to those of stage movement, while some are perhaps slightly different. To mention again only the most important types, we have:

1. Business essential to the action of the play. This is ordinarily prescribed by the dramatist, and the director's task is not so much to invent it as to arrange and supervise it. As in the case of movement essential to the action it is, comparatively, a simple problem. Juliet taking the sleeping potion, Olivia sewing on the curtains in *Mr. Pim*, Flemming's cigarette in *The Bat*, Hamlet's duel with Laertes, Androcles removing the thorn from the lion's paw—all these are examples, if examples are needed.

2. Business for delineation of character or state of mind. This sort of business is especially rich in its possibilities, and so is often overworked. It is most legitimate when the delineation of character is in turn essential to the action of the play. In *Mr. Pim Passes By*, for instance, the plot turns upon the old gentleman's absent-mindedness; when, therefore, he forgets his hat, comes back, and takes the wrong one, it is business for character delineation (as well as for humor) but it is also

162

indirectly essential to the plot. When Liliom spits in the face of Mrs. Muskat, or when Kiki sprays perfume about the room, or when Shylock strops his knife on the sole of his boot, we have character delineation quite as important as the plot itself. Business for delineation of a state of mind may be equally important; that of the Professor at the opening of *The Professor's Love Story* is a good example.

3. Business for background, atmosphere, or local color. Within reasonable limits this also may be made to enrich a play, but again its appropriateness depends upon the extent to which the background is itself important. The business of putting turf on the fire in plays of Irish peasant life is certainly legitimate, and is often suggested by the dramatist. The business of dodging snakes, bugs, and nameless things that "drop on one from above" in the second act of *The Admirable Crichton* is manifestly helpful to the atmosphere; so are the bits of business incidental to bull fighting in *Blood and Sand*, or those suggestive of lower middle-class family life in *The Show-Off*. Sometimes it is the manner rather than the fact that is significant. In *Liliom*, for example, there is a loaf of bread to be cut; an American woman would lay it on the table and cut it downward, but the Hungarian holds it against her body and cuts it toward her. The Belasco productions are generally rich studies in the use of business for atmosphere or local color.

4. Business for emphasis or illustration. Whenever a line, or movement, or character needs "pointing up" in some way for greater importance or greater clarity there is the possibility that a piece of business will do the trick. Pure gesture is the simplest form of business for this purpose, but more elaborate forms are common, as when Yank, in *The Hairy Ape*, emphasizes his curse by hurling a shovel at

Mildred, or when Hamlet points up his lines about Yorick by handling the skull.

5. Business for control of attention. Of this, more in the next chapter.

6. Business for dramatic foreshadowing. The unobtrusive "planting" of ideas that are later to be built up dramatically is a device that every accomplished dramatist understands. Much of the foreshadowing is done in the lines; but occasionally, either because the dramatist prefers it so, or because he has overlooked the matter, the director or the actor must invent business for the purpose. In *The Beggar on Horseback* the distraught composer, just before the doctor gives him an opiate, sits absently toying with an ivory paper knife while he explains his troubles to his friend. This is natural enough, and might be classed as business for delineation of character or state of mind; and it makes only a subconscious impression on the audience. But when in the fantastic dream that follows he slaughters his intolerable relatives-in-law with a huge replica of that same paper knife, the thing seems much more intelligible and inevitable by reason of the "plant". A bit of business is often a better plant than a line. It is generally less obtrusive, for the reason that we accept the lines as representing the dramatist's conscious intention, while the business, if well done, seems casual; at the same time it is less apt to escape the attention of the audience than a line would be, because in the theatre the eye ordinarily misses fewer things than the ear.

7. Business for position. It often happens that a certain stage movement is desirable but lacks apparent motivation because the real reason for it cannot at the moment be disclosed. When the director of *Abraham Lincoln* wanted to keep the left half of the stage clear for Lincoln's entrance he had to find a reason for crowding the visiting neighbors

at extreme stage right. He put the fireplace at stage right and had them warming their hands before it. In the dinner scene of *Erstwhile Susan* it is necessary for Barnabetta to hear some parts of the conversation and not to hear others: since she is the drudge as well as the daughter of the house it is a simple matter to arrange the business of waiting on table so as to bring her on and take her off at the proper moments, and that is what was done in the Fiske production.

8. Business for rhythm. What was said with respect to movement for rhythm also applies here.

9. Business for humor. Humor is one of the motives for much of the best stage business—one of the motives, in fact, for the theatre itself. But outside of pure farce humor *alone* is a very risky purpose either for the dramatist or the director. Humorous business is artistic only when it combines the motive of humor with that of legitimate character delineation, or that of clarifying a line, situation, or state of mind—in other words, when it contributes to the main thought or feeling of the play without distracting the attention. Even the so-called "comic relief" in a serious play may be a source of distraction if at all forced or irrelevant. In a tongue-in-the-cheek farce like *The Bat* we do not especially mind such antics as those of Lizzie with her elderberry wine or the Japanese butler with his sudden opening and closing of doors. But in a play that is something more than nonsense we demand humor that is something more than a device for getting a laugh. Humorous business will help, but only when it is natural and appropriate as well, like that of Frank Craven in *The First Year*, or Glenn Hunter in *Merton of the Movies*, or Lenore Ulric in *Kiki*, or like those delightful bits of by-play with which Erskine Sanford enriched the character of Mr. Pim. *The Taming of the Shrew* is proof that even a farce can be constructed without irrelevancy or distraction.

10. **Business for naturalism or relief.** Under the most favorable circumstances acting involves some measure of strain, rigidity, or self-consciousness. Inexperienced actors have a tendency to seek relief from this in movement or business of some sort. Left to themselves they are apt to take it out in mere fidgeting, relieving themselves but not the audience. It is futile for the director to attempt to suppress this tendency by merely instructing the actors to keep still; but if he can divert their energy into useful channels by suggesting little bits of business, unobtrusive in themselves, and seemingly unimportant, but natural to the situations, he will not only ease the strain but will actually improve the play at the same time. When, for instance, an actor enters ostensibly from outdoors, he may be kept busy taking off his gloves and hanging up his hat, and so will have no time to fidget. When an actor accustomed to smoking cannot keep still on the stage, and smoking is not inappropriate to the scene, it may be better to let him smoke. It will keep his hands at least partly occupied, and attract less attention than the fidgeting; moreover, if he is required to practice the smoking at rehearsals it will give him something to think about and relieve his sense of inaction, and when the first performance comes along he will experience that comfortable sense of knowing just what he is going to do. A woman may be permitted to knit or sew for a similar purpose.

COMBINING PURPOSES

With business, as with movement, it is well to combine the purposes as much as possible for economy of expression and unity of effect. It is also well to combine the purposes of the business with those of the movement, and both with the motives of the play itself. A piece of business that is necessary to the action, enriches the delineation of character, is humorous, excuses a movement of the character to a position where he will soon be needed, and at the same time improves the picture, is clearly an asset to the production.

The real importance of stage business, especially in modern plays, is not always fully understood. Properly managed, it adds verisimilitude, enriches the interest, and helps greatly in the rounding and polishing of the production. The less experienced the actors the more important the latter point becomes. Only the most finished actors can declaim lines convincingly without business, but even beginners can often perform business convincingly under competent direction; and beginners who have difficulty in reading their lines sometimes find them easier to deliver when accompanied by appropriate business well rehearsed. Ability to arrange good business will therefore count heavily when the director's problem is how to get a finished performance from unfinished actors.

At the same time it is obvious that stage business is interesting in its own right, and therefore a potent source of distraction if poorly conceived or over-elaborated. A good deal of nonsense has been written about the "art that conceals art," but if there is any phase of art that needs such concealment it is the designing of stage business. A stirring or impassioned reading of a line may—the point is debatable—just happen. But good business does not just happen; it is carefully and intelligently designed, with consistency of motive and economy of means, and nothing is more important than to keep it within bounds.

It is neither necessary nor possible to arrange all the business of a modern play before the first rehearsal—although, as I have already stated, I believe in arranging as much as possible. Business that has to do with the larger movements and groupings of the characters and the major effects of the play can and should be arranged first. Business that calls for team work should be settled before the actors have had a chance to form very definite conceptions of their parts. Individual business connected with the enrichment of lines and character can be allowed to wait until rehearsals have begun, but even this should be fixed early enough to be learned with the lines.

AIDS TO INVENTION

With all proper regard to the danger of excessive stage business it remains a fact that most amateur performances suffer from too little rather than too much, and that the amateur director often finds himself at a loss how to devise suitable business. The following suggestions may help him to cultivate a little more fertility of invention in such matters:

1. Study the manners and customs of the people and time represented in the play. Remember, however, that the object is to produce a work of art, not a museum of antiquity. Art implies discrimination and selection.

2. Study out the costumes and make-ups in advance. Have the costumes (or adequate substitutes) on hand for trial as early in rehearsal as possible, especially costumes that differ essentially from modern street dress. A Roman toga, a Turkish veil, or a military uniform may suggest business that would otherwise not suggest itself. It may also reveal when and where business is needed, especially business for naturalism, for an actor may seem perfectly easy at rehearsal with his hands in his pockets only to lose his poise when he finds himself in doublet and hose without any pockets.

3. Study the placing and use of properties, including "hand props." As with costumes, have the properties (or adequate substitutes) ready for use at an early rehearsal. The height or depth of a chair, the width of a davenport, the space available between a chair and a table, the length

and weight of a cane, umbrella or parasol, the position of a hat-rack or telephone, the placing of a flower vase, ash tray, or match-box—any of these considerations may suggest a piece of business or affect the character of one.

4. Make use of ordinary objects, especially in devising business for naturalism or relief. Consider the objects men carry or handle: Cigars, cigarettes, pipes, matches, tobacco, pencils, watches, fountain-pens, note-books, wallets, brief-cases, suit-cases, keys, canes, pocket-knives, guns, swords, revolvers, whips, monocles, snuff-boxes, and what not. Or those women handle: Fans, gloves, vanity-cases, compacts, purses, hand-bags, parasols, shawls, scarfs, furs, sewing-bags, needles, thimbles, scissors, knitting-needles, lorgnettes—any woman can extend the list. Or consider the objects in more general use by both sexes: Books, papers, furniture (chairs to be moved, for instance), dishes, knives, forks, spoons, pen and ink, call bells, telephones, lamps, light switches, candles, pictures, hats, coats, wraps, handkerchiefs—and so on almost indefinitely.

5. Study real people, on trains and trolleys, in restaurants and stores, at church, in the theatre, at dances and parties, on the street, in their homes and at their occupations. Note especially what they do with their hands, for an amateur actor needs more help on that point than almost any other.

6. Study bits of business on the professional stage. The best way to do this is to see the same play several times, and to note the care with which certain bits of business are timed and the precision with which they are repeated. Note also the skilful articulation of business with lines. Never miss an opportunity to see two different companies in the same play, whether trained by the same director or not; the experience is highly instructive in either case, though in different ways.

7. Watch the natural movements of the actors in the early rehearsals. In many instances these will not be appropriate, but when they are, make use of them. For example, if a member of the cast sits down without being told, decide at once whether the action is appropriate. If not, rule it out; if so, establish it as part of the play, note it in the prompt-book, and insist upon it at subsequent rehearsals. If a real change of interpretation later requires a change in the business, well and good; but do not allow the actors to keep changing their incidental business with every whim.

8. Have a stage rehearsal as early as possible, and try to have a few friends present to suggest an audience. The behavior of the actors on the stage with even a small audience before them is astonishingly different from their behavior at a private rehearsal in somebody's home.

9. Do not hesitate to experiment in the early rehearsals. Try every possibility and see how it works out. But decide early, settle everything, and have the business learned with the lines. Make copious notes, and study the problems of business between rehearsals; ideas do not come just when they are wanted, and it is futile to hold up a rehearsal while you seek for an inspiration.

One of the most difficult problems for the amateur director is the articulation of lines with business, or business with lines. The amateur actor wants to speak his line first and then carry out the business, or vice versa, and cannot seem to manage the two things at once. The problem can only finally be solved in rehearsal, but in planning the business the director should have regard to the timing and cadence, and should not ask the actor to do impossible things.

For example, it may be appropriate in a certain scene to have an actor light a pipe. The director should time the business so that it does not create an awkward interruption of the dialogue, and so that the dialogue does not interfere with the business, causing the actor to bungle the latter. This piece of business is most effective when it seems to articulate with the line. The skilful actor fills his pipe as he talks, lights a match, finishes a sentence, lights the pipe, speaks another word or two while he throws the match away, and gets in a few more puffs in time to make the pipe draw. The amateur (perhaps a confirmed smoker off stage) creates an awkward stage wait, tangles his words, burns his finger, and lets the pipe go out. American audiences are quick to note such bungling and are not tolerant of it. Amateur actors they can tolerate, but amateur smokers—never!

Even more troublesome is the task of articulating the lines and business of a scene at the dinner table. If the actor fails to eat a reasonable quantity of food the audience notices it at once. If he eats continuously, he cannot speak his lines. If he takes a large mouthful he is almost sure to hear his cue before he can swallow, and there is either a stage wait or a strangulation scene. Unless the actors are very old and capable hands, a scene of this kind must be carefully timed by the director, and each bite of food considered as a separate bit of business to be prescribed, learned, and rehearsed.

THE PRINCIPLE OF BALANCED FORCES

In relation to the problem of stage position and posture there is one very important principle which ought to be mentioned here because it often calls for invention of stage business. It is the principle of balanced forces, somewhat akin to the principle of resultant forces in physics. Most experienced professional actors make constant use of it, sometimes without analyzing or understanding it; but amateurs are not apt to make use of it at all unless the director is prepared to teach it to them.

To illustrate the principle: Suppose a character at stage left (H, in Figure 13) is to speak an important line following a cue from another character (W) at stage right. If he faces

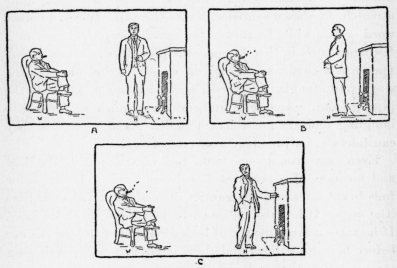

FIG. 13.—BALANCED FORCES IN STAGE BUSINESS

the audience squarely (as in *A*, Figure 13) the line will be pointed up, but the effect may be mechanical and declamatory. If he faces the other character (as in *B*) the effect will be natural enough, but he will be seen only in profile, and his voice will travel across the stage instead of toward the audience. Sometimes this will do no harm, as when the character is rather loud-mouthed and the line a bold or blunt one. But suppose in this case it is important to have the actor's full face seen as he speaks the line, or that the line is of such a nature that it ought to go straight out to the audience, yet with no suggestion of declamation. The solution is to give the character a bit of business at stage left— flicking the ashes from his cigarette into the fireplace, for example—and to time it so that he is pulled left by the business at the very moment when he is pulled right by the cue from the other character. The resultant of these two forces is a force in the direction of the audience. In other words, with his body turned left to perform the business and his thoughts drawn right by the cue, his face is toward the audience (as in *C*, Figure 13), and the effect is perfectly natural. A slight inclination of the head toward the right helps to suggest the direction of H's thoughts without forcing him to turn his face too far.

Trickery? Of course. But a reasonably intelligent amateur can learn to do a trick of this kind in six weeks, and to do it so naturally and at so little cost to his freedom of interpretation that the audience will hardly notice the device; whereas it may take him ten years to learn how to declaim a line straight toward the audience without seeming stiff and unnatural.

Among the types of business most often useful for balancing forces in this way are:

Lighting cigarettes, cigars, or pipes; getting rid of ashes; looking in a mirror and adjusting hair, hat, or tie; opening or closing a door; looking out a window; moving a chair or other object; examining a book or photograph; warming the hands at a fire; smelling flowers or rearranging them; dusting or tidying; lighting lamps; ringing for servants; reading books or newspapers, and writing letters.

SIMPLICITY IN STAGE BUSINESS

All this suggests, no doubt, a great deal of complication and a great danger of over-emphasis. Simplicity is highly desirable in art, for complication is distraction. But simplicity does not mean *sterility*. The best simplicity is not that which results from a paucity of ideas, but that which is resolved by choice out of many possibilities; and one must often find his way through great complexities before he can simplify intelligently. The best stage business is simple, not because the director lacks experience or knowledge, but because from a wealth of ideas he has selected wisely.

CHAPTER IX

CONTROL OF ATTENTION

THE problem of controlling attention is one that persists throughout the period of rehearsal and even after performances have begun; but as certain aspects of it affect the planning of stage movement and business it may best be considered at this point. The problem is really a little more complex and a little more important than the inexperienced director is apt to imagine.

THE KINDS OF ATTENTION

Psychologists do not agree upon the nature of attention—or of consciousness—and they are hardly likely to agree as long as some believe the body to be a piece of soulless mechanism automatically controlled, while others believe it to be controlled through consciousness by an immaterial mind or soul. They do agree, however, upon a practical distinction between two types of attention, which they call *primary* and *secondary*.

Primary attention is the automatic or involuntary attention which we give to a strong external stimulus—a bright flash of light, for instance, or a loud noise, or a sudden slap on the back. The appeal is concrete; that is, it is more or less directly in terms of sense impressions, either real or suggested. Primary attention involves no sense of effort, no conscious intention, no exercise of will power.

Secondary attention is voluntary attention, the sort that

175

one gives to a difficult problem through a sense of duty or by force of great concentration. Whether there is such a thing as real "will power" or not is of course the point in dispute, the mechanists holding that what we mistake for will power is but the reaction to the more remote stimuli in the past experience of the individual; but there is certainly a kind of attention in the giving of which we are aware of conscious effort.

ATTENTION IN THE THEATRE

In the theatre very little dependence should be placed upon secondary or voluntary attention. The teacher or the preacher may conceivably have a right to expect his audience to put forth an effort of the will, but the actor has no such right. The problem in the theatre is how to gain, hold, and control primary or involuntary attention.

The conditions of the theatre make the first part of this —and to a certain extent the second part—easy. People come to the theatre expecting to be interested and entertained; they await eagerly the beginning of the play; the house lights go down, there is a sudden hush, the curtain rises, and out of the darkened auditorium they gaze in fascination upon the lighted stage. This is primary attention at its best, and if the circumstances are reasonably favorable it is likely to continue, simply because the concentration of sound and light on the stage acts as a powerful magnet, and tends to hold the audience spellbound.

There are always, however, two possible enemies to sustained attention, and either of these may operate in the theatre, if not to destroy attention at least to shift it or weaken it. One of them is distraction, and the other is monotony.

CONTROL OF ATTENTION

Distraction may be described as primary attention gone wrong; it is the shifting of primary attention caused by some external and irrelevant demand upon the senses.

The American theatre audience of today suffers from comparatively little distraction, especially distraction external to the performance. This may seem a very rash statement if one has recently been annoyed by the coughers or sneezers, or the people who rattle waxed paper, or carry on conversations, or push their feet into one's back, or the people who arrive late and depart early. But the word is *comparatively*. Things used to be much worse. Only a few decades ago audiences in this country expressed themselves freely by shouting, stamping, applauding, hissing, heckling, and sometimes by throwing eggs or vegetables, by quarreling and rioting, and even (in a few notorious cases) by violence and bloodshed. Not all performances were so interrupted, nor are all performances free from interruption today; but distractions were common a few years ago which today would be almost unbelievable. And even today the European theatres tolerate demonstrations of approval or disapproval—especially the latter—for which a theatre-goer in the United States would be promptly put out, and perhaps arrested.

Even so, there is more distraction than there ought to be. Perhaps conditions will continue to improve as we become more civilized—if we ever do. Much of the responsibility for improvement in the theatre rests with the house manager, the theatre owner, or the theatre architect, rather than the director. If audiences cannot be educated to come on time they can certainly be refused admission while the curtain is up. Seats can be made more comfortable—as in the Goodman Theatre at Chicago—house lights and decorations less distracting, and theatre walls more nearly soundproof. As for those distractions which arise from the bad manners of the audience, the only solution would seem to be a law defining the slaughter of their perpetrators as a trifling misdemeanor instead of a crime.

Very little of this concerns the director. What does concern him, vitally, is that quite as many distractions may be caused by the faults of the production itself as by the defects of the house or the misbehavior of the audience. An actor with E. H. Sothern in *What Never Dies* made himself up to look like a man whose picture had appeared in every newspaper in the country in connection with a famous murder trial; it was a perfect make-up for the part, but the instant he appeared there was a buzz all over the audience and attention was distracted from the play. In the first act of *The Easiest Way* Mr. Belasco introduced such elaborate lighting effects to suggest a sunset on the Rocky Mountains that one temporarily forgot the characters. In *Johannes Kreisler* the constant shifting of scenery and the noise of the wagon stages proved very distracting. In *Six Cylinder Love* the automobile used on the stage ran wild on one occasion and plunged over the footlights; at subsequent performances people who had heard about it could hardly keep their minds on the play for wondering whether the accident would be repeated, and their distraction was hardly lessened when they observed that the car had been moored with a heavy cable to prevent its going too far. The distractions caused by divided or broken scenes, unused exits, or misplaced empathic effects have already been mentioned. A piece of rickety scenery or property, a teaser hung too low or not low enough, a delay in the rise or fall of the curtain, a late entrance or other stage wait, an audible prompt, an uncovered light shining in the eyes of the audience, an actor out of the picture, an illogical entrance or exit, an unexplained movement, a gratuitious piece of business, a forced joke or gag, an awkward gesture, a line spoken too softly or otherwise unintelligibly, a piece of over-acting, a too conspicuous costume or property, a mirror facing the audience, an unnecessary clock or telephone, an unintentional noise back stage, a spotlight badly managed, a shadow in the wrong place—these are just a few of the possible causes of distraction that may be blamed on the director or the actors. There is only one way to combat them, and that is by constant vigilance. There must be careful planning, thorough rehearsal of both cast and stage crew, and the most rigorous censorship of every single element that might catch the primary attention of the audience and lead it astray.

COMBATTING MONOTONY

The effect of monotony is less obvious than that of distraction. There is doubtless very little danger in the theatre of the droning hum-drum which the word monotony ordinarily suggests, but there exists, in the theatre and elsewhere, a subtler sort of monotony which it is well for the director to understand.

The psychologists tell us, after due laboratory tests, that attention cannot be sustained for more than a few seconds at a time; that there is no such thing as continuous attention; that attention which seems continuous is really a succession of fresh perceptions, each the result of a fresh stimulus or a fresh effort of the will. They point out that fixation of attention is equivalent to destruction of attention; that complete concentration on a single, simple, unchanging element is the way to hypnosis or induced sleep. This very important fact is the explanation of why monotony is destructive of attention—not alone monotony of pitch, but monotony of force, tempo, rhythm, line, mass, color, or any other element of expression.

If attention is to be held for any long period of time it must be renewed by a constant succession of fresh appeals to interest.

The director must realize, therefore, that in the attempt to hold attention and keep it fresh he is dealing with a psychological rather than a logical problem. He may know, for example, that a certain scene is of great intrinsic importance in the play, and may suppose therefore that it will prove interesting to the audience. But interest is not governed by intrinsic importance; it is governed by sense stimuli, and the most important scene in the play may fail utterly to hold attention if the effect upon the senses is either too weak or too continuous. There must be a succession of fresh appeals to the eye and ear, striking enough and varied enough to prevent either a relaxation or a too steady fixation of attention.

An audience that is familiar with a play, and fond of it, will contribute some measure of attention as a result of its previous knowledge—the sort of attention known to the psychologists as "derived primary" attention. An object that has little immediate sense appeal may, upon longer acquaintance, grow into the interests of the observer in such a way as to command what is virtually primary attention. A man who has made a hobby of science may take great interest in a formula which to the rest of us would prove quite unattractive. Similarly an audience familiar with Shakespeare may be keyed up with anticipation the moment Hamlet begins his soliloquy, or Mercutio his "Queen Mab" speech, and the task of holding attention may, at least for the moment, be easier.

There are many different ways of freshening the attention in the theatre, some depending upon the dramatist, some upon the director, and some upon the actors. The dramatist who knows his business is careful not to prolong a scene unduly, or use too slow a method of development; when there is danger of monotony he brings in a new character or a new phase of the plot. The capable director supplements this by movements of the characters, variations of the stage pictures, changes of tempo, shifts of emphasis, and injection of stage business. The actor contributes variety in action and delivery as well as business of his own invention; and upon his power to gauge the attention of the audience and to strengthen his acting as needed depends much of the final success of each performance.

Among producers, nobody understands the problem of freshening attention better than Mr. Belasco. In a Belasco production the attention is never allowed to lag for a moment; there is always some fresh movement, some shift of emphasis or change of tempo, some play of light or color to keep the attention engaged. Mr. Belasco has been accused of overdoing it at times to the point of restlessness, or of failing to motivate sufficiently the devices employed, but he has never been accused of monotony.

On the other hand many little theatre and art theatre groups have failed to hold the attention of popular audiences largely because they have not understood how to avoid monotony. Among such groups the commonest and worst form of this fault is simple "talkiness."

When the Abbey Theatre players of Dublin first visited this country they impressed two eminent teachers of dramatic literature in quite opposite ways. One praised highly their simplicity, naturalness, and freedom from artificiality; the other, while admitting the excellence of their diction, found them in other respects quite amateurish. The difference lay, no doubt, in the fact that the first, being a specialist in Irish literature and already familiar with the plays, supplied not only a clearer understanding and a livelier imaginative interpretation, but also a keener "derived primary" attention. The second, a specialist in another field, had no such advance interest; he took the plays as actually presented, and was bored by the talkiness and uneventfulness of the performances.

This difference is typical, and represents one of the director's major problems. It is one thing to produce *Hamlet* before a well established Shakespeare Society which has seen the play many times before, and quite another to produce it before an audience of high school students who are seeing a Shakespearean play for the first time. Whenever a new or otherwise unfamiliar play is produced the director can safely expect his audience to require constant freshening of interest. Neither the intrinsic interest of the play itself nor the intellectual curiosity of the audience will quite solve the problem in the absence of the necessary sense stimuli.

It need hardly be said that both the director and the actors should go as often as possible to observe the work of the best professionals—not for slavish imitation but for intelligent study. Many professionals are extraordinarily clever in freshening interest. Mrs. Fiske, for example, can enrich the flattest sort of part and make every line interesting, and that without the slightest apparent artificiality or strain. Some of it she does by means of business, skilfully articulated with the lines; but most of it by variations of pitch, force, and especially tempo, in the use of the voice, and by the most unexpected and yet natural use of pauses. Walter Hampden does it largely by change of tempo and by unexpected movements. George Arliss and Cyril Maude do it by richness and variety of stage business, while Pauline Lord does it every so often by a sudden welling-up of emotion, quickly suppressed again but leaving strong empathic effects.

CONTROL OF ATTENTION

Another problem of attention arises from the fact that in nearly every play there are certain lines or bits of action so important in conveying the meaning that the audience simply cannot be allowed to miss them. The dramatist of course points these things up as best he can, and when the plot permits he repeats important ideas several times to make sure that they are heard and understood. But sometimes the plot does not permit. An essential point may be of such a nature that it can be given only once, and the play may be spoiled for anybody who misses it. What sort of insurance will enable the director to guard against such contingencies?

The temptation, of course, is to have the actor shout the important line; but that is always painfully artificial and often leads to false accent in the delivery of the line. Sometimes a very slight increase of voice is allowable; at other times the situation may preclude even that, as when one character is supposed to speak the important line confidentially to another in fear of being overheard.

A more practicable plan is so to arrange the business and movement, the stage picture, the lighting, and the contrasts of voice, as to concentrate the maximum attention on the right character at the instant he is to deliver the important line. This will not prevent external distraction, of course; somebody may cough or sneeze just as the line is uttered. But the more powerful the concentration of attention at the instant, the greater the resistance to distraction, even on the part of the coughers and sneezers themselves; and if a listener does miss the line that is so pointed up, he realizes that he has missed something important and so tries harder to pick up the context.

An essential line should always be expressed in easy familiar words with strong vowel contrasts; such a line is less apt to be missed than a line couched in unfamiliar words, or words not easily distinguishable in sound. Unfamiliar proper nouns are the most troublesome of all, and more apt to be misunderstood than any other class of words. While this is undoubtedly the dramatist's business rather than the director's, a good director can often repair some of the damage done by a dramatist unfamiliar with the realities of production.

Clear enunciation is of course a great asset in conveying the points of a play to the audience—not only in its effect on the ear but in its effect on the eye as well. Most people nowadays do a little lip-reading, and confirmed photoplay addicts do a great deal, so that if an actor faces front as he speaks an important line and makes his lip movements distinct, many listeners will catch the line as much with the eye as with the ear. Gesture helps in the same way; and here again we feel the influence of the moving pictures, in establishing something very like a conventional sign language, universally understood. Many dramatists and stage directors today are finding it safer to entrust important thoughts to pantomime than to express them in words—partly because the public is becoming more visual-minded and partly because the eye is not so easily distracted as the ear in a darkened auditorium. Safer still is a combination of both, for it is an unusually violent distraction that causes one to miss an entire line and also the accompanying action; and if one gets a part of the thought and the contributing conditions are helpful he can often piece out the rest. The director's concern is to make the contributing conditions as helpful as possible, without obtrusive over-emphasis.

All of this is ridiculously obvious when one stops to think of it. But how often does an amateur director sit down before the first rehearsal, check over the essential points of the play, and plan a constructive campaign to get those points to the audience even at the sacrifice of minor effects? More often, perhaps, an otherwise good performance is ruined by the practical failure of one important line, when so trifling a thing as a well-planned movement or a well-timed pause might have saved it. In Frederick Lonsdale's *Aren't We All?* the very last line is the key to the title. In Cyril Maude's production that line was beautifully pointed up; but in a certain otherwise good production by a community theatre it missed fire completely, and the final curtain fell flat.

DIRECTING ATTENTION

The necessities of a production often require that the attention of the audience be controlled and directed not merely to the stage but to some particular spot on the stage, or that it be shifted at a given moment from one spot to another. For the accomplishment of this it is possible to devise a more or less complete technique, just a few points of which may be suggested here.

The first step is naturally to consider the various elements in play production, and to study their relative effect in attracting or repelling attention. For example, it will be found that attention generally tends to fall on:

1. People, rather than inanimate things.
2. Speaking persons, rather than silent ones.
3. Moving persons, rather than still ones.
4. Light places, rather than dark ones.
5. Bright colors, rather than dull ones.
6. Converging, rather than diverging, lines.
7. Near objects, rather than far ones.
8. Stage center, rather than stage right or left.
9. Objects at which the characters seem to be looking, rather than objects they seem to ignore.

10. An advancing, rather than a retreating, character.

11. A character in a state of emotion, rather than a character in a tranquil state of mind.

12. A character framed in a doorway or holding a striking pose, rather than one casually or inconspicuously placed.

13. A character on a stairway or other high level, rather than one on the ordinary stage level.

14. A character who is being talked about by other characters.

15. A thing that is being talked about, if visible.

16. An unusual element of any kind, rather than a commonplace one.

These are mere suggestions; the catalogue might be continued almost indefinitely. There will be plenty of exceptions, of course—as when a single silent character draws attention away from many talkative ones, or when a single dull costume stands out by contrast with many brilliant ones—but if one understands the principle of primary attention these exceptions will explain themselves.

The extent to which it is possible to control and direct attention is perhaps best illustrated by the sleight-of-hand artist. Half the secret of his magic lies in his ability to direct the attention of the audience to the wrong place. By talking glibly and looking with great apparent interest at his right hand he practically compels his audience to look at that hand, while he performs the essential part of the trick with his left hand and nobody sees him do it. A great prestidigitator like Keller or Thurston employs for this purpose not only the devices of the actor—speech, gesture, and facial expression—but those of the stage director as well, including position, movement, business, line, mass, scenic effect, light and shade. The student of stage directing who is not too sternly opposed to trickery may learn from such performers a great many facts about the psychology of attention that will prove valuable in actual play production.

Perhaps the most important trick for the ordinary stage

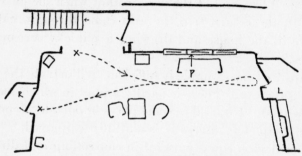

FIG. 14.—A STUDY IN LEADING THE EYE

director to know is the simple physical one of leading the eye to the right place at the right time. This is so common that almost any well directed play will furnish an illustration; but let us take one from *The Bat*, as staged by Collin Kemper. In one scene of that extraordinarily popular play a bloody arm was thrust into view through a broken window pane, and the hand unfastened the catch. For full effect it was necessary that every person in the audience should see that arm the instant it appeared. The arrangement was roughly that shown in Figure 14, with the window up L.C. and the broken pane at P. It was night, and pitch dark outside, and a number of previous incidents had made everybody feel that some awful danger lurked in the garden, threatening the lives of the inmates. Miss Dale Ogden, the ingénue, had just been left alone in that fearsome place, standing near the hall door up stage right, with the attention of the audience concentrated upon her. Had the mysterious arm appeared just then not one person in twenty would have seen it, and the effect would have been lost. But Miss Ogden, apparently fearing an attack from almost any direction, crossed timidly to the door up left, listened there for an instant, then, half reassured, crossed back as if to listen at the door down right—all of this being natural enough under the circumstances. Of course all eyes followed her, and at the very instant when she passed the point P on the return trip the arm came through, catching every eye in the house and drawing a panicky scream from the ladies.[1]

Perhaps this one example is sufficient to illustrate the device of leading the eye. There is hardly a play in which some use cannot be made of it, and in some plays important scenes may miss fire completely unless it is skilfully employed.

Another device, equally useful in controlling and directing attention, is that of anticipation—a device employed both by the dramatist and the director in a great variety of ways, some of which have already been discussed in connection with stage movement. Whether the anticipation be created by the lines of the play, by an expectant vacancy in the stage picture, by the gestures or facial expressions of the actors, or by dramatic foreshadowing, it is one of the greatest possible incentives to attention; and properly understood it is one of the easiest devices to manage. No more need be said of it here.

No amount of theorizing will teach the inexperienced director to control and direct attention unless it is backed by constant study and observation on his part. He should consider again and again the importance of the negative element in technique, and should be as anxious to avoid those things which distract or destroy attention as to create those things which gain and hold it. And always he should beware of excessive and artificial straining for attention—which is itself a cause of distraction.

---

[1] This was true of the Philadelphia performances. In the one performance I saw in Chicago the arm appeared about two seconds late, and at least half the effectiveness was lost.

CHAPTER X

CHOOSING THE CAST

BEFORE the play can be put into rehearsal it is necessary of course to choose the cast—tentatively, at least. Sometimes the director has no option in this matter, the cast being chosen before the play is put in his hands. More often he either aids in the choice or bears the entire responsibility himself.

The first question that arises is whether the choice is to be made solely in the interest of the particular production, or partly in the interest of the organization and its future welfare. In the commercial theatre a production is ordinarily an independent venture, and the producer endeavors to secure the best possible cast to fit the characters—or to shine as stars—regardless of any permanent organization. As a result what is known as "type casting" has come to be the general rule in the commercial theatre; an actor is chosen primarily because he is already identified with the type of part to be filled. But in an amateur or little theatre group, or in a real repertory theatre, it is often necessary to consider the training of a permanent company and the building up of an organization as well as the needs of the particular play.

One thing should be emphasized from the beginning, however, and that is the utter futility of sacrificing the quality of the production for the sake of training the actors. Such a procedure defeats its own purpose, for nothing is more injurious to the training of an actor than a half-hearted production, or a feeling that the production doesn't matter very

189

much as long as some other end is achieved; and nothing is more injurious to a sound *esprit de corps* than the toleration of inferiority. Considerations of permanent policy, therefore, should never be allowed to outweigh the needs of the particular play to the extent of spoiling the play. If the demands of a later production preclude the choice of a good cast for an early one the only honest procedure, artistically, is to omit the early one altogether. If to give the actors variety of experience it is necessary to mis-cast them badly, the exercise should be confined to rehearsals or classroom practice, and both actors and audience should be spared the pain of an inferior public performance.

However, without serious detriment to the excellence of any one production it is quite possible to establish certain general policies in casting that are permanently beneficial to the actors and to the organization; and a few of these may be mentioned.

TYPE CASTING VERSUS MIS-CASTING

The most important point is to steer a middle course between type casting and mis-casting. To choose an actor to represent a character because he seems to be that character himself, or because he has specialized in that type of character, is perhaps to gain a temporary advantage in making the play convincing. But if this method of casting is continued as a permanent policy the actors soon fall into ruts, become identified with their particular types, develop mannerisms, and fail to grow in imagination and sympathy. Meanwhile the audience, if a permanent one, learns to identify each actor by his mannerisms, to regard him always as the same character in a new situation, and to look upon each new play as a mere rearrangement of the old familiar types—very much as the small boy considers each new photoplay by Tom Mix or

Charlie Chaplin not a new story about new characters but a mere continuation of the adventures of his hero. Neighborhood audiences very quickly develop such an attitude toward the actors of a local stock company, and while the result may be a fairly healthy spirit of play it is not likely to encourage a very high order of art.

On the other hand, if actors are chosen arbitrarily and needlessly for parts totally unlike themselves, the result may be ruinous to the quality of the performances, and eventually to the morale of the group and the interest of the audience. Even the mechanical rotation of parts is bad from this point of view. It is a very good thing for the actor to try his skill at a variety of parts within reasonable limitations, versatility being unquestionably a thing to be encouraged, but it should be obvious that some actors are physically or temperamentally unfit for some parts, and if they are cast for such parts they can only meet with failure and discouragement.

The Moscow Art Theatre has successfully steered the middle course. In that theatre the actors are cast for varied rôles, and several different actors are cast in rotation for the same rôle; yet no actor is assigned to a part for which he is seriously unfitted. The best feature of this system is that it educates the actors, but it is almost equally advantageous in its effect upon the audience, as emphasizing the play and the character rather than the actor. This it could not do, did not each actor thoroughly subordinate himself to his part.

CASTING FOR TEAM WORK

A second important point is that good team work has more to do with training the actors and building up a strong group than has emphasis on individual talent. From the standpoint of permanent policy, therefore, it is not always best to choose the actors who show flashes of talent. It is better to choose those who show the most intelligent sense of coöperation with the director and the other actors. As a matter of fact this type of actor frequently gives the better performance in the end, even considered as an individual, though his superiority is not so noticeable in the early rehearsals.

In other words, if there are four candidates for two parts it is better to take the two who are not brilliant but who work well together than to take the brilliant pair who work at cross purposes. In this connection physical fitness is a consideration, of course; one does not want a heroine who is a head and a half taller than the hero, even if they are individually the best actors. Compatibility is another consideration; experienced professionals may act smoothly together though sworn enemies in private life, but amateurs can seldom do so. It is better to sacrifice a little talent than to allow a constant element of friction to disrupt the team work.

An important element of team work is leadership, and in choosing the cast of a play it is wise to assign actors of experience and tried ability to those parts which involve leadership. In this respect it is not always the so-called "leading" parts—those of the hero and heroine—that carry the greatest responsibility. Often there are other parts, long and exacting, but not conspicuous or attractive, which have more to do with sustaining the play. A thoroughly dependable actor in such a part will do much to stiffen and steady the performance, and will exercise a most beneficial influence on the less experienced members of the cast; an untrustworthy actor, on the other hand, even though talented, will ruin the whole performance. Unfortunately, he will also carry off the individual honors, for the audience will note his flashes of good acting and at the same time fail to discern that it is he who is upsetting the others; and they will blame the raggedness of the performance on almost anybody else—which is most exasperating to the director and unfair to the other actors.

When the actors are all young, as in a school or college production, it is usually much easier to cast the juvenile parts than those of old or middle-aged persons. Occasionally a young man, aided by a broad character make-up, can play very acceptably the part of an extremely old man; less often, but for the same reasons, a young girl can play an old woman. But it is usually the hardest thing in the world for a young person of either sex to play a middle-aged part convincingly. The youngster's face, voice, and movements are too youthful, yet he dare not indulge in elaborate make-up and he cannot change his voice without becoming painfully unnatural. It is advisable, therefore, to cast the middle-aged parts first, using the most capable actors for the purpose, even though the younger parts suffer somewhat in consequence. It often happens, fortunately, that the middle-aged parts are also the sustaining parts of the play, so that these last two problems merge into one.

CASTING THE SMALL PARTS

While the most difficult and most responsible parts should always be given to capable actors, the members of the group should never be allowed to regard the small parts as unimportant—mere leftovers to be parceled out among the defeated candidates as consolation. Such a feeling is bad for the production as well as for the spirit of the organization.

Every actor should be made to feel that a small part is just as essential to the play and just as worthy an object of study as a large one, and that it affords him just as fine an opportunity for good acting and good team work. One way of encouraging this feeling is to assign experienced players to

193

small parts every now and then when they are not otherwise engaged, impressing upon them the dignity of doing a small thing well, and the importance of subordinating the individual to the ensemble effect. In the Moscow Art Theatre—if the reader will pardon another reference to that exemplary organization—even the smallest "bits" are carefully cast, and played with the utmost attention to detail. In *The Three Sisters* there is a serving woman who never speaks a word and does nothing but answer the doorbell; but even on tour in this country that part was played by a painstaking actress who made it a finished character study. Stanislavsky himself is not above playing a supernumerary part when he does not happen to be cast for a main one, and by so doing he encourages the subordinate members of the company to sink their individual pride and consider only the good of the play. The spirit of the company is one of self-suppression and artistic sincerity, and the result is not only the best ensemble playing in the world but also the best possible influence for the training of the younger actors.

FAIRNESS IN CASTING

The loyalty and good sportsmanship of a producing organization depends in no small measure upon the feeling that the casting is being done wisely and fairly.

It is a bad plan to give the impression that talent is being overlooked or neglected, but it is even worse to push the merely talented members forward too easily and too rapidly. Service, experience, and reliability should be considered first. When important parts are hastily assigned to comparatively inexperienced players because they have displayed some flash of brilliancy, jealousies are quick to arise among those who think themselves equally brilliant; at the same time less brilliant members are apt to feel the hopelessness of competition and lose heart. Nobody likes to be given a minor part in support of an irresponsible young upstart. On the other hand most people who are at all seriously interested are glad to play in support of an experienced and reliable old-timer. They know they can depend upon him, that he has won his place by hard work, and that they can learn from him what is most likely to help them in their own efforts. The result of such casting is a spirit of loyalty and coöperation very desirable in a permanent organization.

THE NEEDS OF THE PLAY

Granted that the needs and policies of the organization are taken care of, there still remains the problem of casting the particular play as effectively as possible.

The question most often asked in regard to casting is whether ability or suitability should be considered most important as determining the fitness of a candidate. The answer would seem to be fairly obvious: A certain degree of suitability is a necessary prerequisite, but beyond that ability, rather than suitability, should determine the choice.

The first test, then, to apply to a candidate for a part is that of minimum suitability. Is he physically possible in the part? In considering this question one naturally makes allowance for the possibilities of disguise, especially disguise of the face through make-up. There are some things, however, that even make-up cannot do. It can make an average face seem a bit narrow or a bit broad, but it cannot make a very broad face seem narrow, or vice versa. It cannot change greatly the facial angle so important in profile—not unless the part allows a copious application of whiskers. It can make a character face out of a straight juvenile, but it cannot make a straight juvenile face or a straight middle-aged face out of a character face. In a small theatre a heavy make-up

195

is apt to be too obvious, and so to weaken the illusion; and in a play calling for subtleties of facial expression a heavy make-up is a serious detriment anyhow. It is not well, therefore, to put too much dependence upon the possibilities of make-up, or to disregard in casting the facial characteristics of the candidate.

Another consideration is bodily physique. The six-footer obviously cannot play Napoleon, the short fat man cannot play Abraham Lincoln, and the lady who weighs four hundred pounds cannot play the heroine—historical precedents not-withstanding. Little can be done to disguise such physical extremes. Even lesser peculiarities of build, proportion, carriage, and gesture are difficult to disguise, especially in the case of the women. Modern styles may permit a woman to conceal the facts about her complexion, but not about her architectural idiosyncrasies. Time was when a bow-legged actress could play the lovely heroine, but not so today. A grasshopper build, pigeon-toes or knock-knees, even an absence of curves where curves should be will now disqualify an otherwise talented actress for anything but a character part, and if there is any part in the play which calls for a particular physique a candidate must be found who can satisfy the requirement.

The same difficulty of disguise which narrows the choice in casting is from another point of view a protection against error. I remember some years ago choosing an attractive, graceful little girl for a fairy part in which there was some dancing, and then being horrified, at the dress rehearsal, when she appeared for the first time in short skirts, to discover that her dancing extremities were somewhat too substantial to be fairy-like. Times have changed, and the director is not likely to make *that* mistake until they change again.

Even more important than face and figure for certain parts

is a suitable voice. Some voices are flexible and adaptable to many different characterizations, but most voices, especially young voices, have definite limitations which make them totally unfit for some parts. Voices can be trained, and flexibility can be cultivated, but the time required is a matter of months and years. For the sake of the play, therefore, the director must often reject at once the candidate whose voice is inappropriate and who cannot change it sufficiently to make it right.

PROBLEMS OF EMPATHY

Given a candidate who has the physical equipment for a part, the next question is: Will he, or she, create the proper empathic effect upon the audience? This is not always easy to determine in advance, and sometimes the director is badly fooled. An actor who seems warmly human in real life may stiffen up on the stage, becoming cold and mechanical. On the other hand a dowdy frump of a girl who would be described by a smart writer as having "no sex appeal" may sometimes make up to look positively alluring on the stage and, conscious of the effect she is producing, develop a magnetic stage personality and a freedom in emotional acting which nobody could have supposed possible. I have seen this happen in startling fashion on several occasions.

As I pointed out in an earlier chapter, there are two questions of empathy to be considered in casting: the effect of the actor upon those who are to empathize in him directly— especially those of his own sex—and the effect upon those who may empathize in some other character with whom he is involved. Since it is almost impossible for a man to judge how the women in the audience will respond, or vice versa, it is a good plan for the director to consider the problem in consultation with one or two persons of the opposite sex. Two heads may or may not be better than one, but two sets of motor nerves are certainly better than one when the problem is to prophesy motor responses; and a half dozen sets may be better than two, especially if they represent both sexes and several different ages and temperaments. At best the prophecy is uncertain, and for this reason, as for many others, the director should avoid too hasty decisions in casting.

Another question is whether the candidate has the sympathy and imagination necessary to a full appreciation of the part. Possession of these qualities is, to be sure, no proof of a good actor, but absence of them is pretty good proof of a bad one. Without the power to put himself mentally in the character's place, to imagine his sensations and emotions, and to sympathize with them even though they are entirely different from his own, an actor can hardly expect to interpret a part successfully. Fortunately for the casting director these qualities are not so difficult to judge, provided the method of trying out the candidate gives him opportunity to reveal them to the director. An intimate, informal talk about the character will usually afford such an opportunity.

Another qualification which some directors demand in a candidate is intelligence, a reasonable amount of which would seem to be at least desirable. Whether a very high order of intelligence properly belongs to the art of acting is a question long in dispute; there are those who believe that a good memory, a fine voice, a responsive body and a strong emotional temperament are much more to the point, and the history of the stage bears them out in some measure. But the team work and coöperation required in a modern production, and the coöperative spirit of a modern producing organization certainly call for intelligence. It is doubtless still true that the reaction of the audience is largely emotional rather than intellectual, but it is becoming increasingly necessary under modern conditions for the actor to have intelligence himself if he would create the right emotions in others. The more sophisticated our audiences become, the more intelligence the actor needs to enable him to penetrate their intellectual armor and touch their real emotions.

Perhaps the least important quality to look for in a new and inexperienced candidate, though one of the easiest to test, is technical excellence. Not that technique is unimportant in the finished production; but a new candidate who *can* not be expected to have it ready made. A candidate who professes to have had considerable experience should of course be judged a little more severely in the matter of technique. On the other hand a player who shows a facile but superficial technical skill without much background of intelligence, sympathy, and imagination is not usually a person of very good promise. The indications are that he has been overtrained and under-educated, or that he lacks balance. What the director must find out is not how well the candidate knows the traditional conventions, but how well he can adapt himself to whatever conventions may be called for by each new play. This of course *is* technique, in the broadest sense, but it is not what many old actors mean by technique.

THE TRY-OUT SYSTEM

Some sort of a try-out system is often necessary to assist the director in choosing the cast, and is often desirable from the standpoint of competition and morale in the producing organization. It should be understood, however, that such a system is at best a mere makeshift, dictated by policy or necessity.

There is no director on earth who can really tell in one try-out, or five, or ten, what an actor has in him. Only the test of actual performance—of many performances in many parts—can reveal that. It may be true that Belasco picked a school girl and made her a star, or that Reinhardt chose an unknown woman to play the Nun in *The Miracle* because he liked her profile in the moonlight, but for every such case in which the judgment proved correct a dozen could be cited in which equally experienced producers went wrong. One has but to read the biographies of famous actors, past and present, to be impressed with the fact that many of them were themselves misjudged in youth, and had to go through long years of apprenticeship and even failure before their talents were recognized. Sarah Siddons was not only scorned by the managers but was hissed off the stage by the audience in London, to return after years in the provinces as the most popular actress England has ever known. Henry Irving was laughed at for his mannerisms long before anybody began to take him seriously. Many great actors, too, have been utterly different in rehearsal and in performance; Clara Morris, for example, though she often tried, could never give any impression at rehearsal of what she would be before an audience, and was often misjudged in consequence, even by so astute a manager as Augustin Daly. There is only one thing harder to foretell than the future development of an actor, and that is the success or failure of a play. And if commercial managers cannot judge correctly among actors who have had, as a rule, at least some experience, the director of amateurs should have little faith in any judgment he can form on the basis of two or three try-outs.

But to say that is not to solve the problem. When the director has a play to cast and most of the candidates are strangers to him he cannot wait several years to find out what they can do. He must go ahead and choose, as wisely as possible, without hope of infallibility, but with the determination to reduce the probability of error to a minimum.

How, then, can a series of try-outs be planned so as to

come as near the truth as possible in the time available? Among the many methods now in use which are most genuinely helpful?

The commonest method—and the worst—is to have the candidates read at sight the parts for which they are competing, and to pass judgment upon the reading alone. This is, to be sure, the quickest way to eliminate a large number of candidates. But the best sight reading, or at any rate the most spectacular, is sometimes done by the superficially clever elocutionist. With a facility born of much practice and some egotism, he—or she—can give almost any part a broad and lively reading which may or may not be correct, but which positively shines by contrast with the more cautious reading of the careful, earnest student. It frequently happens, however, that the person who puts a great deal of expression into the first reading of a part over-acts it seriously at a later period, and because he forms his conceptions so quickly he forms some misconceptions that are later hard to break. Many of the most capable and finished actors form their conceptions slowly at first, and so read very poorly, giving little evidence of interpretation until they have gone far enough to lay aside their books. To eliminate such persons at the first try-out would be most unfortunate. So deceptive, generally, is a judgment based upon a first reading that if I were compelled to choose a cast by that method I should almost think it safer to reject the good readers and retain the poor ones.

A far better method is the one occasionally used in amateur casting, and sometimes in professional, by which each candidate is required to perform a scene from some play in which he has previously appeared, or a scene especially chosen in advance and rehearsed for the purpose. If the candidate has sufficient notice and some idea of the kind of play and the kind of part for which he is being considered, he can choose a scene that will demonstrate his abilities in appropriate manner. Still better is an elaboration of this method by which the candidate appears in several scenes from several different types of plays.

It is possible, of course, to use actual scenes from the play to be produced, and a great many directors do this. But scenes so used are apt to become tiresome to the actors before the real rehearsals have begun, and the total period of rehearsal is apt to seem painfully long and dragged out. Another difficulty is that some of the candidates will have learned these scenes without proper direction, and will have to make too many readjustments in rehearsal. Moreover, it is sometimes desirable, for one reason or another, to withhold announcement of the play until rehearsals are under way, and defeated candidates are not always the best people in the world to keep a secret.

On the whole it is generally better to keep the try-outs separate from the play itself, giving out the parts only after the cast has been finally chosen. When the competition is very keen, or when the candidates are serious-minded students eager for every scrap of coaching or instruction, it is possible to keep them working on the play for some time with no certainty of making the cast; but with the average group of amateurs it is easier to maintain the competitive spirit through a series of tests distinct from rehearsals. Most young candidates will work hard enough on preliminary try-outs, but they have a strange aversion to doing any real work on the play until they are sure of their parts.

The problem, then, is not so much how to conduct a series of trial rehearsals as how to devise a series of independent tests that will make possible the tentative choice of a cast, or at least the elimination of impossible candidates. Obviously no single recipe will do for all productions; plays and parts are so different in their requirements that the director must be prepared to meet each new occasion, changing his plan much or little according to circumstances.

By way of illustration, suppose we are to produce a play of Barrie—*The Admirable Crichton,* for example. Here is a play about the family of an English earl. It has the humor and whimsy of Barrie, plenty of comedy, a little romance, a little pathos, and a great deal of satirical "kick." Clearly we shall have to eliminate—at least as far as the principal parts are concerned—those candidates who are too uncouth in speech or manners to suggest the English peerage, even satirically; or too persistently American in speech to play English parts; or too naïve to appreciate the values in satire. We shall need some such tests as the following:

1. A reading test, for pronunciation and enunciation.

2. A conversation test, to supplement the reading test, and also for diction and intonation.

3. An improvisation test, for diction, manners, poise, and imagination.

4. A pantomime test, for poise, carriage, technique, and imagination.

5. A special acting test, or recitation test, for satirical feeling.

6. A general acting test, for all-round acting ability.

7. A personal interview, for character, intelligence and sympathy, and to supplement all other tests.

For the reading test the candidate may be asked to read at sight from several different scenes, taken perhaps from another play of Barrie, such as *Dear Brutus.* The material may be varied for different candidates according to their apparent possibilities, but the attention should be upon speech habits rather than character interpretation. The director should note any slovenliness of enunciation or any markedly un-English pronunciation, giving special attention to the long and short *o*, the *a* as in "laugh," "half," and "past," the medial and final *r*, and the more difficult labial and dental consonants, especially *b*, *t*, and *d*. Failure to achieve a perfect English pronunciation on the first reading should not necessarily mean summary dismissal, for a candidate may be very distinctly American in his ordinary speech and yet have the gift of learning dialects other than his own. The director should criticize the first reading, allow a little time for preparation, and then hear the same candidate again. If, after several chances, with criticism and time for preparation, the candidate still seems unable to shake off his most pronounced Americanisms he is not likely to be useful in any important part in this play. And if, even on the first reading, he displays extreme uncouthness of speech—bad grammar, slovenly enunciation, excessive elision of syllables, vulgar intonation, coarse voice, or roughness of any kind—matters which are too serious to be corrected in a few weeks—he may be promptly disqualified for anything but a supernumerary part.

The conversational test is a useful check on the reading test because there are some people who can read fairly well in a school room manner but who revert to Bowery English in conversation. Such persons are not usually to be trusted in sustained parts requiring cultivated speech; they are apt to exaggerate the cultivation when they think of it, and forget all about it when the excitement of acting is upon them. The director should draw the candidate out in conversation, putting him as much at ease as possible, but noting carefully his speech habits. There are matters of tempo, intonation and sentence rhythm that are not revealed in the reading test, for the reason that reading has certain conventionalized inflections of its own; but most of these come out in conversation. Some candidates who can correct their pronunciation and clean up their enunciation are unable to catch the *tune* of English speech as distinct from American. If the director can adopt at least a suggestion of the English intonation in his own speech while conversing with the candidate he will find that the very adaptable candidate will respond with unconscious imitation—though this device is rather subtle and not always reliable.

The improvisation test is hardly a fair test of speech if used alone, because of the added element of self-consciousness, but it does help to reveal the relation of the candidate's speech habits to his manners and carriage. At the same time it tests the imagination much more severely than an ordinary acting test. The candidate may be asked to enter an imaginary drawing room, acknowledge the greetings of guests, place a chair for a lady, retrieve a lady's handkerchief and return it to her, perform an introduction, acknowledge an introduction, give an order to a servant, or what not, improvising his own lines as he goes. Or he may have a more definite and significant dramatic situation described to him, and be asked to enact his part of it, again improvising the words. As a rule it is best to apply this test to several candidates at once, assigning them to the several parts involved. After a group of candidates have floundered through an improvised scene once or twice they should be given a few moments to think it over and then heard again, for unless they are actors of considerable experience they will not do very well on the first attempt and the test will seem a hopeless failure. After two or three trials and a little coaching they will begin to loosen up enough to reveal to the director what he wants to know about them.

The pantomime test is almost identical in method and purpose, except that the emphasis is now on the action rather than the lines. The two tests may, of course, be combined, but I have generally found that I can learn more about a candidate's carriage, poise, manners, and action technique by putting him through a few scenes entirely in pantomime. If he does not have to rack his brains for words he can concentrate his imagination on the action. The director may describe to him a simple situation: He enters a drawing room; tea is being served; he sees Lady Clara on a divan at stage left; he greets her, and expresses his pleasure at seeing her again; he asks if she has had tea; she has not; he gets it for her; he asks permission to present a friend who is in the next room, and goes in search of him; he brings his friend on and introduces him to Lady Clara. Either with or without words the candidate will make an amusing grotesque of this scene on the first attempt, but after two or three attempts he will begin to reveal some social poise if he has any. When, after several rehearsals, he swaggers on with his hands in his pockets and his chewing-gum still in one cheek, stands almost on Lady Clara's feet, and says, "Hullo, Lady Clarrer, wantcher ter meet m'fren' Jones," he can be set down as unavailable for any part in *The Admirable Crichton*.

For a play like *The Admirable Crichton* the test for satirical feeling is especially important. The candidate should be asked to learn and recite a satirical poem or prose sketch, or to act out a satirical passage from another play, and should be judged for his ability to convey the double meaning or the tongue-in-the-cheek attitude concealed behind the lines. Almost anybody can convey sharp, bitter irony, but with Barrie the problem is to keep the whimsical light-comedy effect and the gentle good humor, and yet deliver the wallop. One candidate will fail utterly to detect any satirical meaning and will see only naïve romance; another will detect the satirical intent but exaggerate it and make it bitter; another will keep the comedy, but translate the satire into burlesque. The history of American literature is proof that Americans generally are not quite as keenly alive to high comedy satire as the English, and it is not easy to find young American actors who can act Barrie with just the right flavor. But a candidate who can recite Sir Peter Teazle's famous monologue, or Dickens's description of Mr. Turvey-drop, or Goldsmith's *Elegy on the Death of a Mad Dog*, or one of Gilbert's *Bab Ballads*, or Kipling's *Pink Dominoes*, and do it in such a way as to bring out the humor and satire, is at least a possibility.

The purpose of the general acting test is clear enough. As already suggested, it should consist of an opportunity to act a complete scene thoroughly prepared in advance. Several candidates may be tried together, in a scene from *Dear Brutus*, or *Quality Street*, or *What Every Woman Knows* (with or without the Scotch dialect), or perhaps a scene from some other author of high comedy, like A. A. Milne. Costumes and scenery are not essential, but if time permits there should be several repetitions so that the individual may do himself justice after the first self-consciousness has passed. Inexperienced directors do not always make sufficient allowance for the unusual strain attached to try-outs, a strain that is far greater and more artificial when individuals are competing against each other than when they are working as a group to perform the finished play.

The last test, that of a personal interview, is in many respects the most valuable of all, and yet one that many directors omit altogether. It will not, of course, serve by itself, for one wants to know how the candidate will look and act on the platform, viewed objectively; but on the other hand it will reveal quickly many things that will not appear at all in the platform tests until after weeks of rehearsal. The director may question the candidate as to his previous experience, his knowledge of technique, his knowledge of the drama in general and the play to be performed in particular, his tastes and preferences, his admirations and ambitions; and in a general way draw out his entire character. The candidate's preferences in reading will throw a great deal of light on his possible ability to appreciate satire, as well as on his understanding of literary and social values. Quite obviously this test may be combined with the conversational test already discussed, and the candidate's speech habits tested at the same time; but the director must not be too much concerned with externals, and fail to note those deeper things that cannot be taught.

All this is but a suggestion of method. The several tests may be combined in any convenient way, or still further subdivided, and not all of them will be needed with every candidate. The director who has confidence in his own snap judgement will regard the whole business as fantastic, of course. If he can get along with something simpler that is his good luck. Personally I want to know as much as I can find out about every candidate who applies, and I have found each of these tests helpful in one way or another, at one time or another.

THE TWO-CAST SYSTEM

Nearly every director of experience has felt the difficulty of having to make his final decisions in casting before the best candidates have had a chance to show their fullest development. One method which offers at least a partial solution is that of choosing two complete casts, and having each of them rehearse thoroughly up to the time of actual performance. There are certain difficulties in this system, not the least of which is the fact that it just about doubles the director's work; but there are certain compensations that occasionally make it worth while. For one thing it solves the understudy problem as well as it can be solved, and protects the production against the sudden illness of a member of the cast. It makes the competition very keen, and enables the director to reserve his final judgement until the last possible moment. If the players are inclined to be half-hearted it is not likely that they will relish the prospect of working hard up to the final rehearsal and then being obliged to retire in favor of somebody else, although an earnest group with a good director may be willing to take the chance for the sake of the experience and instruction; but this difficulty can be overcome in the case of a production that is to run for a week or more if each cast is promised a chance to perform. If the casts develop with about equal merit the performances may be divided equally between them. If one turns out to be better than the other it may be allowed more performances, or assigned to the preferred evenings. If the two casts have been rehearsed interchangeably it is possible to establish similar preferences with respect to individual players, and if it happens that one particular player appears at the end to be hopelessly inferior to his rival it is usually possible to induce him to withdraw rather than risk the unfavorable comparison.

When the two-cast system can be managed at all it is highly instructive to the players. Just as long as they do not feel that they are working for nothing they are likely to pay

keen attention to the play, and to watch each other in rehearsal and performance in a constant effort to learn from
each other and excel each other. There is no better way
to stimulate their talents. But it is not a plan to be under-
taken lightly.

CHAPTER XI

THE DIRECTOR AS TEACHER

IN THE study of the play and the planning of the production the director is first of all an artist, and as an artist he must continue to function until the finished performance leaves his hands. But with the assembling of the cast and the start of actual rehearsals he begins to function also as a teacher, and his ability as a teacher is so important an element in the success of the production, and the permanent success of the producing group, that it deserves rather more than the usual amount of emphasis.

THE THEATRE AS A SCHOOL

In the European repertory theatre the regisseur is, as a rule, not only the managerial head of an organization but the headmaster of a permanent school as well. He is interested in the artistic presentation of each play, and in the efficient conduct of the business of production; but he is also interested in the development and improvement of the actors, and the building up of a strong ensemble. He does not go out and hire a ready-made cast for each new play; he adds new recruits to his company because they show promise, and he helps them, through years of training and experience, to develop that promise into achievement. The result is an *esprit de corps*, a group solidarity, and an artistic unity almost unknown today in the American professional theatre.

Now and then, of course, an American producer does succeed in establishing a somewhat analogous relationship.

211

Augustin Daly and A. M. Palmer did so in the eighties; David Belasco has done so at times, and there have been approximations of it in the repertory companies of Sothern and Marlowe, Walter Hampden, and others. But for the most part the strictly commercial theatre in this country is on an entirely different basis. A producer accepts a play, engages a director, and hires a cast. He does not hire learners if he can help it; he hires people who are already identified with the types of parts they are to play. The director starts with the assumption that his actors are finished artists who know their business thoroughly, and the actors generally start with the same assumption. The director tells them where to go and what to do rather than *how* to do it, or *why*. If the actors are good-humored and the director tactful he may give them some hints on acting, or suggestions as to interpretation, but he cannot feel any deep obligation to teach them anything beyond the needs of the particular play. If they are not good-humored, they are likely to resent any instructions beyond the needs of the play. If they are underlings they do as they are told; if they are stars they do as they please. The combination of trades-unionism, type casting, and temporary organization has made almost impossible the teaching relationship so necessary to a permanently fine theatre.

It is in the amateur or semi-professional theatre, the school or community theatre, that the teaching relationship can best exist. The director of amateurs, especially when he is himself a professional,[1] has an obvious responsibility for the training of his actors that the hired director in the commercial theatre is under no obligation to feel; and if the actors happen to be earnest and eager to learn, the theatre soon begins to

[1] I should like, here, to define a professional as one who is making a vocation of the work, and not necessarily as one who has been on the commercial stage.

function as a school and the director as a teacher. It is, I believe, the existence of this relationship in our little theatres that has enabled so many of them to compete in popularity with the professional theatres, and that has caused some of them, on their own merits, to turn into professional theatres of the repertory type.

What the American theatre—amateur and professional— most needs is the constant encouragement of its function as a school. Not, of course, as a school for the audience, and not as a school in the uplift or missionary sense; but as a school for its own development, a school of its own art. For the development of such a function the director—or directors if there are several—must establish in relation to the actors a true teaching attitude.[1]

THE TEACHING ATTITUDE

A true teaching attitude does not mean a didactic or dictatorial attitude, an assumption of omniscience or of superiority on the part of the teacher. Nobody is more painfully aware of how little he knows than the earnest teacher, for the very effort to teach somebody else reveals to him the gaps in his own knowledge. An effective teaching attitude is not, of course, inconsistent with dignity and self-respect, but it is characterized by modesty, sympathy, and tolerance. A good teacher aims to teach rather than to command. He does not pretend to know everything or to be right in all his opinions, and he expects to learn as much from his students as they learn from him. His function is to guide and assist them in their efforts to learn, and to serve as a sort of clearing house through which the experiences of others may be passed on to them.

[1] For an interesting discussion of the theatre as school, see Granville-Barker, *The Exemplary Theatre*.

Perhaps the most essential element of a good teaching attitude on the part of the stage director is a willingness to explain his directions; to give reasons; to teach the *why* as well as the *what*. Tell an actor what to do and it may serve for the needs of the play; tell him why, and you have taught him a principle which he may be able to apply for himself on another occasion. Too often the director begrudges the time or effort involved in giving reasons; or he assumes that the actor is too stupid to understand them, or too indifferent to care; or—breathe it softly—he has no reasons to give. Sometimes he has a conscious conviction that the actors ought not to know why they do things, that they ought to be clay in the director's hands, mere brainless "übermarionettes," expressing the director's art in their own.

It may be said in objection to the teaching of reasons that there is not sufficient time for the director to explain every direction he gives, or to teach elementary principles of acting; and this unfortunately is true. But no one contends that the director should turn his rehearsals into kindergarten classes and permit the work to be constantly interrupted by foolish or needless questions; and no one contends that he should put himself on the defensive and feel compelled to explain himself every time he makes a decision. What he should do is to meet half way the actor who is seeking to improve himself, who is interested in the play as well as in the part, and who is willing and eager to give serious study to the whole problem of production. Sometimes it is necessary to require that questions and discussions be postponed until after rehearsals—but this is a matter of expediency and not of attitude. The important point is that the director shall take it for granted that the actor wants to learn, and shall help him as much as possible.

THE DIRECTOR AS TEACHER

WHAT TO TEACH

Given a teaching attitude on the part of the director, the question arises, What shall he teach?

Clearly he must teach the meaning, lines, and business of the play in hand. Also, if he is to have any permanent success, he must teach the actors an attitude—a learning attitude to correspond with his teaching attitude. But possibly the most obvious need, if we consider the little theatres of the country, is that he shall teach acting,[1] for it is in the acting that our non-professional theatres are most conspicuously inferior. In this connection I cannot refrain from quoting some significant words of Mr. Walter Prichard Eaton. Writing in the *Little Theatre Review* of October 21, 1920, and speaking of the little theatre, he says:

". . . In the matter of plays, it is easy enough for the ambitious amateurs to excel, because they have only to produce what the professional theatre, as at present organized, will not risk. In the matter of scenery and stage adornment, both their inferior income and their generally superior taste and imagination over the average professional manager, help the amateurs to suggestiveness and simplicity. The weak point, and the dangerous point, is the acting.

"I have great sympathy with the ideals of the 'new stage-craft,' with all attempts to catch the peculiar rhythm and style of a play and reflect it in every detail of a harmonious

---

[1] Mr. Granville-Barker (in *The Exemplary Theatre*, page 101) takes the position that acting should not be taught. What he appears to mean is that nothing should be done to encourage young people in the too common notion of acting as a mere surface accomplishment of mimicry or impersonation. In this we must all concur. Young people must not be taught the practice, the trickery, of acting while yet too shallow or immature to appreciate the underlying principles and substance. But if we are to have better acting we must teach it; the thing is to teach the substance and the principles and not the mere technique.

production. Nevertheless, I fear the stubborn fact will not down that 'the peculiar pleasure of the theatre' still resides, as it always has resided, more largely in the presence of living actors than in any other element, and nothing can compensate for poor acting, unskilful acting, acting without illusion. . . . ."

Mr. Eaton offers no analysis of the acting he complains of, but my own observation indicates a greater lack of team work than of individual talent. Amateur actors often show flashes of brilliance or power, and a freshness, a spontaneity, that in itself is good; but they lack technical smoothness, poise, and group coördination.

The director should teach his actors to think in terms of plays, not parts; of scenes, not lines; of stage pictures and stage actions as seen by the audience, not individual movements and business. Such teaching will not confuse the actor, nor will it tempt him to neglect the movements and business prescribed. The better he understands the purpose of what he does and the more clearly he sees his own actions as a part of the general scheme, the easier it will be for him to accept the directions given and perform them with precision, and the greater will be his individual creative freedom within the natural limitations of the play. There is nothing so conducive to real artistic freedom as knowing just how far you can go.

The director should teach his actors how to analyze a play, to find the author's meaning, to catch the mood and rhythm of each act and scene, to visualize the background or period, and to discover the relation of each character to the play as a whole. He should explain the essentials of plot construction, the distinction between comedy and tragedy, and the characteristics of the principal styles and types of plays. He should stress particularly the importance of *theme* and the advisability of toning the acting according to the theme rather than the plot.

The director should teach his actors the essential principles of stage movement and business. He should encourage intelligent discussion and intelligent experiment. He should emphasize especially the element of compensation that so often appears—the necessity for one character to balance another, to give way for another's movement or fill in after it. He should teach them to feel the balance of the stage picture in their own bodies, to correct it, when imperfect, as unobtrusively as possible by slight changes of position; but he should distinguish between an accidentally unbalanced picture and one purposely unbalanced to create suspense or anticipation. He should teach them to take and hold the attention at certain points and to yield it at others, according to the needs of the play. He should teach them how to remain in character and to act when not speaking, yet without distracting attention from the other characters; how to listen effectively to other characters; how to remain in repose when on the stage but out of the action.

He should teach them to maintain what William Gillette calls the "illusion of the first time"—that is, the illusion that the character is uttering his words for the first time and not merely repeating memorized lines.

He should teach them the most important conventions and devices of acting, emphasizing always the principles and purposes rather than the mechanism, but bearing in mind that the stage is not real life and that acting is not just "being natural." He should teach them to play toward, but not to, the audience; to convey meaning without direct communication; to suppress meaningless movement; to cultivate repose; to keep out of emphasis when not emphasized by the dramatist; to heighten effects a little beyond nature; and above all, to simplify—to select essentials and reject useless detail as every artist does.

The director should encourage his actors to train their bodies, to cultivate grace and poise and expressiveness. If they need more instruction than he can give them, he should try to have them get it elsewhere. Some will need courses in dancing, or fencing, or eurhythmics, or plain gymnastics. Others will need drill in gesture and in traditional stage movements, foot positions, turns and the like—although stage drill is capable of abuse and should not be carried to excess. Others will need instruction in etiquette, poise and carriage; for almost no young man to-day can carry himself with the dignity of an earlier generation, almost no young woman can walk across the stage gracefully, and almost no young person of either sex is above reproach in parlor or table manners. The actor can never tell when he may be called upon to play a drawing room part or to dance, fence, box, or play the piano; the greater the number of such accomplishments he has at hand, and the greater his flexibility and adaptability, the better his chance of success.

The director should encourage his actors to practice pure pantomime. It may even be worth while for him to conduct such exercises himself. Numerous articles on pantomime may be found, most of them suggesting lists of subjects; or the director may draw his subjects from bits of pantomimic action in plays with which he is familiar—the checker game in *What Every Woman Knows*, for instance, or the scene depicting a professor's state of mind at the beginning of *The Professor's Love Story;* or the scene in which the hero of *Old English* drinks himself to death.

The director should impress upon his actors the importance of voice and should give them every possible help in voice training. Most young actors fail to realize the need of such training and can only be driven to it by constant urging.

He should teach his actors to observe the life that is about them, to be interested in the speech and the actions of all sorts of people. He should suggest that they carry note-books in which to jot down interesting bits of action, traits of character, mannerisms, tricks or peculiarities of speech, or what not, as observed on trains or trolley cars, in the shops or on the streets. He should, however, caution them against too literal a copy of life with consequent loss of æsthetic distance, and against the danger of dragging in good business for its own sake without regard to relevancy. He should encourage the study of human motives and the cultivation of sympathy and understanding. He should warn his actors against interpreting all human life in terms of their own motives, or the motives of their own age, race, nation, or social level, and should impress upon them the advantage of mixing with all classes of society, of knowing all quarters of the city or country, and of understanding the conditions of other countries and other historical periods.

He should urge them to read and study—to know something of history, philosophy and literature, and perhaps even of science. He should encourage study and appreciation of the other fine arts and should emphasize the similarity of aim and principle in all of them. He should teach the leading theories of æsthetic appeal, especially the principles of empathy and æsthetic distance, and he should make every effort to relate these principles to actual practice. He should strive to make his actors artistically sensitive, that they may learn to avoid false notes in acting to spare themselves pain, as a musician avoids false notes in music.

To teach all of these things is, of course, a superhuman task. There is never any limit to the possibilities; the limits are found only in the equipment, the time available, the capabilities of the actors and the ability of the director himself.

There are those who believe that a teaching attitude and something to teach make a teacher; there are others who consider the technique of teaching a science in itself, and an essential element of any educational process. The problem is too extensive to be considered here. There are, however, one or two controversial questions concerning the teaching method of the stage director which have greatly disturbed the teachers of dramatics and even the critics of the professional theatre, and which therefore deserve some comment.

The first of these is the question of monarchy versus communism, already partially discussed in relation to the planning of stage movement and business. As applied to teaching method, the question is this: Should the director adopt a sort of *laissez faire* policy in teaching, striving to inspire his students to learn for themselves, but leaving them to find the way; or should he assume definite control of their activities, guiding and shaping their studies at every point? Stanislavsky, one of the greatest of teaching directors, suggests that the director should not generate an idea, but should merely preside at its birth. Gordon Craig, on the other hand, would make the actor an "übermarionette," subservient to the director at every point. David Belasco shapes and trains his actors by close personal instruction until they are recognizable as Belasco products; Arthur Hopkins is said to sit quietly at rehearsals, giving no sign until something goes wrong, and then merely indicating that something *is* wrong and leaving it to the actors to find out what, and to correct it.

Clearly the question of which is the better teaching method depends somewhat upon the object to be attained. But it depends also upon the director's own ability and upon the age and temperament of the actor who is to be taught. The beginner may require more definite rule-of-thumb teaching than the experienced actor. In so complex a problem generalization is futile; the director should understand and use both methods, according to circumstances.

Another and more important question is whether the director should make use of demonstration in his teaching—whether he should show an actor how to do a thing and permit him to learn it by imitation. On this subject there has been violent disagreement. Some amateur directors and teachers of dramatics are so afraid of imitation that they will not permit the slightest suggestion of it—not even when the actor is totally at a loss what to do and says, "Please show me." They seem to feel that it means the downfall of his creative freedom and the enslavement of his personality —if not the loss of his immortal soul!

With the essence of their contention one must, of course, agree. Nobody except Gordon Craig wants the actor to be a mere puppet in the hands of the director, and nobody at all wants him to be a pale copy of someone else—a mere mechanical imitator of things he does not understand. But when the extremists insist that imitation is necessarily ruinous to the sincerity and individuality of the actor, one wonders whether their theory is consistent with the psychology of the learning process. The psychologists themselves are divided on this point. Some maintain that the impulse to imitate is inherited and plays a large part in the learning process; others insist that the learning process begins with random movements which are gradually "conditioned" by experience, and that imitation is only possible in the case of activities already learned by accident. If the latter are correct, there can be little danger in imitation, since it cannot take place until the thing to be imitated is already learned through experience. If the former are correct, and imitation is an essential part of the learning process, why be afraid to make use of it?

Our education is built up largely, if not wholly, out of our experiences. We do not create our thoughts out of nothing; we build them out of elements drawn from outside. If the necessary elements are lacking, we cannot create; we must first gain more experience, and it is here that demonstration comes in. When the director tells an actor that he ought to get a certain effect and the actor, after several attempts, says: "I can't do it; I don't know what you mean; please show me"— he is merely saying that he cannot create because he has not the necessary experience. If at that point the director can show him what to do, or have someone else show him, the whole situation may be cleared up. If, after being shown, the actor still does not understand and falls back on slavish, hollow mimicry, it is a very dull director indeed who fails to detect the fault, and a very foolish one who allows it to go uncorrected. But if the effect of the demonstration is to give the actor just that fresh light which he needs—to make him say, "Oh, now I understand; that is a good idea; I wish I had thought of it myself"—I do not believe that he is likely to be ruined by the slight element of imitation that may creep into his playing.

There is still another question of method in teaching which every director must face, and that is the question of the actor's emotions and the extent to which the director is to appeal to them, to exercise them, and to teach the actor to depend upon them. But this is so bound up with the theory of acting, to be discussed in a later chapter, that I shall omit consideration of it at this point.

THE TEACHER AS DIRECTOR

The teaching relationship of the director to his actors is seen at its best, perhaps, in the school or college play. The person who is a teacher in the classroom naturally functions as a teacher in directing a production by his own pupils, whether as part of a course or as an extra-curricular activity. To be sure, he does not always preserve the classroom manner —which is a gain rather than a loss—but he assumes as a matter of course the task of training the individuals as well as the group. To this fact may be attributed the surprisingly high quality—all things considered—of the average school play.

I say "all things considered" because I happen to know some of the difficulties of the school-teacher director. In the first place there is the inescapable youth and immaturity of the players, even among those of college age. In the second place, there is the fact that the boys and girls do not remain long enough under the director's charge to gain the necessary experience; about the time they begin to develop they take their diplomas and go home. In the third place, there is the almost total lack of persons to play old and middle-aged parts. In the fourth place, there is the handicap of an unsuitable place to play and the difficulty of finding time for rehearsals. In the fifth place, there is the financial problem. And finally, there is the fact that in a vast majority of cases the teacher, no matter how good a teacher or how well fitted temperamentally for the work, has had no practical training back stage; has, in many instances, never seen a first-class professional performance, nor been inside a real theatre. This is even truer today than it was twenty years ago, for the moving pictures have driven the road companies out of the small towns, and first rate companies visit only a very few of the larger cities. Under the circumstances, it is no wonder that most school performances are crude and unpolished and immature; the amazing thing is that they show as much intelligence and imagination and taste as they do. At least it may be said that, taking the country as a whole, the school play is about two jumps ahead of the audience.

The teacher as director is, as a rule, more likely to have the right attitude toward his work than most other directors; and, perhaps, more likely to pursue an effective teaching method. If he makes any mistake in his teaching, it is almost sure to be an over-emphasis on the interpretative work of the individual and an under-emphasis on the team work. Most school plays are poorly organized and loosely directed, though excellently "coached"—if the distinction may be permitted. For that reason the teacher who is called upon to direct plays should lose no opportunity to learn of the technical side of the theatre and no opportunity to cultivate the organizing ability so necessary to the director as executive.

EDUCATIONAL DRAMATICS

Of late years a great many schools and colleges nave been making dramatics a part of the curriculum rather than an extra-curricular activity. The educational influence of play production in teaching literary and artistic values, appreciation of the drama, sympathetic understanding of character, control of body, speech, and imagination, has very properly earned it a place in the curriculum. But its classroom values have led some teachers to take a somewhat distorted view of the whole purpose of educational dramatics.

According to these teachers, dramatics in an educational institution should exist for educational rather than artistic (that is, pleasure-giving) purposes. To this end, they say, there should be less attention paid to the excellence of the production as a whole than to the educational effect on those taking part; there should be no attempt to choose the cast for the good of the play by selecting actors according to their suitability for the parts; the students should, instead, be deliberately assigned to characters unlike themselves, in order to correct their faults of personality. Thus, a small, effeminate man should be chosen for a heavy, masculine part, in order to render him less effeminate; an ill-tempered, surly person should be chosen for a courteous, kindly part, in order to improve his disposition. And above all, no attention should be paid to the matter of pleasing the audience, who should be suffered to attend at their own risk.

In this point of view there are really several propositions more or less distinct.

The first is that educational dramatics should exist to educate the person taking part and not to please the audience. At first sight this seems reasonable enough, but the danger lies in the assumption of an irreconcilable alternative. To assume that such methods of production as will please the audience are probably not the best methods to educate the actor, is to distort the problem. The truth is that the very sort of excellence in production which best pleases audiences is also the best educational influence upon the actor. It is true that pure type casting is bad for the actor—as well as for the production—and if students can be given varied experience without ruining the production, the effect is educational. Even deliberate mis-casting may afford good practice to the student if confined to rehearsals without audience, or to classroom exercises. But the purpose of a play is to give æsthetic pleasure to an audience, and any indulgence before an audience in play production which deliberately ignores or sets aside this purpose, is intellectually insincere, and therefore vitiating to the educational purpose. Clarity of purpose, sincerity, and coördination of effort are far more important educationally than facility in interpretation, and to sacrifice the greater to the lesser is to falsify the emphasis in education. If the purpose of the fine arts is inconsistent with sound education, the fine arts ought to be bundled right out of our schools. If not, then the purpose should be given the main emphasis, and every effort should be made to accomplish it with the highest possible degree of excellence.

The second proposition is that the student actor should for his own sake be cast for parts unlike himself. But is it a proper function of the educator to mold character in this sense? Is it right to subdue each individual bent or bias by the neutralizing force of an opposite? Or, if only the bad traits are to be subdued, who is to be the judge to decide which traits are bad and what models to follow in the molding process? The proponents of the plan would take a little, effeminate chap and make a man of him by having him play a masculine part. But would they take a husky, boisterous, young athlete and make a mollycoddle out of him by having him play an effeminate part? And if their purpose is to mold character, what parent would want his son to be cast for Macbeth or Shylock or Iago in the school play? Or are the unpleasant parts to be left out, and educational dramatics confined to the representation of saints and heroes?

Of course the whole idea of molding character in this sense is absurd. It is true that the playing of many and varied parts broadens the sympathies of the actor, enriches his imagination, and enables him to understand all human nature a little better; wide reading and constant theatre-going do the same thing, and if acting does it more quickly, it is chiefly because it demands more of the imagination. But to suppose that the playing of any particular part will mold the actor's character toward an appreciable resemblance to that part is pure nonsense. It is almost a commonplace that the great comedians are serious or even melancholy men; that actresses who depict sweet, innocent young girls are sometimes quite otherwise themselves; that stage villains are often good husbands and fathers at home. It is well known that some of the cleanest and sweetest poets have led dissolute lives; the whole history of art and literature is one long pageant of what Professor Schelling calls "projected emotion"—the artistic representation of verities and sincerities quite independent of the artists' own characters, and absolutely unproductive of any character-molding influence upon them. It all rests on the fact that art is not life, but a more or less idealized imitation of life; and you can no more make a student strong by having him—in the artistic sense—imitate a strong man, than you can ruin him by having him imitate a weak one.

The advocates of specialized educational dramatics are primarily interested in the education of the individual as a human being and not in his training as an actor, but in much of what they say and write they imply that it is best also for the actor as an actor to be given the parts unlike himself, and to be required to work for individual experience without regard to the play as a whole or the pleasure of the audience.

This proposition has already been touched upon in the chapter on casting. Variety of experience breeds versatility, and versatility is desirable; the actor who can play only one part—that of himself—is almost as much to be pitied as the actor who cannot play one part any better than another.

But dramatists do not (or should not) write parts, they write plays; and audiences come to see plays. Good acting does not consist in playing parts; it consists in playing plays.

It is not individual work, but group work. The individual part is the elementary part of acting, and within the limits of talent it is the easy part. It is the team work that is hard, and rare, and that must be learned even by those who have the talent. Above all it is the team work that counts most in accomplishing the purpose of the play. To mis-cast the parts and to ignore the pleasure of the audience is to put a discount on team work right from the start, and it is therefore the worst possible way of training actors.

CHAPTER XII

REHEARSAL: BLOCKING OUT

WE COME now to the director's most active personal responsibility: the conduct of rehearsals.

Rehearsals have at least three different purposes, and it is well to distinguish them at the start. The first is to give opportunity for experiment; the second is to teach the text and meaning of the play to the cast, and the third is to perfect and polish the performance. The division is arbitrary, but useful.

Most amateurs are too busy with other interests, too pressed for time, and too restless, for very much indulgence in experimental rehearsal. The director working with such people must do most of his experimenting in advance, or between rehearsals, and devote the rehearsals themselves to learning and to polishing. A certain amount of experiment is, to be sure, inevitable in the early rehearsals, for no matter how well a production has been planned unexpected problems will arise during the blocking-out period, and changes will have to be made. But it is a common mistake with amateur directors to use so much time in experiment that when the date for the performance begins to draw near it becomes necessary to concentrate on the learning process, and the polishing gets crowded out altogether. The director should realize that a production which is not learned in time to allow for thorough polishing cannot be otherwise than crude in performance, no matter how well worked out in the experimental stage; and if he values his reputation he will sacrifice other

229

things, including his own time, to provide for adequate polishing.

THE SCHEDULE OF REHEARSALS

To avoid the danger of neglecting some phase of production, it is a good plan to work out in advance a definite schedule of rehearsals. The shorter the time, the more important this becomes. If a complete schedule cannot be arranged before the first rehearsal, a tentative schedule may be posted, to be replaced after the play has been blocked out by a corrected schedule, showing the exact number of remaining rehearsals and the exact ground to be covered in each.

Different types of plays call, of course, for differently planned schedules. Some plays are so constructed that they must be rehearsed chiefly for continuity and ensemble; others can be rehearsed by acts; others, by separate scenes. *The Yellow Jacket*, for example, is a series of brief episodes, involving a few characters each; these episodes can be rehearsed separately, and the whole play need not be put together until the last few rehearsals. *The Thirteenth Chair*, on the other hand, is built around ensemble scenes, and most of the rehearsals must be general ones with the whole cast present. Some plays are so dependent for their effects upon costume that they require a number of dress rehearsals; others depend upon lighting effects which must be carefully rehearsed, and others depend so completely upon the recital of the lines that much of the work may be in the nature of individual coaching.

In general, it is a good plan to break up the play into small scenes, and to rehearse these separately in the early stages—partly to allow of more intensive study and partly to save the actors who appear in only a few scenes from sitting about all evening doing nothing. Difficult scenes involving only

230

one, two, or three characters—love scenes, soliloquies, duels, fist fights, quarrels, dances, conspiracies—should be worked out in special rehearsals, with as much individual instruction as possible. Most amateur directors other than teachers fail to realize the importance of individual consultation; they follow the professional method of issuing directions at rehearsals and expecting the actor to perfect himself at home, which is just what the inexperienced actor cannot do. A great deal of time is wasted by amateurs in poorly planned and ineffective general rehearsals.

It is well, also, to vary the emphasis of the general rehearsals, announcing one for meaning, another for business, another for cues, another for tempo, and so on. This helps to insure that each important phase of preparation will be attended to; at the same time it gives the actors a clearer idea of what to work for, and promotes team work.

It is not possible to lay out an ideal schedule of rehearsals that will do for every play, but a sample schedule may be helpful to the inexperienced director as indicating what he may do with the time available. Suppose, for instance, that he has eight weeks in which to rehearse a modern three act comedy, and that most of the cast are so situated that they can spare only two full evenings a week, with perhaps a little more time during the last two or three weeks. Suppose, also, that only three rehearsals can be held on the stage, and that the others must be held in private houses or borrowed rehearsal rooms. A tentative schedule might read somewhat as follows:

First Week

Tuesday, 8 p.m.—Reading of Play. Discussion.
Thursday, 8 p.m.—Blocking out of Act I.

THE ART OF PLAY PRODUCTION

Second Week

Tuesday, 7 p.m.—Review of Act I. 8.30 p.m.—Blocking out of Act II.

Thursday, 7 p.m.—Review of Act II. 8.30 p.m.—Blocking out of Act III.

Saturday, 2 p.m.—Round table conference, for all who can come.

Third Week

Tuesday, 7 p.m.—Stage rehearsal, for positions, distance, voices, etc. (All night, if necessary.)

Thursday, 7 p.m.—Review of whole play, for corrections.

Saturday, 2 p.m.—Special rehearsals of difficult scenes or scenes that need change. Members needed are to be notified.

Fourth Week

Monday, 7 p.m.—Rehearsal for details of interpretation: principals only.

Wednesday, 7 p.m.—Rehearsal for details of interpretation: subordinates only.

Friday, 7 p.m.—Rehearsal for interpretation: whole cast.

Fifth Week

Monday, 7 p.m.—Rehearsal for cues; entire cast to be letter perfect.

Wednesday, 8 p.m.—Special rehearsals—love scenes, or scenes needing change. Members needed are to be notified.

Friday, 7 p.m.—Costume and make-up rehearsal (for experiment, not continuity). Whole cast.

Sixth Week

Monday, 8 p.m.—Rehearsal for tempo and continuity, Act I.

Wednesday, 8 p.m.—Rehearsal for tempo and continuity, Act II.

Friday, 8 p.m.—Rehearsal for tempo and continuity, Act III.

Seventh Week

Monday, 8 p.m.—Special rehearsals or consultations as needed.

Tuesday, 7 p.m.—Rehearsal for mood and emphasis. Whole play. Whole cast.

Wednesday, 8 p.m.—Special rehearsals as needed.

Thursday, 7 p.m.—Rehearsal for speed and polish. Whole play. Whole cast.

Friday, 8 p.m.—Special rehearsals as needed.

Saturday, 2 p.m.—Scenic rehearsal, on stage. No cast.

Eighth Week

Monday, 7 p.m.—Full dress rehearsal, on stage. Friends invited.

Tuesday, 8 p.m.—Special rehearsals, if needed, for correction.

Wednesday, 8 p.m.—Rehearsal for speed and polish. Whole cast.

Thursday, 8 p.m.—Special rehearsals, if needed.

Friday—Rest or recreation.

Saturday, 8 p.m.—Full dress rehearsal on stage, with invited audience and no interruptions.

Ninth Week

Monday, 8.20 p.m. sharp—Performance.

If only six weeks are available, the proper procedure is not to drop out the work of the seventh and eighth weeks, but to condense as far as possible the work of the first two weeks, and of the fourth, fifth, and sixth, as here given.

It will be seen that this schedule requires very few of the actors to attend more than two full evenings a week until the last week, but still gives them opportunity to come out for short additional periods now and then to rehearse special scenes or to join in consultations. The director, of course, must work almost every evening unless he can train a competent assistant to carry part of the burden.

Some groups of experienced amateurs or semi-professionals would, of course, regard such a schedule as absurdly long and exacting. Sufficient, they think, to have genius, experience, ability to commit lines—and about three rehearsals. The players of the Moscow Art Theatre, on the other hand, would regard it as inadequate, and would prefer to labor over

233

the play for additional weeks or months. Doubtless there will always be these two extremes of opinion, with corresponding results.

THE FIRST READING

Many directors like to begin rehearsals with a reading of the play. Whether this is necessary or not depends upon circumstances.

If books are not available and the actors must learn their parts from "sides" a reading is almost essential as a means of telling them what the play is about. It should not be conducted as a rehearsal; there should be no blocking out of the stage positions and no reading of parts by the actors. Instead the reading should be done by some person who can read well and who is already familiar with the play—the author himself, if possible. Interruptions should be permitted only for necessary questions on the meaning, but at the end of the reading there should be a little time for informal discussion.

When printed books are available they should be distributed several days before the first meeting of the cast, and each player should be instructed to read and analyze the play for himself, and to make note of any points he may care to have discussed. Some actors—even experienced professionals—have to be driven to do this, and some cannot be driven. There are actors who prefer not to know what the play is about, being interested only in their own parts. They are nuisances. The only really satisfactory actor is the one who wants to understand the play thoroughly in order that he may become a part of the whole rather than an exploiter of his own powers. The strongest argument for the use of printed books is that they emphasize the play rather than the parts, and so encourage the group attitude.

Whether a formal reading is necessary when the actors are supplied with books depends largely upon the nature of the play itself. If it be subtle or obscure in meaning a reading may be advisable, particularly if the author can be present and can do the reading; the actors are bound to learn from him a little more about his meaning and intention than appears in the text. But if time is very short and the author not available it is seldom wise to use up a whole evening in mere reading.

THE FIRST REHEARSAL

After the actors have read the play or had it read to them the next step is the "blocking-out" process. If the director has done most of his planning in advance, this process will be greatly simplified. If not, it will consist largely of a trial and error method of working out positions, movement, and business, with many halts for head scratching, many false starts and many corrections, and with everybody more or less at sea.

If the action has been carefully planned, the director will open the first rehearsal by explaining the arrangement of exits and entrances in the first scene, the positions of the furniture, and the terminology to be used in giving directions. Some directors like the actors to "walk through" their parts on the first rehearsal to fix the locations on their minds; others prefer to have them remain seated and take careful notes. Some like to show a chart of the stage and indicate the positions of the characters at each point in the text with movable push pins. If there is plenty of time and the actors are earnest this plan is helpful; otherwise it does not work. In most cases, perhaps, the walking method is the best. But whether the actors walk through or remain seated they should be instructed to take notes freely, and especially to mark on their parts every position, movement, and action. It is surprising how many actors will not think of taking notes unless told to do so. The director should insist upon the importance of getting everything right the first time, and of learning the positions and actions with the lines.

If the actors are to walk through their parts the furniture should be placed as accurately as possible, and the entrances indicated by extra chairs or by chalk lines on the floor. Hand properties are not needed at this stage, and would seriously interfere with the note taking; but anything that may help to establish spaces and distances should be included. The actors should read their own parts, moving to position as directed, and the director should interrupt freely to give instructions, and should allow time for the actors to enter them in their notes. Continuity is no object at this stage; care and thoroughness in the preliminaries take time, but they mean smoother and better work later on. When the first rehearsal is held in the evening and the actors have been otherwise employed all day it is best to block out only one act; some directors do this anyway, going over the act two or three times to make sure that the directions are properly understood. When the interval before the second rehearsal is to be long this is undoubtedly the best plan.

The director should permit free discussion at the first rehearsal, and should welcome criticisms or suggestions from the actors if given in good faith and good humor. He should try especially to discover whether any of his directions conflict with the actors' understanding of their parts, and to thrash out all such difficulties at the very start. However, when a knotty point arises involving only one or two actors it is usually best not to delay the rehearsal but to pass over the point, make a note of it, and call a special consultation of the persons concerned, to meet if possible before the next regular rehearsal.

It should be understood that the chief purpose of the blocking-out rehearsals is to give the actors something clear and correct to study; whatever is not ready for study should be postponed until it can be made ready.

REHEARSING THE LOVE SCENES

The love scenes—and any other especially difficult or embarrassing scenes—are best worked out separately before being rehearsed in the presence of the whole cast. Amateurs are naturally self-conscious in the love scenes and afraid of being laughed at. They should be cautioned from the first that the surest way to get themselves laughed at is to look as if they expected it, and that the best way to avoid it is to act their parts boldly, sincerely, and convincingly. But they cannot be expected to do the latter before an audience until they know their parts well, and are sure of every posture and movement; hence the need for the separate rehearsal.

In the days when youth was more bashful and unsophisticated than at present it used to ease the situation somewhat if the first rehearsal of a love scene could be held in the girl's home and in the presence of her mother. Whether this helped the girl or not, it was a considerable relief to the young man, who was usually much more genuinely scared; also it made things a little easier for the director, and from that point of view it has perhaps not altogether outgrown its usefulness. No doubt the professional director would be vastly amused at such a device, but many are the wiles and stratagems to which the director of amateurs must resort if he would coax out of inexperienced actors a performance in any way approaching professional smoothness.

The tendency of amateur actors in a love scene is to keep

too far apart. Often they will attempt to embrace with their arms and shoulders while their feet are separated by a good eighteen inches; and instead of gazing fondly into each other's

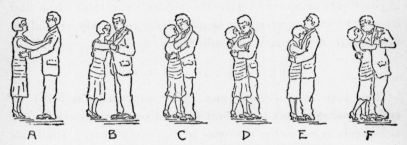

FIG. 15.—BAD AND GOOD POSTURES IN LOVE SCENES

A and *B* illustrate the stiff postures commonly assumed by amateurs. *C* is quiet, but a little more natural. *D* follows the traditional rule for the position of the arms. *E* is calm and conventional, and easier for amateurs than *C*, *D*, or *F*. *F* indicates the impassioned posture often assumed by professionals.

eyes—as it is said real lovers do—they stare vaguely at each other's hands, or coat collars, or at the walls or ceiling. The effect, of course, is ludicrous. The director must attack these and similar faults at the first rehearsal, and if necessary prescribe the exact posture for every minute of the scene. If the actors have had some experience and are known to be reliable he may insist upon their gazing into each other's eyes for a part of the time. This is difficult and embarrassing, and can only be done effectively if well rehearsed, but properly done it often marks the difference between a painfully amateurish love scene and one having professional finish. If the actors are too inexperienced or self-conscious to succeed with it the attempt should be abandoned early and a more conventional plan substituted. The girl may rest her forehead against the man's breast, for example, while he looks down at her hair or off into the distant future (*E*, Figure 15). Such a device is less effective empathically than the direct gaze, but is reasonably convincing and much more certain. A conventional posture of this sort should not be held too long.

Audiences seem especially sensitive to the element of beauty in a love scene, and it becomes necessary, therefore, for the director to give particular attention to the pictorial effect. The postures should be chosen not only for appropriateness and convincingness, but also for line, mass, and color. An awkward or ungainly posture, or a clashing color scheme will just about ruin an otherwise beautiful love scene.

For the very reason that the love scene is usually the weak point of an amateur production a well played love scene will do much to make the whole production less amateurish. It will pay, therefore, to take pains with such scenes in the early rehearsals.

THE FIRST REVIEW

Ordinarily the first rough blocking out will extend to the second and third rehearsals, but a portion of the time at each rehearsal after the first should be devoted to following up or reviewing what has already been blocked out. Otherwise it will grow cold. The director should be cautioned, however, against giving so much time to the first act in review that the other acts never get proper attention.

The chief purpose of the first review is to afford a check on the actors after they have had a chance to do a little studying. Ordinarily they should not be required to be letter perfect at this stage; they should be studying to understand their parts and especially to fit themselves into the team work, and not primarily to commit the lines.

It is in the review rehearsals that tangles and misunderstandings are to be straightened out, questions answered, suggestions received, and broad problems of interpretation discussed. Details and fine shades of interpretation should for the most part be postponed until later, but essential questions of meaning should be settled and the major points of emphasis established. At this stage it is particularly important to remember the fundamental principles of good design: fidelity to the main thought and fidelity to the limitations of material. Irrelevancies should be suppressed, and the central idea of the play given the emphasis over subordinate ideas; and the slightest attempt to transcend the limitations of material should be restrained. The limitations in this connection would include those of space, setting, lighting, equipment, and ability; and the director should restrain his own tendency to attempt the impossible as well as that of the actors. It will develop, perhaps, that some of the actors cannot do certain things assigned to them, and the director may have to modify his plans here and there to keep within their abilities. To know what changes must be made without making unnecessary ones is not so easy.

Useless or meaningless movements should be restrained in the early rehearsals before they get a chance to become habitual, and the actors should be cautioned against fidgeting. They should be instructed to make their movements simple, broad, and decisive in so far as these qualities may be consistent with the meaning. When there is much fidgeting the director should try to ascertain the cause. Sometimes he will find that the action he has planned does not articulate effectively with the lines, or does not allow a sufficient outlet for the expressive impulses of the actors. In the latter case as in the case of fidgeting it is futile to attempt repression; the only solution is to devise new and more significant movements or business through which the restless impulses may be discharged. Sometimes the director will find that the movements he has called for do not fit the stage spaces, and that the fidgeting is due to that fact. A very common instance of this occurs when an actor has been told to perform a certain movement on a certain line, and the line proves too long for the movement, so that the actor arrives at his destination too soon, or else slows down the movement until it becomes painfully hesitant and unconvincing. The smaller the stage the greater this difficulty; an actor having to enter on a line finds himself halfway across the stage before the line is finished, stops suddenly, fidgets, and perhaps backs up a little and comes at it again. Another common fault is for those already on the stage to crowd the entrances, so that the newcomer has no chance to come fairly on. The director should take special pains in his planning and in the early rehearsals to clear the way for each entering character, and to see that the center of action at the moment is far enough away from the entrance to give the actor an adequate excuse for coming well into view. It can hardly be repeated too often that meaningless and irrelevant movements are the bane of amateur theatricals, and that they should be stamped out as far as possible the moment they become evident.

After the first round of review rehearsals another effort should be made to check all doubtful matters and conclude all necessary experiments. A stage rehearsal at this point is very helpful for trying out voices, movements, stage pictures, and the like, and if only two or three stage rehearsals can be arranged this is the time for one of them. If possible the actual furniture and other properties should be used; chairs and sofas should be checked for height, width, and depth; the actors should try sitting down on them and getting up; chairs that are to be moved should be moved to see if they are light enough; hand props should be tried out to see if they can be managed; even costumes and make-up should be tried out if important or difficult effects are to depend upon them in any way—although it is not essential, of course, that all these things be done at the same rehearsal.

In short, it should be the object of the director in the first half dozen rehearsals to make sure, first, that nothing is being learned wrong, and second, that no actor is left in doubt or uncertainty as to what he is to learn, especially in respect to the team work. The next step is the consideration of the meaning and interpretation of the play in detail.

REHEARSING FOR MEANING

Professional actors frequently jump to conclusions about the interpretation much too early, especially when they work from sides instead of books. From the sides each actor studies only his own part, and being eager to make the most of it he begins to feel for the mood of the part before he is at all sure of the mood of the play; and he begins to read meanings into his lines which may or may not have been intended by the author. Experienced amateurs occasionally display the same trait, and the director must be on his guard against it.

For the most part, however, the problem in amateur production is to get the actors to pay sufficient attention to the meaning early enough in the process, and to assimilate the meaning well enough for reasonable freedom of interpretation. Beginners are apt to feel a bit dazed at the first two or three rehearsals. Groping vaguely for their positions on the stage and striving to remember the instructions given them, they are in no mental condition to appreciate fine shades of meaning. Even actors of some experience feel the confusion and uncertainty, and it is not uncommon to find them at the fourth or fifth rehearsal still speaking their lines with a dismal lack of understanding.

Before any errors of interpretation can become fixed the director should begin an intensive study of meaning, quizzing and challenging the actors repeatedly at all doubtful points. When a line does not come easily he may ask the actor to explain it in his own words, or to substitute his own words, temporarily. Or he may ask specific and troublesome questions about the line: Is it a serious line? Is it humorous? Is it satirical? Has it a double meaning? Is it charged with emotion? If so, what emotion? Is it an essential line for the audience to get? Is it a laugh line? Does it call for an answer? If so, in what mood is the answer to be awaited? Is the wording especially typical of the character? If so, in what way? If the line is a long one, how can it be broken up? What changes of tempo can be used? What bits of business? How, in general, can the meaning be enriched without strain or false emphasis?

Every now and then a line turns up which is completely baffling to the actor; he seems utterly unable to grasp the meaning or to express it by his reading. In such cases the director faces a difficult question: assuming that he understands the line himself, should he give the actor the correct reading and seek to have him imitate it? This is the question discussed at some length in the last chapter, and the answer would seem to be that the director should do all in his power to suggest the real meaning of the line to the actor, whether by demonstration or by discussion, but should rigidly check any tendency on the part of the actor to rely upon a mere echo of the director's reading. Now and then an actor will be found who cannot, or will not, learn in any other way; the best remedy in such cases is probably homicide, though if no understudy is available it may be unwise to apply it until after the performance.

To illuminate a line for the actor's better comprehension the director must sometimes resort to the device of "bridging"—that is, interpolating an explanatory passage in such a way that the meaning of the original line will become clear. The following examples illustrate how this may be done, and also show how many different meanings may be drawn from an apparently commonplace line:

1. We must not forget.
    We must not forget (, though others may).
    (To forget would be suicidal;) we *must* not forget.
    (They count on our forgetting, but) we must *not* forget.
    (We may forgive, but) we must not *forget*.

2. How many?
    (I know you want some, but) how *many?*
    (There are many, of course, but) *how* many?
    (What's that you say?) *How* many?

3. I don't know how.
    (Why ask me?) *I* don't know how.
    (You say I know how, but) I *don't* know how.
    I don't *know* how (, but I can learn).
    (I'd do it if I could, but) I don't know *how*.

It is, as a matter of fact, the apparently commonplace line that causes most of the trouble. The unusual line challenges attention and dictates its own inflections, while the commonplace line which has several possible meanings is as likely to get the wrong inflection as the right, and so to convey a wrong meaning or no meaning at all.

When bridging is used, the actor sometimes catches the meaning immediately, gives the line its proper inflection, and has no further trouble. More often he must repeat the bridging with the line—either mentally or aloud—at a half dozen rehearsals before it begins to sink in. In the latter case the device is of questionable value, especially if the actor shows a tendency to revert as soon as he drops the interpolated line, or to have difficulty in dropping it. On the whole it is best to avoid too much mechanism in rehearsal, and if bridging fails to bring almost instantaneous results it is better to abandon it and try something else. In any case the director should make sure that all interpolated phrases not to be retained as part of the text are dropped out before the polishing rehearsals begin.

In all study of meaning the director should bear in mind the construction and theme of the play as a whole, and should guard against the actor's tendency to interpret individual lines irrelevantly. Very early in rehearsals he should begin to emphasize the varying moods of the different acts, and to point out that a line correctly interpreted one way in Act I might bear a very different interpretation in Act III. This is a difficulty which amateurs find it very hard to master; the constant rotation of acts in rehearsal confuses them, and they cannot remember what the characters they represent are supposed to know, or not to know, at each point in the action. Accurate study of the meaning and mood of each line in a play calls for an alertness of mind and an unceasing vigilance scarcely comprehensible to those who have not tried it.

MEMORIZATION

At what point in the preparation of a play should memorization begin, and at what point should the director require his actors to be "letter perfect"?

To answer these questions properly one must first understand that there are two distinct methods of memorization, and that the answer is not the same for both. By the one method the act of memorizing is made a purely mechanical process having no relation to the study of meaning; the two things are, so to speak, carried on independently by two separate portions of the mind. By the other method the words, actions, and meanings are memorized coördinately, and all associations built up from the start.

The first method is employed by a great many professionals as a matter of choice, and is almost essential in stock company work when a new play must be learned every week with only three or four rehearsals. It has one important advantage: the memorizing may be done early and quickly—even before the first rehearsal—and the actor need not be hampered at rehearsal by the necessity of carrying a book and reading his part. But to use the method successfully the actor must be able to separate the memorization from the interpretation, and to refrain from forming any impressions during the memorization which he may have to unlearn later. No actor can do this without some experience, and many can never learn to do it. Moreover, those who succeed in memorizing mechanically are not always able to throw off the mechanical effect when they come to interpret. On the whole the method is to be recommended only when circumstances necessitate a very hasty production, or when the actors happen to be fitted for it by temperament and experience.

The second method is the better one for those who have time to learn a play slowly and thoroughly, and is the only one suitable for beginners. By it the interpretation precedes the memorization, and lines, business, and meaning are memorized together. The advantage lies in the fact that nothing is learned incorrectly or mechanically, and that the elements of acting are coördinated from the start. The disadvantage lies in the impediment put upon the early rehearsals by the actors' dependence upon their books, and the consequent delay in reaching the polishing stage. By this method it is obvious that memorization cannot even begin until the meaning and the action are understood.

To answer our questions, then, we may say that when the

mechanical method is used the memorization should begin with the distribution of parts, and the actors should be letter perfect at the second or third rehearsal; but when the associative method is used they should not begin to memorize until absolutely sure of meaning, movement, and business. They should be letter perfect as soon after that as possible.

Some actors have a good deal of trouble with memorization, and some make themselves a nuisance by pretending to know their parts before they do know them, thereby overworking the prompter and disrupting the rehearsals. Often, of course, the failure to memorize is referable to mere laziness or procrastination, or to a lack of will power; but when an actor who really tries hard is unable to memorize it is commonly because of a tendency to straddle between the two methods. Seeking to memorize the words he allows himself to be distracted and delayed by considerations of meaning; or seeking to study the meaning he tries too hard to memorize at the same time, and the memory process interferes with the thinking process. It is better to do one thing or the other. If the mechanical method is to be used he should rigorously shut out of his mind all thought of the meaning, all play of imagination, establishing visual or auditory images rather than ideas. Sides are better than books for this kind of study, which is why stock-trained professionals so often prefer them. But if the associative method is to be used the actor should not hurry or force the process. He should get at the memorization through the understanding, assimilating the meaning and action so well as to remember them subconsciously and involuntarily. The mechanical method may be practiced in an arm chair, or the actor may pace aimlessly up and down as he commits the lines; but the associative method is best practiced in actual rehearsal, and even when studying at home the actor should speak the lines aloud with the proper expression and should move about as on the stage, rehearsing the actions with the lines. When lack of privacy makes this procedure impossible, he should try to do it in imagination.

In memorization, more than in any other phase of play production, the youngsters have the advantage. It is the older, and especially the elderly men and women who find it hard to remember their lines, and who often forget them in actual performance—although with professionals the facility born of experience often compensates for the difficulties arising from increasing age. It seems especially hard for elderly amateurs to coördinate lines and movement, and to remember them together, and the director must often devote hours of extra rehearsal to drilling such actors. It is usually best to rehearse them by short scenes, going over and over each scene until the coördination becomes subconscious. The greatest difficulty is ordinarily met with when the intervals between rehearsals are long, and when the actors in question have only occasional speeches as part of the ensemble. The poise of these older actors is often valuable to an amateur company, but to get the best out of them without making everybody else nervous at their uncertainty requires patience and skill on the part of the director.

All actors have more or less trouble with the memorization of parallel passages or passages having similar associations. For example, if Smith and Jones converse about Brown in Act I, with Smith standing at stage right and Jones sitting at stage left, and then converse in much the same way in Act III, a single wrong line in Act I may start them off on the scene that belongs in Act III. Many of the serious disasters in amateur performances result from such transposition of lines. The director should guard against this, first, by arranging different movements and positions for parallel passages (except when symbolism requires similar movements and positions), and later by checking up such passages to see that the actors are keeping them straight. When the actors show any tendency to transpose lines, he should point out to them the differences rather than the similarities, and should try to establish contrasting associations in their minds as mnemonic aids. A little ingenuity will solve the problem if applied in time.

No single recipe or formula for successful memorization can be laid down, and actors of different temperaments will swear by different methods. But one general principle is always sound, and that is the principle of kinesthetic coördination—coördination in the sensations of activity involved in expression. The actor who acts all over remembers his lines more surely and with less conscious effort than the one who memorizes a page of print and then reads it off from a visual image alone. As indicated in an earlier chapter, he is also more convincing.

CHAPTER XIII

REHEARSAL: POLISHING

I T IS an unfortunate fact that most amateur productions never get any real polishing. The chief reason for this is that the learning process has a way of drawing itself out indefinitely; the play never seems quite ready for polishing, and the director postpones the latter until it is too late. There is only one way to overcome the difficulty, and that is to announce certain rehearsals as polishing rehearsals, and to carry them out as such no matter how many details of study and experiment have to be left unfinished.

A professional producer planning a New York opening often relies upon public performances in a "dog" town to do the necessary polishing for him, and there can be no doubt that actual performance before an audience brings, by compulsion, a kind of polish that cannot be attained in any other way. But as amateurs seldom give more than three or four performances of a play altogether they cannot very well depend upon this sort of polishing. As a rule they must expect to be judged upon the merits of the very first performance —sometimes the only one. Any polishing that is to be done under these circumstances must be done in rehearsal.

The presence of an interested "gallery" at the polishing rehearsals is a fairly good substitute when trial performances are impossible. An invited audience at the final rehearsal is nearly always advisable. The designation of certain rehearsals as "speed rehearsals" or "continuity rehearsals" serves to concentrate energy upon the polishing, and the elimination of unnecessary interruptions and unnecessary prompting helps to keep the emphasis. Sometimes it is a good plan to banish the prompter altogether. It is said that Augustin Daly purposely employed a Frenchman as prompter; the actors could not understand what the man said, and so were forced to know their lines. Any device that will exert upon the actors some of the pressure of a public performance is likely to be an aid in polishing.

SPEEDING THE DIALOGUE

One of the chief problems in polishing is the problem of speed. Amateur performances nearly always drag. The actual dialogue moves too slowly, and the chief causes are inadequate memorization and tardiness in taking up cues.

Inadequate memorization may be a matter of incorrect method, as discussed in the last chapter, or of inability to articulate lines and business, or of pure neglect. The fact that amateurs really can memorize if they are put to it is well demonstrated whenever there happens to be a keen competition under the try-out system. But with the best of intentions many amateurs totally underestimate the degree of memorization required for freedom in acting. They suppose it sufficient to be able to recite the lines without marked hesitation or serious error. Experienced actors know that the real study just about begins at this point; and the less experience an actor has the better he must know his lines to achieve an equal degree of freedom. Sometimes the best thing a director can do to make the polishing process effective is to scare, or shame, or cajole the actors into studying their parts all over again.

Nearly all amateurs are slow about taking up their cues. First Brown speaks his line, pronounces the cue, and waits. There is a perceptible pause. Then Smith wakes up, and answers. In real life we do not waste time in this way; we pause only when there is some uncertainty about the answer, or some need for special emphasis, or when action intervenes. In the ordinary run of real conversation we make our answers promptly, often slightly anticipating each other, and sometimes frankly interrupting in our eagerness to get ahead with the thought. Stage dialogue should proceed in the same way; if anything it should move more rapidly than in real life, since art is selective and does not attempt to represent all the clumsiness and accident and friction of reality.

Perhaps the chief reason why amateurs are slow about taking up cues—aside from insufficient study—is their tendency to literalness. The book gives a certain word or phrase as the cue; therefore the actor waits until he has heard that word or phrase before beginning his line. And since it takes him a perceptible fraction of a second to hear and recognize the cue and to respond—even when he knows his lines well— there is a hiatus in the dialogue, not very marked in itself, but serious enough when it is repeated several hundred times in one play.

An experienced actor, or an actor properly directed, overcomes this tendency by a slight overlapping of line and cue. Instead of waiting for the last word of the preceding speech he takes as his cue the second or third word from the end, and so begins to speak almost at the instant his colleague ceases speaking—perhaps even a fraction of a second before. As a general rule this produces the effect of a smooth and continuous conversation. Of course it may be overdone, and snappy professionals sometimes reel off their dialogue with so much rapidity and so much overlapping as to make the whole performance mechanical and unconvincing. Robert Milton, writing in the New York Times, decries the speed fetish of the old professional producer who was forever getting his actors to talk louder or faster. Moderation is the best rule; but moderation for most amateurs means more, not less, speed.

The extent to which overlapping is permissible with any given line depends upon the meaning. When the meaning of the line is not complete until the last word is uttered, the actor who is to reply should wait for that word; but when the meaning becomes clear some time before the last word he may safely anticipate a little and begin his line. Even in such cases, too much or too frequent overlapping suggests impatience and impoliteness on the part of the character, and should be avoided unless these qualities are to be portrayed. The actor should consider carefully the mood of the character, and his relation to the other characters. A character in a thoughtful or absent mood will be slower in response than a wide awake, eager or impatient character, or one who is in a hurry to end the conversation or turn it into another channel. A polite or deferential character will make prompt replies, but will not anticipate or interrupt. A master may interrupt a servant, but a servant may not interrupt his master without suggesting impertinence; all differences in age, social position, or official responsibility call for similar variations.

BROKEN LINES

A very marked interruption is usually indicated by the dramatist with the aid of a broken line and a dash. The broken line however, sometimes makes trouble for the amateur actor, and occasions a special type of delay. When Brown's line is broken and Smith is supposed to interrupt him, Brown stops abruptly at the dash and waits for the interruption which he too evidently knows is coming; Smith, on the other hand, waits until he hears Brown stop, and then opens his mouth to speak. Brown, of course, should be taught to speak as if he had every expectation of finishing the sentence—

should in fact, be taught to finish it unfalteringly in the event of Smith's failure to interrupt; while Smith should be taught to take his cue a word or two earlier and get started in time to interrupt at the exact point indicated by the dramatist. Even when the interruption takes place on schedule, Brown should be taught to think out the rest of his line, or at least a few words of it—a nice little point in acting that some professionals neglect. Broken lines cause no end of trouble, and do much to make amateur acting unconvincing, and for that reason they should be most carefully timed and rehearsed.

Another source of delay is to be found in the entrance and exit cues. Here again it is the tendency to literalness that causes most of the trouble. When Brown and Smith are talking and Jones is to join them, the dramatist usually finishes a speech by Smith or Brown and then writes, "Enter Jones." The literal-minded actor waits in the wings until he hears the last word of the cue speech and then starts on; but as it takes him a few seconds to cover the intervening fifteen or twenty feet, Smith and Brown have to stand around doing nothing until Jones arrives. The actor should determine by study the exact point in the dialogue at which he is to arrive at a certain spot on the stage, and then take a cue sufficiently in advance of that to get him there in time. Amateurs rehearsing in parlors and living rooms are apt to forget the greater distances of the real stage, and especially the three or four steps which they must usually take off stage before coming into full view of the audience. All exits and entrances should be carefully timed by the director at the first stage rehearsal —which should be held early for this if for no other reason— and then carefully re-checked in the polishing rehearsals. In most instances they will need constant speeding up. Poorly timed entrances and exits will make an otherwise good performance seem very crude and unfinished.

CADENCE

Inexperienced actors should be frequently cautioned against depending for the timing upon the inspiration of the moment —even when they know their lines perfectly. Once the correct timing is determined for a given line it should be rehearsed again and again, so that the actor will remember not only the words and meaning but the rhythm and cadence as well. Perfect cadence teaches a platoon of soldiers to respond automatically to orders, and helps a motorist to change gears or apply the brakes instinctively and accurately, even in emergency. In the same way it helps the actor to remember his line through bodily rhythm rather than through conscious effort; it helps, in other words, to educate the motor responses, and insure the actor against the effects of excitement. The conscious mind is too variable and too easily distracted to be entirely trustworthy, but the motor responses, properly trained, can be depended upon.

It is a good plan to memorize each cue as if it were part of the line, running the two together mentally until the cadence is established. Lines that have a strong natural cadence are more readily memorized and retained, and less apt to get out of timing. Actors generally take up their cues more promptly in verse than in prose, for if the poet has been sufficiently skilful the meter itself suggests the proper timing.

EASING THE DIALOGUE

After the dialogue has been speeded up sufficiently it is still apt to remain artificial and unconvincing. Amateurs are inclined to deliver their lines as if they were reading instead of speaking; there is no illusion because there is no conversational quality.

The conversational quality is hard to define, yet it is one

of the most essential elements in good acting. It does not necessarily include naturalism, or conversational style. A natural or commonplace style would just about ruin a poetic or symbolic play; the characters of classic drama are not everyday persons, and their speech is a matter of poetic convention rather than reality. Yet even in poetic plays the characters who address each other must seem to be *speaking*, rather than reading or reciting. The most heroic language can be made to sound convincing if the actors are able to speak it with directness and imagination.

A good conversational quality includes, of course, such physical matters as variation of tempo, promptness in taking up cues, articulation of speech with action and gesture, significant use of pauses, live facial expression and active vocal tone. But the essential element is imagination.

The actor must have imagination in order to realize the feelings of the character he portrays, to grasp the implications of plot and situation, and to feel a sense of communication with the other characters. Moreover it must be the right sort of imagination. A good reader may have imagination, and yet be unmistakably a reader rather than an actor. The reader's imagination is, in a sense, detached and objective. He preserves his æsthetic distance as one of the audience, and is not part of the play. The actor is part of the play, and his imagination must be of the subjective kind, enabling him to believe in himself as a character in the play and to address the other characters as if he were speaking, not at them, but to them.

How to stimulate the imagination is not so easily told. Questioning helps, especially when the characters are questioned about their thoughts and feelings: "Where are you going?" "What brought you here?" "What room did you come from?" "Which act is this?" "Has such-and-such an event happened yet?" "Have we passed the climax?" Addressing the actors as *characters* rather than as actors also helps the imagination. Costume and make-up rehearsals help—or better, full dress rehearsals with scenery, lights, and properties. But something depends also upon the will power of the actors and no director can provide them with imagination if they lack the will to imagine.

The greatest difficulty in easing the dialogue appears, logically enough, in those passages which are inherently least natural. It is not hard to get natural delivery of colloquial dialogue, full of current slang and commonplace informality. But the moment an actor is required to deliver an extra long speech, or one that is a bit literary in flavor—not to mention one that is stilted, or heroic, or poetic—the trouble begins. Anybody can speak a colloquial phrase in a colloquial way, and anybody can speak a stilted passage in a stilted way. But to speak a heroic or poetic passage with heroic or poetic effect and yet with naturalness and conviction is not so easy; and to speak a really stilted passage in such a way as to conceal the stiltedness and make the speech seem dignified and natural calls for positive genius.

OPENING OUT THE LONG SPEECHES

A good director can ease the dialogue of inexperienced actors considerably if he can help them to open out their long speeches, to vary the tempo, and to articulate lines and business.

To open out a long speech it is usually necessary to devise additional business, or at least to suggest some changes of gesture or facial expression; otherwise the pauses will seem artificial and meaningless. Variations of tempo within the sentence do much to break up a speech that is too long, and variations of tempo throughout a stretch of dialogue do much to ease the whole. The variations, however, should not be arbitrary; they should be in keeping with the meaning. Variations of pitch and force are occasionally necessary, but are of less general use than one might suppose. There is plenty of pitch variation in the very reading inflections we are trying to escape, and in the affected or elocutionary style of delivery —so much so that a positively monotonous delivery is sometimes a relief by contrast. Extreme variations of force, on the other hand, are open to the objection that they tax the ear of the listener, and make it difficult for him to hear without strain. Variations of tempo, and of timbre, or quality, are better.

Another matter that sometimes requires attention is the laugh or cry that sounds strained and artificial. If the book says, "Ha, Ha!" the actor thinks he has to say "Ha, ha!"— which for him may not be a natural way of laughing at all. Such words are merely a convention by which the dramatist indicates that the character is to laugh, and the director should see to it that the laugh is made natural and convincing in whatever way is best adapted to the capability of the actor. Sometimes that will mean an attitude, a facial expression, or a bit of business instead of a loud laugh, or in addition to it. It is usually best to keep the laughter and the weeping well within the bounds of moderation; amateurs have a tendency to overdo both.

The problem of easing the dialogue calls for some rather heroic and intensive work, even in the last stages of rehearsal. In the case of particularly refractory passages it may be necessary to resort to bridging or paraphrasing of some sort, or to actual modifications of text. General rehearsals should not be too frequently interrupted for this sort of work; the result would be confusion rather than polish. Instead the bad spots should be noted in passing, and worked out in special rehearsals or private conferences.

POINTING UP

In spite of careful planning it will often be found that certain portions of the play fail to work up properly, and seem, in the later rehearsals, to lack point. Significant lines are delivered too casually, and escape notice; lines that should be theatrically effective seem to fall flat, and humorous lines fail to get laughs. It is always difficult to know how much of this is due to the lack of a proper audience and will correct itself in performance; laugh lines, especially, often fail to amuse the director and the cast, but succeed very well with the first audience. The presence of a few strangers at each rehearsal makes it easier to determine which lines need pointing up.

In general, lines that are highly dramatic or theatrical in effect, or that convey strong passion or emotion are likely to come up very well in the mounting excitement of actual performance; while smart lines, farcical lines, and broad character lines—especially in dialect—are likely to need toning down. Lines that are subtle but significant, lines that "plant" ideas necessary to the plot, satirical lines, and high comedy lines are the ones most likely to need pointing up. Lines that are to convey repressed emotion sometimes require a combined treatment—a somewhat excessive pointing up, followed by a careful toning down.

The method to be used in pointing up will vary according to the nature of the fault to be overcome. When a line is delivered too casually it is sometimes because the actor himself has failed to realize its significance, and the remedy may lie in pointing it out to him. When a line that ought to convey a great thought or feeling fails to strike fire it may be the actor's imagination which is at fault; or it may be the team work, or the director's own work in planning movement or business for emphasis. The distribution of emphasis is supposed to be taken care of in the planning and the early rehearsals, and when it needs attention in the polishing stage it is because something has gone wrong. The problem is to find out what, and how, and to correct it.

It is important to remember that the pointing up of a line does not always rest solely with the actor who delivers it. No matter how well a line is spoken it may fall flat if the listening actors do not play up. It is always harder for amateurs to listen effectively than to speak effectively, harder to keep still than to move about. Yet the slightest irrelevant movement at the instant an important line is spoken may ruin its effectiveness; and the slightest tendency of the listening actor to drop out of character may spoil some other actor's best bit—a fact which is occasionally turned to account by a jealous actor eager to take unfair advantage of a rival.

Too much pointing up is as bad as too little and results in what is generally called "playing to the gallery." The deliberate attempt which some actors and directors make to evoke direct applause for a line is usually not good art, because it is destructive of æsthetic distance. Any attempt to get a laugh which is recognized as such by the audience tends to defeat its own purpose, and even to give pain instead of pleasure. Nevertheless, some pointing up is sure to be necessary, and when the dramatist's purpose is to give pleasure through laughter it is the director's business to see that the actors get the laughs.

GETTING THE LAUGHS

When a laugh line misses fire it is usually from one of two causes: lack of appreciation on the part of the actor, or faulty technique.

Lack of appreciation in this connection does not necessarily mean stupidity; nor does it mean absence of a sense of humor. Indeed, one often finds it among the most intelligent beginners, and those with the keenest sense of humor off stage. It is the "comedy sense" that is lacking—a very different thing from the sense of humor.

The comedy sense is easily recognizable in those who have it but very hard to define. The sense of humor is subjective. The comedy sense is *pro*jective. To appreciate humor subjectively one must possess a sense of values and must be quick to note relations and catch implications; at the same time he must preserve an attitude of detachment. To enact comedy one must invoke empathy in others, while seemingly not implicated himself. He must preserve their æsthetic distance and his own as well, but the two must be different. The comedy sense, more than any other phase of the actor's art, implies a dual psychology. But of that, more in the next chapter.

As for technique, the most important point is to avoid killing the laugh at the moment of its inception. Too often the actor spoils a good laugh by dropping the voice just as the point is reached, or by executing a sudden movement which distracts attention, or by failing to give the audience time to laugh. Since the most effective humor is conveyed to the audience by half-concealed means it is necessary as a rule for the actor to be well down stage and facing front when he speaks his line, in order that the audience may see his face and detect that subtle something which reveals the comic element; also that they may witness his ostensible effort to conceal his own appreciation and remain in character. Laugh lines are seldom effective when the actor turns away from the audience. When Smith is talking to Jones, if Smith faces Jones and Jones faces front, Smith's funny line will fall flat—unless the humor lies in the *effect* of that line on Jones and Jones registers clearly. When the humor is in the line itself, Smith should face front to speak it while Jones faces him. This is a good general rule, though it should not be applied too sweepingly.

The tendency of the inexperienced actor is to drop the emphasis too quickly at the end of a line, to turn away too quickly, or even to stop acting and drop out of character. He should be taught to "follow through" as the golfer puts it—that is, to keep up the tension at the end of each line and go on acting out the thought just as vividly after the last word as before. Audiences are usually a little uncertain whether to laugh or not, but inclined to do what is expected of them; and if the actor speaks what would seem to be a funny line but turns away casually at the end, as if he did not expect a laugh, they are quite likely to restrain themselves and perhaps to suspect themselves of having misunderstood the thought. They are eager enough to laugh if given a chance, but the actor must give them the chance.

He must also give them the time. When he hurries on to the next line the stupid listeners will not get the point and the clever ones will choke back the laugh in order to hear the next line. Now and then it may be good policy, with a succession of funny lines, to hurry the audience a little in order to pile up a cumulative effect, but this will only work when the humorous element is in crescendo. The listeners will not enjoy holding back a hearty laugh for the sake of a more moderate one. If the pace is just right so that every point is clear, and there is just time for the listener to begin a laugh and then catch his breath for a better one, the result is sometimes worth the risk. As a general rule, however, the actor should be taught to "hold everything" after a humorous line until the laughter subsides; and should be warned at rehearsals to be ready for unexpected laughter at the public performance.

The technique of getting laughs is thus largely negative—a matter of not doing the wrong thing. There is, however, one constructive element which deserves mention, and that is the skilful use of a pause just before the main point is reached. Mark Twain's famous essay on *How to Tell a Humorous Story* stresses this element, and much of what he says in that essay is valuable to the actor. The pause serves to some extent as a conventional symbol labelling the laugh line as such; but its chief function is that of intensifying the suspense. It creates a little element of surprise, and at the same time lessens the chance of confusion or misunderstanding; but it must be correctly timed and there is no rule for timing it. The timing of pauses, in this and other connections, should be given careful attention in the polishing rehearsals.

REHEARSING FOR SMOOTHNESS

While attention to detail is a necessary part of the polishing, too much of it at the expense of continuity will tend to make the performance ragged rather than smooth. To guard against this it is a good plan to devote some rehearsals entirely to the cultivation of smoothness. If time permits it may pay to run several of them as regular performances, with no interruptions and no criticisms. If time is short much the same result may be attained by omitting the interruptions but retaining the criticisms. For this the actors must be taught to go right on playing while the director shouts occasional comments at them—a difficult matter for beginners, who are easily distracted by criticisms and likely to forget their lines and stop. When the actors have learned the trick, and can stay in character while making mental notes, the director can conduct his rehearsals as an orchestra leader conducts a concert, and can do a good deal of coaching without loss of smoothness.

In rehearsals for smoothness the more general problems of emphasis, tone, mood, and tempo should be given the major consideration, and individual criticisms kept to a minimum, although individual actors may occasionally be reminded of points previously discussed with them. "Watch that turn!" the director may say to an actor who usually turns the wrong way on a certain line; or, "There you go again!", or "Better that time!" The favorite remark of one successful director, always spoken in cheerful tones, is "Rotten—go on!" The actor goes on, but he remembers that spot in the next rehearsal and tries to do better. Not all of the comments given in this rapid fire way bear fruit, but if detailed rehearsals or special rehearsals of troublesome scenes are sandwiched in between the rehearsals for smoothness, the general plan will, as a rule, be effective.

In regulating the emphasis the director should see that the main climax is sufficiently vigorous, and that no sub-climax is confused with it and given too much emphasis. He should caution the actors who have heavy scenes late in the play not to outdo themselves in the first act, but to hold some of their powers in reserve. He should see that the relative emphasis of the several acts is properly preserved, and that the climactic effect within each act is properly worked up.

In regulating the tempo he should see that the casual moments are not allowed to drag and that impressive moments are not unduly hurried. At the same time he should see that expository passages are played deliberately enough to be clear, and that the rushes of action approaching the climaxes are sufficiently spirited. In some instances he will be able to discern characteristic rhythms in certain scenes, and to adjust the tempo in such a way as to bring these out. Secondarily, he should see that the tempo is varied enough to avoid monotony.

In regulating the tone and mood he should look for two things: the characteristic mood of each scene, and any contrast of mood that may exist between different characters in the same scene. Harmonization of these two things is not always easy. There may be one melancholy character in a rollicking scene; and to bring out both moods in contrast without destroying the unity of the larger requires a nice sense of balance. Toward the end of the rehearsal period the actors are apt to become a little weary of the play, and so to lose their sensitivity to mood; and the director will find that they need constant reminding on this point. The continuity rehearsal accompanied by coaching without interruption is much more effective in regulating the mood than intensive rehearsal with frequent interruptions.

THE DRESS REHEARSAL

The so-called dress rehearsal is one of the cherished traditions of the theatre, but as ordinarily conducted it is futile and demoralizing. The trouble is that two quite different purposes are confused, with the result that neither is fully accomplished.

Theoretically the dress rehearsal is a complete rehearsal with full equipment, run without interruption and intended to be as nearly like an actual performance as possible. In this sense it is the final step in the process of rehearsal, and is naturally scheduled for the last available date before the public performance. Unfortunately it is also, as a rule, the first try-out of scenery, properties, costumes, and make-up, and as such is anything but a polishing rehearsal; it is an experimental rehearsal of the most rudimentary sort, and it usually goes to pieces, leaving the actors with the feeling that the play is only half learned on the day before the opening. True, the fright sometimes induces them to work a little harder in the few remaining hours, and the performance turns out better than expected; but that is no defense of a bad system.

The logical procedure is to try out the scenery, lighting, costumes, and make-up early in the experimental rehearsals—not necessarily all at once, but in plenty of time to make adjustments. If the equipment is hard for the actors to manage in any way it should be used at a number of rehearsals, some early, some late, so that the "dress" part of the play gets its polishing gradually along with the lines and action. When this is done a full dress rehearsal at the end is no longer a mere experiment, and can serve its proper purpose as a polishing rehearsal.

Sometimes, to be sure, this arrangement is not entirely possible. The equipment, or part of it, may not be available until the last rehearsal. When this is the case it is best to abandon frankly the idea of a smooth dress rehearsal and to rehearse only those portions of the play which involve the use of equipment. If possible the stage crew should be rehearsed in handling the scenery and properties before the actors are asked to rehearse with them. If the one experimental rehearsal can be held two days before the performance instead of one day, it may be followed by a continuity rehearsal either with or without the costumes; such a rehearsal helps to restore the smoothness so often shattered by the confusion of the so-called dress rehearsal.

The important point is to distinguish the two purposes; to accomplish the experimental purpose as early as possible; to work for polishing towards the end, and to make the final rehearsal a good topping-off rehearsal whether a full dress rehearsal or not.

STUDYING THE AUDIENCE

As already suggested, the last stage of polishing is that of actual performance, with the audience as collaborator. In this stage all sorts of unexpected things happen. Audiences are not passive, but active; they contribute their own imaginations as colored by their experiences. Sometimes they show real creative power, and more than one dramatist has expressed the thought that a play is not finished until it has been properly "re-written" by the audience. Audiences occasionally insist upon an interpretation of some episode, situation, or character, entirely different from the one intended by the actor. Otis Skinner's famous experience in *The Honor of the Family* is a case in point; he did not know he was supposed to be funny until he heard the audience laugh.

This raises the question of whether the actor, author, and director should aim to give the people what they want, or make them take what is good for them. Is the actor properly the "servant" of the public, as it is so often put? The Elizabethan actor undoubtedly so regarded himself, and his point of view has been more or less the prevailing one ever since. "We aim to please, and hope you will like us," is, and in a sense has to be, the motto of professional entertainers everywhere. On the other hand some producers, following Gordon Craig, take the position that the actor, or the director working through the actor, should be an independent interpretative artist, catering to no one, and letting the audience pick up the pearls or leave them as they choose.

In this, as in so many other things, the truth lies somewhere between the two extremes. The attitude of the Elizabethan actor was inherited from the strolling players and minstrels who preceded him—mere vagabond entertainers, living on the bounty of their occasional patrons, and proud to be retained from time to time as actual servants to this or that nobleman. While the social status of professional actors has been steadily improving, something of the menial attitude has survived, and has hampered the development of a dignified independent spirit. Worse even than the menial attitude is the purely commercial attitude which too often replaces it, and which is seen in its most vicious form today in the manager who panders to the lowest public taste and the actor who "plays to the gallery." From an artistic point of view there can be no defense of such truckling.

But to suppose that the proper alternative is a lofty disregard of the audience is to ignore the psychological fact that the most sincere creative effort is meaningless except in terms of its effect upon others. A painting is but a mixture of chemicals on canvas; its effectiveness as an object of art is in the thought or emotion it engenders in the observer. A piece of music is but a vibration of the atmosphere; its beauty is in the ear of the listener. In the same way a play is not what is written on paper or what is done on the stage, but what takes place in the imagination of the audience. It is right that the actor should try to guide that imagination to the appreciation of the best, but this can be done only through a sympathetic understanding of audience response. "You must make your audience act for you," said Salvini. But to do so you must first bring what you have to offer within their experience and comprehension.

The study of the audience should begin, of course, long before the first performance. The director, like the dramatist, should learn to know the tendencies of audiences in general, and which tendencies are most subject to variation. He should determine, if possible, for what type of audience he is preparing his production, and what limitations he must meet. He should prepare to meet the most probable emergencies, and should have his actors prepare.

WHAT AUDIENCES LIKE

Nearly all audiences demand surprise, suspense, action, love interest, something to root for, something to hate, something to laugh at, something to sympathize with, some satisfaction of poetic justice, and a chance to feel that they have understood the dramatist with remarkable sagacity. These things are as much the director's concern as the dramatist's, since it is the director who is responsible for the final contact with the audience.

Surprise need not always be sharp or startling, but a little of it now and then is needed to freshen interest; it may come at almost any appropriate point in the play, early or late. Suspense, however, must begin early. Unless an audience is in some way made anxious before the conclusion of the first act the succeeding acts are pretty sure to fall flat. Action is needed to freshen interest, and also to act empathically as a relief valve for the motor activities of the audience.

Love interest is of many kinds, and romantic love is not the only kind that appeals to an audience; but very seldom does a play without any love interest at all prove satisfying. Professor Quinn, in his *History of the American Drama from the Civil War*, has pointed out that the wide appeal of *Abie's Irish Rose* may be partly due to the fact that it has almost every conceivable kind of love in it—romantic, conjugal, filial, parental, grand-parental, and altruistic—and that the audience is permitted to sympathize with all of them at once.

269

In working up the love interest the director must keep constantly in mind the probable empathic responses of his audience, and must not ask them to empathize in impossible situations or impossible people.

The instinct to take sides is bred into the very nature of the human animal; it is part of his pugnacious disposition. Children always want to take sides, to root for some hero, or country, or idea; and grown people, despite their restraints, crave the same right. Audiences cannot comprehend neutrality, or empathize in a neutral character—which is why some indeterminate problem plays fail in popular appeal. The director, in so far as the dramatist permits him to do so, should leave his audiences in no doubt as to where their sympathies and loyalties belong.

The appeal of alternate laughter and tears—of what Belasco calls the "emotional alternating current"—is very well known, and some dramatists and producers make a fetish of it. In plays like *The Old Homestead,* or *Shavings,* or even *Lightnin'* it is so manifestly overdone as to be painful, and second rate actors of the older generation are apt to carry it to absurd extremes whenever the opportunity offers. Yet within proper limits it is a legitimate and very effective appeal. The director should study carefully the transitions.

As for the community of understanding between the dramatist and the audience, some producers think it the most important appeal. People like to be taken into the confidence of the author. They do not mind being fooled now and then within the rules of the game—in a mystery play, for example —but for the most part they like to feel a sort of superior intelligence in understanding what the author means without being told, and in perceiving or foreseeing what the characters do *not* perceive or foresee. This involves the matter of dual personality in acting, to be considered in the next chapter.

There are limits to all things, and the director should see that these various appeals are not all made at once in too hectic a fashion. That master showman Dion Boucicault put a great deal of wisdom in two sentences when he said to Clara Morris a half-century ago: "Never rack your audience. Touch 'em—thrill 'em—chill 'em—but never s-t-r-a-i-n 'em."

HOW AUDIENCES DIFFER

In studying the particular audience for which he is preparing a production the director should consider its probable social, racial, and national characteristics, creed, occupation, degree of intellectuality, education, sophistication, and experience in playgoing. He should consider also whether it is likely to include an unusual proportion of men, or of women, or of children; whether it is likely to be familiar with the play in advance; and whether it is likely to be critical in its attitude. Audiences differ greatly in these and many other respects.

It is amazing what different audiences one can see in New York City alone. At a matinee performance of Clemence Dane's *Will Shakespeare* I saw an audience of elderly and middle-aged persons, chiefly white-haired ladies, whose refined speech and settled manner suggested a Colonial heritage. In the evening of the same day, at a performance of the German expressionistic play *Johannes Kreisler*, I saw the greatest collection of swarthy, unwashed "intelligentsia" that ever came over in the steerage. Leaving the theatre I ran into a crowd of over-dressed big-town sports and their country cousins, coming from the latest musical revue at an adjoining theatre. And the next afternoon, way over on the East Side, I sat in the Neighborhood Playhouse with the most cosmopolitan, most intelligent, and most genuinely appreciative audience I have ever seen.

The same differences, in lesser degree, may be found in

other cities, together with local differences too numerous to mention. Local interests and local prejudices must be reckoned with, and accepted as natural limitations. Many plays that succeed in New York fail on the road, and vice versa. The director cannot always change the appeal of the play, but he can often modify it by slight cuttings, changes of emphasis, or modulations of mood. Small-town audiences generally respond better than metropolitan audiences to romantic appeal, or to the appeal of the moral. They are, as a rule, less jaded, and less insistent upon smartness or novelty. But they do not respond as well to subtleties of humor or satire, especially the latter. Little theatre audiences are sometimes community audiences, drawn together by gregarious instinct or civic spirit rather than by a real love of art; and in such cases they are far less discriminating than the patrons of the commercial theatre.

In most American audiences—except at the motion pictures—there are more women than men; and matinees, especially mid-week matinees, are very largely patronized by women. Women, as a rule, yield themselves more completely to the illusion of a play, and are less sensitive to æsthetic distance than men, and more apt to lose it when their own emotions are stirred. They are less restrained than men, and will respond empathically to a much more expressive type of acting—even to what most men would regard as over-acting. They are less critical than men on the technical and artistic side, but more critical on the human side. They cannot brook a cold actress, or a cold character. Molnar's *The Swan*, for example, did not appeal to the women, because the heroine was a cold person who allowed romance to escape from her. The romance, too, was made fun of, and that no woman can forgive. Romance is almost sacred; it may be blasted tragically, but it must not be satirized or ridiculed. The empathic responses of the women are naturally quite different from those of men. When the hero in Frank Craven's *New Brooms*, suddenly overcome by filial emotion, kissed his father full in the mouth, the women in the audience burst into spontaneous applause, while the men shuddered. Doubtless the men approved the sentiment, but they could not escape an unpleasant empathy, because men—American men at least— do not make a practice of kissing each other.

One reason why comedy is more popular than tragedy today is to be found in the decline of religious faith. People who believe in an after life can preserve their æsthetic distance better in the presence of tragedy than can the materialists. To the latter death is of this earth; it is the end of things, and is depressing. They relate everything to their own lives, and are unable to idealize. The faithful feel that this world's disasters are relatively unimportant, and that justice and mercy will prevail in the end.

Perhaps the most important question for the director to ask himself about the audience is whether they can be presumed to have seen the play before; or if it is a new play, whether they can be expected to see several performances or only one. Some plays are like symphonies: they are hard to appreciate on one hearing, but reveal new beauties with each repetition. When the New York Theatre Guild first produced *He Who Gets Slapped* there was a violent controversy about its merits. Mr. Gilbert Emery, himself a dramatist of note, wrote a letter to the New York Times in which he condemned the production as baffling and incoherent. He was answered, politely but intolerantly, by Mr. Lee Simonson, scenic artist of the Theatre Guild, by Mr. Richard Bennett, the leading actor in the production, and others, who accused him of being strangely blind to great art. But Mr. Emery had seen the play only once, whereas his opponents had studied it thoroughly and seen many rehearsals and performances. My own impression, on one viewing, was much like Mr. Emery's, and from the blank expressions I saw about me in the audience I am sure most people felt the same way. Doubtless three or four viewings would put most of us on the other side. But how often has a director the right to assume that an audience will see his production more than once? And how often, today, can he assume that his audience is already familiar with the play? In the days of classic repertory this was always assumed, and it can be assumed today in connection with a very few of the best known Shakespearean plays; but generally the director must reckon with the fact that the great majority of his audience have never seen the play before and will probably not see it again.

It is never possible to predict the reactions of an audience with absolute certainty, and it is never possible to please everybody. In the midst of a highly appreciative audience at a performance of *What Every Woman Knows*, with Helen Hayes in the leading part, one man and woman sat with an air of sad resignation. At the conclusion they put on their coats in silence, and then the man said to the woman: "Yah, dey always has a gyp show at dis t'eayter!" Such is the reward of excellence.

NOTES ON POLISHING

So many elements need attention in the polishing of a play that anything like a complete discussion of them all is out of the question. A few practical hints in condensed form may, however, be useful, and I offer them as a sort of appendix to this chapter:

1. Direct the polishing rehearsals from the auditorium, not from the stage. Move farther and farther back.

2. Try the visibility and audibility from all parts of the house, including the balcony and gallery.

3. Check up on the settings, exits and entrances, sources of light, and arrangements of furniture, as seen from all angles.

4. Test out the stage pictures from all angles. Squint at them.

5. Remember what has been said about the time element in stage pictures. (See page 149). Polish the transitions.

6. Remember the principle of grace—that is, economy of effort. Try to eliminate unnecessary effort, or the suggestion thereof. Check grace of plan from the balcony or gallery.

7. Watch for detrimental empathies of any sort, and eliminate them. (See page 32). Rehearse carefully all scenes in which actors carry heavy weights. Teach those who are carried to relax. Watch all moving of furniture, and all such actions as sitting, kneeling, or rising, to see that there is no unnecessary suggestion of effort.

8. Bearing in mind the charge that directions learned in advance inhibit the actor, check up to see whether any movements seem stiff or mechanical. If so, find out why. If necessary, allow the actor a little more freedom, or change the movements for him. As a rule he will need the change rather than the freedom.

9. Seek out and remove all distractions. Watch especially the actors who are not speaking. Eliminate fidgeting. When there is too much movement or business, select and reject, but retain that which is relevant rather than that which is clever. Check up constantly on the principle: "No movement without a purpose." Challenge any new movement or business introduced by the actors, and accept it only when the purpose is sound.

10. Aim constantly to simplify. Work for strength rather than elaboration.

11. Watch for violations of unity, both in the play as a whole and in each act and scene. Watch especially for diffusion of interest, a very common fault in amateur production. Keep the balance between unity and variety.

12. When the play seems "talky," introduce one or two significant bits of action at critical points rather than many unimportant ones.

13. Check up again and again to see that the most essential and significant lines are reaching the audience.

14. At the same time suppress any over-emphasis, and any misplaced accent growing out of attempted emphasis.

15. See that the play as a whole is coming over the footlights; that the actors face the audience often enough and play far enough down stage, and speak with sufficient volume.

16. See that the actors are creating the "illusion of the first time."

17. Combat the tendency of some actors to shorten their movements, failing to use the full stage space. Make the performance fill the eye. But guard against restlessness; work for bold broad movements, but not too many of them.

18. Study carefully the matter of æsthetic distance. Consider it from all parts of the house. Suppress any tendency on the part of the actors to establish communication with the audience, or to step out of the picture in any way. Check excessive realism, especially unpleasant realism. (See Chapter III).

19. Watch the acting at the points of strongest emotion. Guard against false or exaggerated emotion, and against painful empathies. But remember that the emotional phase is the hardest to judge correctly before the actual performance. When the emotional acting is false or unconvincing consider the possibility of simplification, especially by subsitution of significant business. (See page 25).

20. Remember the "James-Lange theory." (See page 134).

21. Suppress any tendency of the actors to show consciousness of the "fourth wall."

22. Consider the tone and mood of the acting at all times.

23. In a comedy, no matter how serious, see that an optimistic tone prevails—not necessarily a happy tone all of the time, but a tone that foreshadows the ultimate triumph of the protagonist.

24. In a tragedy see that a sense of inevitability is planted and maintained, and that there is a crescendo effect as the tragic forces gather. Guard against any interruption or letdown that may break the climactic force.

25. Beware of what Stark Young calls "the tragic goose step," especially in poetic and heroic plays. Do not let the actor strut or pose.

26. Nurse the rhythms—at least in so far as they express the moods correctly—and make the most of them.

27. Try to have the actors avoid the commonplace and give a touch of distinction to their parts.

28. Check the tempo constantly. Guard against the tendency of the actors to slip back to the wrong tempo, especially the tendency of each actor to take the tempo of his line from that of the actor who speaks before him.

29. Teach the actors to "hold the picture" and stay in character when interrupted by laughter or applause; also when taking receptions and curtain calls.

30. If curtain calls are ruled out as a matter of policy, see that everybody is so informed, and that a statement to that effect is printed in the program.

31. If curtain calls are to be allowed, decide what actors or groups are to take them, and in what succession. Rehearse the curtain calls as carefully as the acts. Insist, how-

ever, upon modesty and reserve, and see that the actors remain in character. It is always painful to see a group of amateurs take curtain calls in a stagey, ostentatious manner, with elaborate bows and smirks; but it is almost equally painful to see them caught unawares by the raising of the curtain, and to see them running every which way and bumping into each other like a lot of frightened sheep.

32. Finally, study the audience at the first performance; note the responses, especially the unexpected ones, and prepare immediately to make any necessary changes or readjustments.

In other words, be omniscient and omnipotent; let nothing escape you, and perfect every detail. Outside of that there is very little to do.

CHAPTER XIV

THEORIES OF ACTING

IN ANY study of the art of acting it quickly becomes apparent that there is no one true theory, no one best method. Different plays and different conditions call for different styles of acting, and different actors develop their talents in different ways. For all this variety we should be thankful; it is part of the charm of the theatre.

The taste of the public changes in a general way from generation to generation, and what was thought the very finest acting in Shakespeare's time, or Garrick's, or Kean's, or Forrest's, or Booth's, may not be so considered today. It is doubtful whether a modern audience would enjoy the direct declamation of an Elizabethan actor or the roaring passion of a Forrest; we prefer a more consistent illusion and a greater measure of restraint. We are learning, also, to think less of virtuosity for its own sake, and more of artistic unity and sincerity. We welcome a company of Russian actors playing in the Russian language, and admire them for their self-suppression in the interest of team work; but I doubt whether we should care to hear a French or Italian actor playing in his native language with a supporting company playing in English—a kind of exhibition in which our theatre-wise ancestors delighted. In spite of our star system, our personality actors, and our hero worship, we are coming more and more to feel that it is the play as a whole which matters, and that the satisfactory actor is the one who fits in rather than the one who stands out.

EMOTION IN ACTING

But while times are changing and variations of technique multiplying, certain fundamental questions of principle in acting remain always with us, and persist in getting themselves discussed, even to the point of controversy. Most irrepressible of such questions is the one raised in 1770 by Diderot, the French philosopher and critic, in his famous *Paradoxe sur le comédien*—that is to say, the question of how much real emotion an actor should feel in playing his part.

In contending that the actor should be completely insensible to emotion Diderot so far overstated his case that he cannot be taken quite seriously. His theory is remembered today chiefly because Constant Coquelin revived and defended it in a widely read essay, *L'Art et le comédien*, published in 1880-81. Without quoting Diderot, Coquelin endorsed the *Paradoxe* as "literal truth," but a study of his whole essay reveals a general attitude so much more temperate than Diderot's that one is inclined to wonder whether he had read the *Paradoxe* before endorsing it. "Extreme sensibility," says Diderot, "makes middling actors; middling sensibility makes the ruck of bad actors; in complete absence of sensibility is the possibility of a sublime actor." What Coquelin says, in effect, is that acting is an art with certain natural limitations and conventions to distinguish it from reality; and that for effective creative work in that art the actor must "remain master of himself throughout the most impassioned and violent action on the part of the character which he represents; in a word, remain unmoved himself, the more surely to move others . . ." He does not say, as Diderot does, that the actor should be insensible to emotion—merely that he should neither give way to it, nor depend upon it. "I am convinced," he says, "that one can only be a great actor on condition of a complete self-mastery and ability to express feelings which are not experienced, which may never be experienced, which from the very nature of things never can be experienced."

Coquelin's essay aroused a great deal of protest, and led to a spirited controversy in which Henry Irving became the leader of the opposition. The controversy interested William Archer, who, with the coöperation of Longman's Magazine, undertook to assemble and analyze all the available opinions on both sides. He distributed an elaborate questionnaire, asking several hundred actors and actresses whether they were in the habit of giving way to genuine tears, blushes, or laughter on the stage; whether their acting of emotional scenes was affected by their memory of personal sorrows or other experiences; whether they found it necessary to prepare for exacting parts by working up their emotions beforehand; whether they experienced a kind of "double consciousness" in acting, and whether they believed in making use of sudden inspirations. The results of his study were published first in the magazine and later (1888) in the form of a book entitled *Masks or Faces.*

I shall not attempt to detail all of Mr. Archer's conclusions; every actor and every stage director should read *Masks or Faces* for himself. It is sufficient to say that although he is by no means unbiased in his attitude and starts out with the evident purpose to prove Diderot in the wrong, he ends by accepting a compromise position. He brings overwhelming evidence against the notion that a temperamentally insensitive person makes the best actor, but he finally agrees that a measure of self-control is essential to good acting, even in highly emotional scenes. This, after all, was Coquelin's main point, if not Diderot's, and it is admitted by Irving, Booth, Barrett, Clara Morris, and many other players quoted by Mr. Archer as supporters of the emotional theory. Clara Morris

—who shed tears profusely on the stage and "felt" her parts with exquisite agony—states the compromise view clearly. "As to really losing oneself in a part," she says, "that will not do; it is worse to be too sympathetic than to have too much art. I must cry in my emotional rôles and feel enough to cry, but I must not allow myself to become so affected as to mumble my words, to redden my nose, or to become hysterical." Lambert's famous phrase, *Le coeur chaud, la tête froide* ("a warm heart but a cool head") expresses the same idea in epigrammatic form, and offers perhaps the best statement of the true paradox of acting.

EMOTION AND TEAM WORK

From the standpoint of the modern director, William Archer's book has, I think, one or two limitations for which the student must make due allowance. The most serious is that he appears to consider acting as an individual matter, ignoring the problem of team work. When an actor under stress of emotion produces an effect which not only electrifies his audience but startles his fellow actors out of their composure, one may properly ask if he is not achieving a personal triumph at the expense of the team work. Mr. Archer cites incidents of the kind with implied praise, and in accordance with the prevailing taste in 1888 he appears to measure excellence in acting largely by intensity of emotional effect upon the audience. The good actor, to him, is the one who "stops the show." He admits that a complete loss of self-control is bad, but he appears to think of it in terms of the individual actor and the effect upon his acting. The modern director must think in terms of the whole play, and to him the great danger in excessively emotional acting is that it will throw the actor out of his stride, disrupt the team work, disconcert the other actors, and unbalance the production.

A second limitation in Mr. Archer's discussion is the fact that he conducts it without definition of terms, and without knowledge of the psychological principles involved—or at any rate without reference to them. Had he believed, as most psychologists now believe, that emotion is the effect rather than the cause, of bodily activity, he would doubtless have attacked the problem in a different way. Diderot's conception of a great actor simulating perfectly the bodily manifestations of emotion and yet feeling no emotion himself is clearly improbable under the James-Lange theory.[1] But equally improbable is Mr. Archer's conception of emotion as an inner urge, an actuating cause, moving the actor to outward expression.

Emotion, according to the James-Lange theory, is but the realization in consciousness of certain bodily activities— laughter, tears, trembling, dryness of the throat, and so on —the activities themselves being induced by sensory stimuli. The emotion aroused by one set of motor activities may, of course, play a part in shaping the next set, since the motor activities are governed by past experience as well as by immediate stimuli; but that means a procession of horse-drawn carts rather than a cart before its own horse. Every emotion felt by the actor will undoubtedly affect his *subsequent* motor activities; but it cannot affect the motor activities out of which that particular emotion is built, since they precede it. From the fact that many great actors weep and suffer in sympathy with the characters they portray, William Archer seems to infer that they are great actors because they are able to weep and suffer. William James would doubtless have said that they weep and suffer because they are great actors—because they simulate the bodily activities of suffering so completely that they cannot help feeling the corresponding emotion.

[1] See page 134.

EMOTION AND IMAGINATION

If the James-Lange theory is correct, emotion on the stage is not in itself a thing to be especially cultivated—or avoided. The thing to be cultivated is imagination.

Imagination is the power to conjure up unrealities in terms of reality; to see in the mind's eye, or hear in the mind's ear; to draw present sensations out of past experiences, and to assemble them in new combinations. In the actor it is the power to conceive in his own body the significant motor activities of a fictitious character. In so far as emotional experience, on or off the stage, helps him to cultivate his imagination it is good; and in so far as a lack of sensibility hampers the development of his imagination it is bad. "In my opinion," said Lawrence Barrett, "the prime requisites of an actor are sensibility and imagination. But he must have these under perfect control. The moment that they become his masters instead of his servants he ceases to be an artist." What is called sensibility includes, I take it, a general responsiveness to sense impressions, and also a keenly active sympathetic system by which the experiences of one part of the body are felt associatively in other parts. Mr. Archer seems to use the terms emotion and sensibility almost interchangeably, but sensibility is, I think, a very different thing from emotion. Emotion is sensitivity to one's own bodily state; sensibility is sensitivity to one's environment. Emotion does not always breed imagination; emotional people are often self-centered, narrow, or unsympathetic. But sensibility, in the broadest sense, enriches the imagination by enriching the experience.

Actors are notoriously poor analysts, and most of what they have written about acting is not very intelligible or very trustworthy, but if there is any one point upon which they have generally agreed it is the importance of imagination.

It was surely imagination—not emotion—that Garrick was thinking of when he made his much-quoted remark to a young actor who had complained of inadequate inspiration in his surroundings: "If you cannot give a speech, or make love, to a table, chair or marble as well as to the finest woman in the world, you are not, nor ever will be, a great actor!" [1] The time-worn story of Madame Modjeska reducing an audience to tears by reciting the Polish multiplication table is more likely to be quoted in illustration of the power of imagination than in defense of real emotion in acting—as is the similar story of three actors in a restaurant, one of whom made the others weep by reading the menu aloud. Of the latter story Mr. Alexander Woollcott disposed by offering the opinion that the three actors "were all soused to the gills"; but one hesitates to accept the frightful implication that imagination and sensibility were keener—or emotion more sincere—in the days before Prohibition. Perhaps it is only that the audiences were more gullible. Seriously, whatever truth there may be in either story bears out the power of imagination.

A great many actors, past and present, have felt the necessity of spending some time before each performance in seclusion in order to get into adjustment with their characters. It is said that Salvini always dressed and made up an hour or two early and gave himself over to meditation, while other actors smoked or chatted. Clara Morris found him one evening pacing up and down on the dark stage. "You walk far, signor, she said. "Si, signorina," was the reply, "I walk me into him!" Stanislavsky does the same thing. He calls it "getting into the circle," and in the Moscow Art Theatre each actor is supposed to think of nothing but his character before and during the performance, and no ir-

[1] It is said, by the way, that Diderot based his *Paradoxe* partly on his observation of Garrick.

relevant conversation or diversion is permitted back stage. This sort of thing is often cited to prove the importance of emotion or sensibility in acting, but it really has little to do with either. It is a matter of imagination. Some actors need more help than others in order to set their imaginations going, and some are more easily distracted than others by irrelevant things. Talma, one of the strongly emotional actors, could laugh and chat in the wings, but at the sound of his cue jump instantly into the most impassioned scenes. Whether a young actor should follow Salvini's method or Talma's is a question of temperament, affected somewhat by the character of the part, and by its familiarity to the actor.

THE ÆSTHETIC BALANCE

A great deal of confusion on the subject of acting seems to me to disappear when we do our theorizing in terms of empathy and æsthetic distance. At the risk of repeating what was said in an earlier chapter let me try to restate the problem of "masks or faces" in those terms.

The actor's purpose is to create something not so much on the stage as in the imaginations of his hearers. He is there to give them æsthetic pleasure, and to do so he must give them something in which they can empathize—something into which they can feel themselves imitatively—but toward which at the same time they can maintain an attitude of personal detachment. The more realistically he portrays the bodily activities of the character he represents, the more completely will the audience feel those activities imitatively in themselves, and when the activities happen to be those which give rise to emotion, the more keenly will the audience (and incidentally the actor) feel the emotion. It is a part of our pleasure in the theatre, as in all fiction, to share empathically the emotions of the characters; but only when the balance of emotions in the play or book as a whole is satisfying, and only when we are able to maintain our æsthetic distance. If the actor portrays unpleasant scenes too vividly there are too many unpleasant emotions aroused in us, and the experience becomes too harrowing; and if his portrayal reminds us too painfully of ourselves and our real troubles we lose our æsthetic distance. It should be obvious that if the actor throws himself into a part with so much realism as to break down emotionally he has destroyed his own æsthetic distance; and if he has done that there is a fair probability that he has done the same thing empathically for his audience.

It must be remembered, too, that art is not life, and that even in the most realistic drama there is a convention of unreality, felt by the audience, consciously or unconsciously. When an actor is so far carried away by his part as to show real emotion there is danger that the audience will detect that fact; and the moment they discover that it is the actor rather than the character who is laughing or weeping, the illusion vanishes and again æsthetic distance breaks down. It is quite true that some actors can experience more real emotion than others without detection, and that some audiences are less able to distinguish between real and acted emotion; but the difference is merely relative and the principle holds good.

There is, of course, no rule of proportion for preserving the balance between empathy and æsthetic distance. Neither element is measurable. But there are certain variable factors which affect the proportion in ways that can be understood.

In general it may be said that a play dealing with exotic or unfamiliar places and characters will bear stronger empathies than a play dealing with everyday life. The greater the resemblance to familiar reality the greater the danger to æsthetic distance. Many people did not like *The Show-Off*, for instance, because they could not maintain the necessary detachment; it was too much like real life. One student of mine wrote: "We have a man just like that in our own family, and I do not care to be reminded of him any oftener than is necessary."

Similarly, a play that is fancifully or idealistically treated will bear more empathy than one realistically treated. The material may be familiar enough, but if the spirit is one of idealization, that in itself helps to preserve æsthetic distance. All other things being equal, a costume play is less likely to break down under excessive realism than a play in modern dress; a play in verse is less likely than a play in prose; a play in the heroic mood is less likely than one in a plaintive or pessimistic mood. A little study of such contrasts will reveal a great deal about the balance of empathy and æsthetic distance. Incidentally it may reveal why the great poetic tragedies have more universality and permanence than the drab, depressing dramas of the realistic school, and why the great actors of the last century could go so much farther in the display of passion than most actors can go today.

Physical conditions, too, may affect the æsthetic balance. Empathic responses are harder to get in a large theatre than a small one, but æsthetic distance is easier to maintain. Make-up, in so far as it disguises the actor, helps to maintain æsthetic distance; but in so far as it becomes painfully obvious it weakens empathic appeal. A platform stage, being less realistic than a proscenium stage, is less likely to destroy æsthetic distance through excessive illusion of reality; on the other hand it may destroy it through *weakness* of illusion or through establishment of direct communication between actor and audience. At its best the platform stage permits of the strongest possible empathic appeal, but its technique is much more difficult than that of the "picture frame" stage, and the æsthetic balance more precarious. On either type of stage the lighting effects play a very important part in maintaining the æsthetic attitude. But the management of the physical conditions is not our concern here; the point is that the actor must regulate the degree and nature of his empathic appeal in accordance with the conditions.

The prevailing taste of the public today is for a good deal of realism in acting; but the prevailing opinion of the liveliest modern critics of the theatre, from Gordon Craig to Kenneth Macgowan, is that realism is all wrong. It should be the actor's business, they say, to create, not to imitate. They object to the whole conception of art as imitation or representation, and insist upon presentation, or expression, or abstraction, as the proper aim. In accordance with this view they condemn every attempt to counterfeit nature or create illusion.

There can be no doubt that representative or imitative realism has often been carried to excess in the modern theatre; but before condemning the *principle* of realism let us try to define our terms, and to discover if possible the motives involved.

If by realism we mean absolute one-hundred-percent reproduction of reality, then of course realism is not art. But I cannot find that anybody does mean this. The most ardent realists in all branches of art agree that art is not reality— that some principle of limitation, or selection, or emphasis, or interpretation, or conventionalization must enter into the work of the artist in order to distinguish it from the work of the scientist or reporter. Virtually all artists claim that their purpose is to suggest, rather than to portray, or to suggest more than they portray—even the ones who portray a great deal. All artists aim to stimulate imagination. The

289

difference is that some try to do so by abstract symbolism, others by concrete representation.

In order to stimulate imagination through suggestion it is necessary to represent (that is re-present) certain elements of real experience. Suggestion is not possible in any other way. We think, feel, and imagine in terms of past experience and we cannot do these things at all unless some germs of past experience are presented to our senses to stir up our mental and emotional associations. If the elements presented are singly and collectively quite unfamiliar, they have no meaning for us, arouse no associations, and leave us baffled and blank.

Realism, then, is not absolute, but relative. The question for the artist is what proportion of reality, what degree of concrete representation, is necessary to accomplish the desired suggestion. In the comparatively abstract art of music the sound of a thunder-sheet may be thought unnecessarily realistic; but in a play the sound of the same thunder-sheet back stage may be laughed at as too unconvincing to carry the illusion. Acting is of necessity one of the most realistic of the arts, because it is in terms of human beings, the realest things we know. The most abstract or stylized acting, even the pantomime of the ballet, is more representatively realistic than the most obvious of "program" music. Let us understand, therefore, that realism as a principle is neither good nor bad; that what is to be condemned is its excessive application. But let us also understand that the very inevitability of realism in acting is in itself a temptation to excess.

The consistent realism of detail which we sometimes find in the modern theatre is, of course, relatively new in history. It is variously said to have begun with Betterton, or Macklin, or Garrick, or Booth, or Appia, or Irving, or Belasco. But to suppose that realism as a principle began with any of these is to misunderstand the problem completely. There were ele-

ments of realism in the Greek theatre, including stage properties, some painted scenes, mechanical effects, and attempts
—especially on the part of Euripides—to humanize the drama
itself. I have no doubt there were moments of realism in the
acting, despite the masks and choruses and poetic conventions; certainly there were such moments in Roman acting at
a time when the ambition of the Romans was to imitate the
Greeks. There were moments of realism in medieval times
and in the age of Elizabeth. There was more attempt at
realism of effect in Shakespeare's time than is generally supposed, even in the public theatres; and in the private theatres
there was more than in some of the little theatres of today.
There was, of course, no such completeness and consistency
of illusion as we find in the modern theatre, either in setting
or acting. The realistic stage effects were sporadic and inconsistent. The actors declaimed most of their lines in conventional manner, dropped out of character between times,
and were sadly interrupted—at least in the public theatres—
by disorderly members of the audience. But we may well
believe that their conception of the highest achievement in
acting was "to hold the mirror up to nature," and that their
moments of greatest triumph were the moments of greatest
realism in the portrayal of thought and feeling. If this was
true in the comparatively idealistic plays of Shakespeare it
must have been even more so in the plays of Marlowe and
Webster and in the so-called "domestic murder plays," which
for stark realism of situation can hardly be matched in
modern drama.

The same impulse to realism of portrayal on the part of
the individual actor persisted through the eighteenth and
nineteenth centuries. It was that impulse which made Garrick
clutch at the imaginary dagger in Macbeth, which made Macready and Clara Morris study the inmates of asylums the

better to portray insanity, and which made Edmund Kean chew red madder during his death scenes in order to drool blood. But realism of this kind is less common today than it was in the days of heroic declamatory acting, and when it appears it is usually less intense. Most good actors now have some feeling for æsthetic distance, whether or not they know it by name, and they are aware that excessive realism destroys the proper attitude of the audience. Clara Morris found this out for herself, and in her *Stage Confidences* she cites many instances in which scenes on the stage came too close to real life. In one play she portrayed incipient madness by clasping her arms about her knees and swaying, as she had seen a woman inmate of an asylum do; but at the first performance a young girl in the audience fainted and had to be carried out. She had recognized her mother's symptoms. A hundred years earlier Sarah Siddons' exploit in making people faint had been hailed as a triumph of acting; but Clara Morris had the good sense to see that such effects were not those of legitimate art, and she took pains to avoid them in her later years. Nearly all the great actors of the last two generations have recorded similar experiences and similar conclusions.

But if the impulse to excessive realism in acting is on the decline, what is it that gives rise to the charge that the theatre is being ruined by realism? What is it that began with Betterton and Garrick and Macklin, that has been growing upon us ever since, and that has made the modern theatre and modern acting so different from the Elizabethan?

CONSISTENCY AND COMPLETENESS

First of all it is the idea of consistency—not realism but *consistency* in realism. It was the idea of consistency, as a reaction against *in*consistency, that caused Betterton to stay in character between lines and to strive for a more continuous illusion. It was the idea of consistency that caused Macklin to play Macbeth in Scottish costume instead of the usual British general's uniform. It was the idea of consistency that led Garrick to drive the audience off the stage, and to demand of his actors a greater degree of artistic unity and imaginative sincerity than the English stage had known before. And it is the idea of consistency—growing with sophistication and constantly subjected to fresh challenge through improvement of material equipment—that has forced upon the modern theatre an increasing regard for scenic realism, for natural lighting, for smooth mechanical effects, for team work and restraint in acting, for perfection of detail in every department of play production.

Consistency, like everything else, can be carried to excess; but in so far as it represents the natural revolt against stupid inconsistency it is good. The more civilized we become, the more sensitive we grow to inconsistency and the more certainly it becomes for us a source of distraction. We may regret this, and long for the more rugged, naïve imaginations of our ancestors; but they can be brought back only through a reversal of the process of civilization. In the present order of things we must expect to demand more and more consistency.

But does this mean that art must become more and more representatively realistic, more and more punctilious in detail? It most certainly does not.

The trouble is that we have got two ideas rather badly mixed—the idea of consistency and the idea of completeness. Inconsistency and incompleteness often go hand in hand, and they did so in the early days of the theatre. So, when actors and producers began to feel the need of more consistency they quite naturally failed to distinguish between consistency and completeness, and in working for the one they worked also for the other. Sometimes completeness has seemed the only apparent means to consistency—as when the improvement in stage lighting disclosed the incompleteness and inconsistency of old style scenery; or when the increasing interest in contemporary domestic drama necessitated a little more attention to make-up, dialect, and stage business. And now the process has gone so far that some of our realists are simply floundering; they are straining for representative completeness when they should be aiming at consistency of illusion. A degree of consistency appropriate to our civilization is essential to art and to the illusion of art. But art is selective, and representative completeness is therefore undesirable—besides which it is impossible.

Good acting, then, is neither wholly realistic nor wholly unrealistic. It is always sufficiently realistic to be intelligible and suggestive and to arouse the necessary empathy; it is always sufficiently consistent to be convincing; and it is always sufficiently *un*real to preserve æsthetic distance and to leave something to the imagination. Within these limitations of principle it is capable of great variation in style, from the painstaking yet spiritual realism of the Moscow Art Theatre to the pure make-believe of the Chinese.

ABANDON VERSUS REPRESSION IN ACTING

The question of style in acting is almost as troublesome as that of principle. Some theatre-goers, for instance, will always prefer the actor who plays with abandon; who seems to "wear his heart on his sleeve," and to put all his powers of expression into his part. Others will prefer the actor who plays more quietly and seems to hold something back.

The extreme abandon of the romantic age, with its "grand manner," its furious display of passion, its orotund declamation, its bursts of harrowing realism and its consequent destruction of æsthetic distance, is gone, let us hope, forever.

But there are still many people who feel that the repressed style of acting so common today, especially among English actors, has taken some of the life out of the theatre. Such acting, they say, is cold, conventional, unexciting. It fails to stir the soul.

If this charge is true, repression in acting is bad. The only real test, of course, is the effect upon the audience. But no actor *aims* to be cold, conventional and unexciting; if his acting lacks abandon it is either because he is unimaginative or self-conscious, or because he believes in restraint as more effective than abandon. If he is unimaginative or self-conscious his acting is merely bad acting and need not be discussed; but if his restraint is intentional we must consider whether he is right in believing that restraint is—or ought to be—effective.

It has been suggested that comedy and tragedy call for different styles of acting, and that the English type of restraint is only suitable for comedy. Stark Young [1] thinks that the English actor, starting with a handicap of racial inexpressiveness, is not capable of acting tragedy effectively. Lester Wallack [2] thought that comedy was naturally self-conscious and technical; tragedy, spontaneous and abandoned. There is clearly some truth in this point of view. But the terms are relative, and all we can safely say is that comedy will bear a little more self-consciousness than tragedy. Neither should be obtrusively self-conscious, and neither should be abandoned to the point of hysteria.

A certain increase of restraint in acting is a natural and inevitable accompaniment of our increasing sensitivity to æsthetic distance. Sometimes, too, repression is more poignantly suggestive of deep emotion than the wildest sort of rant. It is a commonplace of real life that those who con-

[1] *Theatre Practice,* p. 26.   [2] *Memories of Fifty Years,* p. 172.

ceal their grief suffer more deeply than those who give way to it; true or false, the idea is so widely accepted that it is bound to shape our empathies. When an actor succeeds in giving us the impression of emotion bottled up, our empathic response is very strong, and the more civilized we are the stronger it is. Civilization trains us to repress and conceal our emotions; so when a character in whom we are empathizing gives way to his emotions we feel it in ourselves as a weakness. There are times, to be sure, when a vicarious release from our inhibitions is just what we most desire; but we do not like to feel, for any considerable time, that we are losing our grip. If we weep too freely or laugh too loudly we are a little ashamed of ourselves; but we are never ashamed of having *felt* deeply if we have retained our self-control.

Sarah Bernhardt, who could rant well enough on occasion, was never more effective than when she conveyed a whole tumult of feeling with a single significant gesture. In *La Tosca*, for example, when her lover was understood to be undergoing torture in the next room, she did not beat upon the door with both fists and shake her hair loose, as any good movie queen would do. She stood close to the door with her arm against it and her forehead against her arm, and the only movement was a convulsive twitching and clenching of the free hand. Repression of this kind is not uncommon with great actors in emotional scenes. With the French it is a matter of studied technique, a part of their classicism; with the Russians of the Moscow Art Theatre, and with many Americans, it is a phase of realism; but with the English it is a definite convention, partly ethical and partly æsthetic, comparable to the toning down of a too garish painting. Much of the complaint against it comes from those whose taste is for more lurid coloring.

Repression at its best really *is* convention—the convention

of selection—in short, art. It is the unessential that is repressed; the essential somehow gets through. A painter
selects a few harmonious colors to convey the mood of his
picture, and suppresses the rest. An illustrator draws a
few telling lines and a graphic story appears on the page.
An actor seizes upon a significant gesture, represses all meaningless movement, and a wave of emotion sweeps over the
audience. In such repression there is actually a kind of
abandon—the abandon of the artist whose judgement is so
sure, whose hand is so practiced, that with three or four bold,
broad, apparently careless strokes he can paint a whole picture. It is this kind of abandon, not the abandon of indis-
crimination, that we really want in art.

PERSONALITY VERSUS IMPERSONATION

Another important question is whether the actor should
cultivate a personality of his own, recognizable through all
his parts, or sink himself so completely in his parts as to
be unrecognizable. Nearly everybody professes to admire
the perfect actor, who changes himself with each part and
disappears in the characterization; yet more people patronize
the personality actor than the impersonator. Unusually
skilful impersonators, specialists like Ruth Draper and H. V.
Granville, command a certain following, but it is nothing
compared to the following of a Forrest, a Bernhardt, or a
Duse. Run over the names of the popular stars of the past
few years—John Drew, Francis Wilson, William Gillette,
Billie Burke, Raymond Hitchcock, Frank Bacon, Helen
Hayes, George Arliss, William Hodge, Ethel Barrymore,
George Cohan, Frank Craven, Francine Larrimore, Ina
Claire, Grant Mitchell, and so on—and consider which of
them can compare with Erskine Sanford or Henry Travers or
Alfred Lunt as character actors. Erskine Sanford's Mr.

Pim will be remembered for a long time; but who thought of Mr. Pim when he saw Erskine Sanford in *St. Joan* or *Johannes Kreisler?* Henry Travers' Stogumber was almost the high spot of *St. Joan,* but who recognized the same actor in the Androcles of the Theatre Guild's *Androcles and the Lion?* Both of these actors disappear so completely in their parts that they hide themselves from their audiences to their own professional disadvantage; and there are many others like them. Alfred Lunt has been better advertised, and is more widely known, but he too is unrecognizable in different parts. As a result he has more admirers than personal devotees. Even on the screen the ablest and most versatile character actors are seldom featured as stars or remembered by the audience; while Mary Pickford, Douglas Fairbanks, Charlie Chaplin, Pola Negri, Buster Keaton, Clara Bow, and a score of other "screen personalities" are always sure of a following.

Advertising, of course, plays an important part—indirect advertising, especially. The very fact that a personality actor is recognizable in several parts fixes his identity in the minds of the producers as well as the audience, and both begin to advertise him. People talk about the actor whose name and face they can remember; and they remember the one who is advertised, or who advertises himself by consistent tags or mannerisms. Producers in turn advertise the actor they find the audiences talking about; and a kind of vicious circle is established. In the cleverest impersonation there is an element of impermanence which disconcerts memory and discourages investment; and nobody can be blamed for clinging to the more comprehensible and more profitable element of personality.

In each of us, too, there is a streak of conservatism. We distrust the thing we do not know about, and hold fast to that which is sure. If an actor is good in two or three similar parts we begin to cherish his stage personality as one of our familiar possessions, and we patronize him in preference to some upstart newcomer. Had Erskine Sanford followed Mr. Pim with two or three other characterizations of gentle old men he might have become as popular a stage personality as Mrs. Thomas Whiffen.

Of course, a great deal of what we call personality is not personality at all, but merely the accident of getting into a rut—the natural result of type casting. As such it is in no way admirable. The actor who is always the same because he has never tried but one type of part, or because he is simply himself and no actor at all, is not a great artist. But the perfect impersonator is not necessarily a great artist either. The great actor is more than a clever impersonator; he is an interpreter, and to be a real interpreter he must be a personality as well. To skill in changing his character he must add depth of understanding, individuality, creative imagination, greatness of soul. These are figurative, not scientific terms; but they represent what, in the best sense, is meant by personality in acting.

DUAL PERSONALITY IN ACTING

The chief difficulty in respect to the theory of acting lies in the fact that the actor is *both* impersonator and interpreter at the same time. When we say that the great actor is a personality, an interpretative, even a creative, artist, we are saying something which is theoretically in conflict with the idea of acting as exhibition or illusion; the distinction between reading and acting in terms of æsthetic distance [1] seems, in that connection, to break down. If the actor is part of the illusion of the play, with the æsthetic distance between him

[1] See Figure 1, page 40.

and the audience, how can he serve also as an interpreter? Does not interpretation imply a sharing of experience with the audience, and does not that put him in the place of a reader, on the audience's end of æsthetic distance? The answer is that he must be in both places at once, for he is two persons at once—the artist and the character.

Other artists have instruments and materials outside themselves with which to work, but the actor is his own medium. As the musician plays upon his instrument the actor plays upon himself.

Considered in this way, the dual function of the actor becomes fairly clear, but the difficulty of adjustment and emphasis remains. How can the actor be in character as a part of the exhibition or illusion, and still exercise the function of interpretative artist? How can he, in the words of Stark Young, be "technically able to inject into the movement his own witty comment upon it?" [1] How can he serve as the mouthpiece of the author or as a critic of the play without losing his place in the illusion? How can he take his audience into his confidence without establishing communication with them and so destroying æsthetic distance?

Well, good actors do these things constantly. Few of them, perhaps, can explain how. The most obvious thing that can be said about it is that the actor's two functions are not equally evident to the senses. His function as a character in the play is frank, open, and above-board; it is that function which the audience observes—the only one, in fact, which it should be permitted to observe, consciously. It is that function which defines acting with respect to æsthetic distance, and distinguishes it from reading. But the actor's function as an interpretative artist, critic, or leader of the audience should be unseen, subtle, almost telepathic. Since

[1] *Theatre Practice,* p. 21.

he must use himself as the medium of his art he must keep himself as artist in the background—behind the scenes so to speak. You know he is there but you do not see him. You feel his personality, but you feel it through the character's personality, and you observe no conflict between them.

Two dangers confront the actor who seeks to perform this dual function. The first is that he will overdo the effort at interpretation, injecting too much of his own personality and spoiling the impersonation. The other is that he will fail to distinguish between *projection* and *communication*. Direct communication with the audience is indefensible under modern theatrical conditions—at least for legitimate drama. It destroys æsthetic distance, and it destroys the "illusion of the first time." But the actor's appreciative attitude can be projected to the audience without direct communication, and the trick of doing that is the real trick of acting. It is the power of projection which distinguishes the so-called "comedy sense" from the sense of humor. The actor may have ever so keen a sense of humor, but if he cannot project his appreciation to the audience he has not the comedy sense. And if he cannot project his personality along with his impersonation, or if he has no personality to project, he is not, in the deepest sense, a great actor.

CHAPTER XV

VOICE AND DICTION

NOT much can be done to improve the voices of the actors in the limited time devoted to any one production, but when the director and the group are to be together for several seasons, or even for several productions, some attention to voice and articulation is distinctly worth while.

The importance of voice to the actor can hardly be overstated. The great actors who have written of their art have, almost without exception, stressed that point. "The voice is the most important of the actor's possessions," said Sarah Bernhardt; "By means of the voice the attention of the public is riveted; the voice it is which binds together actor and auditor. An actor's voice must run the whole gamut of harmonies—grave, plaintive, vibrating, metallic." Bernhardt's own voice was one of the greatest—"liquid music" people used to call it. Edwin Forrest's voice had such power and such depth of vibration that his outbursts of passion almost terrorized his audiences. Of James E. Murdoch, Professor T. C. Trueblood writes, "He had incomparably the finest voice I ever listened to. It was of wide range, powerful, a clear ringing baritone." Salvini's voice was, in the words of Bernhardt, "a whole orchestra." There have been fine voices, too, in recent years—not so many great tragic voices, perhaps, as in the last century, but flexible, responsive voices, capable of force and variety in expression.

For every good voice, however, there are many bad ones, and what with the prevalence of type casting and of realistic colloquial plays, the proportion of good voices is diminishing.

A good vocal equipment includes adequate volume, resistance to fatigue, good tone, good articulation and flexibility. Practically all of these qualities, and especially the first two, rest upon good breathing.

BREATHING

Teachers of voice disagree violently as to what constitutes correct breathing in voice production, and the problem is greatly complicated by confusion of terminology. Not all of those who advocate "abdominal breathing," for example, mean the same thing by it. To avoid both the controversy and the confusion I shall limit my discussion to the presentation, in non-technical terms, of a few fundamentals about which there is little dispute.

The best authorities are generally agreed that correct breathing is natural breathing, in the sense that it is free from physical restraint and conscious self-control, like the breathing of a child. Such breathing involves a maximum of physical action, but a minimum of physical strain. It is perfectly controlled in the sense that it is responsive to the demands of expression, but the control is subconscious, not studied. Most of us do not breathe naturally in this sense; our childhood freedom has been warped and restricted by training and habit, by poor ventilation, cramped posture, and tight clothing; so that very little of our natural bodily freedom is left. Improvement of the breathing habits is, therefore, a matter of trying to restore a natural function.

Good breathing is not confined to the action of a few muscles or to one portion of the body; it involves the coördinated activity of a large part of the trunk. Just which muscles participate, and in what proportion, I shall not attempt to state, since that is one of the matters in dispute. It is fairly safe, however, to assert that the diaphragm plays an important part, and that any method of breathing which gives inadequate play to that muscle is probably wrong. The diaphragm is an internal muscle, and its action is not easily felt, but since the external muscles about the upper abdomen are closely coördinated with it, an active diaphragm brings about a sensation of muscular tension at the center of the body. Good breathing is neither so high in the chest nor so low in the abdomen as to be grotesque; it is centered in what the pugilist calls the "mid-section." The strain is thus carried by some of the largest and strongest muscles of the body. At the same time, and most important of all, the throat is relaxed. A feeling of strain in a healthy throat during voice production is a sure sign of some fault—usually incorrect breathing.

Numerous exercises for the correction of faulty breathing may be found in the books on public speaking and on voice, and need not be repeated here. One of the best is the so-called "sipping and packing" exercise, by which the air is inhaled in small sips, and packed away until the lungs are full. Another is the "panting" exercise, which is just what the name implies. In general, those exercises which tend to develop the diaphragm and to encourage full open breathing are best; but no exercise should be employed which occasions the slightest strain or irritation in the throat. The actor should be cautioned to take his breathing exercises regularly but on the side, and not to think of the breath or its control when actually speaking.[1]

[1] For a further discussion of vocal and breathing exercises, see the author's *Handbook of Public Speaking,* p. 127.

VOCAL QUALITY

Many of the common faults in vocal quality are really faults in breathing, and clear up satisfactorily when the breathing habits are corrected. Others are referable to poor resonance, poor tone placing, or poor selection of pitch; and the worst are referable to poor coördination of mind and voice.

Resonance has much to do with the carrying power of a voice as well as its quality. Poor resonance may result from malformation of the chest, throat, or head, or from a catarrhal or other obstruction; or it may result from faulty coördination of the parts involved. When it is due to malformation or obstruction the case is one for the physician or surgeon. When it is due to faulty coördination it may sometimes be corrected by properly chosen exercises. Chest resonance [1] is usually improved by good breathing exercises tending to increase the lung capacity and the responsiveness of the diaphragm. Head resonance may be improved by relaxing the throat and forwarding the tone so that the upper teeth and the hard palate vibrate; also by practice in singing "*dans la masque*"—that is, humming well forward in the nose with the lips very lightly closed and the whole front of the face tingling with the vibrations. Good resonance at any pitch requires instant adjustment of the soft or movable parts involved, and is greatly impaired by fatigue or irritation; a flat or wooden voice is often simply a tired voice, or a voice that has been strained or abused. The actor should never be allowed to shout or to force his voice in any way, but should be encouraged to seek an easy, open, relaxed utterance. He should strive to decrease the effort and improve the quality without loss of volume, rather than to increase

[1] Assuming that there is such a thing. The matter is in controversy.

305

the volume; if he succeeds in the former, the latter will take care of itself.

Poor resonance is often associated with poor tone placing. If the actor will pronounce in rotation the vowels *oo, oh, aw, ah, ă* (the latter sound as in "at"), he will soon notice a sensation that the *oo* is very far back, the *oh* a little less so, the *aw* in the middle of the mouth, the *ah* just behind the teeth, and the *ă* very far forward, almost out of the mouth. He will also notice that the mouth is opened wider as the sound comes forward. The resonance is usually poor on the *oo* because the mouth is nearly closed, and any incipient resonance is smothered before it gets out. As the mouth opens and the tone comes forward, the resonance increases and the tone improves until it reaches its best on the *ah*, with the maximum vibration in the mouth, the nasal passages, and the front of the skull. Usually the *ă* is not so good in quality; it is too far forward and the sound escapes into the air without having set up the proper head resonance. Constant practice on these vowels in rotation, with occasional variations of pitch within the natural range of the voice will help the actor to acquire a sense of the relation between vowel quality, position, and resonance, and to form a concept of the sort of voice he wishes to cultivate.

In the effort to get volume with untrained voices, amateurs often strike too high a pitch. The higher the pitch the greater the volume for a given amount of effort, but the greater the strain on the listener. Most voices are poorer in quality in the upper half of their range than in the lower, and therefore less pleasant to the ear; moreover a high pitch is emotionally associated with fear, desperation, impatience, or frazzled nerves, and is thus empathically disturbing. The actor should be taught to cultivate the lower middle tones of his voice, and to use them ordinarily in preference to the higher. There will still be occasional need for the higher tones to express the states of mind mentioned, and they will be all the more effective by contrast. There will also be need for the very lowest tones to express the deeper emotions. Both extremes of pitch express emotion, but the higher expresses excitement, weakness and loss of self-control, while the lower expresses depth and sincerity coupled with a measure of restraint. Either may be effective in its place, but the average pitch level should be a little lower than most amateurs make it. Women especially are apt to pitch their voices too high, or at any rate to offend more by doing so—perhaps because their voices are a full octave higher anyhow. It is noteworthy that the great stage voices have nearly all been rich and flexible in the lower registers.

RESPONSIVENESS

The most important quality of voice for the actor is not pure tone, but responsiveness—flexibility accompanied by perfect coördination of the voice with the mind. Nearly all voices are in some degree expressive of character or mood. A rough, hard voice, for instance, may reveal a hard character; or a high-pitched, frantic voice a nervous one. The actor's voice, however, must reveal, not his chronic disposition, but the varying moods of all the different personalities he portrays. It must be a free and flexible instrument, responsive at all times to his imagination.

The actor should work for both variety and adaptability, and should distinguish between them. Some voices are full of variety yet not adaptable to different parts. The actor playing Hamlet should be able to vary his voice in pitch, force, and tempo to express the many moods of the character, yet it should always be recognizable as the same voice—the voice of Hamlet. The same actor playing Shylock should have a different voice—the voice of Shylock—varying again within its own range, but always consistent with itself. There are many great personality actors who can read their lines with variety of interest, but who cannot, or will not, change their voices for different characters. The voice of George Arliss is always the voice of George Arliss; those of William Gillette, Ethel Barrymore, Francis Wilson, Frank Craven, Judith Anderson, Grant Mitchell, and Francine Larrimore are always recognizable as their own. Walter Hampden, on the other hand, can change his voice considerably for different parts; so can O. P. Heggie. Actresses are generally less able to adapt their voices than actors, doubtless for purely physical reasons; Helen Hayes and Lenore Ulric are reasonably successful, but more through variation of dialect and manner than through actual change of timbre.

A change of timbre, or quality, can only be achieved through a change of resonance. That means that the tone must be differently placed, or that different portions of the chest, throat, and head must be brought into play as resonators. Timbre is dependent upon the number and character of the overtones, and the overtones are determined by the resonance. There is only one way in which an actor can learn to control the timbre, and that is by experiment in variation of resonance followed by abundant practice, preferably under guidance and criticism.

One of the best possible exercises for the development of vocal responsiveness is the following: Choose a lyric poem embodying some strong emotion—love, grief, pathos, indignation, or mirth. Read it over to get the thought; then read it aloud to an imaginary audience, putting your whole soul into your voice, and a little more. Exaggerate the mood and its expression; if pathetic, sob over it; if humorous, chuckle over it; if enthusiastic, rave over it. Try to make your voice and body vibrate with the emotion. As soon as you have succeeded in expressing one selection with sufficient abandon, drop it and try another in an entirely different mood. Vary the mood four or five ways each time, and try in the course of a week to run the whole gamut of possible emotions. Do not concentrate on any one mood too long, or mannerisms may develop. Remember that it is all mere exercise, and that the exaggeration should not be carried into real life or into the theatre.

Not all actors, of course, need this exercise; some of them slop over quite sufficiently without any encouragement. But for the actor whose voice is inhibited and unresponsive it is really very helpful, especially when the inhibition has grown out of shyness or constraint.

Both variety and change of voice may—like everything else in the theatre—be overdone. Too much variety within the part weakens its consistency, and gives the impression of straining for effect. Too much change for a new character that does not call for any special vocal quality likewise suggests strain. Straight parts require less adaptation of voice than character parts, and actors playing to a succession of strange audiences on the road have less need to change their voices than those playing in stock or repertory, whose audiences know them too well.

ENUNCIATION

No production can be effective unless the actors make themselves heard and understood, and in this connection good enunciation is even more important than great volume. The two things, however, are not entirely independent; a certain amount of volume is a necessary part of the enunciation, and insufficient volume often induces mumbling. The latter fault is surprisingly common, even on the professional stage, and some of our best actors and actresses have been roundly scolded for it by the critics. The smaller, more intimate theatres of today have something to do with this; they encourage the actor to speak more quietly, and when he happens to find himself in a larger theatre he cannot shake off the habit. But the chief cause is the tendency of the actors, both amateur and professional, to rehearse in conversational tones, or even undertones. Professionals do this as a matter of tradition; they are supposed to know how to project their voices when necessary, and consider it beneath their dignity to put forth unnecessary effort at rehearsal. Amateurs speak in undertones because they do not know any better, or because they are obliged to rehearse in private houses where full stage volume would annoy the occupants. The director should know that habits formed in rehearsal are hard to break later, and that the only way to be sure of adequate volume in public performance is to have it learned with the lines and thoroughly rehearsed.

There should be enough volume from each player to make him audible, and in addition there should be a reasonable degree of uniformity. It is always distressing to hear one actor shout while another mumbles; the listener cannot adjust his ear to either, and so misses many lines. Directors often fail to detect such variations in rehearsal because they remain too close to the stage; they should listen occasionally from the parquet circle or balcony.

Individual actors should be warned against excessive variation of force in their own delivery. No one, perhaps, has been more successful in enriching dialogue with variety of force and tempo than Mrs. Fiske; but the critics often complain of her poor enunciation. When an actor does not speak loud enough or does not form his consonants distinctly the condemnation is unanimous, but in the case of Mrs. Fiske there is great difference of opinion; some people have no difficulty in understanding her, while others have a great deal. The reason is that her somewhat jerky outbursts, unexpected pauses, sudden changes of pace and shifts of emphasis are difficult for certain ears to follow, though other ears follow them readily enough. In other words Mrs. Fiske's trouble is not slovenly enunciation, but somewhat excessive variety of enunciation. Very few amateurs, however, need be cautioned against this fault.

An important element in good enunciation, especially when for dramatic reasons the volume must be subdued, is a forward placing of the voice. People marvel at the power of some actors to make themselves heard with no apparent effort and no perceptible raising of the voice. As a rule, these are the actors who speak well forward in the mouth, with the maximum activity of lips, tongue, and teeth. Francis Wilson is a remarkable example. He speaks in a quiet, confidential, half-nasal tone, but every word is distinctly audible in the last row of the balcony. He seems to have the power of projecting the sound straight from his lips to the ear of the listener; he keeps his chin high, and the words go out into the audience instead of dribbling down his shirt front. A great many of our older actors and actresses share this power, but it is rare enough among the younger American players.

Another essential of good enunciation is correct vowel quality. Some speakers blur the vowels, failing to distinguish one from another; all their vowels tend to become indeterminates. The several values of *o*, *a*, and *u* are almost reduced to a common *uh*, and the distinction between *e* and short *i* is lost even in accented syllables. Contrasts of vowel sounds are a great aid to clarity of speech, and when a speaker levels his vowels his syllables tend to become indistinguishable. "Uh wunna gutta Phulladulphia" is not the clearest way of saying "I want to go to Philadelphia," but it is about the way some people say it. American speakers are especially careless in this respect, and also in respect to the duration of sounds; they shorten their vowels to such an extent that they frequently seem to be speaking in consonants only. Consonants are noises; vowels are tones; and since much of the beauty and expressiveness of a voice is in the tones, the actor should learn to give full value to his vowels. He will find that in so doing he also makes easier the enunciation of consonants.

The enunciation of consonants is, of course, the stumbling block for many actors. There are various reasons for this. One is poor breath control. Another is inadequate or excessive flow of saliva, usually induced by nervousness. Another is failure to sustain the vowel long enough for the muscles to get into position for the next consonant. But the worst and commonest cause is "lip laziness," or, more politely, lip sluggishness, especially sluggishness of the upper lip. Here again the English usually have the better of us. Their habit of speaking forward in the mouth enables them to cultivate responsiveness and flexibility of lips and tongue, without the excessive mobility of countenance that so often accompanies a self-conscious attempt to enunciate distinctly. The actor who is badly troubled with lip sluggishness may profitably exercise his lips and jaws by practicing in rotation such widely divergent sounds as *ee, ah, oo,* or *ip, it, ik,* or *el, are, em,* or *fun, pun, shun;* but he should be warned against making faces and cultivating lack of repose. When the lips have been limbered up to a reasonable degree such exercises should give place to exercises in forwarding the tone.

VOICE AND DICTION

The problem of correct stage pronunciation is a difficult one, involving both the choice of a standard and the practical task of training the actors to follow it. It has been said that the best English in America is heard on the stage, and there is some truth in the statement, but when it comes to explaining just why and in what respect it is best all sorts of complications arise.

Some plays, of course, do not call for standard English. Realistic plays with strong local color must be played in the dialect of the region depicted, or at least in a fairly suggestive approximation of it; and sometimes several different dialects must be spoken by different characters in the same play. But literary plays or plays of an abstract or universal character, not especially representative of locality or social class, must be played in a sort of English that is at least reasonably free from dialectal limitations and reasonably acceptable to all those who come to hear it.

Standards of pronunciation vary considerably, off the stage as well as on, and for that reason the stage English of New York or London is not always necessary, or even desirable, in an isolated community. The very best Oxford English may, indeed, sound like an affectation to the ears of a small-town audience in Iowa or Utah, and so distract attention from the play. On the other hand the small-town people do not expect even their local actors to play literary drama in the casual everyday speech and manner of the neighborhood. They expect some slight heightening of effect, some suggestion of universality in the artistic medium employed, including the language. How to get the universality without the affectation is the problem.

313

Since the American theatre derives historically from the English theatre, and English actors have been playing in this country on and off for more than a hundred and fifty years, it is natural that the traditional standard in stage pronunciation should be slightly more English and less American than the standard of the streets. Up to a certain point this is a good thing, as tending to preserve the unity of English and American dramatic literature; and up to a certain point it is not offensive. A tradition is mellowed in a hundred and fifty years, and the pronunciation of our older actors, learned in the school of experience, does not sound affected in the ears of the Iowan or the Californian, or even that linguistic outcast, the Philadelphian. What does sound affected is the pseudo-English of the younger actors who have learned their pronunciation by phonetic rule. The standard they follow is, for the most part, very distinctly English; but it is artificially so, lacking both the spontaneity of our native speech and the settled moderation which characterizes the traditional speech of the theatre.

The phoneticians who teach this standard deny, it is true, any attempt to imitate the speech of England, and point out that every sound which they advocate is to be found native somewhere in the United States. The Italian or broad *a*, for example, in words like "half," "laugh," and "master," is common in some parts of New England and elsewhere. The dropping of final *r* in words like "mother" or "father," and of medial *r* in words like "hardly" or "courthouse," is common all over New England and in most parts of the South. But the same New Englander who omits the *r* in "mother," "father," and "dear," supplies it gratuitously in "idea" and "law" ("idear" and "lore"), and the one who says "It is hahf pahst two," often says "Let's take the ca-a to Ha-a-vud" —using the so-called short *a* (as in "fat"), prolonged in duration, to which he objects when the Philadelphian uses it.[1] The Philadelphian, curiously enough, though he says "lā-ăff" for "laugh" and "hā-ăff" for "half," reverses the New Englander on "cahr" and "Hahrvard." And while the phonetician is trying to persuade the Philadelphian to use an open *o*[2] in words like "not," "got," and "on," the Middle Westerner is busy turning "daughter," "water," and "automobile" into "dotter," "wotter," and "ottomobile," while the Vermonter is turning "nought" into "naht." The truth is that the so-called "standard English" of the New York elocution schools, taken as a whole, does not represent the native speech of this country or any part of it, but does roughly imitate the speech of the upper classes in southern England. Nobody outside of New York has any illusions on this point.

The heightened conventions of the stage, however, demand a standard of pronunciation somewhat above the carelessness of ordinary speech, and one may well ask what standard, if not the standard of southern England, is to be accepted. The only safe standard, it seems to me, is that of normal English. Normal English is simply the kind of English that is reasonably acceptable wherever English is spoken. It differs from local speech chiefly in the omission of localisms. It is, in fact, a negative thing; its acceptability lies rather in what it leaves out than in what it includes. It leaves out the peculiarities that are familiar in one place but unknown in another, and especially those that are in some regions thought ugly or offensive. It includes the elements that are

---

[1] In phonetic script the sound is [æ:], as in [kæ:], [hæ:vʌd]; it cannot be correctly represented in ordinary English type. Students of pronunciation should make themselves familiar with the International Phonetic Script, which provides the only satisfactory means of indicating speech sounds on paper. (See O'Neill and Weaver, *The Elements of Speech,* or Woolbert, *The Fundamentals of Speech,* revised edition.)

[2] The sound of *aw* as in *"awful"*, but shortened. The phonetic symbol is [ɔ].

uniform, or nearly so, everywhere; and when it must express what is expressed differently in different regions it does so by compromise, choosing a middle ground.

Some such standard is exemplified in the speech of Otis Skinner, Francis Wilson, Haidee Wright, O. P. Heggie, Edith Wynne Matthison, Julia Marlowe, E. H. Sothern, Roland Young, Doris Keane, Eva LeGallienne, Walter Hampden, and Ethel Barrymore, all of whom, despite their individual differences, sound reasonably natural and inoffensive to the ordinary listener almost anywhere. Some of these actors are English and some American, but it is difficult to tell by their speech which are which. Most of them have played successfully in both countries. It is the speech of such persons that the director should have in mind when training a group of amateurs, rather than a preconceived artificial standard.

Two qualities are essential to good speech: intelligibility and freedom from distraction. The trouble with localisms and other peculiarities is that they do distract; they call attention to the actor's limitations when the audience should be thinking of the play. But affectations distract attention quite as much as localisms, and should be avoided for the same reason. Even beauty, in itself a desirable quality, is capable of becoming a source of distraction when overstressed. The problem of stage pronunciation is not primarily a problem of beautification. It is a problem of clarification. A maximum of intelligibility with a minimum of distraction is the proper goal.

NOTES ON PRONUNCIATION

All this is perhaps too general to be of immediate practical assistance to the inexperienced director, who will want to know just what types of pronunciation to encourage and what types to discourage. There is no room here for a pronouncing dictionary, but certain fairly definite suggestions may be offered, as follows:

1. Suppress any marked individual peculiarity of pronunciation, unless needed for character delineation.

2. Suppress or modify any ugly or unpleasant pronunciation not unmistakably the preferred one, or only one, in common usage. But be sure the ugliness is real, and not merely a matter of personal distaste.

3. Discourage any variant pronunciation based primarily on *slovenliness*, such as the substitution of *oo* for long *u* (properly a diphthong *iu*) in words like "stoodent" or "institoot" (although in some words like "blue" and "true" this change is inevitable); the substitution of a cough through the nose for the true dental *t* before *n* in words like "Tren(t)'n" or "impor(t)'nt"; the practical elimination of medial *t* in other words like "men(t)al" or "in(t)eresting"; the substitution of *n* for *ng* in present participles; the transposition of sounds in words like "calvary" (for "cavalry") or "irrevelant" (for "irrelevant"); or the insertion of relief sounds in slightly difficult words like "stastistics" (for "statistics") or "athalete" (for "athlete").

4. Discourage on the other hand any pseudo-learned pronunciation which takes its authority from the *spelling* rather than from the speech of educated persons. This sort of "eye pronunciation" is very common in the present age of literacy without learning, and has been widely fostered in this country by inadequately prepared teachers of English. Common examples include the reinsertion, under influence of the spelling, of sounds long omitted in good usage, like the *t* in "often," "fasten," or "waistcoat," the *h* in "forehead," or the *th* in "clothes"; the substitution of a *t* sound for the well

established *ch* sound in words like "picture," "literature," or "fortune"; the unscrambling of *sh* into double *s* in "passion" or "issue" ("iss-you" is bad enough, but "iss-oo" is worse); the punctilious separation of syllables in words like "uninteresting" or "extraordinary"; and the painfully artificial sounding of unaccented syllables in words like "lev-el" (for "lev'l") or "cap-tain" (for "capt'n").

5. Discourage any pronunciation so narrowly local as to identify the user with a particular town or community, like the "boid" (for "bird") of the Bowery New Yorker, or the "sitchyation" (for "situation") of the Pennsylvania German.

6. Of the dialectal peculiarities representing large sections of the country discourage first those which have generally incurred ridicule in other sections, such as the prolonged *ă* of the Middle Atlantic and Middle West sections ("lā-ăff," "mā-ăn," etc.); the somewhat exaggerated Italian *a* of New England; the drawl of the South, especially when emphasized by the omission of final *r;* the hard short *ah* for *aw* of the Middle West ("dotter," "wotter," etc.); the Hoosier twang; the Yankee snarl; and the Bowery slur—which is by no means confined to New York.

7. Discourage any American pronunciation commonly ridiculed in England, such as "jun'lmen" for "gentlemen," "Amurrican" for "American," or "N'York" for "New York."

8. Suppress any dialectal peculiarity of recognizably foreign origin, such as the Irish *oi* for long *i,* or *a* for *e* (as in "fate" for "feet"); the German confusion of *v* and *w; the* French *ee* for short *i* (as in "eet ees" for "it is"); the cockney English or Australian long *i* for long *a* (as in "lye-dy" for "lady"); the Swedish long *a* for long *i* (as in "Ay" for "I"); the Yiddish hard *g* in *ng* combinations; and the common Continental substitution of *t* or *d* for English *th.*

9. Discourage any tendency to break single vowels into

diphthongs, as in "mā-ăn" for "man," "proo-un" for "prune," or "lowered" for "lord."

10. Discourage also the opposite tendency to shorten diphthongs into single vowels, as in "ahr" for "our."

11. Encourage any pronunciation which, though not universally employed, is universally admired. In this respect so much depends upon association, intonation and manner that it would be dangerous to cite specific examples. Some of the less extreme values of *o* and *a* in England and New England, some of the clarities of the Middle West, and some of the softnesses of the South are quite generally pleasing. But a pronunciation is not "universally admired" unless admired by all classes; if widely admired by purists or pedants but scorned by ordinary mortals it should be discouraged.

12. Encourage a moderate or middle sound of *a* in words like "laugh," "class," "after" or "dance"—a sound between the *ă* and the extreme Italian *a*. Such a sound is common in England as well as the United States, and can be learned by most people without affectation, whereas a complete shift from the nasal short *a* to the Italian *a* usually cannot. The phonetician will cry out that this is a cowardly compromise; but the stage director's business is to avoid distraction, not to make or shape the language.

13. Encourage a general cleaning up of unaccented syllables—not, however, an artificial precision in the vowel sounds. Unaccented vowels are bound to weaken and become more or less obscure, as in "Trent(o)n," "cap(a)ble," or "c(o)mplete." The obscure vowel is usually a sound between English short *u* (as in "shut") and French *eu* (as in "*peu*"),[1] and it is usually brief in duration; sometimes the vowel practically disappears. In some cases the short *i* sound (as in "it") can be appropriately employed in the unaccented syllables; and

[1] The phonetic symbol is [ə].

as far as possible this should be encouraged, because the short *i* is a clean-cut sound which carries well in the theatre, even when spoken very quickly. It is much less apt to sound muddy than the obscure vowel, and less apt to induce poor enunciation of adjacent sounds. Thus "po-im" is better than "powum" (for "poem"), and "pro-ibition" is better than "prowubition" (for "prohibition"); while "Trentin," "captin," "valit" (for "Trenton," "captain," "valet") are often heard from careful speakers. More important than the exact shade of vowel sound in unaccented syllables is the clear enunciation of the consonants.

14. Encourage a reasonable modification, rather than an abrupt dropping, of untrilled final *r* on the part of those individuals who say "mother-r-r," "father-r-r," "dear-r-r." The sound is undoubtedly ugly when given full value, being little more than a growl, but it is so widely prevalent in this country that its complete elimination, even on the professional stage, is impracticable. Many persons who fully appreciate its ugliness cannot drop it suddenly from their speech without seeming affected and unconvincing. Moreover, the complete dropping of final *r* is just as certainly a dialectal extreme as is the exaggeration of final *r*,[1] and has no greater sanction in usage—less sanction, in fact, from a numerical standpoint, for comparatively few people, even in England, eliminate the sound as completely as certain teachers of elocution would have us do. If the director can get his actors to bring the *r* up out of the throat, shorten it, and limit it

[1] Dion Boucicault, speaking in England in 1882, said: "There is no more splendid letter in the whole alphabet than the letter *r*. Some people pronounce it like *w*. That is a misfortune that they cannot help. But the majority of you, and I dare say a great number of you who are now laughing at those who pronounce it like *w* do not pronounce it at all. Some of you pronounce it as if it was an *h*, and when you are speaking of the Egyptian war you say 'the Egyptian wah!' and you say 'that is rathah!' when you mean 'rather', and 'mothah' when you mean 'mother'; whereas there are no such words in the English language."

to a slight curl at the end of a clear vowel he will be doing very well indeed.

These suggestions may be useful, but they are no substitute for good taste and good scholarship on the part of the director. Any director who means business will want to know something more about standards of pronunciation than is here set down; for references on the subject he should consult the Bibliography at the end of the book.

DIALECT PLAYS

Plays in local or foreign dialect involve serious difficulties for inexperienced players. As a rule, the less an actor knows about a dialect the thicker he tries to lay it on—often with distressing results. A certain degree of exaggeration is proper and necessary in the theatre, but on the other hand nothing is more painful to the audience than an obvious straining for effect. The more extreme dialects are usually easier to render than the subtler ones; they sound so strange to the ear anyhow that inaccuracies pass unnoticed. Similarly the dialects of comic or burlesque characters are ordinarily less troublesome than those of serious characters, for exaggeration is expected in burlesque, and laughter disarms criticism. It is the rendition of slight dialectal shadings in serious plays that presents the most difficult problem.

Many of the plays produced in this country are English in subject matter and authorship, and the question naturally arises whether such plays should be rendered in full English dialect. When a play is universal in theme and character, and the choice of English names and an English setting seems arbitrary or accidental, it is often advisable to ignore the dialect and to render the play as if it were American; occasionally it is possible to change the locale and the names

321

and to omit all English allusions. When, however, a significant element of plot, theme, or character is essentially English, some suggestion of an English dialect is almost imperative if the point is not to be lost. No indication of dialect appears, of course, in the text—except in the case of rural, or cockney, or other type characters—and so must be supplied by the director or the actor.

In training a group of American actors to do an English play the first point is to suppress, more rigorously than usual, any Americanisms of speech—especially the excessive final *r*, the extremely nasal short *a*, the Western *ah* for *aw*, and the neglect of medial *t*. The second point is to introduce the English values of long and short *o;* the long *o* is almost a diphthong consisting of short *e* (as in "get") followed by *oo* (as in "soon"), and the short *o* is a short *aw* ("not" being simply a quicker "nought"). The third point is to work for a suggestion of the English sentence tune, which makes use of more rising inflections and fewer falling ones than the American. It is seldom wise to attempt any general changes beyond these three, though many individual words or phrases will require attention as they occur. The purpose is always to suggest rather than to portray, and if there is no marked inconsistency to create distraction a very little positive suggestion will be sufficient. The director should never suppose that a complete representation of English speech as actually spoken in England is desirable before an American audience. Even English companies playing in America do not give us that; they find some modification almost necessary for intelligibility and for avoidance of distraction.

Plays in Irish dialect involve a somewhat less troublesome problem, especially the plays of Synge, Yeats, and their followers. The tendency of the amateur actor in an Irish part is, of course, to assume the Irish brogue of the comic strip or the vaudeville stage, and this tendency must be suppressed. Some slight modification of long and short *a*, a slight suggestion of *th* on medial *t*, and an occasional tongue trill on *r* may be permitted, but again it is the sentence tune that is most important. Synge, especially, catches the flow of Gaelic rhythm in English words; the sentences are long and loose, with many participial constructions and many appended clauses. For this dialect the actor must have plenty of reserve breath, and must conquer the urge to hurry and to skimp the enunciation. But the beauty of the language at its best is a great incentive to mastery, and with sufficient practice amateurs often do very well with it.

German and Yiddish dialects are among the easiest for most amateurs. The substitution of *v* for *w*, and of *s* for *z*, and the pronunciation of *th* as *d* or *t* are the changes most needed. There is less modification of sentence tune in these dialects than in English or Irish, but a little more difference in manner. For the German a more explosive utterance is usually desirable, together with a freer use of guttural sounds. For the Yiddish more gesture is required, together with a husky or slightly nasal tone. The chief danger in these dialects, as in the Irish, is that of presenting vaudeville types instead of real people.

A French accent is usually suggested by an equalization of syllabic stress, and by a squeezed quality of tone accompanied by freer use of the lips (but not the jaws). The squeezing changes some of the vowel qualities, especially that of short *i* which becomes *ee*. Sometimes a slight suggestion of lisp (*th* for *s*) is helpful, though the *th* sound itself tends to become *t* or *d*.

Plays written in some of the local dialects of this country are more difficult than those involving foreign accents—except, of course, for actors native to the districts represented.

This is partly because dialectal differences within our own country are apt to seem more strange and less convincing to most of us than those that are frankly exotic. We see nothing astonishing in the fact that a foreigner speaks a dialect unlike our own, but when an American does so we are a little inclined to suspect exaggeration.

Many of the best American plays written in recent years depend so much upon local color as to require careful study of dialect. The Carolina Folk Plays and others of their type use both the negroid dialect of the South and the modified Elizabethan dialect of the mountain whites. The plays of Eugene O'Neill involve a number of dialects, including those of the negro, the Bowery rough-neck, the 'longshoreman, the tramp sailor and the Yankee farmer. Other writers have found their material in the Ozarks, in Texas, in the corn belt, or on the prairies. Unfortunately, some of the most important writers are peculiarly amateurish in representing dialect on paper; no department of the dramatist's art requires more professional skill than this. The amateur actor can hardly be expected to deliver lines convincingly when they are not written convincingly; yet the director who is to produce modern plays—those of O'Neill for instance—must undertake to teach his actors to do just that thing. If he does not know the dialects thoroughly himself he is almost sure to fail.

How shall he go about studying them? A few of the most characteristic local pronunciations have already been mentioned in this chapter, but a complete catalogue of dialectal variants would occupy a large dictionary. Actual sojourn in the region to be represented, with intelligent observation and analysis of the local speech habits, is obviously the best method of study. Often it is not possible, and the director must depend upon the printed page. Dialect dictionaries sometimes help, as do certain books and articles by trained philologists or phoneticians. For background reading, novels are generally more helpful than plays; Mark Twain, Bret Harte, George W. Cable, Booth Tarkington, Joseph C. Lincoln, John Fox, Jr., Gene Stratton Porter, Harold Bell Wright, Winston Churchill, Jack London, Zane Grey, and a score of others—like Dickens and Hardy in England—have been far more successful in conveying dialect to the reader than have most of the dramatists.

The director should strive to pick out the most suggestive features of each dialect, but should be careful not to let his actors exaggerate them unduly. At the same time he should check the probable tendency of each actor to revert to his own native speech between times; nothing is more certain to render the dialect unconvincing than excessive contrast between the points selected for emphasis and the rest of the language.

Dialect plays add considerably to the director's task, and so should be attempted only when plenty of time is available for study.

CHAPTER XVI

ORGANIZATION BACK STAGE

MORE amateur performances are ruined by bad management than by bad acting. Most of the calamities depicted in George Kelly's amusing satire on amateur theatricals, *The Torch Bearers*, are the result, not of lack of talent, but of managerial incompetence. Good management does not in itself make a play; there must be good acting too. But good management helps to make good acting. The sense of security that an actor feels when he knows that all the properties are in place, that everybody will make his entrance on time, that the prompter is awake and alert, and that the curtain will come down when it is supposed to come down, is the best possible cure for stage fright and a very real aid to freedom of interpretation. The director of an amateur production should see that such conditions obtain, even at the cost of some time and energy on his part.

THE DIRECTOR AS EXECUTIVE

A successful executive back stage, as elsewhere, is something more than a hustler and an enthusiast. He is also a technician, a diplomat, and an organizer.

As a technician he must know everything about the theatre; about the mechanical, electrical and scenic equipment of theatres; about the organization of companies and of stage crews; about methods of conducting rehearsals; about union rules, and underwriters' rules, and theatre licensing systems; about back-stage traditions and customs; in short, about

326

everything pertaining to the whole business of production, professional as well as amateur.

As a diplomat he must know human nature, and be able to exercise tact in the handling of actors and stage crew. Knowledge of human nature is one of the most difficult things in the world to acquire, and a great deal of nonsense has been written about it. The "efficiency expert" type of executive who can line up a row of candidates for a position and pick out the right one at a glance by the color of his eyes or the shape of his chin is either a great liar or a great fool. Snap judgement is of no use to the stage director. The kind of understanding of human nature he needs begins with humility and patience. It rests upon a sense of reciprocity, an ability to grasp the other fellow's point of view, and a willingness to study people carefully. With such an equipment the director can face difficult situations with some chance of lasting success.

But it is as an organizer that the director as executive meets his severest test. Organization is the act of bringing things into organic, or functional, relationship; of uniting otherwise independent parts into a coöperative whole. The organizing type of mind is the type which is always hunting out relationships, seeking to discern order in apparent chaos, demanding not only rules but reasons for them. Such a mind is often spoken of as analytic; but it is more. It is both anaytic and synthetic; it tears down only that it may learn to build up. It is logical, but not theoretical; it is imaginative, but not visionary. It is capable of evolving new schemes of relationship, but only out of an understanding of the old; it does not ignore its materials or its limitations. It is surely in some fashion methodical; yet method alone is not organization. One may be methodical without intellectual curiosity or constructive enthusiasm, and live out his life as a butler or bookkeeper or telephone operator. To the organizing mind method is but a means to satisfy an all-powerful passion to construct.

The director cannot, of course, provide himself with a new mind; but he can cultivate some of the habits of thought which are conducive to organizing ability. Any study which helps to develop curiosity, any hobby that calls for constant rearrangement, classification and coördination of elements, will be found beneficial.

There are two quite opposite plans of organization, and two quite opposite types of executives, one of which might be called the egocentric, and the other the mechanistic. The egocentric executive builds an organization about himself; a highly unified, smooth-working machine, which, however, needs his brain to run it. Gordon Craig's ideal director would be of this type; it is inconceivable that the masterpiece of such an artist could go on tour without him. The mechanistic type of executive seeks to build up a system that will function automatically, and will be independent of any individual, even himself. The average professional director has to be of this type, for circumstances do not permit him to remain with the play after the run begins. The amateur director may choose either method, or he may compromise. Necessity often compels him to build about himself for the sake of insuring a good performance, the inexperience of his assistants making any other course an invitation to disaster. But the wise director who values his own time and health will seek, at least gradually, to establish an organization which will not be too dependent upon his personal presence.

PROFESSIONAL ORGANIZATION

Professional organization is not by any means uniform, especially in regard to the duties and powers of the stage director. In some instances the director is the producing manager or proprietor himself; in others he is the author of the play; in others he is the principal actor or star, and in still others he is two or three of these things at once. More often—in New York, at least—he is a hired specialist with such powers and responsibilities as the producing manager may have delegated to him.

The producing manager who directs his own productions is of course a very busy man, bearing as he does the financial and executive worries of the enterprise as well as the artistic. But he has certain advantages. Since all persons concerned in the production are his employes he can count upon a maximum of subordination and of unified effort, and a minimum of jealousy and friction. The stage attracts many temperamental persons, and there is no other method so efficacious for holding them in check as a firm grip on the purse strings. If the manager is at once a true artist and a sound business man he can perhaps harmonize the artistic and business interests of the enterprise with the least detriment to either; and though the worries of the manager may interfere with the concentration of the artist, there is compensation in the healthy freedom and the no less healthy restraint that the artist feels when he is gambling with his own money.

The producer-director is as old as the history of the theatre. So likewise is the actor-director. Both have their ancestors not only in Garrick and Shakespeare, but in the poet-actor-producers of ancient Greece.

The actor-director works under an obvious disadvantage— especially when he plays a major part. If he gives his attention to the directing he is apt to neglect his part; if he concentrates on his part he cannot maintain the broad perspective and sense of detachment that a director ought to have.

But the disadvantage is not insuperable, and sometimes the actor who has the experience, the versatility and the scholarship to head a repertory company has also the qualifications of a good director. When this is the case an understudy may be employed to act the leading part at rehearsals. This does not relieve the actor-manager of the burden of learning his part, but it does enable him to give proper attention to the directing; and many actor-managers have used the method successfully.

Most of the plays produced in the modern commercial theatre, especially in New York, are staged by hired directors who are more or less free lances. Some of them are actors or ex-actors who happen to be unemployed; some are producing managers who have been unsuccessful in their own ventures; some are playwrights or play-doctors who have turned to directing for practical experience or for economic reasons; some are ex-amateurs who have drifted into professional production on the crest of some little theatre movement; some are scenic artists; some are imported European *régisseurs;* and some—perhaps the majority—are former stage managers. In the latter group are some of the worst and some of the best.

The stage manager is the responsible official back stage during the run of the play; he is the representative of the producing manager, and both the company and the stage crew are responsible to him. Until comparatively recent years it was customary for the stage manager to handle the routine work of directing, larger questions of interpretation being left for decision to the producing manager, leading actor, or visiting star. In the days when an oratorical manner of production was in vogue and classical or standard plays the rule, there was less need for close-knit direction than at present; the work of the actors was more largely individual, and where team work was called for it tended to follow established tradition. There were no hired directors in the modern sense, and the stage managers had to be more capable as directors than they do today. Under the old repertory system these men received an excellent training, and the few who survive are among our best directors.

Under modern conditions, however, the stage manager is subordinate to the director, and is sometimes a technical man rather than an artist. Some of the younger theatre-trained stage managers who have become directors are decidedy lacking in background. They are responsible, in some measure, for the kind of mechanistic performances so often seen in the commercial theatre. As artists they are generally inferior both to the old stagers and to the better educated directors drawn from the little theatres, universities, and technical schools, and from abroad.

When a special director is hired for a production, his duties and powers are fairly well defined. It is his business to stage the play. He seldom chooses the cast or designs the settings, though he may be called into consultation on both points. Sometimes he is not even hired until after the cast is chosen. He is given the script with certain stipulations as to the manner of production; he lays out the stage movements and proceeds to conduct the actual rehearsals; and his work ends with the final rehearsal or with the first performance. The stage manager acts as his assistant, holds the script, marks it with notes and corrections, works out the technical problems, and assumes the entire responsibility when performances begin. Often the director has the assistance of the author and the producing manager, the amount and value of such assistance depending of course upon the persons. Sometimes his chief duty is that of a pacifier, a sort of buffer between the producer and the author, or between the author and the star. For his services, lasting for from two to ten weeks, he receives a single fee, usually agreed upon in advance.

The whole system in the commercial theatre is temporary and kaleidoscopic. The production of a play is a speculation, and nobody concerned knows how long the associations formed will last. The director is, as a rule, the first to go. If the play runs a while on Broadway and then goes on the road some of the actors drop out; the younger ones especially decline to leave New York. As soon as the road tour is ended the whole organization breaks up. Hardly one-tenth of the associations formed last for a year.

The strength and the weakness of this system are evident. It makes, of course, for standardization, quantity production, and interchangeable parts. The result is a kind of all-round practical working efficiency such as is observable in cheap watches or cheap automobiles; they go, and go surprisingly well; but they are not works of art. There is nothing hand-made or custom-built about them. Plays produced under the commercial system have a certain professional snap and precision, an atmosphere of reliability which suggests that everybody concerned knows his job. Everybody *has* to know his job, or the system would break down completely; its very life depends upon the maintenance of uniformity and efficiency. But uniformity and efficiency alone do not make great art.

REPERTORY ORGANIZATION

The artistic aspects of repertory have already been sufficiently discussed. In the matter of organization it is worth noting that the elements of leisure and permanency that make for good acting also make for efficiency back stage.

Many of the European theatres are subsidized. Nearly all are permanent institutions. The *régisseur* is usually an all-round man—an artist, a manager, and a teacher. He surrounds himself with a permanent staff of capable assistants, assembles a permanent company, a permanent repertory of plays, and even a permanent stage crew. As a rule he does not rent or purchase scenery or costumes; he maintains a complete stock of equipment, and when new equipment is needed he has it designed and constructed by his own staff. Sometimes—as in the Moscow Art Theatre—he builds up as an adjunct to the parent theatre a studio theatre or school, in which the beginners in all departments can gain preliminary experience under the guidance of veterans.

There is a tendency in this country to over-rate the European director. With one or two conspicuous exceptions he is probably no better than the American, and when he tries to produce an American play he is often stupid. But he has the advantage of a far better system.

Various phases of the European system have been imitated in this country, especially in the semi-professional little theatres and professional schools. The Neighborhood Playhouse developed a repertory system and maintained it successfully for a time. But most of our attempts to establish strictly professional repertory theatres have been unsuccessful, even when subsidized, and we have no one theatre doing for the drama what the Metropolitan Opera Company or the Chicago Civic Opera does for opera. We have stock companies in many cities, but these are for the most part very different from repertory companies. They are devoted to the somewhat hasty production of a succession of plays, most of them just released for stock production after running themselves out in the larger cities; these are played, as a rule, for one or two weeks, and then shelved, and so rapid is the process that there is no time for careful study or careful direction. All too frequently the members of such companies are either young learners or old failures. Some of the so-called stock companies of an earlier period, however, were real repertory companies, playing chiefly standard plays, reviving them frequently, and adding to the repertory only now and then after a reasonable period of rehearsal. Such companies as those of Daly and Palmer in New York in the eighties, or the Arch Street Theatre Company in Philadelphia in the fifties and sixties, or the travelling companies of Booth and Barrett, were, in the opinion of many old theatre-goers, almost as steady and finished as the Moscow Art Theatre Company. In the last few decades the tradition of repertory has been kept half alive by the Shakespearean companies of Mansfield, Sothern and Marlowe, Mantell, Forbes-Robertson, Hampden, and others; but most of these have been travelling companies with no permanent theatre behind them and no permanent organization. Whether a permanently organized repertory theatre on the European basis is possible in America under present economic and industrial conditions is problematical, especially in New York; but in recent years attempts to found such a theatre have been growing more and more numerous.

AMATEUR ORGANIZATION

The amateur or little theatre director can learn much about organization from the repertory system, as well as from the Broadway system. If he wishes to achieve the highest in artistic sincerity, if he seeks spirituality rather than mere efficiency, he will do well to study carefully the organization of such a theatre as the Moscow Art Theatre. From it he may learn the importance of stability and permanence, of a close personal relationship among the players, of harmony on and off the stage, of careful, intelligent study and long, patient rehearsal, and of complete subordination of the individual to the artistic purpose of the group. If he is direct-ing amateurs he may be unable to realize all of these things in their entirety; there will be limits to the amount of time he can demand of his players, and other interests on their minds; there will be petty jealousies to be suppressed and triflers to be weeded out; and there will be constant changes of per-sonnel, especially if the group is a school or college group. But there is no rea on why he should not preserve the ideals, at least, and strive to approximate them as closely as circum-stances permit. If he cannot keep the same people together year after year he can at least try to keep the same spirit; he can discourage selfishness and jealousy, and emphasize the group idea, insisting that even beginners shall think of the whole play rather than their own parts; and he can conduct rehearsals with the idea of doing each play thoroughly and well. In this way he may be able to keep alive an *esprit de corps* very much like that of a famous regiment which, al-though it may have been shot to pieces in every war for a hundred years, is somehow still the same regiment.

FIXATION OF RESPONSIBILITY

The division, delegation, and fixation of responsibility is the most essential part of organization back stage, and the part most commonly neglected by amateurs. Amateurs often feel that because play production is a communal activity it should be communistic; that it should be run as a sort of inspired democracy, every member contributing according to his ability and sharing equally in the joys and benefits derived. So far as the central essence of this feeling goes, nothing could be finer; out of a truly coöperative spirit grows the best dramatic art. But in art, as in politics, democracy, to be successful, must be organized; there must be not only a division of labor, but some subordination and a very definite fixation of responsibility.

In amateur organizations there is too much loose committee work and not enough individual responsibility. The matter of properties, for example, is often entrusted to a "property committee." The committee meets, and tries to make up a list of properties required; certain members of the committee promise to furnish needed articles, somebody volunteers his automobile to haul them, and everything looks very promising. But if the director is foolish enough to wait until the night of the dress rehearsal or of the first performance, as so many do, he may find that certain articles are missing.

"Where is the sofa?" he inquires of the chairman of the property committee.

"Why, I don't know. I thought Smith was getting that."

Smith is found, but he has an alibi. "Why no," he says, "I was going to bring mine, but Jones said he had one that was more suitable, so I left it to him. Where's Jones?"

Jones, it turns out, has been called away on a business trip. Mrs. Jones is reached by telephone, and agrees to lend the sofa if some one will come and get it. Smith goes with his automobile, but the sofa is too big, and the local expressman cannot be found. The director comes to the rescue by persuading a friend in the ice business to send one of his ice wagons to haul the sofa, and the day is saved: Saved, that is, so far as the sofa is concerned, but in the excitement the telephone bell is quite forgotten, and remains forgotten until it is supposed to ring in the middle of the second act. It doesn't ring, and there is a case of suspended animation, until the bright young hero, stepping into the breach, says, insincerely, "Wasn't that the telephone bell?" While the audience titters he proceeds to answer the imaginary summons, and just after he gets the telephone off the hook a zealous committeeman back stage finds the bell and sets it off with a whang!

This is not exaggeration. Worse things than these occur in amateur theatricals, and occur so often that they have come to be regarded by some people as inevitable. But they are not inevitable. They do not grow out of amateur organization but out of *bad* organization; and bad organization can occur on the professional stage as well as the amateur. In one performance of the *Greenwich Village Follies* at a theatre in Philadelphia I saw no less than five major "breaks"; in one instance the curtain was run up with the scene half set and the stage carpenter in a very undignified position at stage center. The same thing occurred at the same theatre during a performance of Balieff's *Chauve Souris*. Even the Moscow Art Theatre is not immune—on tour, at least. In a performance of *Tsar Fyodor* in Philadelphia the back stage lights were so arranged as to throw on the rear wall of the Tsar's palace a huge shadow of a stage hand manipulating a bunch light. I once saw a professional stage manager take half an hour to place properties for the first act of *The Admirable Crichton* because he did it by guesswork, memory, and head-scratching, when he could have done it in ten minutes with a regular property-plot.

These things are exceptional, of course. Usually the professional performance is smoother and surer than the amateur, not because it is professional but because it is better organized; and the chief difference is in fixation of responsibility.

THE PRODUCTION STAFF

Instead of a group of irresponsible committees the director should surround himself with a firmly organized production staff.

The head of the production staff is the stage manager, and a reliable stage manager is the greatest possible help to the director. The stage manager takes entire charge of the production subject to the director's orders. He organizes the stage crew, arranges for the making or hiring of scenery, properties and costumes, summons the actors to rehearsal, sees that they are called for their cues, holds and marks the prompt-book, and in every way relieves the director of executive detail. He bears the same relation to the director that the executive officer bears to the captain on a ship or in the army, and the efficiency of the system is well attested by the fact that it has been retained in the armies and navies of the world. The best thing a director can do for his organization is to train and develop a good stage manager.

The stage manager, in turn, will require one or more assistants, the number depending upon the degree of elaboration in equipment and production. In an organization that is necessarily subject to constant change of personnel, as in a school or college, the assistants should be definitely trained to succeed the stage manager in order of seniority. Each assistant should have some one part of the work of production delegated to him, and should be directly responsible to the stage manager for its efficient execution. He should be given credit in the program for his particular contribution.

When an organization designs and builds its own equipment the production staff must, of course, be fairly large. There must be someone to design the scenery, a stage carpenter to build it; and a property man to make the properties. There must be someone to design the costumes, and a master (or mistress) of wardrobe to care for them, and to be responsible for having new ones made. There must be a technician to supervise the stage lighting, and a musical director to arrange the incidental music. Each of these officials may need one or more assistants, and in elaborate productions the stage manager himself will need an assistant not otherwise engaged to divide responsibility with him and to act as prompter. The actual stage crew may vary in size with the needs of the production, but will always include a stage carpenter, a property man, and an electrician, with as many assistants as are needed.

If the organization is strictly amateur, playing at all times in its own theatre or club-house, these various duties may be combined or doubled up in any way that seems to fit the personnel. But if the organization wishes to articulate at any time with the commercial theatre, even to the extent of hiring a licensed theatre for a single performance, the division of labor should be as nearly like that of the professional stage crew as possible; otherwise there may be a disastrous conflict with union rules.

UNIONIZED STAGE CREWS

The matter of union rules, and of iron-clad division of labor, is a serious problem in the commercial theatre, and no amateur stage manager or director who expects to come in contact with that theatre in any way can afford to be ignorant of the situation.

In most cities of the United States the stage hands are thoroughly unionized, and entirely committed to the principle of the closed shop. In each theatre there are three so-called "heads of departments," the stage carpenter, the stage electrician, and the property man. In some cities the law requires that the first two of these shall be licensed artisans. The heads of the departments are members of the union, and will not work with non-union help; they dictate to the stage manager how many assistants they are to have for each play, and the union backs up their demand. The electrician uses as many assistants as in his judgment are necessary to handle the various lights placed about the stage without compelling him to leave the switchboard himself. The general rule is a man for every light. The property man engages enough "clearers," as his assistants are called, to carry off all the movable properties of one act and carry on those of the next simultaneously; he seldom carries anything himself, though he does design and make properties, and sometimes condescends to manipulate back-stage effects which he is unwilling to trust to persons of inferior intellect. Between acts he bosses the clearers, and flourishes a hammer, with which he nails rickety objects in place. The stage carpenter is in charge of the actual settings, that is to say the walls and ceilings, the flats, wings, drops, and curtains. He has two classes of assistants, the "flymen," who remain in the fly gallery above the stage to raise and lower such parts of the set as are hung on the "lines" and to manipulate the curtain or curtains; and the "grips," who handle the pieces of scenery upon the stage floor. A grip to every flat is not an uncommon rule in elaborate productions where quick changes are necessary; and union flymen are never asked to strain themselves by lifting too much weight single-handed. The stage carpenter is usually regarded as the general head of the entire crew, and in some cities is held responsible under his license for all mechanical arrangements back stage. Like the property man he often carries a hammer, but his chief symbol of office is a long pole, with which he clears the drops or ceilings as they are lowered by the flymen upon the flats or wings.

The three classes of labor performed by these three divisions of the crew are very sharply defined. The carpenter and his crew handle only the actual settings. The property men handle all movable objects, including "hand props," furniture, bric-a-brac, and even such heavy set pieces as fireplaces, rocks or trees; they also provide all back-stage effects, except electrical ones. The electricians handle only electrical effects. No self-respecting grip would so much as lay a finger on a table or chair, much less move it; and if a clearer were to remove the electric bulb from a fireplace he would be liable to a heavy fine or expulsion from the union.

The entire stage crew, under the direction of its department heads, takes orders from the stage manager, or from the assistant stage manager if there is one. The stage manager is not a union man; he represents the employer—in effect, *is* the employer. Union rules cannot prevent the stage manager or his assistants from moving or adjusting or otherwise handling articles on the stage, so long as sufficient stage hands are employed and paid, but let it once appear that the stage manager is employing a number of assistants and doing bodily work himself by way of economy, or by way of a subterfuge to replace union with non-union help, and there is likely to be a strike on the spot.

The plan of organization is in general not unlike that in a closed-shop factory. The head of a department is analogous to the foreman of a gang of laborers; he is a union man, but is classed a little above the rest, and receives a little more pay. The stage carpenter is in some instances analogous to a head foreman. The stage manager, however, is equivalent to a factory superintendent; he is an employe, but a salaried employe rather than a wage earner. The director, in the modern scheme of organization, is a little like the engineer in industry—a professional expert, standing a little apart from the direct organization, but having certain powers over it.

When an elaborate production goes on tour, the producing manager often finds it advisable to send the heads of departments along with it, and sometimes even the complete crew. The handling of intricate scenery, and especially of lighting effects, requires practice, and it is not always safe to depend upon the house crew in a road theatre. In such cases the company crew and the house crew work together, the men taking orders from their own heads, and the house heads taking orders from the company heads. The house electrician always runs the house switchboard; the company electrician may stand by him and tell him what to do. Some producers provide portable switchboards to travel with the production; these may be handled by the company crew. It goes without saying that the company crew must be unionized; otherwise the house crew would not work with them. As it is, there is sometimes much jealousy, especially if the company crew is large and it appears that local hands are being kept out of employment. Local unions often demand the employment of a full crew by the house, even if the company crew is large enough to handle the entire production. So serious is the problem that managers who can afford it occasionally arrange to have the full house crew paid to sit around and do nothing while the company crew, familiar with the production, does all the work. Naturally, this is an expensive luxury.

The stage hands' unions are of course affiliated with the American Federation of Labor, as are the musicians' unions and the Actors' Equity Association. The musicians, like the stage hands, insist upon a closed shop; and these two groups support each other. The employment of a non-union orchestra, or even of an amateur orchestra, may therefore result in the stage hands going out on strike just when the play is about to open; conversely the orchestra may refuse to serve if it discovers that no union stage crew is employed. A hired orchestra composed of union musicians will sometimes accept engagements to play at strictly amateur affairs outside the regular theatres; but if a delegate of the stage hands' union comes to them and says, "Look here, these people are handling a lot of scenery and we have a lot of men out of work. We are going to make them hire a union crew, and it's up to you fellows to back us up," the orchestra is likely to quit at the most inconvenient moment with an ultimatum to the management demanding the hiring of a union crew. In some cities the stage hands will not touch scenery that is hauled to the theatre by non-union expressmen; and in some instances have declined to handle scenery not built by union labor.

The attitude of the unions officially, and of the men personally, is not generally unfriendly to amateurs, but here and there will be found a local union leader who is not above holding them up for whatever he can get out of them. I know, for I have been held up myself. I was once compelled by a union leader to use eleven paid stage hands, in addition to the three heads of departments, to work a theatre that I can handle, and have handled, with a crew of five or six college students. In the light of such possibilities the amateur director with executive responsibilities must be constantly on his guard. He will find it expedient to make all his arrangements and contracts some time ahead, and to get them all down in writing.

The Actors' Equity Association did not at first stand for a closed shop, or for a great deal of active coöperation with the other unions; but in 1924, it went upon a closed shop basis. The attitude of Equity, however, has been, and probably will be, friendly to honest amateur effort. The members of Equity are professional people, some of whom at least have a profound distaste for trades-union methods, and accept such methods only because they have been forced to do so by the conscienceless behavior of a few powerful managers. They have nothing against the amateur, and less against the student player in school or college. They very naturally object when a commercial manager employs too many amateurs as "extras" while Equity members are out of employment, especially if they have reason to think he is doing so rather to save money than to provide deserving students with experience. But they do not object to the occasional employment of non-union extras, nor to the occasional association of professional actors as guest players with semi-professional or amateur companies. In other words they do not object to the professional amateur, but do object to the non-union professional. As for the rival association, the Actors' Fidelity League, it is not affiliated with the American Federation of Labor, and is not a closed shop organization.

In respect to the attitude of the unions, conditions vary somewhat in different parts of the country, and the director will do well to familiarize himself with those of his own locality.

BUILDING AND FIRE LAWS

Besides the union rules the director should know the rules of the local fire marshal, the underwriters, and the city police, and perhaps the building laws. In many cities amateur clubs and playhouses are not licensed, and not under control of the fire marshal. The buildings are of course subject to the building laws, and can only be insured under the rules of the underwriters. There are usually some restrictions regarding seating capacity, and there is usually a rule requiring a four-foot aisle, and perhaps a rule requiring exit lights. But generally speaking the amateur club in its own clubhouse can do about as it pleases.

The commercial theatre, however, is nearly always subject to license, and under strict inspection. The construction and arrangement must be approved by the building inspectors, underwriters, and fire marshal. The safety appliances must be tested before each performance, and in some cities a fireman is stationed behind the scenes at every performance. Smoking is usually prohibited except in special smoking rooms of fire-proof construction, or when necessary on the stage to portray character, and in the latter case the actor is sometimes required to report to the fireman in the wings before going on. All exit doors must be kept unlocked. Scenery must be fire-proof; and many an amateur company has had artistic settings spoiled by a hasty last-minute application of chemicals.

The fire-proofing of scenery is a troublesome problem, especially in the case of curtain settings. Canvas flats can be fire-proofed from the back (preferably before painting) by spraying with a saturated solution of alum, and the process has little effect upon their appearance; but curtains and draperies tend to stiffen up when sprayed, and sometimes to show stains or changes of color. When expensive draperies are to be fire-proofed it is a good plan to consult a textile chemist, who will know the best method of treating the particular fabric. In renting scenery it is always wise to make sure that it has been fire-proofed. It is never wise to neglect the fire-proofing or let it go till the last minute. The fire marshal has a very effective method of testing the scenery: he holds a match to it. If it is not properly fire-proofed the asbestos curtain does not rise, and the audience goes home.

As a rule the fire marshal requires that the scene be struck between performances and a fire light left burning at stage center so that a patrolman on the street can see right through the theatre to the back of the stage. Asbestos fire curtains are almost always required; they must be up when the house is empty, but down when the audience is admitted and until they leave, except during the actual performance; in some cities they must be down between acts. Exits, both in front and back stage, must be kept clear, and over-crowding is prohibited; in some theatres the sale of standing room is not permitted.

For the non-enforcement of these and other rules heavy fines are provided; and amateurs playing in a licensed theatre are held responsible for observing them on the same basis as professionals.

SCENE, LIGHT, AND PROPERTY PLOTS

In planning the work of the stage crew it is usual to employ written outlines or lists known as "plots." The stage carpenter gets a "scene plot," which shows, by acts and scenes, how the stage is to be set; often it includes sketches or diagrams, as well as lists of the needed items. The property man gets a "property plot," listing both the "stage props" (properties to be placed upon the stage by the property men) and the "hand props" (properties to be furnished to the actors who carry them on), also by acts and scenes. In some modern realistic plays the property plot reads like the catalogue of a mail order house. The electrician gets a "lighting plot" stating clearly how the "foots," "borders," and "pros" (proscenium or side lights) are to be set for each scene; where the bunch lights, flood lights, and spot lights are to be placed; and how all those lights are to be manipulated if changes are called for during the scene.

Light changes, quick shifts of scenery or properties, off-stage and trick effects are governed by "cues" in the lines of the play, and these cues should always be entered on the proper plots. Difficult effects, of course, should always be well rehearsed.

For purposes of checking up, the stage manager should keep a copy of each plot. In amateur productions it is a wise plan for the director to keep an extra copy himself, so that he can go quietly about just before the first performance and check up. Any extra trouble that this may give him will be more than compensated for by his ensuing peace of mind.

Extreme care should be taken to see that every correction of a plot is entered on all copies.

Besides the plots for the three heads of departments some directors like to employ a costume plot, a make-up plot, a curtain-call plot—in short a plot for every problem of management involved. Others dislike so much rigmarole; but a certain amount of rigmarole is far better than something forgotten.

RUNNING THE PERFORMANCE

Some time before the dress rehearsal the director should see that the prompt copy is properly annotated with call warnings, curtain warnings, and all necessary warnings and cues for off-stage effects. Strictly speaking, this is the stage manager's responsibility, but unless the stage manager is a very capable and experienced person the director will do well to see to it himself. For each entrance of a character there should be a marginal note, perhaps a page in advance, reminding the prompter to "call So-and-So," and during the performance the prompter should have a "call boy" at his elbow to go after each actor in plenty of time for his entrance cue.

The call boy is an ancient and useful institution in the professional theatre, and it is a pity that amateurs do not know him better. Before the performance he goes about back stage and among the dressing rooms calling the time intervals —"Forty-five minutes!"—"Thirty minutes!"—"Fifteen minutes!"—"Ten minutes!"—"Overture!" Before each act he checks up on the actors who are supposed to be "on" for the next curtain, or ready to enter shortly after. Having seen that these actors are ready he reports back to the prompter, who thus knows when it is safe to ring up the curtain. During the act the call boy stands by the prompter so that he may be sent to call the actors as they are needed, to check up on the stage hands who are supposed to execute off-stage effects, and to do any other necessary errands for the prompter.

These are little things, but tremendously important, and commonly neglected by amateurs. If attended to at all they are usually attended to by the stage manager or the director himself, but since both of these officials have other responsibilities and either may be interrupted or called aside at any moment it is not safe for them to depend upon themselves for routine tasks. A good stage manager will keep a watchful eye on his prompter and his call boy, and a good director will keep a watchful eye on the stage manager as well; but a good call boy and a good prompter would save many an amateur performance from raggedness.

The work of the prompter is in itself an art. No one can prompt effectively unless he has attended a number of rehearsals and followed the text carefully. He must learn to know each actor's style, and to know whether he is pausing for effect or has forgotten his lines, for nothing is more annoying to the actor than to be prompted unnecessarily. He should note carefully the probable danger points, the lines on which the actor repeatedly stumbles, and should be ready to help him. Sometimes an actor prefers to have an understanding with the prompter and a method of signalling to him when he needs a prompt. In general the prompter should not be *too* helpful at rehearsals, but should plan to be infallible at the first performance. With the help of the actor on the stage and the director in the auditorium he should try out his voice in advance, to determine how best to project it to the actors at various points on the stage with the least likelihood of its being heard by the audience.

The wise director will assign every back stage task to some one else, leaving no specific duty for himself except to check up on the others. But unless his people are thoroughly experienced he will trust nobody, especially at the first performance. He will check up on the stage manager to see that the actors and crew are all present and accounted for, and that all last-minute managerial tasks have been performed. He will check up on the stage carpenter to see that the scene is properly set, on the property man to see that all properties are in place and all effects ready, and on the electrician to see that the lights are in place and that he has his cues; and he will repeat this process before each act. He will check up on the costumes and make-ups before each act, and upon the hand props which the actors are to carry. He will check up on the prompter and call boy to see that all actors are ready before the curtain is rung up; and during each act he will check up on the calls and warnings to see that nothing is missed. In all of this work he will be greatly assisted if he has before him written memoranda systematically prepared in advance. But on no account should he let his subordinates know that he is going to check them up in this way, lest they depend too much upon him.

It is needless to say that the necessity for such careful supervision varies inversely with the experience of the group. Most professional directors would regard the scheme here outlined as unnecessarily elaborate. But a little excess of care in managerial matters sometimes gives an amateur production a smoothness that is highly pleasing—even astonishing—to the audience, and elicits words of thankful praise from any newspaper critics who may, in their martyrdom, have been obliged to attend.

When amateur directors, generally, begin to realize that the obligation to good management and smooth performance is even greater upon them than upon professionals, as being the only possible compensation for their natural shortcomings and the only means of bringing out their best talents, then amateur dramatics will begin to be taken seriously by those who really love the art of the theatre and are not content with good-natured inferiority.

CHAPTER XVII

THE GENESIS OF SCENIC ART

WE HAVE now to consider what to some modern directors is the most important problem in play production: the problem of scenic investiture. In recent years
so much attention has been given to this matter, and so many
styles and movements have developed, that an adequate study
would occupy several volumes. I shall attempt merely to
summarize the problem. But for the most elementary understanding of modern scenic art some slight notion of the past
history of the theatre is necessary.

The drama is always beginning over again somewhere in
the world, and almost always in the same way: as an out-
growth of religious ceremonial. First there is a festival cele-
bration of some kind, with tribal dancing, musical or
rhythmic accompaniment, song, and spectacle, the purpose
being to honor or placate some god, or through magic
incantation to bring about good crops or success in battle.
The theatre, at first, is but an area set apart for the par-
ticipants, with the spectators standing round about. Costume and decoration are at first purely religious or magic
in significance. After a time the mimetic element begins to
creep in; there is symbolic movement in the dancing, then
direct pantomime, and finally acting. At some point in the
process the people begin to discover that the performance is
interesting in itself apart from its religious meaning, and
from that point the secular element grows rapidly and the
religious purpose is soon replaced by a more or less frankly

351

theatrical one. So often and so independently has this process recurred in different countries and different ages that we are forced to regard it as natural.

At what point in the process the playing space becomes a theatre and the decorations a setting depends upon definitions and circumstances. The modern drama is said to have begun in the religious ritual, not of a primitive tribe, but of the highly organized medieval church; and for that reason, unlike most drama, it began indoors. It used the church for its first theatre, and later the space outside the church, with the church as background. But the modern theatre, in its architectural and scenic arrangements cannot be explained in terms of this origin; it has its roots in an older theatre, and to trace its development we must go back to ancient Greece.

THE GREEK THEATRE

Greek drama originated in the ceremonial dances and choral singing in honor of Dionysus, the god of wine, who was conceived to imbue his devotees with a kind of spiritual (perhaps not unmixed with spirituous) ecstasy. For the purpose of these ceremonial dances a circular space called an *orchestra* (ὀρχήστρα, or "dancing place") was marked out on the ground at the foot of a hill. That circle was the beginning of the Greek theatre, and so of the modern theatre.

The evolution of the Dionysian festival dances into the classical drama was a matter of centuries, and little is known about it. Tragedy and comedy appear to have had separate origins, the latter growing out of ribald mummeries and street processions and only appearing in the orchestra at a later stage. The introduction of the actor, as distinct from the chorus, is generally credited to Thespis, a poet who lived at Icaria about 535 B.C. Some time in the sixth century the custom arose of holding contests and giving prizes for the best dramatic choruses, and it may have been in connection with such a contest that Thespis made his innovation. The idea of acting was probably not his invention, for there had

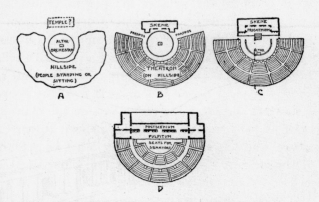

FIG. 16.—EVOLUTION OF THE GREEK AND ROMAN THEATRE

A indicates the probable beginning of the Greek theatre in the *orchestra*. *B* shows a typical theatre of pure Greek design; *C* a Greek theatre remodeled by the Romans; and *D* a typical Roman theatre.

been strolling clowns and entertainers before his time, but he seems to have been the first to see the possibilities of the mimetic element in relation to the Dionysian festival. What he did was to provide a single actor (probably himself) who, assuming several different masks in succession, engaged in dialogue with the chorus and illustrated the thought with pantomimic action, thereby achieving variety and giving the chorus an occasional rest. It was Æschylus (525-456 B.C.), the first of the great Attic dramatists, who added the second actor, and Sophocles (497-406 B.C.), the last of the great ones, who added the third. At no time in the Golden Age were more than three actors employed in the tragic drama, although by changing their masks these three represented many characters.

The orchestra in the true Greek theatre was circular; it is

so, for instance in the theatre at Epidaurus, one of the few preserved today supposedly not modified by the Romans. At first there was nothing but the orchestra, with an altar in the

FIG. 17.—A GREEK THEATRE

Conjectural sketch, showing the probable arrangement in the late fifth century. The side doors in the *paraskenia* are doubtful, and may not have appeared until much later. Note, however, that the seats unmistakably face the *orchestra* rather than the *skene*.

center, and the spectators merely stood or sat about on the hillside. Later, wooden seats were built, and the auditorium came to be known as a *theatron* (θέατρον, or "seeing place"). Later still—probably not until after the drama had reached its height—the wooden benches were replaced by stone.

The *orchestra* and the *theatron* existed for a long time before the introduction of the actor made necessary a dressing room to which he could retire to change costume. The dressing room built for the purpose was called a *skene* (σκηνή, a "hut" or "shelter"), and was at first a very simple temporary structure, placed near the orchestra circle on the side opposite the audience. Later it was made more elaborate, and its possibilities as a background for the action came to be recognized; but it was still of wood in the time of Æschylus, and perhaps as late as the time of Sophocles. After the decline of Attic poetry the theatres were greatly elaborated, and the scene buildings were built of stone and ornamented with columns. At an unknown date a second story was added, and the roof of the first story made to project in a sort of ledge known as the *proskenion;* in some scenes actors representing the gods may have spoken from this ledge, and for a long time it was believed that the Greeks used it regularly as a very high stage. The action of the great classic drama in the fifth century, however, certainly took place on the ground, either in the *orchestra* or in the space between it and the scene building; and the first use of the raised *proskenion* was doubtless comparable to that of the balcony in the Elizabethan theatre or the window representing "heaven" in the Chinese, rather than to that of a regular stage.

The typical *skene* of Sophocles' time was rectangular in shape, with small side wings or *paraskenia,* and with three doors opening on the ground level, the center one of which was the focal point of the action. There is no evidence that the Greeks ever attempted to represent scenic background in other than a roughly symbolic way, but that they did use something in the way of painted scenery at least for suggestion even Aristotle bears witness. What it was like nobody knows. In late times they made use of three-sided prisms called *periaktoi,* placed at either side of the playing space, and capable of being revolved so as to show three different painted decorations. There are enough references to change of setting in the Greek drama to indicate that they knew the use of stage properties and furniture as suggesting place; and there are many references in ancient writing to the elaborate mechanical devices of the Greek stage. These include the *eccyclema*, by which bits of indoor setting or furniture appear to have been rolled out of the scene building on a wagon or turn-table; the *exostra*, a similar device (perhaps the same one under a different name); and the *machine*, or crane, by which actors representing the gods were brought down from the roof of the *skene*. There were, in other words, many attempts in the Greek theatre to startle or impress the audience with realistic exploits, but there was never any attempt at complete representative illusion.

THE ROMAN THEATRE

In Rome the theatre was not a public religious institution as in Greece; it was an institution for entertainment. But it borrowed heavily from the Greek theatre, both in its scenic arrangements and in its drama.

Prior to the Greek influence the Romans were familiar with the entertainment provided by strolling clowns and jugglers, who performed as a rule upon improvised platform stages with the audience standing about on the ground level. To the Romans, therefore, entertainment implied a stage, and the most important modification they made in the Greek theatre when they came to adapt it to their own uses was the addition of a wide stage and the elimination of the *orchestra* as a playing space. In the later Greek theatres built or rebuilt under Roman influence a compromise plan was adopted, both stage and *orchestra* being used; but in the true Roman theatres the action was confined to the stage, and the *orchestra* used as seating space for the senators.

The typical Roman theatre was semi-circular in shape, with the stage, scene building and auditorium constructed as a single unit. The scene building was much larger than in the

Greek theatre, with massive side wings, and with an elaborate proscenium wall decorated with columns and pediments. Usually there were three doors in this wall, with two more in

FIG. 18.—A ROMAN THEATRE

Conjectural sketch. Note that the seats face more nearly toward the proscenium wall than in the Greek theatre.

the side wings, taking the place of the open passageways between *skene* and *theatron* in the Greek theatre. A sloping roof usually covered the stage, and in hot or stormy weather an awning was stretched over the audience.

There is no trustworthy evidence as to the amount of scenic decoration used by the Romans in addition to the architectural background, but it is supposed that they sometimes used painted cloths hung against the proscenium wall or in the doorways, and they may have used *periaktoi*. In some cases they used curtains to conceal the whole stage, as in the modern theatre (except that these rolled up from the bottom instead of down from the top), and this would hardly have been necessary unless the setting was to be changed. Certainly Roman writings suggest even more elaborate attempts than in the Greek theatre to startle with bits of realism, though it is likely that these involved the use of stage properties rather than true scenery. In Rome, as in Greece, there was no realistic completeness.

In late Roman times the drama degenerated, the theatre growing more elaborate as poetry declined. Intricate stage machinery and realistic spectacles like mimic sea battles, parades, and triumphs took the place of real plays; these eventually gave way to animal-baiting and gladiatorial exhibitions, and the drama practically died out.

THE MEDIEVAL THEATRE

Through the so-called dark ages there was little real drama in Europe, though the classic tradition in this and other matters was never as wholly lost as historians used to believe. There were strolling minstrels, clowns, and jugglers in ancient Rome, and it is probable that these never ceased to exist even in the darkest centuries. The idea of public entertainment in some form persisted, and

FIG. 19.—A PRIMITIVE PLATFORM STAGE

with it the idea of a rough platform stage set up in the street or public square. The simplest form of platform stage, with a curtained retiring space at the back (Figure 19) appears to have been known from the earliest times in many countries, and has doubtless been re-invented independently whenever the need has arisen.

When the religious drama came out of the churches and was taken over by the guilds the platform stage was thus already familiar, and was quickly adapted to the new purpose. The guilds elaborated it, of course. On the Continent they developed various types of booth stages, and also the long platform stage with simultaneous settings representing various localities in Biblical history from Heaven at one end to Hellmouth at the other, like the one at Valenciennes so often illustrated in books on the theatre. In England they developed the wagon stage, which could be dragged about from place to place, setting and all. Except, however, for the elaboration of stage properties and set pieces, the guild stages had very little influence upon the subsequent history of scenic art.

THE RENAISSANCE THEATRE

During the Renaissance there was a great revival of interest in all things classical, including the drama, and the architects who were called upon to design theatres naturally attempted to imitate the classical mode. They had two chief sources of inspiration; the writings of Vitruvius and the ruins of the buildings themselves. But the Roman ruins were more familiar than the Greek, and Vitruvius, a first century Roman architect, had interpreted the Greek and early Roman theatre in terms of his own age, so that both these sources of inspiration were distinctly Roman. The result was that the Renaissance theatres came to be Roman also, with one important modification; they were indoor theatres, completely roofed over, and artificially lighted.

The first Renaissance theatres were those of the Italian courts, and were often merely converted ball-rooms with temporary stages. On these stages were set up elaborate scenes in false perspective, erroneously supposed to conform to the practice of the ancients. Vitruvius had described the principles of perspective, and had attributed its invention to

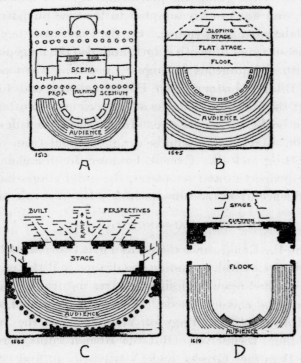

FIG. 20.—EVOLUTION OF THE RENAISSANCE THEATRE

A represents an Italian artist's misconception of the Roman theatre (Fra Giacondo, 1513). *B* shows the essential features of the perspective setting as described by Serlio, 1545. *C* shows the plan of the Olympic Theatre at Vicenza, with the perspectives built by Scamozzi. *D* shows the arrangement of the proscenium in the Farnese Theatre at Parma.

the Greeks. He had also made reference—in a somewhat obscure passage [1]—to the three types of ancient settings, the tragic, the comic, and the satyric. This passage is now believed to indicate the ancient method of decorating the *periak-*

[1] Quoted in Cheney's *Stage Decoration,* Allen's *Stage Antiquities,* and Nicoll's *Development of the Theatre.*

toi or other painted panels for suggestive symbolism, but the Renaissance architects took it to mean that whole settings in the ancient theatre were built up in artificial perspective; and with that understanding they proceeded to indulge in an orgy of perspective that swept over the theatres of Italy, England, and the whole of Europe, and dominated the history of scenic art for three centuries. An Italian architect named Serlio, writing in 1545, described the three types of ancient settings, and gave explicit directions for the arrangement of a perspective stage; his book exercised a wide influence, and was translated into several other languages, the English edition appearing in 1611.

Next to the writings of Serlio the most important influence in spreading the craze for perspective scenery was the Olympic Theatre at Vicenza, designed by Palladio, and built between 1580 and 1585. It was a direct imitation of a Roman theatre, with the auditorium made slightly wider and shallower, and entirely roofed over; it was substantially constructed, and is still in excellent condition. Palladio having died before its completion, Scamozzi, another architect, added in 1585 the famous perspective vistas which were seen and admired by visitors from many lands, and are still an object of curiosity to tourists. Behind each doorway in the proscenium wall Scamozzi set up a series of built units representing the corners of buildings on either side of a receding street, suggesting by their diminishing size a distance much greater than the actual distance to the artificial vanishing point. The central doorway was larger than the others, and the vista more elaborate, and this feature seems to have greatly impressed Inigo Jones, the English architect, who visited Vicenza in 1613. A sketch of his, found in his copy of Palladio, indicates that he thought of still further enlarging the center door into a kind of proscenium arch, with the space within the vista added to the playing space (*C*, Figure 21). Some historians regard this sketch as the progenitor of the modern proscenium arch, but there is no evidence that Jones ever built the stage so designed; on the other hand he had undoubtedly built temporary proscenium arches for his court settings as early as 1605, and similar arches had been used in the court theatres of Italy in the sixteenth century. In any consideration of the genesis of the proscenium arch it must not be forgotten that the whole framework of the Roman stage, with its roof above and its side walls, was fairly suggestive of the modern proscenium or "picture frame" stage, and that the Roman theatre, unlike the Inigo Jones project, sometimes had a curtain at the line of this framework. The first Italian theatre known to have had a regular modern proscenium arch with flush curtain was the one at Parma (*D*, Figure 20), built between 1618 and 1628.

It was in connection with the development of perspective in stage setting that the first attempts were made to provide complete representative illusion as a background for acting. It is noteworthy that such attempts were made rather in relation to opera and masque than in relation to the drama proper. Within the limits of formal perspective a high degree of realism was reached in sixteenth century Italy, and the idea prevailed that whatever lay within the proscenium frame should be as consistent and as convincing as possible. The mechanical equipment of the Renaissance theatre was far from crude, judged even by modern standards. Candles and lamps supplied the lighting, but they were skilfully used, and in large numbers. Sabbatini, writing in 1638, describes methods of placing them to light the houses and streets of the perspective, and of using them as footlights behind a low parapet at the front of the stage. He also describes colored lighting effects obtained by placing lamps with reflectors behind glass bottles filled with wine or other colored liquids. He illustrates a method of dimming candle lights by means of cylindrical covers suspended on cords and pulleys. He mentions cranes or machines for enabling characters to fly, and methods of simulating the billows of the ocean by agitating green cloths. There were provisions for changing scenes quickly, and several methods are described by Sabbatini; but the one that came finally to prevail in the eighteenth century—that of flat wings sliding in grooves— appears to have been the invention of the Englishman, Inigo Jones.

THE ELIZABETHAN THEATRE

The Elizabethan public playhouse, built in imitation of an English inn yard, has been so frequently pictured and discussed that its probable features are familiar to every casual reader. Primarily it was an open courtyard surrounded by galleries for the spectators, and the stage was a bare platform occupying one end of the yard. A curtained inner stage, two or more proscenium doors leading to the "tiring room," and a balcony above the inner stage which might on occasion be used "for Juliet" were the essential stage equipment. The importance of this type of theatre in determining the form of the drama cannot be denied; but its importance in relation to the history of theatre architecture has been somewhat exaggerated, while that of the so-called "private" or aristocratic theatre has been overlooked. It was in the temporary court theatres and university theatres that Inigo Jones did most of his experimenting, but it was in the private theatres that the results of these experiments were worked out into a tradition sufficiently permanent to carry beyond the Restoration.

Of the private theatres—which were not private at all, but

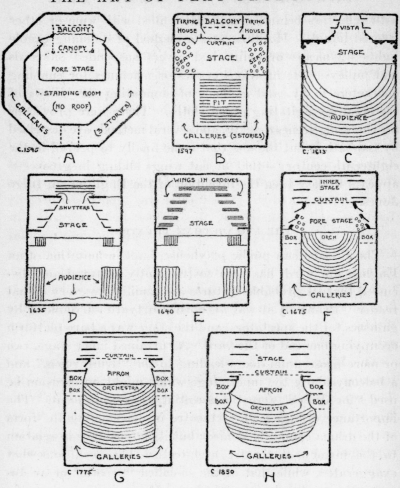

FIG. 21.—EVOLUTION OF THE ENGLISH THEATRE

A shows a conjectural plan of an outdoor public theatre during the reign of Elizabeth. *B* is a conjectural plan of the Blackfriars Theatre after the description by Professor C. W. Wallace. *C* is a plan of Inigo Jones's project for a modification of the Olympic Theatre. *D* shows the type of setting Jones was using on ball-room stages up to 1635, and *E* the radical change which he made about 1640, introducing sliding wings. *F* is a conjectural Restoration theatre plan; *G* a typical theatre plan of Garrick's time; and *H* the nineteenth century theatre plan which developed from it.

merely aristocratically high-priced—the most important was the Blackfriars of 1597, the direct ancestor of all modern English and American theatres. It was an indoor theatre, located in the priory building of the dispossessed Franciscan friars, parts of which had already been occupied by the Office of the Revels. From 1597 to 1603 it was operated under the patronage of Queen Elizabeth with a company of boy actors from the Queen's Chapel. On the accession of James I the Children of the Chapel, as they were called, lost the royal patronage, and in 1608 they were driven from the theatre by royal edict. The theatre was then taken over by Burbage and Shakespeare, the former being already the owner of the property, and for several years the most popular and most important of the professional men's companies gave its regular performances therein. This means, of course, that some of Shakespeare's last and greatest plays had their first production in an indoor, artificially lighted, aristocratic theatre, a fact sometimes lost sight of by enthusiastic advocates of the sunlit platform stage.

The Blackfriars Theatre was of stone construction, rectangular in shape, sixty-six feet long and forty-six feet wide.[1] The stage was perhaps twenty-five feet deep and forty-six feet wide, occupying the whole width of the room. There were tiring rooms behind the stage, proscenium doors, a balcony above the stage, and "traverses" or curtains, presumably concealing a small inner stage. There were galleries for the spectator as in the public theatres, but these ended where the stage began, so that the entire audience, with the exception of the privileged persons who sat on the stage itself, faced the stage from the front, and not from three sides. The custom of sitting on the stage began in the court theatres, but was first popularized at the Blackfriars. It was later copied at

[1] See Wallace: *The Children of the Chapel at Blackfriars.*

other private theatres, and was carried over into the Restoration period; but it was not permitted in the public open-air theatres in Elizabeth's time, and perhaps not even later.

Performances at the Blackfriars, both before and after 1608, were given with more attention to decoration and stage equipment than in the cheaper public theatres. They were not, of course, as elaborate as those at court, but some of the devices of the court theatre were undoubtedly used, including "pieces of perspective." Whether these were set up on the outer stage, or only within the recess or inner stage behind the curtains, is a question that has not yet been settled. There are indications that footlights were used at the Blackfriars, and they were certainly used in other private theatres before the Restoration. The chief source of light was doubtless the overhead chandelier. Elaborate stage properties were used; the costumes were finer than in the public theatres; and the audiences seem to have been more genuinely appreciative. It is recorded definitely that they were more orderly—this in spite of the gallants on the stage. Altogether it seems reasonable to believe that something more like the atmosphere of the modern theatre existed at the Blackfriars than in any previous theatre or any other theatre of the time; more in fact than in the later English theatre until the time of Garrick.

What the Blackfriars Theatre was to modern theatre architecture, Inigo Jones was to modern scenic art in the narrower sense. It was he who introduced, to England, and so to America, the perspective setting, and with it the idea of representative illusion. At first he set up his perspectives in the Italian manner, each unit representing the corner of a building and being much too substantial for quick changing. He made one experiment with *periaktoi* at Oxford, in 1605, but in most of his settings up to 1635 he allowed the side wings to stand, and made changes during the performance only at the rear of the stage, where the elaborate properties of the masques were set up. To conceal such changes he employed shutters, sliding in grooves (*D*, Figure 21), and it may have been these shutters that led him to the idea of using flat wings and grooves for the whole stage setting. About 1640 he began setting up his wings in sets of four (*E*, Figure 21), each wing running in a groove, so that on a given signal all the wings of the first setting could be pulled back simultaneously, revealing the second setting, and so on until all four settings had been shown. This method had such obvious advantages in ease of handling as well as in rapidity of change that it came into general use in the public theatres after the Restoration, both for indoor and outdoor scenes; and it remained the standard method until the realistic box setting displaced it late in the nineteenth century.

THE THEATRE AFTER THE RESTORATION

The first performances after the Restoration were given in hastily constructed, or reconstructed, theatres, of which no clear descriptions remain. These soon proved inadequate, and between 1670 and 1675 several new theatres were built, including the famous Drury Lane Theatre of Christopher Wren. Through the next hundred years these underwent numerous alterations, and most of the authentic sketches of them represent later steps in their evolution. It is unmistakable, however, that the foundation of all seventeenth and eighteenth century theatre architecture in England was the Elizabethan private theatre of the Blackfriars type. The influence of the Italian opera house and court theatre is equally unmistakable, but the greater part of that influence had already been felt before the Commonwealth, and what took place after the Restoration was rather a logical working out of forces already in operation than an introduction of new forces. If there was any new influence in the theatre it was the licentiousness of the age, but this had more effect on the drama itself than on scenic art.

The Restoration theatre retained the seating galleries of the Blackfriars type of theatre, but these soon began to encroach upon the stage in the form of proscenium boxes. The custom of sitting on the stage persisted even after this change had made it more of a nuisance. The double stage of the Blackfriars, with the traverse concealing the inner stage, survived in the Restoration theatres, but the traverse soon became a full width curtain, the inner stage expanded to make room for more pretentious wing-and-drop settings, the outer stage became a simple forestage, and finally a mere apron. The proscenium arch of the court theatre was elaborated into a permanent gilded picture frame as early as 1671 in the Dorset Garden Theatre, although the Dury Lane Theatre of 1674 had merely a very simple hanging to mark the proscenium line. The proscenium doors of the Elizabethan theatre existed for a long time after the Restoration in the form of side doors between the stage boxes and the proscenium frame, two on each side at first, and later one on each side; but in the nineteenth century they gradually disappeared, the apron shrank, and the action of the play retired behind the curtain line.

As for the scenery proper, the methods of the court masque and the Italian opera became, after the Restoration, the regular practice of the public theatre, but with far less elaboration. From the days of Charles II to the days of Victoria, background was considered of very little importance, and it was not until late in the nineteenth century that any consistent attempt was made to outdo the exploits of Inigo Jones.

Such, in very sketchy outline, is the history of the theatre up to the coming of brighter lights and greater realism in modern times. It will be useful to us only if we can discern in it some permanence and logic of motive that will help us to evaluate the various reforms of the past and the proposed reforms of the future.

There are three essential parts of the theatre: the playing space, the place for the audience, and the scenic background. Of these the playing space undoubtedly came first.

THE EVOLUTION OF THE PLAYING SPACE

For the arrangement of the playing space visibility was of course a very early motive; but I do not think it was the first. Ritual preceded spectacle in the primitive history of the drama, and the impulse that made primitive man scratch a rude circle on the ground to define the limits of the ceremony preceded even his consciousness of observation. That circle was a magic circle. Within it was the ritual of religion; without was the commonplace world. That the mere spectator should not intrude within was a secondary—though important—thought.

The impulse thus to separate the drama from the reality surrounding it, and incidentally from the observer, grew and manifested itself in different ways. The Greek emphasized his *orchestra* with a stone curb or coping. The Roman put his actors on a raised stage—partly, of course, for better visibility, but partly to make them less commonplace. Statues are placed on pedestals for a similar reason, and pictures in panels or frames; and the Romans were great enthusiasts for pedestals and panels. It seems, therefore, that the sense of detachment common in the modern theatre is not so new after all; that it had its parallel even before the dawn of art in the unreality of religious ritual, the spell of the magic circle, and that it existed in the formal, non-illusive theatres of Greece and Rome. In course of time the relative positions of actor and audience have been frequently altered, as have the conventions of acting, but the feeling that the actor should be *set apart* in some way from the audience is the oldest and most basic tradition of the playing space. Every attempt to break it down by mingling actors and audience—from the wretched intrusions of stage-seated dandies in the seventeenth and eighteenth centuries to the false "intimacy" of some modern productions—has given offense to people of true artistic sensibility. Every such attempt will continue to give offense because it is a fundamental attack on the magic of the theatre.

Separation from the audience, then, is the first consideration in determining the arrangement of the playing space. Visibility is probably the second, and audibility the third. All three of these motives affect primarily the relation of playing space to seating space. The size and shape of the playing space are determined naturally by the requirements of the production, by the space available, by the methods of construction, and to some extent by pure accident. The Greek playing space was a circle because the chorus danced about an altar. The Roman was a platform for reasons already set down, and it was rectangular because platform stages are naturally constructed in that shape. The Elizabethan playing space was suitable for its purpose, but its form was determined partly by the accidental influence of the inn yard. The curtained inner stage developed because it was needed for interior scenes requiring stage properties which could not have been set up on the fore-stage without interrupting the continuity of the action. The inner stage expanded in size after the Restoration because the wing-and-drop settings required more room. In the nineteenth century the apron gradually became shallower because a growing sense of consistency and a growing feeling for æsthetic distance required that the actor should stay in the picture and not get too far away from his background. Theatre construction is too expensive to permit of a change in the playing space every time the producer wants to experiment, but whenever the drama changes in such a way as to create a continuing need the playing space sooner or later changes to satisfy that need. Doubtless it will change many more times in the future; but no change that runs counter to the basic motives of detachment, visibility, or audibility is likely to be an improvement.

THE EVOLUTION OF THE SEATING SPACE

There is no great mystery about the place for the audience. It began as a mere location where people might stand about and watch what was going on in the playing space; and its development has been guided by three main motives: visibility, audibility, and comfort.

When a few people stand about a circle on level ground they can see well enough, but when the numbers grow, some find their view obstructed. To solve this problem the Greeks built their *theatron* in the hollow of a hill, and by making it surround the *orchestra* on three-fourths of its circumference they enabled an amazingly large number of people to see and also to hear. The strolling players of Rome and elsewhere, having to play in open squares with no provision for seating their audiences, achieved visibility by raising the playing space. When the Romans imitated the Greek theatre and modified it by adding a stage, they cut the seating space to a semi-circle because the actor was no longer in the center of the audience, but in front. The raised seating space might not have been necessary with the raised stage for visibility alone, but it undoubtedly improved the audibility, which may be one reason why the Romans retained it. The Elizabethans found their problem of visibility and audibility already solved for them in the inn yards with surrounding galleries. Most, though not all, of the major changes in the shape of the seating space have thus been dictated by some real or fancied gain in visibility or audibility; and when visibility or audibility has been bad it has usually been because of the failure of the architect to accommodate the auditorium to altered conditions on the stage.

The third motive, comfort, brought the theatre indoors— and will continue to keep it there in most parts of the world, in spite of Gordon Craig and other fresh-air enthusiasts. The outdoor theatre served well enough in Greece for one or two annual festivals at a season when the weather could be depended upon. In Rome, with more frequent performances, sometimes in stifling hot or very stormy weather, it did not serve so well; hence the awnings, and eventually the roofs. In England the open inn yard served well enough for the "groundlings" and the vagabond players, so long as the gentlemen in the galleries were sheltered from the sun and rain; but it would not do for the court and aristocratic theatres, and in the more comfort-loving times after the Restoration it would not do for the public theatres. Outdoor performances have their charm, and will always be popular in favorable climates; but in most regions—including England and the eastern United States—they are too uncertain to be relied upon.

In addition to the three main motives, one or two others have occasionally affected the arrangement of the seating space. The love of display which led the Elizabethan and Restoration dandies to demand seats on the stage is doubtless responsible for the proscenium boxes of the modern theatre and the private stalls of the opera house. The cupidity of managers has undoubtedly led to occasional over-

crowding and other abuses; and the stupidity of architects—
if that can be called a motive—has made some theatres places
of torment rather than of entertainment. But these matters
have little to do with scenic art.

THE EVOLUTION OF THE SCENIC BACKGROUND

In the genesis of scenic background five main motives are
discernible. In chronological, and perhaps logical, order
they are: concealment, decoration, suggestion of mood, suggestion of place, and portrayal of place.

The origin of the background is that of the Greek *skene*,
or of the backing curtain of the primitive platform stage:
a shelter or retiring place for the actor, to conceal him from
the audience during changes of costume or intervals in the
action of the play. The word *skene* itself—from which we
get our word scene—means "hut" or "shelter." A great deal
of nonsense about scenic art would be avoided if we could
remember that the most fundamental purpose of scenery is,
and always has been, to conceal from the audience what would
prove irrelevant or distracting if seen. All other purposes
are incidental, and of later growth.

The second purpose, decoration, is, however, very old.
Background cannot be used at all without being observed by
the audience, and what must be seen may as well be beautiful.
The Greeks soon found this out, and began to decorate the
scene building as they decorated all their architecture; unlike
the Romans, however, they seem to have had the restraint
to avoid over-decoration. A background that distracts attention from the play by its excessive beauty violates the
fundamental principle of good design; nevertheless, a fairly
pleasing background is generally less distracting than one
that is even slightly ugly, since it does less violence to the
æsthetic attitude. Decorative background, properly sub-

ordinated to the action, is therefore generally preferable to representative background which by its tawdriness offends and distracts. It is in keeping with the magic and glamour of the theatre.

The third purpose, suggestion of mood, is often confused, under the general idea of symbolism, with suggestion of place. It is probably much older, and more fundamental. Before background had been in use very long the ancients must have discovered that an appropriate decoration, in keeping with the mood or atmosphere, heightened the dramatic effect. There is little need for suggestion of place in religious ritual, nor in the early forms of drama dealing with religious and national themes already well known to the audience. But emotional symbolism of some sort is a natural part of religious ritual, and in that sense must have antedated the scene building itself. It was probably suggestion of mood rather than suggestion of place that led the Greeks to differentiate the tragic, comic, and satyric scenes; and the remarks of Vitruvius indicate that even in Roman times changes of background were dictated rather by the requirements of mood than by the logic of place.

Just when the fourth motive, suggestion of place, began to affect the scenic background is not clear; but it is obviously less basic than the three already mentioned. The ancient drama required little suggestion of place, and that little was accomplished by the use of properties, by the explanatory remarks of the chorus, and by such conventions as the use of the central door to indicate a palace, of the adjacent doors to represent guest chambers, and of the two side approaches to represent the city and country respectively. The Elizabethans, except when influenced by the Italian court theatre, contrived to suggest place through the words of the characters or prologue, through the posting of placards, and through the use of symbolic stage properties. The more concretely the drama concerns itself with life, and the farther it gets from the familiar themes of race or religion, the greater the need for suggestion of place as an aid to understanding. Suggestion of place must not be ruthlessly condemned; without it some of the best drama we have would be unintelligible. But a great deal can be suggested without being portrayed, and a great deal can be suggested—or even portrayed—in the acting and the properties without change of scenic background.*

Of the five motives affecting the background the last, and least basic, is portrayal of place. Between suggestion and portrayal no absolute line can, of course, be drawn; the one thing develops into the other very gradually. The first attempts at a complete portrayal of place through representative illusion in the background appear to have been those of the Italian Renaissance; and it is noteworthy that they originated in a mistake—a misunderstanding of ancient writings on perspective. It was the craze for perspective that led to the spectacular illusions of the English court theatre, and eventually brought the painted canvas wing-and-drop setting into the public theatre. But the impulse to portray background realistically did not flourish in the public theatres— except in grand opera—until the nineteenth century. Through the Restoration and the eighteenth century the emphasis was on the actor; and the background, though casually representative and fashioned, for convenience, after the court setting, made no serious attempt at illusion. The wings were conventional; furniture was painted on the back drop; the inner stage was poorly lighted; and settings were used over again for widely different plays. It was not until the brighter lights and the shrunken apron of the nineteenth century made the scenery more conspicuous that the motive of portrayal began again to dominate the scenic artist, and not until the coming of Belasco that it reached its height. The logical continuance of this motive in the theatre of today will be considered in the next chapter.

THE EVOLUTION OF STAGE PROPERTIES

Although stage properties have often associated themselves with scenery, and in the modern theatre are virtually a part of it, they appear to have had a different origin, and their development to have been influenced by different motives. The stage property evolved from the hand property, and the fundamental motive of the latter was illustration or symbolism. The first hand properties were doubtless the weapons and totems carried by warriors and medicine men in tribal dances, and their use was to illustrate action or to symbolize magic. The first stage property was probably the altar. All of these things antedated the beginning of actual drama; but when the drama evolved from ritual the symbols of ritual became the symbols of pantomime. Scenery is background, but properties are those objects needed and used by the actors to explain or illustrate their actions in some way. It is but an accident that some of them are light enough to be carried by the actors, while others—chairs, tables, beds, altars, rocks, trees, boats—are large enough and heavy enough to seem like part of the setting.

The actor antedated the scenery, and, except in an occasional perversion, has always been far more important in the eyes of the audience. For that reason the properties used by him to illustrate or symbolize his actions have always commanded more interest than the scenery; they are not of the background but of the foreground—of the very essence of the action. Naturally, therefore, they have developed more rapidly, and have lent themselves more readily to the purpose of realism.

Symbolism and illustration are closely associated, and it is not always easy to distinguish them; nor is it safe to say which came first historically. Of the two, symbolism seems the more essentially dramatic, and therefore more fundamental. Symbolism is suggestion through the display of a concrete symbol, conventionally accepted as standing for something else. Illustration is pictorial exposition. Illustrative stage properties are those which, like gesture, help to clarify the thought and enable the audience to understand otherwise unintelligible actions. There are, after all, very few situations in which properties are absolutely essential for explanatory purposes, gesture alone being usually sufficient, as the Chinese actors know; and how far we choose to employ explanatory properties is largely a matter of taste. For symbolism, however, they have a distinct dramatic value. Visible symbols often stir the imagination as mere words do not—witness the effect of a flag, a mace, an altar, a crucifix, or a statue of the Virgin.

With properties, as with acting, therefore, effective symbolism has always been a sounder motive than portrayal, though a certain measure of realism may be necessary for intelligibility. Excessive realism in the choice of properties involves the same dangers as excessive realism in the acting; but it does not involve the distraction incident to excessive realism of background.

THE EVOLUTION OF STAGE LIGHTING

The Greek theatre was lighted by the sun and the Elizabethan public theatre by the misty gray of a London afternoon. But those who on that account insist that daylight is the only truly theatrical light, and the outdoor theatre the only true theatre, are curiously undiscerning. Daylight is *less* theatrical than artificial light, for the obvious reason that it is more natural, more commonplace, and therefore less magic. Primitive tribes have sometimes felt this, and have often—if not usually—conducted their ceremonial dances in the mystic glow of the camp-fire. Demons and spirits, and even gods, may be more readily imagined in artificial light than in the disillusioning light of day—which may be one reason why we put stained glass windows in our churches, and candles on the altar, and why our Boy Scouts save their ghost stories for the camp-fire at night instead of telling them at the lunch table. Even the outdoor stage is more magically impressive at night, under the spell of one or two calcium lights, than it can ever be in the daytime.

Logically, artificial light belongs to the very genesis of primitive drama. The daylight of the Greek theatres was a matter of expediency; the Greeks had no adequate method of lighting their huge theatres, or of lighting the streets; and it probably never occurred to them to hold their public assemblies at night. For similar reasons the strolling players of the middle ages performed by daylight, as did their descendants, the vagabond Elizabethans in the inn yards. But wherever and whenever, in the history of the theatre, artificial light has been practicable, it has generally proved to be more dramatically effective than daylight.

From the very first, artificial light in the theatre has been *frankly* artificial. It is not basically an imitation of daylight; it is an escape from daylight. There are those who complain of the footlights on the ground that they are not natural, since natural light comes from above. Of course they are not natural. They were invented—probably in the Italian Renaissance, but possibly earlier—for the sole purpose of emphasizing the actor and lighting up his face. There was precedent for them in the glow of the camp-fire on the faces of dancing savages, and there is much of the same magic in both.

The discovery that light is emotional, a great instrument of mood, is not new. It goes back, in fact, to those same ancient camp-fires. The cathedral builders of the middle ages understood the principle; and the use of colored lights in the sixteenth century suggests that the Italian theatre artists understood it also. It fell into neglect after the Restoration— when everything else romantic fell into neglect; the artificiality persisted, but with little relation to particular mood. Since the invention of gas and electricity, however, the emotional possibilities of light have been re-discovered and greatly widened.

THE EVOLUTION OF COSTUME AND MAKE-UP

Costume and make-up, like other elements of the drama, have their origin in primitive ritual, with magic symbolism as the first motive. Primitive man adorned his body, smeared his face, or donned a mask, to frighten evil spirits, impress or honor the gods, or symbolize some force or element of nature.

The second motive was disguise. The sense of magic unreality that prompted him to mark off his playing space prompted him also to conceal the identity of his performers. He early felt that the recognition of the individual actor, or dancer, as his own commonplace self destroyed the magic spell.

Symbolism and disguise are thus earlier and more fundamental motives than representation or impersonation. That is why masks have been so popular with primitive races. For symbolizing extremes of abstraction or of magic, or for disguising the individual, they are far more potent than make-up or costume. Make-up itself was conventional and grotesque long before it was realistic; it is still conventional in the classic Chinese drama.

The conventional identification of characters by mask or costume is at least as old as the Greek drama, but in its early stages it is almost indistinguishable from pure symbolism. Only in comparatively recent times have costume and make-up been made realistically representative. The Elizabethan actors wore the costumes of their own time, varying them only to represent extremes of character or social position. In the eighteenth century it was not always thought necessary to do even that, and actresses representing servants often wore frocks more appropriate to ladies-in-waiting. Not until the beginning of the nineteenth century was there any consistent effort to make the costumes historically authentic.

There is perhaps less objection to realism of costume and make-up than to realism of setting because costume and make-up, like properties, have to do with the actor. But it is well to remember that symbolism is more basic than representation, and that disguise is almost as basic as symbolism. This fact seems often to have been lost sight of, with consequent destruction of æsthetic distance. There seems to have been very little disguise of the actor in the seventeenth and eighteenth centuries, and little more in the early nineteenth; and one must feel that the magic of the theatre suffered. Realistic representation has little to do with the magic of the theatre; but mystic symbolism and the suppression of the real and the commonplace have a great deal.

SUMMARY

The genesis of scenic art is, then, the genesis of the theatre itself in religious ceremonial. The theatre's hold upon our imaginations and emotions rests upon its origin in the spirit of magic; and to retain that hold it must continue to cast its spell upon us in terms of the unreal; and must avoid the casual and the commonplace. Detachment, disguise, and symbolism are the most basic motives. Visual beauty is good, but secondary; suggestion of place is sometimes helpful if kept subordinate, while realistic portrayal is the latest and least basic motive. With these motives in mind let us examine the modern tendencies in scenic art, and consider which of them represent the soundest theories of play production.

CHAPTER XVIII

MODERN TENDENCIES IN SCENIC ART

WE HEAR frequent reference to the "modern movement in scenic art," but there is no one movement that can be properly so described. There is, rather, a great seething activity in experimentation, out of which six or eight different movements have so far developed, along with a tangled miscellany of influences and counter-influences too complex for analysis. Most of this activity has been in the nature of a reaction against false realism, as seen in the painted canvas settings of the last century.

Hardly anybody now defends those settings, with their flimsy doors, flapping walls, painted shades and shadows, false perspective, and hideously unconvincing wings and drops. The revolt against them had quite sufficient provocation. But it has been from the first a curiously confused revolt— a revolt against realism and against artificiality at the same time; and its supporters are still advocating all sorts of inconsistent things, on the general principle, perhaps, that any change is bound to be an improvement. They condemn quite opposite faults for similar reasons, and similar faults for opposite reasons. They denounce the attempt to make the theatre realistic, and in the same breath complain that it is unreal. They ridicule the flapping canvas walls, but deplore the attempt to build more convincing walls of panels or plaster. They seek to abolish the footlights as unnatural, but they criticize the realistic lighting effects of Belasco—who was one of the first to abolish the footlights. They condemn the whole indoor theatre as hopelessly artificial, and eulogize the more natural sunlit theatre of the Greeks; but they praise the architectural background of the Greek theatre in contrast to our representative scenery on the ground that it was frankly artificial. They glorify the power of fluid theatrical light as an abstract instrument of emotion, but complain that the light used to represent daylight is not sufficiently white and diffused to be convincing. They complain of the "picture frame" stage as two-dimensional and unnatural and advocate the platform stage as "frankly theatrical." In short, though they frequently display excellent taste, they mix their motives appallingly.

In their attempts to develop a satisfactory theory of scenic art the experimenters have, of course, been considerably influenced by contemporary movements in the other arts, as well as by the underlying social and educational influences of the time. Realism has fallen into disfavor in painting, sculpture and music, as well as in the theatre; and various types of stylization and abstraction have been tried in all the arts.

In the theatre the most significant anti-realistic movements have been those based upon symbolism, stylization, formalism, plasticism, expressionism, cubism, and constructivism. These involve some overlappings and some confusion of terminology, but broadly interpreted they cover most of the important experiments in twentieth-century scenic art. To understand them properly, however, we must first give some attention to the more recent developments in realism itself.

REALISM IN SCENIC ART

As already suggested, realism began very early in the occasional impulse to startle or impress, and for a long time that was its only motive. Later came the motive to suggest place; and later still the motive to portray place consistently and convincingly. The last motive grew out of the other two and was at first largely defensive. As soon as some elements in the theatre were made realistic other elements were thrown into unfavorable contrast, and were criticized as unreal and unconvincing. Criticism of that sort began very early; there are hints of it, for example, in the comedies of Aristophanes. In Elizabethan times there was much ridicule of the unrealistic methods of the public stage, especially from those who had seen the more elaborate settings of the court masque or the Italian opera. The inconsistencies of the Italian perspective setting were ridiculed almost from the time of its invention. In the eighteenth century, with the setting far in the background and poorly lighted, the challenge was not so great; but in the nineteenth century with the shrinkage of the apron and the improvement of stage lighting the unconvincing character of the painted setting became more and more apparent, and the criticism more and more severe. Harassed managers called upon their stage carpenters and scene painters to meet this criticism, and the stage carpenters and scene painters did the only thing they knew how to do: they built more substantially and painted more carefully. They modified or abandoned perspective, devised the box setting to replace the wings and drops for indoor scenes, and substituted real properties for painted imitations. But still the lights grew brighter and the critics more discontented.

Then came the day of the mechanician—the stage carpenter glorified. The Continental mechanician, especially, began to substitute modern scientific efficiency for the slipshod methods of the old theatre. He developed and perfected the hydraulic elevator stage, the sliding stage, the revolving stage, the cyclorama, the built setting, the Fortuny lighting system, and a host of lesser devices.[1] Although most of these have since been adapted to non-realistic purposes it must be clearly understood that they first came into common use as instruments of realism. The elevator stage was developed chiefly to facilitate the elaboration of spectacle in grand opera. The revolving stage was designed to permit the use of substantial built settings without delay in the changing of scenes. The cyclorama was a reaction against the unreality of the painted back drop and the canvas sky border. The Fortuny lighting system—by which the white light of arc lamps was indirectly reflected

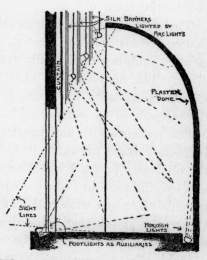

FIG. 22.—THE FORTUNY LIGHTING SYSTEM

from silk banners against the diffusing surface of a dome cyclorama—was devised to make more convincing the representation of daylight in the theatre; and the abolition of footlights, though now commonly associated with the anti-realistic theatre, was actually prompted by the sudden and remarkable discovery that real sunlight shines down, not up.

All the mechanism, however, failed to satisfy the rebels; the theatre was still unreal, they said. At that point they began to disagree. Some said, "Let us abandon altogether the

---

[1] Some of these were not, however, new inventions. The revolving stage had been used in Japan, and perhaps the Greek *exostra* was in effect a revolving stage. The elevator stage and numerous other devices were used in this country by Steele Mackaye in the 'nineties. Many of these things were but adaptations of the machines used in the Renaissance theatres.

attempt to portray background realistically, and go back to the frank theatricality of earlier times." Others said, "If the stage is too artificial let us spare no pains to make it more real." Thus realism and idealism became divergent tendencies in the theatre.

The modern realist is generally much more clear-headed and consistent than the idealist. The latter is still an experimenter, jumping uncertainly from one new movement to another. The realist knows what he wants. According to his view the purpose of the drama is to reflect or picture life, and the purpose of the setting is to reflect the background. He has no patience with half-heartedness, and if the setting is to indicate a room he wants it to look like a room. He hates the obviously painted imitation of a room, and he will go to any length in solidity of construction and detail of furnishing to make the room seem real. If he is a practical man of the theatre he knows that some deception is possible, and even necessary; that things can be made to seem real which are not real. But representative illusion, consistent and complete, is always his objective.

It will not do to condemn off hand what is after all a natural growth and the accepted mode of the commercial theatre— to say nothing of the moving pictures. Let us rather consider its merits and demerits in terms of what we have seen to be the basic motives of the theatre.

The charges against realism are many, but the three most important are: that it distracts attention from the actor, weakens illusion by challenging comparison, and tends to destroy æsthetic distance.

The first charge applies to realism of background rather than of properties or action, and is most serious when the background is not only realistic but elaborate. There is no essential distraction in reality as such; if there were we should

REALISM

No producer can equal David Belasco for completeness and consistency in realism. In this setting, designed by Joseph Wickes for the Belasco production of *Lulu Belle*, we see a photographic copy of "San Juan Hill," the downtown colored district of New York. The perfection of detail is amazing. The false shadows made by the flashlight are absent, of course, in the production.

never be able to avoid distraction in real life, or to concentrate on important things. It is when the reality of the background becomes insistent in some way that it distracts attention. Too much detail, where detail is unnecessary or unexpected, is distracting. Unduly conspicuous or striking elements in the background are distracting. Successful imitation of reality when such imitation is seen to be difficult or remarkable is distracting. The very effort to startle or impress out of which realism originally grew had in it the potential sources of distraction, and the most distracting form of realism today is that which is clearly intended to evoke admiration or applause for its cleverness, or completeness, or deceptiveness.

The second charge—that realism weakens illusion by challenging comparison—applies to realism both of background and of properties, though it is more serious in respect to the former. The fault arises in the failure to distinguish between the illusion of imagination and the illusion of deception. In the attempt to stimulate the imagination by suggesting place the producer is safe so long as the elements of reality are acceptable symbolically, without hint of deception. But the moment they become so numerous or so unnecessarily real as to imply deception, a vicious circle is set up; each element of unreality arouses unfavorable comparison and provokes further effort at realism; and each gain in realism raises the standard of comparison, so that deception becomes more difficult. Since no imitation of life can quite equal reality the whole process becomes futile, and results only in dissatisfaction.

Among the elements of attempted deception that have proved themselves most disturbing in the theatre are: false perspective; false shades and shadows, especially painted ones; flat painted representations of three-dimensional objects;

accurate but lifeless imitations of trees, bushes, or animals; representations of boats, ships, railroad trains and the like, especially in motion; realistic yet unreal properties, especially imitation foodstuffs of wax or *papier mâché;* direct representations of the sun, moon, or stars; realistic, rather than symbolic, sunrise and sunset effects; representations of floods, tornadoes and forest fires; and picturizations of real places, so well known to the audience that comparison is inevitable.

The third charge—that realism endangers æsthetic distance—applies even more to the acting than to the setting, but in some degree to both. When any phase of a performance so arouses the spectator's sense of reality that he feels himself involved in its implications or is too vividly reminded of his own personal experience, he loses his sense of detachment, and his æsthetic attitude is destroyed.

Against these charges the realists have offered several pleas in their own defense. In the first place they point out that we have long been committed to the idea of scenic representation of place and that it is better to have it truly and effectively realistic than half-heartedly so. They say that to abandon realism altogether would be to discard many excellent and enjoyable plays that have been written for realistic production and could not be given intelligibly in the Greek, or Elizabethan, or Chinese manner. They insist that unreality is often more distracting and disturbing than reality; and they claim that perfect realism, properly subordinated, is actually less obtrusive than expressionism or stylization, because it is more like the life we are accustomed to.

There is considerable justice in these pleas. If realistic methods in scenic art had always been confined to realistic plays, and had always been convincing rather than unconvincing we should have heard less of anti-realism. We hear relatively little objection now to the realism of the moving pictures—a realism far more pretentious than that of the stage—because the accuracy of the camera disarms, to a certain extent, the critical attitude. But we hear violent objection the moment a moving picture audience discovers that something supposedly real has been faked. On the whole it seems clear that the distraction lies more in some recognition of futility or inconsistency than in realistic accuracy *per se*.

The great evils in realism on the stage are, it seems to me, the constant effort to achieve completeness without regard to relevancy—which is bad design in any mode—and the effort to achieve realistic effects that are not honestly within the capabilities of stage equipment. If we examine the objections to realism we find that most of them are based on one or the other of these faults. Yet neither fault is essentially a part of realism; with a realistic play and adequate equipment, a truly artistic director can go pretty far in the representation of reality without committing either.

SIMPLIFIED REALISM

One objection to detailed completeness in realism is that it is unnecessary; and therein lies the key to the best type of simplified realism.

It is very significant that detailed completeness played no part in the early history of realism, but developed later as a defensive measure, and then only by confusion with consistency. The defensive attitude of the realist is justifiable: he simply tries to correct the faults that have accidentally arisen. When something is obtrusively inconsistent and unconvincing he tries to make it consistent and convincing. If the inconsistency is associated with incompleteness he tries to achieve consistency through completeness; and after a while he acquires the habit. The habit is bad; but the underlying impulse is good, and should be encouraged, subject to the limitations of good taste and good judgement.

Some of the greatest artists have understood that it is possible to apply realism negatively, or defensively, without indulging in orgies of representative elaboration. What may be called simplified realism consists in the avoidance of unreality where unreality might be distracting, or misleading, or destructive of illusion; but it achieves that avoidance through the elimination of unconvincing details rather than the addition of convincing ones.

In the balcony scene of *Romeo and Juliet* there are good reasons for avoiding unreality. The necessities of the plot demand that Juliet shall appear on the balcony and be seen by Romeo, and any obvious unreality in the appearance of the balcony will at once distract attention from the characters, and perhaps raise a doubt as to Juliet's safety. On the other hand nobody cares at all whether the rest of Juliet's house is realistic in detail, so long as it does not demand attention. Rollo Peters, who designed the settings for the production in which he and Jane Cowl played the title parts, handled this problem with good taste. He eliminated the usual shaky trellises and paper flowers, made the balcony severely plain and substantial-looking, and placed it, as part of a single panel, at the center of the stage. The rest of the setting consisted of soft, neutral draperies, hardly noticeable in the semi-darkness. All the light was directed at the balcony and the actors, and the attention of the audience concentrated on the action. The immediate background of the action was realistic in the best sense; while the rest of the background was not realistic at all, and did not have to be so because its unreality was never obtrusive.

In the setting for the second act of *The Road to Rome*, as designed by Lee Simonson, a similar kind of realism was

DECORATIVE SYMBOLISM

A setting by Lee Simonson for the Theatre Guild's production of *Marco Millions*. It symbolizes a gate in the Wall of China, and is not far removed in spirit from simplified realism. The scene was omitted after the dress rehearsal in order to shorten the performance, and this beautiful setting went to waste.

employed to suggest the headquarters of Hannibal in a Roman temple. The greater part of the set consisted of heavy draperies, not realistic at all. But to convey a sense of actuality two realistic elements were introduced: a huge fluted column in the foreground, and a very substantial door at stage left. The door was called for by the action, and if not realistic would have been unreal and distracting. The column was not actually required, but its presence was somewhat reassuring; and the fact that it did not sway when a soldier casually leaned against it did much to preserve the imaginative illusion.

The same principle has been successfully employed by Livingston Platt, Norman Bel Geddes, Claude Bragdon (notably in his flexible settings for Walter Hampden's Shakespearean repertory), and by many others. It has been especially serviceable in amateur and little theatre work, and a review of the files of the *Theatre Magazine*, the *Theatre Arts Monthly*, and the *Drama* will reveal many interesting examples.

Simplified realism lends itself to a wider variety of uses than almost any other style of setting, and combines well with other styles. It is not always easily distinguishable from others, and some of the settings properly classed as essentially realistic are loosely spoken of as decorative, or formal, or symbolic. At times simplified realism comes very close to symbolism; indeed its chief function is to suggest a place or a mood at a moment when unreality would falsify the place or shatter the mood.

SYMBOLISM

Symbolism is not generally recognized as a separate movement in scenic art, but it is certainly distinguishable as a motive; and as a motive it plays an important part in the general effort to get away from photographic realism.

A symbol is something that stands for something else, not representatively, but conventionally—that is, by common understanding and agreement. Most of our communication is carried on by means of symbols, including our written or printed words, and even our commonest gestures. Many symbols—like the characters in Chinese writing—originate in pictorial representation, but later become so far conventionalized that there is no suggestion of realism about them, and their meaning depends upon recognized association. What I have called simplified realism suggests a great deal of reality by selecting a little; true symbolism goes a step farther and substitutes a pure convention.

There is a power in symbolism that is very close to the magic of the theatre, or of religion. The churches make frequent use of it. An image of Christ or the Virgin Mary is very different in function from one of Washington or Napoleon. Neither, of course, is intended to deceive—to be mistaken in any actual sense for the reality. But the historical statue is a mere picture or memorial, while the religious one is a symbol intended to suggest a spiritual presence. This sort of symbolism is at once more real, and less real, than realism; and it is far more emotional.

In the theatre symbolism has been more generally and effectively applied to the properties than to the scenic background. In the Chinese theatre, for example, a stick of wood with a bit of cloth attached symbolizes a baby; since the audience is familiar with the convention nobody laughs, and when the player impersonating the mother addresses the symbol in words of mother love, the effect is actually more emotional than if a real baby were used. When the same device is used in the pseudo-Chinese play *The Yellow Jacket*, the

American audience first laughs at the property, and then gives attention to the mother; and when, a few moments later, she kills herself for the sake of the child and ascends an absurd ladder into "heaven," the American audience weeps and laughs at the same time.

In respect to the background, it may be possible under certain conditions to suggest the atmosphere of a forest better with a single tree, frankly displayed as a symbol, than with a dozen trees arranged realistically. Logically that is no more absurd than the attempt to suggest it with six printed letters on paper—F-O-R-E-S-T. It is all a question of what we are accustomed to. Elizabethan audiences accepted a tree —or even a single branch—to symbolize a forest. That particular convention may be difficult for us; but we can easily accept two potted evergreens and a wall as symbolizing a garden, or a single Gothic window as symbolizing a church.

That we do not hear more of symbolism as a distinct movement in scenic art is due, I think, to the fact that it combines well with other motives which are more strikingly distinct—especially with formalism and stylization.

STYLIZATION

Stylization, though often associated with symbolism, is very different in purpose. Symbolism establishes the thought or mood; stylization establishes the *mode*.

The stylist endeavors to provide a scheme of decoration in some way characteristic of the particular author, or his theme or intent, or the period, or the nation, or the occasion of production. Stylization is, in this sense, external to the play itself, though it should not be irrelevant. Sometimes it is applied in a decorative way to the background only, while the acting remains realistic; sometimes the costumes and properties are stylized also, and sometimes even the acting. Usually the style is constant for the whole play, though the scene may change several times; and here again stylization differs from symbolism, which is concerned with each mood as it arises.

One of the earliest of the modern stylistic settings—and one of the best—was that designed by Robert Edmond Jones for *The Man Who Married a Dumb Wife*. Another was the setting for Granville-Barker's production of *Twelfth Night*, designed by Norman Wilkinson. Many of the settings for Russian opera and ballet—notably those by Leon Bakst—are stylistic. The Moscow Art Theatre employed one famous stylistic setting in its production of *The Blue Bird*. Most of the settings used in the *Chauve Souris* were stylistic, though not all of them were in the same style. Several of them—those for *Katinka*, the *Wooden Soldiers*, and *La Tabatiere Musicale*, for example—were stylized in the spirit of Russian toys; others in the spirit of French porcelain, or of futuristic painting. Stylistic settings were employed in Otis Skinner's production of *Sancho Panza*, in the dream scenes of *The Beggar on Horseback*, in the Theatre Guild production of *Androcles and the Lion*, and in the Winthrop Ames revivals of Gilbert and Sullivan operettas.

Stylization seems to be at its best in connection with artistic child's play. It was thoroughly delightful in the *Chauve Souris*, and lends itself admirably to the presentation of fairy tales; story-book plays like *Alice in Wonderland;* exotic plays like *The Yellow Jacket* or *Sakuntala;* allegorical plays, or fables, like *The Blue Bird;* satirical plays like *Androcles and the Lion* or *The Man Who Married a Dumb Wife;* archaic plays like *Fashion* or *The Beggar's Opera*, or even *The School for Scandal;* fanciful plays, humorous plays, ballets, operettas, and extravaganzas. It does not lend itself so well to seriously realistic plays or to poetically tragic plays.

Bruguière

STYLIZATION

A setting by Miguel Covarrubias for the Theatre Guild's production of *Androcles and the Lion*. All the settings were in the same mode, and very highly colored.

White

PARTIAL STYLIZATION

A setting by Watson Barratt for the Garrick Theatre Players' production of *The Taming of the Shrew* in modern dress. All the settings were fantastic, but they were not all strictly in the same mode.

Most stylistic settings are abstractly conventional rather than realistic, though even a consistently realistic setting may establish a characteristic style or mode for a play. In extreme stylization there is a kind of frank naïveté, not innocent, but intentional—an attitude both childlike and sophisticated at the same time. Therein lies the chief usefulness of stylization, which is the preservation of æsthetic distance, the heightening of the æsthetic attitude. Realism serves chiefly to strengthen the empathic appeal; symbolism to reach the emotions through the imagination. Stylization serves to accentuate the unreality of the theatre and to encourage the spirit of play.

FORMALISM

Many anti-realists, however, are not content even with stylization, and demand the complete suppression of the stage setting as such, and the substitution of a purely formal background. The background, they feel, should be neither representative nor suggestive; it should belong to the theatre and not to the play, and should signify nothing except the essential theatricality of the playing space. Some formalists approve of a decorative element in the background, provided it is kept subordinate, but fundamentally they disapprove of any attempt to make the setting part of the play.

The chief inspiration for this movement comes, of course, from the Greek and Elizabethan theatres, and the strongest thing that can be said in its favor is that many of the world's greatest poetic dramas were written for formal stages and successfully produced on them. There is a vitality about the formal stage that is not always equalled on the representative or stylistic stage.

It should be understood, however, that when we see a Greek play performed in a modern replica of a Greek theatre the effect upon *us* is not that of pure formalism. An element of stylization inevitably creeps in through the fact that the theatre is not our own theatre but an exotic one appropriate to the particular play. The same thing happens when we see a Shakespearean play performed in an imitation Elizabethan theatre, or when we see *The Yellow Jacket* in a setting representing a Chinese theatre. Not that the element of stylization is bad—but it does tend to defeat the real purpose of formalism.

True formalism is possible only when the background is accepted by the audience as the normal, customary one of its own familiar theatre; or when the background is so far subordinated as not to engage the attention. A formal background may be decorative in an unobtrusive way, as the Greek *skene* was; and a permanent stage to which a regular audience has become accustomed can carry more decoration without obtrusiveness than a stage to which the audience is not accustomed.

Most of the attempts at formalism today are really compromises—accidental compromises with stylization like those mentioned, or intentional compromises with realism or symbolism. The famous *Théâtre du Vieux Colombier* of Jacques Copeau, in Paris—often cited as a successful example of formal staging—is really a compromise; for though the forestage and surroundings are permanent, the architectural units of the rear stage are movable, and are changed for different plays, suggesting, though not actually portraying, changes of place. One of the most popular forms of compromise is that of the skeleton setting, in which a formal architectural structure occupies the major part of the stage throughout the play, while the backings seen through various openings or archways are changed for each act. This device is not new; in effect it is that used by Inigo Jones prior to

FORMALISM AND SYMBOLISM

A compromise setting by Woodman Thompson for the Winthrop Ames production of *The Merchant of Venice* (with George Arliss). The fore-stage was formal and permanent, but the inner stage was re-set for alternate scenes. Both inner and outer settings were substantial, but simple.

1640, and by the Italians of the preceding century. Perhaps the Greek *periaktoi* were not essentially different in principle.

Three types of modern stages have, it seems to me, been reasonably successful in accomplishing the true purpose of formalism. One is the outdoor stage with a backing of trees, shrubbery, clipped hedges, or non-stylistic architectural features, readily accepted by the audience as appropriate—almost inevitable—to the place. Another is the indoor stage backed by simple draperies, used consistently and with very little change for different plays, and merely designed to provide a neutral background for the action. The third is the so-called "space stage," the essential feature of which is light, so controlled as to reveal only the significant action and to suppress the background altogether in a void of darkness. The methods of the space stage are, it is true, adaptable to the purposes of expressionism, or even of simplified realism; but they help to accomplish at the same time the purpose of formalism.

The power of light to control attention and achieve subordination is tremendous, and even when a strictly formal background is not available, or not desirable, the proper manipulation of the lighting effects will go far to accomplish what the formalist aims to accomplish—that is, the defeat of realism, the disarming of the critical attitude, the freeing of the imagination from dependence upon externals. Even a stage with representative painted settings may, under certain methods of lighting, become more neutral and less challenging than a supposedly formal stage over-decorated and too brightly lighted.

Formalism, like stylization, functions largely to preserve æsthetic distance. Symbolism, stylization, and formalism all tend to perpetuate the essential magic of the theatre; the first two by aiding the actor, the last by keeping out of his way and putting him squarely on his own resources.

PLASTICISM

Among the critics of the older theatre are many who find their chief objection in the two-dimensional quality of the "picture frame" stage; and who insist that what the theatre most needs is to get away from the whole idea of a painted picture and develop a plastic or three-dimensional quality.

In its earlier manifestations this movement was at least partly associated with realism. Among the first reforms accomplished were the abolition of flat painted shadows, the substitution of three-dimensional set pieces for painted flats, and the improvement of the lighting system to give a sense of depth. Later came attempts to revive the forestage or apron; attempts to modify or abolish the proscenium arch and to establish a platform or sculptural stage; and finally the development of the space stage—which, because the background is in darkness, may be sculptural in effect regardless of whether it is within a proscenium frame or not. In these later developments, however, the realistic purpose has practically disappeared and plasticism has become associated with formalism, or expressionism, or constructivism.

There are two somewhat divergent views among the plasticists, some holding that the production should be synthesized and plastic as a whole—action, properties, and setting; others holding that the action should be plastic, but the background flat, the better to emphasize the sculptural quality of the action. The latter group appear to favor a kind of bas-relief rather than outright sculpture. They employ a formal or stylistic background and put the action very close to the background on a shallow stage—a stage that is little more than a ledge. Whether this method emphasizes

FUTURISTIC SYMBOLISM

A sketch by Mr. Yarnall Abbott of his setting for the second act of *Hades Incorporated*, as presented by the Musical Clubs of the University of Pennsylvania. The setting consisted of very simple canvas flats, and the effects were achieved by means of the lighting. A red glow at the back threw the jagged flats into relief, and floods of red, yellow, and green, in changing ratio, were used above and at the sides. During the Dance of the Furies red and yellow flashes on the swirling robes of the dancers created the effect of a sea of flame.

the plastic effect of the action or results in greater flatness depends chiefly upon the lighting.

The attempt to get plastic effect by reviving the forestage or apron stage in conjunction with a proscenium frame has been generally unsuccessful, and for a very good reason. When there is a proscenium frame, that frame fixes the limits of the composition and establishes the æsthetic distance; and when the actor steps through the frame and out on to the apron he seems to step out of the picture. It was the gradual growth of this feeling that led to the abolition of the apron; and no artistic purpose can be accomplished by merely going backwards.

The true platform stage without a frame is another matter; and plastic effects can be achieved on such a stage without destruction of æsthetic distance, provided the actor is able to maintain the magic spell of illusion. Again light plays an important part, and the more nearly we approach the technique of the space stage the more completely plastic the effect. Even the central stage, when used as a space stage, with only the essential action picked out by the light, can preserve æsthetic distance effectively; and it is the most plastic of all stages.

EXPRESSIONISM

Many different motives have been confused under the general name of expressionism, and many different styles and methods lend themselves to the expressionistic purpose; but the purpose itself is fairly distinct.

Expressionism in the theatre is a borrowing from the other arts; and in those arts—especially painting—it came about in some degree as a reaction against *im*pressionism. Impressionism as a distinct movement does not seem to have had much effect on the theatre, perhaps because it had played itself out in painting before the revolt in the theatre attained its full growth. In painting it was both a theory and a style. As a theory it was anti-realistic, and involved the attempt of the artist to represent nature, not as it was, but as he thought he saw it—to represent, in a word, his impression of life. This led to sketchiness, and to the development of a particular style involving the splotchy application of crude colors. Other styles not generally called impressionistic were equally in keeping with the theory.

The theory, however, did not satisfy some anti-realists, who said, "What we want is not the artist's *im*pression of nature, but his *ex*pression of himself. We want his vision, not his observation. We want abstraction not alone in the means but in the purpose. We want something that will transcend nature, free the spirit, enable the artist to reveal his emotions and reach those of his public directly, as the lyric poet does —something greater, not less, than reality."

So began expressionism, and so it was transferred to the theatre. But the expressionist, no less than the impressionist, got himself tangled up with particular styles—post-impressionistic, cubistic, futuristic, and what not—and frequently confused his purposes with his peculiarities of technique. As a result he has been generally misunderstood, in the theatre as well as in painting; and his messages of the spirit have often failed to reach the audience.

Expressionism in the theatre can hardly be illustrated photographically; the style can be shown, but not the emotional effect. The true expressionist uses not only the setting but all the elements of the production, including the acting and the lighting; and by fluid, emotional manipulation of light he makes the light itself an actor. The slave ship scene in *The Emperor Jones*, as done by the Provincetown Players,

Bruguière

EXPRESSIONISM IN LIGHT

A scene from the Theatre Guild's production of *From Morn to Midnight,*
designed by Lee Simonson. The absconding cashier beholds a snow-laden
tree, which gradually takes the form of a skeleton before his eyes.

Bruguière

EXPRESSIONISM THROUGH DISTORTION

A scene from *The Adding Machine,* as produced by the Theatre Guild
and set by Lee Simonson. The expressionistic setting is less an indication
of place than a reflection of the character's mental state.

was a fair example of expressionism; so was the ant scene in *The World We Live In*. The German production of *Masse Mensch* attained world-wide fame for its expressionistic power, some of which was retained in the Theatre Guild production in New York. The Theatre Guild productions of *Morn to Midnight* and *The Adding Machine* were good examples of expressionism, the scenery in each of these symbolizing the character's state of mind rather than the place. Expressionism in the theatre is as elemental in its appeal as lyric poetry, and quite as difficult to describe or analyze; but unlike lyric poetry it is in its infancy, and its greatest possibilities are yet to be realized. In its purpose to transcend life and to reveal the artist's own dream or vision it is very close to the essential magic of the theatre, and so is theoretically sound; but it is open to several practical objections and perhaps one theoretical one.

The theoretical objection is that after all neither the artist nor the observer can really vision anything except in terms of this world; that imagination is but a conjuring up and reassembling of memories, or impressions. Expressionism therefore can only be a kind of larger impressionism—something carried a step farther and made a degree more abstract, but still essentially the same. This objection is no stronger than the expressionists' own objection to impressionism.

The practical objections include the difficulty of separating the methods of expressionism from the methods of other schools, the absence of an established language of abstractions for the theatre, comparable to the language of music (the most truly expressionistic of the arts), and the almost prohibitively high order of technique required to convey a pure mood or a lyric emotion without distortion or distraction. Because of these difficulties the expressionists—like the symbolists and formalists—have usually found it expedient to compromise; and so we find many so-called expressionistic productions involving elements of realism, or symbolism, or even stylization.

One type of so-called expressionistic painting which has often found its way to the stage is the type sometimes described as primitivism. It consists largely of distorted angles and reverse perspective and resembles more than anything else the drawings made by insane persons. Right angles are ignored; doors and windows are made triangular or trapezoidal; houses appear top-heavy and unbalanced; and perspective lines diverge when they should converge. One of the most effective settings of the kind was used in the photoplay *The Cabinet of Dr. Caligari* to express the insanity of the principal character. On the stage such settings are seldom effective as pure expressionism, though sometimes quite effective as stylization—notably in the *Chauve Souris*. Even the Caligari settings owed much of their effectiveness to the stylistic flavor, and to the extraordinary excellence of the composition.

The most effective instruments of expressionism in the theatre, apart from the actor himself, are music, rhythm, color, and light. The use of music in this connection is not new; the soft music accompanying sentimental or pathetic scenes in the theatres of yesterday was really a form of expressionism. Rhythm, apart from music, is tremendous in its possibilities, and as yet almost undeveloped except in the ballet. Color has been used decoratively and symbolically, but its potentialities in connection with light have only recently been recognized. It is with light, of course, that the expressionist designer chiefly works, and his greatest achievements so far have undoubtedly been those of the space stage, in which light is virtually the only setting.

FUTURISTIC FORMALISM

A Russian setting for *Uriel Akosta,* emphasizing the structural composition of the playing space, but lacking the anti-decorative quality of true constructivism. Russian and German settings make liberal use of steps and platforms at different levels.

CUBISM AND FUTURISM

Scenic artists have borrowed so heavily from the cubist and futurist painters, that a word about the relation of cubism and futurism to the theatre seems necessary.

Cubism began, apparently, as a kind of expressionism. It was not a motive in itself, but a method of attaining the necessary abstraction to serve an expressionistic purpose. The cubist made use of line, mass, and color in illogical arrangements of squares and rectangles, hoping to express emotion or mood through pure composition. The futurist carried the same idea farther by adding triangles and other geometric figures, and finally by abandoning as far as possible all recognized forms and using only the most meaningless combinations of line, mass, and color that he could devise. Both, however, became stylists as well as expressionists, and eventually stylists rather than expressionists. Much of the best futuristic painting is really pure design, with a decorative rather than an expressionistic purpose.

Transferred to the theatre, cubism and futurism have usually been stylistic in their chief effect, though often hailed as expressionistic. The typical futurist setting is far too obtrusive, too puzzling, too challenging, to be directly emotional. It may be decorative, and parts of it may be symbolic; but it lacks the subordination necessary to the most powerful expressionism.

CONSTRUCTIVISM

What is supposed to be the last word (to date) in futurism and formalism is the type of setting originated by Meyerhold, in Russia, and known as the constructivist setting. Meyerhold calls it a step beyond expressionism and speaks of it as "biomechanical"—whatever that means.

The constructivist setting ranges from a fairly substantial but inconsequential grouping of platforms and steps that lead nowhere to the most amazing collection of torn and twisted junk, suggestive of wrecked sky-scrapers and exploded machine shops. There is usually no scenery in the ordinary sense, no background except the brick wall of the theatre with its iron ladders and hanging lines.

Needless to say, constructivism is anti-realistic—more violently so than any other movement. In addition it has three distinctive motives: To provide the most varied and flexible arrangement of the playing space; to free the inner meaning of the play from the entanglements of decorative beauty; and to reflect the spirit of the machine age.

That these motives are not as new as they sound, a little thought will quickly reveal. The first motive has been that of experienced directors for generations; they have sought variety in the arrangement of the playing space for the sake of variety in movement and grouping. Even the use of different heights and levels, of ramps and stairs, did not originate with constructivism; these have been used for years by the realists, and have been highly developed by the formalists and plasticists. The second motive is just another attempt to subordinate decoration to meaning—the original fundamental principle of good design—but the method chosen, that of deliberate *anti*-decorativeness, is unsound, because it ignores the fact that insistent ugliness is even more distracting than beauty. The third motive—to reflect the spirit of the machine age—is pure stylization.

Of the several anti-realistic movements, constructivism is the only one, it seems to me, which is essentially bad. It is bad because it obtrudes and distracts; because it violates the most fundamental purpose of the background by revealing the back-stage uglinesses which we do not wish to see; because

Courtesy of the Theatre Magazine

From Nash Mir (Berlin)

CONSTRUCTIVISM

Typical "bio-mechanic" settings of the Meyerhold school. The lower (for Alexis Tolstoi's *Revolt of the Machines*) is intended to convey the atmosphere of Soviet industrialism. The inscriptions are suggestive: "The Universal and Artificial Workers," "Each for himself," etc.

it creates unpleasant empathic effects by deliberately ignoring the laws of gravity, balance, and proportion, and by stationing crowds of actors on apparently flimsy platforms and ladders; and finally because it makes use of stage materials which, though they look convincing in pictures, show up in the theatre as more false and tawdry than the worst painted scenery. The setting used by the Moscow Art Musical Studio for *Carmencita and the Soldier*, for example, consisted of arches, steps, ramps, and bridges, the bad joints and painted surfaces of which were more disturbing than the bad joints and painted surfaces of a realistic box setting, because they were supposed to be structural, and had to bear the weight of a large chorus.

SUBORDINATION

A comparison of the various anti-realistic movements, including simplified realism, and a consideration of their best features, seems to lead us back to the old utilitarian basis of good design, the principle of subordination. Subordination of the unessential to the essential is after all the one thing upon which the best designers of all schools agree. True, they sometimes disagree as to what *is* essential, but that is the inevitable human factor. The best realism is simplified realism; the best symbolism is that which captures the significant mood; the best stylization is colorful, but subordinate; the best formalism keeps the background neutral and accentuates the action; the best plasticism vitalizes the actor and makes him dominate the playing space; and the best expressionism is that which creates a vision with the least possible interference from non-essentials.

The type of setting that seems to follow most closely this common principle of subordination is that of the space stage; and its chief instrument of subordination is the manipulation of light. The true space stage, however, has one serious limitation. When the background is a complete void and all the light is concentrated on the action, the emotional power of the light—as well as its command over attention—is tremendous. The result is a sustained intensity which is not suitable for all plays, or for all scenes of some emotional plays. To make all scenes of all plays emotionally intense is to weaken the power of emphasis by destroying contrast, just as habitual profanity weakens the power of expression in emergency. It seems probable, therefore, that the truest form of scenic art for the future will turn out to be a kind of modified space stage, flexible enough to include elements of symbolism or stylization when these are called for, and even elements of simplified realism; but with the light so controlled as to achieve any necessary degree of subordination, from the mere toning down of a too obtrusive stylistic background to the most intense expressionism.

SPACE STAGE METHODS IN SIMPLIFIED REALISM

A setting by Norman Bel Geddes for Gilbert Miller's production of *The Patriot*. The setting is substantial and realistic, but only the essential portion is lighted.

SPACE STAGE METHODS IN STYLIZATION

A scene from Max Reinhardt's production of *A Midsummer Night's Dream* (Courtesy of Charles Frohman, Inc.).

CHAPTER XIX

AMATEUR STAGECRAFT

BOOKS on play production have generally offered more help on the problems of stagecraft than on those of acting or directing; some of them, in fact, are almost entirely devoted to stagecraft, as if it were the whole problem. The elementary side of it has been particularly well covered, and no amateur stage manager need now be ignorant of how to nail boards together to make the frame of a flat, how to tack the canvas on, how to mix and apply the paint, how to color the electric light bulbs, how to stencil costumes or construct properties. It seems unnecessary to repeat very much of this. But there are certain elementary matters which must, for the sake of clearness, be discussed.

STANDARD THEATRE EQUIPMENT

The amateur director should know the usual working equipment of the commercial theatre, not only because he may some time have to work in one, but because that type of theatre represents better than any other the accumulation of practical experience, and is of necessity made adaptable to the widest possible variety of productions.

The standard theatre stage today is flat, or nearly so, with no obstructions in or near the playing space. The floor is of soft wood, to permit of the use of screw braces, and is built in sections, certain of which may be taken up to provide for trap doors; in very elaborate theatres or opera houses the sections are capable of being raised or lowered mechanically

407

to give several different playing levels. The stage space is always much larger than the visible playing space; in the best theatres it is as large again behind, above, and on either side.

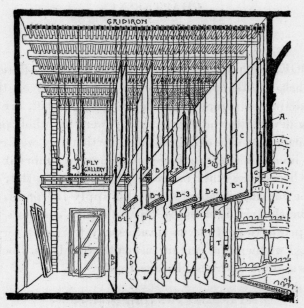

FIG. 23.—STANDARD THEATRE EQUIPMENT

A, asbestos fire curtain; *B-1,* first border, or teaser; *B-2-3-4,* other borders, set; *B-B,* other borders, flied; *B-D,* back drop; *B-L,* border lights; *C,* curtain, or act drop; *C-D,* cut drop; *C-P,* ceiling piece for box set, flied; *D-1,* drop used as backing for scenes "in one" (*i.e.,* shallow scenes); *D-D,* other drops, flied; *F,* flats, stored for next act; *G-D,* grand drapery; *P-B,* prompt box; *S-B,* switchboard; *S-S,* sand bags, on idle lines; *T,* tormentor; *W-W,* wing flats.

Above the stage, usually a little more than twice as high as the proscenium opening, is the gridiron, a most important item in standard theatre equipment. It is a skeleton platform of wood or iron, and on it are mounted rows of pulleys to carry the lines on which certain pieces of scenery are hauled up out of sight when not in use. The space above the stage is known as the "flies," and the "fly gallery" is a gallery at one side of the stage, about as high as the proscenium frame; from it the lines are operated. The lines are rigged in sets of three (or more in very large theatres), and are tied to the drop or other piece of scenery at as many points. Each line is carried straight up to a pulley on the gridiron, then over to the gallery side and down over another pulley to the fly gallery. The gallery rail, known as the "pin rail," is like the rail of a ship, with rows of belaying pins for the lines. The three lines of each set are handled and belayed as one. When a set is not in use, the three loose ends are tied together, and weighted with a sandbag, which is hauled up in the flies and belayed.[1] There are many sets of lines in a large theatre, spaced as closely as pos-

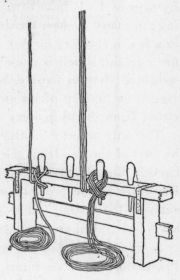

FIG. 24.—PIN RAIL

sible from the proscenium to the rear wall of the stage, so that vast quantities of scenery can be hauled up out of the way. Most of the scenery, however, is brought in and mounted for a particular play, and carried away afterwards; the only pieces in the flies that belong permanently to the theatre are the fire curtain, the regular curtain or "act drop," the "teaser" or first border, and perhaps a decorative "grand drapery" either before or behind the act drop. The grand drapery is often omitted, and sometimes the teaser is known

[1] Persons who are to handle the lines should know how to make knots that will not come loose; otherwise somebody may be killed by a falling sandbag or drop. The Boy Scout and Girl Scout Handbooks contain excellent instructions for tying knots. Most important is the "sheet bend", the only safe method of tying a thin rope to a thick one.

by that name. The teaser, however, is behind the act drop, and may be adjusted between acts to fix the height of the proscenium opening. It is handled on an ordinary set of lines. The act drop is usually counter-weighted and operated by a geared windlass to permit of rapid raising and lowering; in many modern theatres it is operated electrically, and in a few of the very largest all the lines are so operated. The fire curtain, which is usually very heavy, is partly counter-weighted; but in most cities the law requires that it be so rigged as to drop of its own weight when released by hand, either from the fly gallery or the prompter's box.

The only scenery on the stage floor that remains in place as part of the theatre is the pair of wing flats just behind the curtain line, known as "tormentors", and used to regulate the width of the proscenium opening as well as to mask the sides of the setting. The rest of the stage is clear until a set is brought in and mounted.

A standard outdoor set consists of a back drop and several "borders," which are hung in the flies and handled from the gallery, and a number of "wings" [1] which are handled on the stage floor. Each wing is a painted flat, with a hinged flap to give it stability; it is merely dragged into place and braced from behind with one or two stage braces, screwed to the floor. In addition to the wings, borders, and drops, there may be set pieces or special pieces—trees, rocks, houses, fences—which are handled in various ways according to their nature, some as properties, some as flats, and some as fly pieces. Occasionally a whole setting is "flied" for convenience in making a quick change.

A standard indoor setting consists of canvas flats, handled

---

[1] Strictly, wing *flats*—the wings being properly the spaces off stage to the right and left. In stage lingo adjectives often come to be used as nouns; the border lights, for example, are commonly spoken of as "the borders".

on the stage floor, set up, lashed together, and braced, to-gether with a ceiling piece let down from the flies and opened out to lie on top of the flats. Doors, and sometimes windows, are mounted in separate frames; these are set into openings in the canvas flats and inde-pendently braced, so that they will stand firm when opened or closed, and not shake the walls.

The standard lighting sys-tem consists of footlights, sev-eral rows of b o r d e r lights (strips of lights hung in the flies), portable "bunch" lights and spotlights, portable strips, and perhaps a few floodlights for overhead use. The port-able lights m a y be plugged in at various points on t h e stage floor, and in some in-stances m a y b e controlled by dimmers o n t h e regular

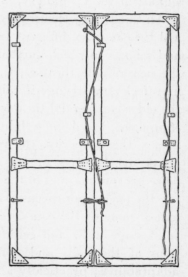

FIG. 25.—METHOD OF LASHING FLATS

switchboard. The footlights and borders are usually con-trolled in four circuits for separate colors, white, amber, blue, and red. They are operated from the switchboard and are connected with dimmers, which are usually interlocking, so that all the colors may be dimmed at once, or all the circuits of one color. The footlights are also divided in some theatres into three sections, right, left, and center, which may be operated separately. The borders are seldom divided in that way; but the first, second, and third rows of borders may be controlled separately.

The switchboard is located behind the proscenium frame at one side; usually it is elevated, with a platform for the operator high enough to be out of the way of the actors using the tormentor entrance. The prompter is usually stationed on the same side as the switchboard—sometimes right under it—and is provided with a small reading desk close to the proscenium frame. Over the desk are push buttons operating signals in the fly gallery, orchestra pit, and dressing rooms.

All this is very elementary, but the equipment of the standard theatre is so different from that of the club-houses, halls and schools in which amateurs usually play, or from that of the newer little theatres, that even an experienced amateur may feel very strange if called upon to play in one. Few of the older commercial theatres in this country have, as regular equipment, the flexible lighting units, the cycloramas or sky domes, the draperies, the revolving or wagon stages of the newer art theatres or the finer little theatres, though the more prosperous ones in the larger cities are gradually adopting the major improvements in lighting. On the other hand, almost none of the commercial theatres are afflicted with the solid stage walls and ceilings, or mis-designed lighting systems of the halls and club-houses. Their virtue is their adaptability; practically any kind of equipment usable elsewhere can be mounted and handled in a standard theatre, while standard equipment cannot always be handled in the art theatres and can seldom be handled in halls and club-houses.

UTILITY SETTINGS

A question often asked by amateurs is, "If we can only afford one or two settings at first, what do you advise us to build?"

So many modern plays call for interior scenes, and so few are purely poetic or expressionistic, that some sort of a box setting is almost indispensable. Its usefulness, however, will be in proportion to its adaptability; and that will depend upon two things: the possibility of varying the arrangement

of the walls, doors, windows, and set pieces, and the possibility
of changing the decorative scheme.

When a box setting is constructed in the standard manner

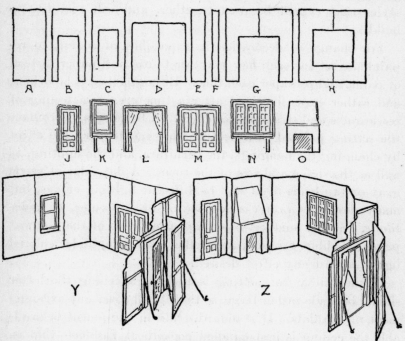

FIG. 26.—AN ADAPTABLE BOX SETTING

A to *H*, types of flats; *D*, a backing; *G, H*, hinged flats; *J* to *O*, framed
pieces to go with flats. As least two each are needed of *B, C, E, J*, and *K*,
and four or five each of *A* and *D*. The sketches at *Y* and *Z* show widely
different arrangements of the units.

the flats are interchangeable, and may be lashed together in
any order. This makes it possible to vary slightly the shape
of the room, and to vary considerably the positions of the
doors and windows. For maximum adaptability, however, the
set should be constructed with a few extra units, including
some plain flats and some odd doors and windows. With the
aid of these the shape and size of the stage room can be
altered in almost any conceivable way, and the number of

doors and windows can be altered, as well as the arrangement. A single set with extra sections will permit a much greater variety of effects than two complete sets of different styles that cannot be used together, and will cost less to build.

For change of decoration it is possible, of course, to repaint the set for each new play; or to use wall-paper instead of paint, and re-paper each time. Either method is laborious, and rather expensive, and after a time creates a feeling of restlessness and straining for effect. A better plan is to have the setting painted in a neutral tint, and to vary the effect by changing the hangings, the furniture, and the lighting, as well as the shape and size of the room. A flat color of warm gray or tan lends itself well to different lighting effects, but many designers prefer a surface of broken color, or *pointilage*. Such a surface, especially if made up of the pigment primaries, blue, crimson, and yellow, will give, under colored lights, almost any effect desired.

If the utility box setting is to have a ceiling the latter should be made rather large, so that it will cover any arrangement of the flats. If standard gridiron equipment is available the ceiling is best handled pocketbook fashion—that is, it is hinged in the middle and the lines attached at the joint, so that when they are pulled up the ceiling folds flat. An extra set of lines attached to each outer edge facilitates opening the ceiling when it is to be set. If there is no gridiron and no space above the stage the handling of the ceiling becomes an awkward matter, and some producers feel that it is not worth bothering with under such conditions. Audiences seem to pay very little attention to the absence of a ceiling, even on an indoor stage; they accept the convention of an open setting; and in the outdoor theatre they expect it.

Next to the utility box setting, the most useful equipment

for ordinary stages is an outdoor set of wings, borders, and drop—unless a sky dome is available, in which case the back drop and the borders can be discarded, and the wings used merely as masks at the sides, if at all. With a sky dome the chief equipment needed is a supply of set pieces and horizon pieces of various kinds—rocks, bushes, fences, corners of houses, and the like—and these are also useful with the wing-and-drop set. Even the conventional set can be more simply and artistically painted than it usually is in the old commercial theatres; simplification without stylization is the end to be sought. With the wing-and-drop setting, as with the box setting, a few extra units in the same unobtrusive style will greatly increase the range of usefulness.

SCREEN-AND-DRAPERY SETTINGS

Some amateurs have found the greatest usefulness in an adaptable screen-and-drapery setting. This type of setting shows its indebtedness to Gordon Craig's designs for *Hamlet*, at the Moscow Art Theatre in 1912;[1] but in common practice follows more closely the well known settings of Sam Hume. It consists of a collection of movable units, including a number of hinged screens, several flat panels, one large arch, two smaller arches, several sections of platform, and several sets of steps, with enough draperies to mask the sides and fill in the gaps between the units. The screens are simply tall narrow flats hinged together in threes, so that when stood up they look like square columns or pylons. All the units are painted in a uniform neutral tone, or in broken color, and the draperies are of a darker neutral tone.

Such an equipment can be rearranged in an almost endless variety of forms, and with variations in the color, intensity, and direction of the light, can be made to suggest many dif-

[1] See Craig: *Towards a New Theatre*

ferent moods. It can be used as a purely formal background to stand throughout the play, or as a solid but unobtrusive background for simplified realism, or as an instrument of

FIG. 27.—SCREEN-AND-DRAPERY SETTINGS

The built units are shown at *A*. *B, C, D,* and *E* suggest the possibilities of varied arrangement.

symbolism, or—with the aid of perfectly controlled light—as a background for modified space stage effects with a more or less expressionistic purpose.

Unless very heavy or very fine materials are used, the

equipment is not unduly expensive; and when the taste of the group is for symbolic, or poetic, or fanciful plays, it will give a great deal of service in proportion to the cost. It does tend, however, to become monotonous, if used continually, in spite of the rearrangements. The units are so conspicuous that they cannot escape attention, and they tend to establish themselves as a kind of stylization, appropriate enough for some plays, but not for all. For unobtrusive neutrality the simple arras setting is probably better.

ARRAS SETTINGS

The most elementary form of arras setting is the plain curtain, hanging in loose folds across the entire stage, and masked at the sides by the tormentors or by the proscenium itself. If the playing space is shallow this may constitute the whole setting. If a deeper stage is required, there will be additional draperies to serve as wings and borders; or the side curtains may be hung longitudinally like the walls of a box setting.

On a regular stage with gridiron equipment the curtains are usually hung from the lines. If the setting is tall and the stage shallow no borders are needed, other than the first border or teaser. When borders are to be used, they should be of the same material and should be hung in folds like the rest of the curtains, to escape any suggestion of realistic intent.

Arras settings are particularly useful for broad, bare platforms, such as are found in many halls and assembly rooms. When there is no proscenium a regular painted setting looks fragmentary and incomplete; but an arras setting in quiet tones provides an unobtrusive formal background against which illustrative or symbolic properties can be used very effectively. If the lighting equipment is sufficiently under control, and the curtains fairly dark, the arras setting can be made to serve the purpose of the space stage.

There are two ways of rigging an arras setting on a bare

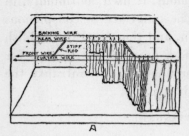

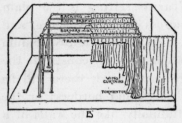

FIG. 28.—METHODS OF SUPPORTING ARRAS SETTINGS

platform. One is to support it with piano wires stretched taut from wall to wall (*A*, Figure 28). The other is to use a framework of wood or metal (*B*, Figure 28). Several manufacturers of curtain settings now supply such frameworks, made of iron pipes, and capable of being set up on any open platform or floor space where there is room. They are, however, rather elaborate and rather expensive. For most amateur purposes a home-made framework or a set of wires will be just as satisfactory and less costly. With the wire rigging the worst problem is to find an adequate method of anchoring the wires to the walls; if that can be done, and the curtains used are not too heavy, the scheme is quite satisfactory. If the curtains tend to sag, they can be supported at the corners of the setting with wooden props, which should, however, be guyed to prevent their wobbling. With the wire rigging no borders or ceilings are needed; the wires are inconspicuous, and the audience readily accepts the convention of mere hangings. At least four wires are needed: one for the curtain, one for the front of the setting, one for the back of the setting, and one for any backings to be used behind rear doors or other openings in the setting. The sides of the setting, if hung box-fashion, may be sup-

418

ported on rods or poles hooked to the cross wires; wires would not do at the sides, as they would tend to draw the cross wires together.

When used on an open stage and without a ceiling, the

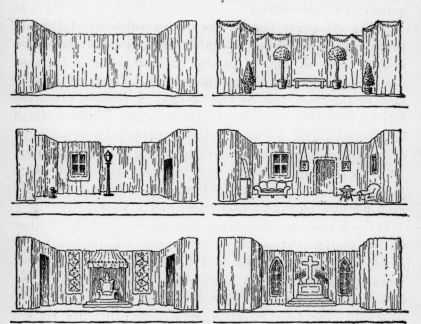

FIG. 29.—ARRAS SETTINGS

Suggesting the many different effects obtained with simple units.

arras setting should not be over ten feet high, so that it may be used to suggest outdoor as well as indoor scenes. The curtains should be in sections, so that openings can be arranged at any desired point, and a few extra sections should be provided, some of them suggestively decorated. It is amazing how much can be symbolized with a few changes of hangings and a few significant properties. Two or three potted plants and a bench suggest a garden; a rectangular opening suggests a doorway, and the lighting determines whether you are looking in or looking out; a lamp-post and a fire-plug make a street corner; a little furniture and a few hangings make a room; a throne and canopy transform it into a palace; a Gothic arch, an altar, and a couple of hangings suggest a cathedral (Figure 29).

There are great possibilities in symbolism or stylization through the use—either separately or in conjunction with a neutral arras setting—of painted curtains, hung in folds, as curtains, and not flat like painted drops. The frank acceptance of the folds disarms any thought of realistic representation, while the symbolic values remain. Whole settings have been painted and hung in this way; but with an ordinary arras setting it is only necessary to use an occasional painted panel or backing in order to get the suggestive effect. Distant backgrounds are very well suggested in this way, and even pictures on the wall, or doors and windows.

It is obviously possible to combine the arras setting—either on the platform stage or in the regular theatre—with elements of simplified realism or stylization in the form of built units or painted flats. A fairly realistic back drop, if set at a distance and not too brilliantly lighted, may be effectively used with a curtained forestage; or a single panel, like Juliet's balcony in Rollo Peters' setting, or like the gate of the Wall of China in Lee Simonson's setting for *Marco Millions,* may be introduced as the central element of what is otherwise an arras setting. This type of combination has been especially popular with little theatre groups.

SKELETON SETTINGS

Another type of setting that has worked out effectively for many plays, on the professional as well as the amateur stage, is the "skeleton" setting. It consists of a fairly substantial setting occupying the fore part of the stage and remaining throughout the performance, but with several archways or other openings at the back through which are disclosed different backings for different scenes (Figure 30). The outer structure may be neutral in design and formal in purpose; or it may be stylized for the whole play.

In the true skeleton setting the action takes place on the forestage, and the changing panels function merely as symbols to suggest change of place or change of mood. In modified forms the openings are sometimes made larger, and part of the action placed within them. When there is only one large opening, as in the Arliss-Ames production of *The Merchant of Venice* (Page 396), it functions as a kind of inner proscenium, disclosing an inner stage, and harking back in spirit to the

FIG. 30.—A SKELETON SETTING

double stage of Elizabethan times. In that case there is usually a panel curtain which shuts off the inner stage during changes of setting while transition scenes are being played on the outer stage.

The skeleton setting has two distinct advantages: it makes possible a rapid succession of different scenes without overelaboration on the one hand or tawdriness on the other, and it establishes a certain unity of effect in the play as a whole. It is obviously more economical than a complete outfit of different settings for the same play, each occupying the full stage; but to be most effective it should be tastefully designed and substantially built, and so is not altogether cheap. If stylized to suit the particular play it can seldom be used again for other plays, and from the amateur standpoint this is a serious disadvantage. There are, however, excellent possibilities of compromise between the skeleton setting and the screen-and-drapery setting, by which the unity of the one can be combined with the economy of the other; and there is always the possibility of a permanent formal stage with the panel feature of the skeleton setting.

DOMES AND CYCLORAMAS

For the modern little theatre some sort of cycloramic equipment is highly desirable; and a sky dome is to be preferred.

The ordinary cyclorama, or *Rundhorizont,* is merely a concave backing to take the place of the painted back drop; it is approximately semi-cylindrical in form, and is painted white, light gray, or light blue. Its purpose is to suggest distance by diffusing the light instead of reflecting it directly, and to obviate the need of wings by encircling the playing space as far as the eye can see on either side. It must be very tall, however, to make the use of borders unnecessary. The cyclorama may be a permanent structure of wood or metal and plaster; or it may be of canvas stretched on some sort of metal frame. The latter form has the advantage of light weight and easy handling; it can be hauled up out of the way when not needed, as in the Yale University Theatre; or it can be made to roll up on a kind of vertical shade roller at one side of the proscenium; or it can be taken down completely, and stored away. But it is always inferior to the plaster cyclorama in the fact that its joints and wrinkles engage the eye, establish the distance, and destroy the illusion. Perhaps, after all, it is little better than a canvas back drop, which does exactly the same thing. If the wrinkles must show, it may be better to hang a cycloramic curtain frankly in folds, with no attempt at illusion. But the plaster cyclorama, if well made and properly lighted, defeats every attempt of the eye to gauge its distance, and gives only the illusion of limitless space. It is more convincing when realism is the object; it is also more ethereal, more spiritual, more poetic.

Even better than the cyclorama is the sky dome, or *Kuppelhorizont*, which is simply a cyclorama in three dimensions. The upper part is curved in spherically above the playing space in such a way as to conceal all back-stage machinery, and to present a reflecting surface for the light as nearly as possible perpendicular at every point to the spectator's line of vision. If the surface is smooth, but dull, the curvature uniform, and the lighting well controlled, the effect is like infinity itself—vast, moving, transcendent.

The one objection to the dome, aside from its cost, is the fact that it limits to some extent the available space for handling other scenery, and obstructs the entrances and exits. A dome of canvas, to be rolled up when not in use, is hardly practicable; in fact, the whole effectiveness of the dome is dependent upon good construction and smooth finish. When the eye is ranging over infinity, the slightest imperfection creates a distraction and destroys the illusion or the mood. It is possible to build a plaster dome that can be moved back out of the way, but it is not practicable unless the theatre is heavily endowed, and a great deal of space is available. When the space is available, however, even a permanent dome can be made large enough, and set back far enough, to leave a normal amount of space for handling ordinary scenery; the gridiron must, of course, be placed very high in that case, so that hanging scenery does not interfere with the view of the dome.

Some theatres employ a modified type of dome, partly flat-

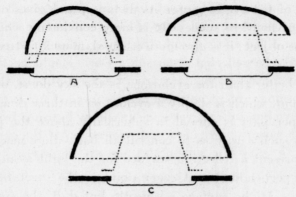

FIG. 31.—TYPES OF SKY DOMES

tened out, and curved more sharply at the edges (B, Figure 31). This is fairly effective, and entirely so for scenes in which the sides of the stage are masked by draperies or set pieces and only the central portion of the dome is seen. For such scenes even a flat plastered wall is satisfactory, and is certainly a great improvement on the painted canvas drop. But for open sky scenes—desert, or seashore scenes, for example—the spherical, or nearly spherical, dome is best. A too rapid curvature, or a curvature that is not uniform, as in the small experimental theatre at Yale, or the Goodman Memorial Theatre at Chicago, makes a perfectly even distribution of light impossible, and is readily detected by the eye. A uniform curvature helps to diffuse the light; and a large dome, set some distance back, helps to create the effect of spaciousness (C, Figure 31).

Some domes and cycloramas are painted in *pointilage*, or broken color, and this makes possible an amazing variation of lighting effects; but unless the theatre is very large and the dome a long distance from the observer, the eye readily detects the patches of color and gauges the distance correctly. An even tone of pale gray is better. It takes the light well, and gives no hint of its exact distance. The dome is usually lighted from above and below (Figure 22, page 385), and the more diffused the light, the better, though it need not necessarily be reflected from silk. Care should be taken to avoid casting direct shadows from the footlights on the dome or cyclorama, except as these may be needed for expressionistic or symbolic effect; yet some auxiliary lighting from footlights or balcony lights is usually necessary if the characters are not to be seen as silhouettes against the sky.

MODERN STAGE LIGHTING

Modern lighting equipment is extraordinarily flexible, and with patience and experiment almost any desired effect can be obtained. The most important improvement in recent years has been the perfection of high powered, concentrated filament, incandescent lamps, which give a light almost as bright and white as that of the arc, but unlike the arc can be controlled with dimmers, and can be depended upon. These, in turn, have made possible the many different types of portable floodlights, spotlights, and "baby spots," and also the screened spotlights and floodlights mounted on the front of the balcony and operated from the switchboard.

Ordinary footlights, proscenium lights, and border lights are still used, and still useful, even in little theatres. There is a tendency to do away with color-dipped bulbs, because the color deteriorates with the heat, and to substitute boxed lamps with glass or gelatine color screens (*B*, *C*, Figure 32). But these are individually bulkier, especially the square kind, and being fewer in number and higher in power are more apt to create unwanted shadows than the old-fashioned strip lights (*A*, Figure 32). The latter, if too bright, have a way of casting blurred shadows of the actors on the scenery;

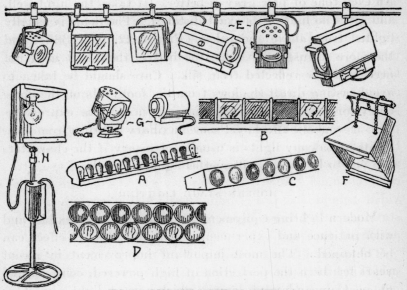

FIG. 32.—MODERN LIGHTING UNITS

A, strip lights; *B*, square boxed foots; *C*, round boxed foots; *D*, round boxed foots, banked close; *E*, a concert border of spots and floods; *F*, a hanging floodlight; *G*, typical baby spots; *H*, a floodlight on a floor stand, with separate dimmer.

but when boxed footlights are used they cast several distinct shadows instead. In a recent production of *The Devil's Disciple*, with boxed footlights, no less than twelve separate shadows of Dick Dudgeon marched across the back drop in lock-step formation every time he moved. Another difficulty is that the color screens of boxed footlights cannot be changed during the performance, and color changes must be accomplished by turning on different units; but when the units are large and far apart, individual splotches of color appear on the nearest furniture and on the actors' legs. Boxed footlights give purer colors than dipped lamps, and hold their colors permanently, but unless they are made very compact and banked close together (as at *D*, Figure 32) they do not blend the colors and diffuse the rays as well.

For the first, or "concert" border, a row of adjustable spotlights and floodlights, mounted on an iron pipe (*E*, Figure 32), is now the preferred equipment; and similar units may be mounted on vertical pipes at the sides to replace the old proscenium lights. These units, being behind the curtain, can be re-set, if necessary, for each act, and the color, position, and focus of each light changed. They can be controlled and dimmed from the switchboard during the act; and those at the sides can be hand-operated, and even the color changed. In a large theatre, where a bridge is provided behind the proscenium, individual operators can be stationed at all these lights, manipulating them during the action of the play.

The modern baby spotlights (*F*, Figure 32) are especially useful in little theatres, and comparatively inexpensive. They can be mounted almost anywhere and in any position, and operated with dimmers from the switchboard. Many of them are provided with focussing devices, and can be used either as spotlights or floodlights.

For high-powered floodlighting, the old-fashioned bunchlights of low-wattage bulbs and the arc-light "olivettes" have been largely superseded by single high-wattage incandescent lamps in suitable housings. They may be mounted on stands like ordinary bunchlights, and may be dimmed from the switchboard, or by means of special dimmers mounted on the stands (*G*, Figure 32). Color changes may be accomplished, as with the bunchlights, by means of gelatine screens, which can be fed slowly into place by hand. Floodlights can also be hung in the flies (*H*, Figure 32), and in some theatres they have largely displaced the strip borders for overhead lighting. In this position, however, the colors cannot so readily be changed, except by the use of separate units separately controlled.

Floodlights and modified spotlights mounted on the front of the balcony are in high favor with some producers, and they are certainly a great improvement over the old hand-operated balcony spotlights. Unlike the arc spots they are noiseless; and because there are no operators moving about, the audience is hardly aware of their existence. For much variation of color effect, however, a considerable number of them are necessary.

The tendency in many little theatres is to elaborate the lighting equipment unnecessarily. For ordinary purposes a very simple outfit will serve. A few portable units, easily adjustable and provided with dimmers, will give greater flexibility than a much more extensive outfit permanently installed. On a small stage great brilliance is seldom required, and there is no use in having so many lights that they must be kept half dimmed at all times.

The most essential part of the lighting equipment is a good bank of dimmers. The older installations did not have enough dimmers, and those they had were tied up with permanent circuits in the footlights or borders, and could not be used for other purposes. A modern switchboard is built on the unit plan with interchangeable connections like the plug-and-jack connections on a telephone switchboard, so that any circuit in the theatre, permanent or temporary, can be connected to a switch and a dimmer, and disconnected when not in use. Since the dimmers are provided with interlocking devices and master handles, the interchangeable feature makes it possible to group the circuits in any desired way for operation in unison. With a switchboard of this type—even a small one—a great deal can be accomplished. Six or eight dimmers will take care of the most pressing needs on a small stage, provided none of them are tied up with idle circuits.

For outdoor lighting effects where ordinary equipment is not available, also for emergency lighting or supplementary lighting indoors, it is sometimes possible to use automobile headlights and spotlights. From four to eight headlights, mounted behind the audience on tall posts, will light a woodland stage fairly well; and a twenty-one candle power spotlight will pick out a point of emphasis quite acceptably. Dimming equipment is not so readily available, but for single lamps some of the more substantial six-volt rheostats made for the radio trade can be used. The power can be drawn from six-volt batteries, or from small transformers connected with regular house current, but the latter are not usually able to carry very many lights at once. Some ingenuity is required in mounting and handling such equipment, but ingenuity is the amateur producer's particular talent.

COLOR IN STAGE LIGHTING

Those whose experience with colors has been confined to the mixing of pigments have little conception, as a rule, of the problems involved in stage lighting. Lights and pigments do not mix in the same way at all. For example, red and blue pigments mixed together give purple, but a red light on a blue pigment gives black. Red and green lights mixed together give yellow light, but red and green pigments mixed together give a dirty brown.

Theoretically, the visible spectrum includes an infinite number of color variations. Practically, the human eye is only sensitive to three colors of light: red, green, and violet; and all our color sensations are in terms of these three colors, singly, or in composition. They are known as the light primaries, or additive primaries—additive because the three kinds of light added together give the sensation of white.

When a red glass or gelatine is used to screen a white light, its effect—provided, of course, it is a true primary red—is to suppress the green and violet rays and to let only the red through. When a green glass is used—a true primary green—its effect is to suppress the red and violet rays and let only the green through. If two screens are used together, on one lamp, both of them true primary colors, they will not let any light through; but if they are used on separate lamps, and the two colors played together on a white surface (no other light being present), they will show a color different from either. Red and green rays, in equal proportions, will give yellow; green and violet will give blue; violet and red will give crimson. In other words, what we call yellow is simply the sensation of seeing red and green rays simultaneously and indistinguishably, in the complete absence of violet rays. What we call blue is the sensation of seeing green and violet rays simultaneously; and crimson is the sensation of seeing violet and red rays simultaneously.

A yellow pigment is a pigment which, in a white light— that is, a light made up of all three rays—has the peculiar property of absorbing the violet rays, and reflecting only the red and green. A blue pigment is one that absorbs the red rays, and reflects the green and violet. A crimson pigment is one that absorbs the green, and reflects the red and violet. These three colors, each of which absorbs one kind of light completely, are known as the pigment primaries, or sub-tractive primaries. They are also known as the complementaries of the light primaries, a complementary of any color being that other color which represents the missing portion of white light.

When a light primary is played upon a pigment of its com-

COLORS OF LIGHT

COLORS OF PIGMENT

	RED	GREEN	VIOLET	RED AND VIOLET	GREEN AND VIOLET	RED AND GREEN

LIGHT PRIMARIES

BLUE

CRIMSON — PIGMENT PRIMARIES

YELLOW

GREEN

RED

VIOLET

ORANGE

BLUE-GREEN

PURPLE

EFFECTS OF COLORED LIGHTS ON COLORED PIGMENTS

plementary color, it should be obvious that black will result—black being the complete absence of light. Since there is only one kind of light present, and the pigment is one that reflects any other light but not that one, no light will be reflected. Thus a red light on a blue pigment shows black; a green light on a crimson pigment shows black; and a violet light on a yellow pigment shows black.

When a pure primary red light is played upon the stage, no green or violet rays being present, it is obvious that only red can be reflected. Different pigments, however, will reflect it with different intensities, the yellows, reds, and crimsons reflecting a great deal, and the blues little or none. This creates an illusion of white and black, and some of the books on color state that a red light on a red surface gives white, a red light on a green surface, gray, and a red light on a blue surface black. In reality there is no white light present, nor any other color except red; but in the presence of a single primary color one loses his sense of color discrimination, and sees only variations in intensity. When only green light is present, with no red or violet, one sees only light and dark green, and thinks of them as black and white; and when only violet light is present, he sees only light and dark violet. It is seldom possible, of course, to find sources of light or color screens that give true primary colors, or even to find pure pigment primaries, so that one seldom sees a perfect demonstration of these principles in the theatre. It is practically impossible to demonstrate them adequately on paper, and the accompanying color chart is merely a suggestive approximation.

On the chart I have tried to show the effect of red, green, and violet light, thrown separately on the primary pigments, and on various common mixtures of pigments; and also the effect of crimson light (a mixture of red and violet rays); of blue light (a mixture of green and violet rays) ; and of yellow light (a mixture of red and green rays). In spite of the inevitable inaccuracies in reproduction this may be useful in suggesting the most serious pitfalls in color lighting. It will certainly show how completely a color may be blacked out by light of its complementary color.

The colors most often used in the older theatres, in addition to white, are blue, red, and amber. But the red is rather a crimson than a vermilion; it is more nearly the pigment primary than the light primary, but is not quite either. The blue is neither the violet of the light primary nor the clear blue of the pigment primary; it is a dark blue, perhaps half way between. The amber is much darker than the yellow of the pigment primary, and contains more red rays. The mixtures obtained with such impure colors are more accidental than scientific. For that reason there has been a tendency in the newer theatres to introduce color units as nearly like the primary red, green, and violet of light as possible, and when this can be done it is possible to mix and control the colors much more accurately, and with more widely varied effects.

PROPERTIES

A good property man is a great asset to an amateur organization, but is not so hard to find if there is a real opportunity for him. It is nearly always a mistake to rent or borrow properties unnecessarily, or to buy expensive ones. The chance to make things, to exercise ingenuity in inventing, constructing, or improvising effects is just what the property man needs to maintain his interest.

Amateurs have found the five-and-ten-cent chain stores a godsend in the matter of properties. They not only offer cheap, but good-looking, jewelry, bric-a-brac, glass and china ware, draperies, and fittings of all kinds, but they offer *suggestions*. The inspiration for many a clever device or effect has been found on the counters of such stores, where articles are spread out in plain sight. The mail order catalogues are equally helpful; so are the windows of the army-and-navy-goods stores. A few trifling purchases, a little wire, or lumber, or canvas, and an *idea*, will often enable the property man to improvise what would have cost dollars to hire, and scores of dollars to purchase. Money paid out for renting properties gives no permanent return; on the other hand there is great satisfaction in building up a permanent stock of properties which, with occasional alterations, can be utilized again and again.

In the matter of alterations, the quick-drying brushing lacquers, with which objects can be given a new color and a fresh appearance in a few minutes, are most useful. The older gilt and aluminum lacquers have long been used for stage purposes, but the many bright new colors are bringing a new note into stage furnishing. Canvas or *papier mâché* set pieces, like canvas scenery, are usually painted with calcimine water colors, or tempera colors, and these also dry very quickly; but they are not suitable for painting furniture or hand properties. A very useful article is a can of drop black, or dull black lacquer, with which tin or wooden objects can be made to look like wrought iron.

As suggested in an earlier chapter, too many properties are confusing and distracting. On the other hand, too few sometimes weaken the illusion, and create another kind of distraction by failing to convince. Well selected properties help tremendously, for example, in the difficult matter of making a dinner scene convincing. But wax fruit and *papier mâché* roast chickens should be forbidden by law; they do more to create ruinous distraction in the theatre than whisky which is obviously cold tea—and in a prohibition country that is a great deal. Artificial flowers can be very distracting also, if handled by the actors or referred to in any way, though they are usually unobjectionable if used merely for background decoration.

A property often called for in realistic plays is a practicable clock, which registers the time to suit the dialogue. Since the dialogue cannot be timed accurately enough to coincide with the clock, the clock must be regulated to coincide with the dialogue. One method of doing this is to extend the shafts of the clock through the back wall of the setting, and turn them by hand from behind. A better method, which permits of the clock being placed at any position on the stage, is to rig up an electric control. An ordinary clock is used, but with the pendulum or balance wheel removed so that it will run very fast; and this is controlled by a spring brake, so arranged that it can be released by the pull of an electro-magnet. The operator stands in the wings or out front, where he can see the clock, and by pressing a button for an instant every few seconds he slips the clutch, so to speak, and allows the clock to move as rapidly as he desires. With a little practice he can make the motion quite imperceptible to the audience, and yet bring the hands to the right place for a given crisis in the play.

Another useful device is a board on which several kinds of electric bells are mounted, with the necessary batteries and push buttons. One should sound like a telephone bell, and another like a door bell; and the same bell should not be used for both purposes.

Off-stage effects in constant demand include wind and rain machines, automobile horns and motors, hoof-beat effects, and thunder sheets. The latter are usually made of sheet iron, but are not very convincing unless of large size and deep tone. Better effects are sometimes to be had with a bass drum or hollow cask, or with heavy shot on a wooden floor. The conventional wind machine is a wooden cylinder over which a piece of heavy silk has been hung, with one edge anchored and the other weighted, so that it will shriek when the cylinder is turned with a crank. An electric motor, or vacuum cleaner, operated at varying speeds with a rheostat, makes a fairly good substitute. Rain can be suggested with pebbles or shot in a round wooden cheese box. Hoof-beats are easily simulated with two blocks of wood. Automobile horns are usually the real thing. These and other off-stage effects are quite commonly operated too close to be convincing; the sound of an automobile too often bursts on the ear suddenly and obtrusively, and even when a real motor is used it does not sound real. A great many off-stage effects are mere stunts, and are unnecessary to the dramatic purpose; such effects might well be dispensed with. When effects are necessary they should be muffled or removed to a distance; the best place for an automobile supposed to be heard from the street is *in* the street, with the stage door slightly open.

COSTUMES

There is far more joy in amateur play production if the costumes, as well as the properties, are designed and made by the group. Certain articles, of course, cannot readily be made by novices, and have to be rented or borrowed—men's tailored suits, military uniforms, fine brocaded gowns, and so on. But most of the costumes for symbolic or fantastic plays can be made quite satisfactorily, and out of comparatively inexpensive materials. Skill in dyeing and decorating, together with skill in stage lighting, can make cheap fabrics look like silk and velvet.

In the selection of costumes the director should be clear about his motives. Costume may be realistically representative of a character, a type, a social caste, a race, a country, or a period of history—or any, or all of these things; or it may be stylistic, or expressionistic, or symbolic, or merely decorative. Some of these motives may be combined, but others are inconsistent and contradictory. The motives should be determined first, and should be determined for the whole play, before any individual costumes are designed.

To represent realistically a period other than our own the designer must have accurate information, and until very recently that has been rather hard to get. Historical costuming used to be done very crudely. Most of the costumers who rented to amateurs had large stocks representing just a few periods—the Greek and Roman, the Elizabethan, the Colonial, the Civil War, and the modern. One hired costumes, let us say, for *Hamlet*, and in due time returned them. A month later he desired costumes for a medieval fantasy like *The Man Who Married a Dumb Wife*, and the costumer would send him the same costumes. The costumer had no standard except stage custom, and the amateur had no means of knowing when he was being fooled. Books on costume were expensive, and hard to find, except in the largest libraries; most of them were in foreign languages, and very poorly illustrated. Now, however, there are several readily available and relatively inexpensive books, clearly illustrated and very helpful. At the same time the audiences have learned to demand more accurate costuming, for they have been witnessing historical moving pictures the producers of which have spent thousands of dollars in research. The little theatre director, if he attempts historical costuming in a realistic way, must expect, therefore, to take pains.

For fanciful or poetic costume plays, however, literal accuracy is seldom necessary. Effective stylization or intelligible symbolism is usually better. But to catch the particular flavor of a period, or to express a particular mood, in costume, requires both knowledge and judgement. The director should not only study the history of costume, but should analyze it philosophically, and in this he will get little help from the books, and less from the historians than from the anthropologists. Man's notion of what constitutes appropriate dress, in different periods and on different occasions, is a very important key to his thought and culture, and so to the essential elements of drama.

In designing costumes it is exceedingly important to choose the colors wisely. Each costume should be appropriate in color, as well as in line, to the particular character, and mood, and theme, and at the same time it should fit in decoratively with the color scheme of the stage picture as a whole. To take care of this adequately is no small task, especially if changing colored lights are to be used. Knowledge and theory will help one to avoid the worst mistakes, but only actual experiment with fabrics and lights will finally solve the problem. One way of solving it is to drape the uncut fabrics on the actors at the first stage rehearsal, and try out the lights. Another is to make all the costumes in white and then dye them the desired colors after the stage pictures have been worked out. Even if this is not done, it is well to have a supply of dyes on hand for making last-minute corrections of color, and some member of the group should be delegated to make a special study of dyes and dyeing processes. Commercial dyes put up in small packages usually carry printed instructions, but if dyestuffs are purchased in large quantities without such instructions the purchaser will need to know what he is about. The best dyes for silk do not work on cotton, and vice versa; and the very finest dyes for deep, rich effects under artificial light fade rapidly under sunlight, and will not do for outdoor performances. Flat colors obtained with single dyes are not the most pleasing on the stage; better effects are obtained by several dippings in different colors.

Every director should know something about the æsthetics, as well as the physics, of color. There are two approaches to this study. One, the psychological, is based largely on the idea that color affects us associatively; that red is exciting because it is the color of blood and the symbol of danger; that blue is pleasing because it is the color of the clear sky, and green because it is the color of living vegetation; that black is the color of night, and fear, and sadness, and yellow the jaundiced color, and so on. Such associations are inescapable, and there is a great deal of truth in color psychology; but its importance has been somewhat exaggerated, and some writers have indulged in rather far-fetched attempts to establish a mood for every color, and a color for every mood. The other approach is more directly scientific, and is based on the theory of color itself. It is admirably explained and illustrated by Michel Jacobs in his book on *The Art of Color*.

For the study of color harmonies and contrasts it is convenient to arrange the three primary colors and their opposites, or complementaries, in the form of a wheel (Figure 33), and to indicate the intermediate colors by subdivision. A color wheel of twenty-four hues is adequate for most purposes.

Color harmony is obtained by the use of adjacent, or nearly adjacent, hues, as they appear on the wheel. Color contrast is obtained by the use of a color and its complementary. Both harmonies and contrasts are pleasing, if used in proper proportion, but there is a difference between a contrast and a clash. Colors approximately ninety degrees apart on the color wheel give the worst clashes.

Unmodified hues, either in contrast or in harmony, are crude and barbaric, though effective enough for certain purposes. For more subtle contrasts and harmonies, neutralized or partly neutralized colors are used. A neutralized color is one with which a portion of its complementary has been mixed; a little of the complementary softens it and makes it

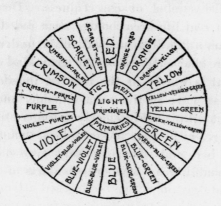

FIG. 33.—COLOR WHEEL

less garish; a little more darkens it; and an equal mixture blacks it out. Colors can also be softened by tinting; that is, by lightening them off with white. The best painters use no black pigments, depending for their darker effects upon neutralized colors.

Some of the most beautiful color effects are obtained by using two or three adjacent or harmonious colors, each partly neutralized, together with the complementary of the middle color, also partly neutralized; or if two basic colors are used, the complementary may be a "split" complementary—that is, a color between the complementaries of the two basic colors.

In considering the psychological effect of color, the director should remember that there are certain associations connected with the theatre itself which are especially apt to influence an audience. Real moonlight is yellow, but in the theatre moonlight has been blue for so many years that we should not recognize it in any other color. Yellow light outdoors, in the daytime, creates an ominous dread, foretelling an uncanny storm of some kind, but yellow light on the stage is accepted as the symbol of cheerfulness. Demure, modest young girls in real life occasionally wear red dresses, but if an actress wears a red dress she will not be understood to represent a demure character. Costume has a kind of established symbolism that is purely of the theatre, in addition to any meaning it may have in the world outside, and not always quite consistent with it. The elderly dowager still wears gray silk on the stage, with skirts to her ankles, though the actress who portrays her, and who is perhaps even older than the character, probably wears knee-length skirts of Alice blue on the street.

MAKE-UP

The most important thing that can be said about make-up for amateurs is that most of them use too much.

The books on make-up, with one or two recent exceptions, follow the practice of the professional stage in the period of brightest lights and largest theatres, when it was practically necessary for an actor to rebuild his face in bright colored grease paints in order to counteract the glare of the footlights and produce an effect at a distance.

With the smaller theatres and more subdued lights of today very little make-up is needed except for character purposes. For straight parts, unless the actor's face needs actual correction, only enough is needed to restore the natural hues and shadows under the lighting conditions of the particular scene. One director, asked by a young actress how much make-up to use for a certain part, replied: "About half as much as you use on the street." The advice would hold good for many parts, and for many young actresses. An overdose of lipstick and rouge is one of the most serious obstacles to the right kind of empathic response on the part of the audience.

There are three general types of straight make-ups: the full grease make-up, the dry make-up, and the mere touch-up.

For the full grease make-up the actor first applies cold cream, rubs it well into the skin, and then wipes it off thoroughly. He uses a ground color of grease paint, light or dark according to the character, and to the lighting effects to be used; this he heats until it is soft, and applies generously to the whole face, neck, and ears, and if necessary to the hands and arms. He then heightens the color of his cheeks with red grease paint, blending it gradually with the ground color; sometimes he uses red also on the forehead, or chin, or nose, or neck, for individual character effect. It is usually necessary to darken the eyelids slightly to restore the natural shadows killed by the footlights. The face is then dusted with powder to set the grease paint and dull the surface; and as the powders change color somewhat when applied, and do so differently on different skins, nothing but experiment will tell the actor what color to use. A lining pencil is then used on the eyelids and eyebrows, black for the eyelids, and black or brown for the eyebrows, according to the general complexion. A dot of carmine at the inner corner of the eye brightens it up a little, as does the laborious process of beading the eyelashes, but neither is worth while unless bright lights are to be used. Wrinkles are also put in with a lining pencil, or with a lining stub dipped in black, brown, or blue grease paint; the proper color is a matter of dispute among actors, and depends somewhat upon lighting conditions, but it may be useful to remember that a shadow on any color goes toward its complementary. Even with a full make-up the process is not an established ritual, as some of the books seem to imply; there are many variations of method, and many different ways of getting good results. There is only one test of a good make-up, and that is its appearance on the stage under actual lighting conditions. The advantage claimed for the full grease make-up is that it blends consistently and is easily managed to give any desired effect in any known light. Its obvious disadvantage is that it encases the fact in a mask and interferes with the play of facial expression. Incidentally, it is messy, soils the linen and even the outer clothing, and is hard to touch up if damaged.

The powder make-up is managed in the same way, except that the grease foundation is omitted, and dry rouge substituted for the red grease on the cheeks. The cold cream may be used beforehand, and unless it is used the powder make-up is apt to be blotchy and hard to get off; but the cream should be wiped off thoroughly before the powder is applied. At best the powder make-up is dependent upon the quality of the actor's skin. On a smooth soft skin it blends evenly, is less obtrusive, and is altogether preferable to the grease make-up except in one respect: the perspiration comes through it more easily, and it needs more frequent touching up. On a rough or uneven skin it is more difficult to manage than the grease make-up.

For most amateur purposes in small theatres a full make-up is not necessary. On anything but a very florid skin some heightening of color is usually necessary unless the lights are to be very dull; but a little dry rouge is often enough. The girls will usually want to pencil their eyebrows, and perhaps to bead their eyelashes, and if the footlights are the chief source of light the shadows under the eyebrows will have to be restored. But a very little make-up judiciously applied and smoothly blended is generally more effective than a full mask of color, and does not interfere with the facial expression.

The director should take particular pains to see that there is uniformity in the make-ups—not uniformity of method, necessarily, but uniformity of effect. It is always bad to have one member of the cast made up as if for the stage of the Metropolitan Opera, while another has but a shading of rouge; or to have some players made up realistically and others stylistically. There is a strong tendency among the men to use too dark a powder, and among the women to use dead white. There should be some difference in color between the sexes, but not too much. Nearly all amateurs of both sexes use too much lipstick.

For character make-ups, wigs, crêpe hair, nose putty, and lining pencils are the chief instruments. Wigs should be avoided as much as possible, since they must usually be hired, and seldom fit well. The joints of bald-headed wigs are especially troublesome. No cold cream or grease paint must be allowed to get under the edge of the wig, or the joint will slip constantly. Often the hired wig is already greasy on the under side; it should be cleaned with high test gasoline in time to dry thoroughly before being worn. A little spirit gum may be used under the edge. After the edge is firmly fastened the grease paint may be rubbed over the joint, and a coat of powder applied.

Crêpe hair is usually applied too hastily. The spirit gum should be allowed to set a moment or two, and become tacky. A quantity of hair should be clipped from the braid in lengths of an eighth of an inch or less; this should be gathered in a wad and dabbed on the tacky spirit gum, until it gives the effect of a stubby beard or mustache. If a longer beard or mustache is required, a quantity of longer hair should be pulled out and loosely matted, and then applied over the stubble with a second coat of spirit gum. This gives a more natural effect than if the matted hair is applied directly, and the hair is less likely to come off. The whole may be trimmed with the scissors when the gum has dried. For very long beards which must bear close inspection it is usually best to depend upon the wig-maker.

Nose putty should be applied to the dry skin before any cold cream or grease paint has been used. Some actors first apply spirit gum, and then a little loose cotton, to serve as an anchorage. The fingers must be kept moist while the putty is being molded. Putty noses are always a little risky, and should be used only when really needed.

Character lines are the real test of the actor's skill in make-up. Some of the books advise the beginner to study photographs and practice copying them in make-up; but nothing is more difficult to read for lines than a photograph. It is far better to follow crayon or pen sketches, caricatures, or cartoons, picking out the significant lines and practicing with them in exaggerated form until a measure of skill is acquired. There has been a tendency in the non-realistic theatre to experiment with grotesque, or symbolic, or stylized make-up; and if such experiment bears no other fruit it will at least serve to demonstrate the significance of certain bold lines in establishing character or expression.

Nobody can learn make-up by reading about it; the thing is to procure the materials and practice. It is not a matter of formula, but of skill, experience, taste, and judgement. Elaborate equipment will not do the trick, nor is it always necessary. One of the best make-ups I ever saw was improvised at a seashore resort out of talcum powder, a burnt cork, a match stick, a piece of manila rope dyed in a mixture of coffee and ink, and some liquid court plaster. The match stick and the burnt cork supplied the lines, and the rope was turned into a fine pair of side-whiskers, fastened with the liquid court plaster; and when the impersonator appeared in a room full of guests he was promptly mistaken for the local minister—somewhat to that gentleman's annoyance.

It is highly desirable for each actor to learn to make himself up, subject to inspection by the director; but the actor who practices only on himself labors under a disadvantage. He cannot check up on his own work. He cannot see himself at a distance, under the conditions of actual stage lighting. He should seek, therefore, all possible criticism of his work from those who can see him from out front, and every opportunity to make others up, and to watch the results.

THE CURTAIN

And now, before we ring it down, let us give some attention to that very important item of theatrical equipment, the curtain.

The curtain, like everything else in the established theatre, has been under fire in recent years. Some critics, on the theory that it represents a fourth wall removed, have wanted to correct the evil by removing the curtain. Others have objected, not to the curtain, but to the method of operation, having made the astonishing discovery that when the curtain is raised the actor is disclosed feet first, and when it is lowered his head is cut off before his heels. The Romans, of course, did it the other way, dropping the curtain into a slot at the beginning of the play, and raising it into place at the end; and some critics have wanted to restore the Roman method. In the New York Hippodrome a curtain is actually used which rises from the bottom, but the motive is a purely practical one. A semi-cylindrical curtain is required to conceal the whole of a huge apron, and it is more convenient to drop it out of sight when not in use than to haul it up to the roof of the auditorium. There is no gain in unobtrusiveness, however—which is presumably what we are seeking; nor is there any gain in logic. It is just as absurd to cut off the actor's feet as his head; moreover, the rising curtain gives a curious sensation of seeing the actor swallowed up in a cave-in or quicksand. Most of the objectors to the drop curtain, therefore, have advocated, not a rising curtain, but draw curtains.

Draw curtains, as we know, are more informal, and more suggestive of real life; and their advocates point out that these make no discrimination between the actor's head and his feet. But they fail to note the appalling fact that draw curtains do discriminate between the actor's right hand and his left, and that at a certain instant only half of the actor may be visible to the audience; the poor fellow may be split right up the middle! This has led a few adventurous souls to propose a more revolutionary scheme: a curtain opening like the iris of a camera, in all directions at once, and from a central point. The mechanical difficulty has prevented any serious attempt to put it into practice; but the same purpose can be achieved, much less obtrusively, by another moving picture device: the "fade-in." With the house lights out, the curtain can be taken up unseen, and then the lights can be fed in slowly with the dimmers, beginning with the spotlights focussed on the center of interest. This was done in *Johannes Kreisler*, for example; and also—somewhat unexpectedly— in Gillette's 1923 revival of his *Sherlock Holmes*.

There is much to be said for the use of lights in lieu of a curtain, provided they can be controlled perfectly; they are silent, sure, and intensely spiritual. But there is little merit in the attempt to replace the conventional drop curtain with queer mechanical devices, or even with draw curtains. The curtain has no significance of its own; its purpose is concealment and revelation at the proper times, with the least possible distraction. Any kind of curtain that moves swiftly and silently, and without calling attention to itself, is good; and any kind that is awkward, or noisy, or obtrusive in any way, is bad.

Amateurs must often use draw curtains as a matter of necessity, no regular curtain, and no space for one, being available. But draw curtains are just as distracting to the eye as a drop curtain, and are usually far more distracting to the ear. A drop curtain, if properly rigged, can be raised or lowered silently, surely, and at any desired speed, and if the spectator is in any danger of meditating too extensively on the actor's feet, speed is the best corrective. I have yet to see a set of draw curtains that operate silently. Most of them scrape and rattle, move jerkily, stick occasionally, and fail to close completely in the middle.

To those who wish to establish a formal stage with no curtain at all, I have nothing to say. There is a place for the formal stage. But those who try to persuade the builders of little theatres to install rich, beautiful draw curtains, as being more refined, more cozy, more artistic than a drop curtain, are leading them straight into error. The drop curtain can be made as refined and beautiful as any draw curtain; its descent at the end of the play is as logical as the falling shades of night; and its silent efficiency is one of the most comforting experiences in the theatre.

BIBLIOGRAPHY

THE following list of references is not intended to be exhaustive in any sense; only a few of the most useful and most readily available works are included, and only those in the English language. Most of the books mentioned are in print, and the one or two that are not are in most of the public and college libraries. No references are given in the field of dramatic literature; for that subject the reader is referred to other volumes in the present series.

GENERAL WORKS ON PLAY PRODUCTION

TAYLOR, EMERSON. Practical Stage Directing for Amateurs. (Dutton, 1923)
The first and best of the very short and very general books.

SMITH, MILTON M. The Book of Play Production. (Appleton, 1926)
The most comprehensive of the elementary books, especially on stagecraft.

STRATTON, CLARENCE. Producing in Little Theatres. (Holt, 1921)
Many illustrations of amateur settings. Good chapters on rehearsing.

MITCHELL, ROY. Shakespeare for Community Players. (Dent-Dutton, 1919)
More comprehensive than the title suggests. Good chapters on properties, costumes, and arras settings; also on rehearsing.

DRUMMOND, A. M. Play Production for the Country Theatre (Cornell Bulletin, 1924)
Elementary, but extremely practical. By a specialist in country theatre work. Especially valuable for those who must work with little equipment.

BOSWORTH, HALLAM. Technique in Dramatic Art. (Macmillan, 1926)
Chapters on directing, stagecraft, and management, but largely a discussion of acting.

DEAN, ALEXANDER. Little Theatre Organization and Management. (Appleton, 1926)
A very practical discussion by a successful organizer.

BIBLIOGRAPHY

CLARK, BARRETT. How to Produce Amateur Plays. (Little, Brown, 1921, 1927)
Very elementary, but has some good material on rehearsing.

WISE, CLAUDE M. Dramatics for School and Community. (Stewart Kidd, 1923)
Elementary. Accent on educational dramatics. Lengthy bibliographies.

ÆSTHETICS AND DESIGN

ARISTOTLE. Poetics.
A natural starting point for the student.

BOSANQUET, BERNARD. A History of Æsthetic. (Sonnenschein, 1910)
A readable and comprehensive account.

HEGEL, GEORGE WILHELM FRIEDERICH. Introduction to the Philosophy of Fine Art. (Trans. Bosanquet) (Paul, 1886)
The starting point in modern æsthetics.

SANTAYANA, GEORGE. The Sense of Beauty. (Scribner, 1896)
One of the most interesting discussions.

PUFFER, ETHEL. The Psychology of Beauty. (Houghton Mifflin, 1905)
A standard textbook, emphasizing the theory of repose.

LANGFELD, HERBERT S. The Æsthetic Attitude. (Harcourt, Brace, 1920)
The most helpful single book on æsthetics for the stage director.

FLACCUS, LOUIS WILLIAM. The Spirit and Substance of Art. (Crofts, 1926)
A new philosophical treatment with much concrete illustration.

BATCHELDER, E. A. Design in Theory and Practice. (Macmillan, 1910)
Practical and interesting. Good treatment of primitive art.

JACOBS, MICHEL. The Art of Colour. (Doubleday, 1926)
Clear, helpful, and generally sound. Beautifully illustrated.

DRAMATIC CONSTRUCTION AND PLAYWRITING

FREYTAG, GUSTAV. The Technique of the Drama. (Trans. McEwen) (Scott, Foresman, 1894)
World-famous, and the basis of most modern works.

ARCHER, WILLIAM. Playmaking. A Manual of Craftsmanship. (Small, Maynard, 1912)
Still one of the best books, and full of hints for the director.

BAKER, GEORGE PIERCE. Dramatic Technique. (Houghton Mifflin, 1919)

Professor Baker's famous course in book form—minus the laboratory work.

MALEVINSKY, M. L. The Science of Playwriting. (Brentano's, 1925)

Interesting, and different. By a man with ideas of his own.

HOPKINS, ARTHUR. How's Your Second Act? (Goodman, 1918)

A penetrating and valuable essay by a practical producer.

LEWIS, B. ROLAND. The Technique of the One Act Play. (Luce, 1918)

The most popular book in this limited special field.

EATON, WALTER PRICHARD. The Art of Playwriting. (Harper. In preparation.)

THE THEORY OF ACTING

(Books on the subject of acting are numerous, but very few are really helpful.)

ARCHER, WILLIAM. Masks or Faces? (London, Longmans, 1888)

A digest of many opinions, and the most valuable book on acting.

CALVERT, LOUIS. Problems of the Actor. (Holt, 1918)

Probably the best book on acting by an actor.

HORNBLOW, ARTHUR. Training for the Stage. (Lippincott, 1916)

Elementary advice for the ambitious actor, much of it very practical.

YOUNG, STARK. Theatre Practice. (Scribner, 1926)

A general discussion of the theatre, but the best chapters are those on acting.

LEWES, GEORGE HENRY. On Actors and the Art of Acting. (Brentano's, n.d.)

A penetrating analysis of many of the best actors of the nineteenth century. Old, but still valuable.

(For other discussions of acting see the publications of the Dramatic Museum of Columbia University, especially WILLIAM GILLETTE's article on "The Illusion of the First Time," and the articles by COQUELIN, IRVING, BOUCICAULT, TALMA, and other actors. Numerous articles are to be found also in the periodicals mentioned below. Bits of very valuable material are tucked away in the biographies and autobiographies of actors and managers, of which there are literally hundreds. Among the best are those of CLARA MORRIS, MACREADY, SALVINI, FORREST, MRS. SIDDONS, BETTERTON, (by Lowe) GARRICK, (several), AUGUSTIN DALY, LESTER WALLACK, JOHN DREW, OTIS

BIBLIOGRAPHY

SKINNER, and STANISLAVSKY. Many of the books listed below on theatre history contain side lights on the philosophy of acting.)

THEATRICAL HISTORY AND SCENIC ART

MANTZIUS, KARL. A History of Theatrical Art. (Duckworth-Lippincott, 1903-09)

Not a piece of exact scholarship, but the most comprehensive work available in English. Six volumes of valuable information. Illustrated.

NICOLL, ALLARDYCE. The Development of the Theatre. (Harcourt, 1927)

A scholarly history of theatrical architecture and scenic art in one large volume, profusely illustrated. Contains a tremendous bibliography, especially rich in foreign references.

CHENEY, SHELDON. Stage Decoration. (Day, 1927)

Historical and analytical discussion, with 256 illustrations. Covers ancient and modern scenic art, but gives more space to the modern.

HAIGH, ARTHUR E. The Attic Theatre. (Oxford, 1907)

Standard, and widely read. Contains many statements disputed by later writers.

FLICKINGER, ROY C. The Greek Theatre and Its Drama. (Chicago Press, 1922)

More general, but reports the result of later researches.

ALLEN, JAMES TURNEY. Stage Antiquities. (Longmans, 1927)

A most useful handbook, reporting briefly but accurately the existing knowledge on the Greek and Roman theatres.

SMITH, WINIFRED. The Commedia dell' Arte. (Columbia Press, 1912)

The most complete work in English on this interesting subject.

BROADBENT, R. J. A History of Pantomime. (Simpkin, Marshall, 1901)

More general. Covers the Harlequinade and the English Pantomime.

CHAMBERS, SIR E. K. The Medieval Stage. (Oxford, 1903)

The standard work, but more concerned with the drama than the stage.

CAMPBELL, LILY B. Scenes and Machines on the English Stage During the Renaissance. (Macmillan, 1923)

Scholarly and comprehensive. Covers the Renaissance theatre.

CHAMBERS, SIR E. K. The Elizabethan Stage. (Oxford, 1923)

A companion work to the one on the *Medieval Stage*. More about the theatre.

ADAMS, JOSEPH QUINCY. Shakespearean Playhouses. (Houghton Mifflin, 1917)
The most complete study of stage arrangements and equipment in Shakespeare's time.

THORNDIKE, ASHLEY H. Shakespeare's Theatre. (Macmillan, 1925)
Less comprehensive, but later, and contains good bibliography.

WALLACE, CHARLES WILLIAM. The Children of the Chapel at Blackfriars. (U. of Nebraska)
An intense piece of scholarship, containing most of the trustworthy knowledge on the Blackfriars Theatre.

THALER, ALVIN. Shakespeare to Sheridan. (Harvard Press, 1922)
Primarily on the drama, but covers also the stage methods of the period.

WATSON, ERNEST B. Sheridan to Robertson. (Harvard Press, 1926)
A companion volume.

DORAN, JOHN. Annals of the English Stage. (Widdleton, 1865)
Contains chapters on theatres and audiences, as well as accounts of the famous actors. Not very accurate.

ODELL, GEORGE C. D. Shakespeare from Betterton to Irving. (Scribner, 1920)
Follows the changing methods of production through two centuries.

CRAIG, EDWARD GORDON. On the Art of the Theatre. (Small, Maynard, 1924. Re-ed.)
The prophetic book which stirred up much of the modern discussion.

CRAIG, EDWARD GORDON. Towards a New Theatre. (Dutton, 1913)
A book of designs for the theatre, with stimulating comment.

CRAIG, EDWARD GORDON. The Theatre—Advancing. (Little, Brown, 1919)
More comment, not always consistent with that in the first book.

CRAIG, EDWARD GORDON. Scene. (Oxford, 1923)
More designs.

WAXMAN, S. M. Antoine and the Théâtre Libre. (Harvard Press, 1926)
Covers the beginning of the new movement in the French theatre.

MODERWELL, HIRAM K. The Theatre of Today. (Dodd, Mead, 1914, 1924)
The first comprehensive account of the modern movement, especially in the Continental theatres. Extremely valuable. Well illustrated.

MACGOWAN, KENNETH. The Theatre of Tomorrow. (Boni, 1921)
Reviews what Moderwell covered, and adds much stimulating discussion and prophecy. Beautifully illustrated.

BIBLIOGRAPHY

MACGOWAN, KENNETH, and JONES, ROBERT EDMUND. Continental Stagecraft. (Harcourt, 1922)
The record of a summer in the European theatres. Illustrated by Jones.

BELASCO, DAVID. The Theatre Through Its Stage Door. (Harper, 1919)
Informative, and ably representative of the realistic viewpoint.

CHENEY, SHELDON. The New Movement in the Theatre. (Kennerley, 1914)
Special attention to stage decoration.

CHENEY, SHELDON. The Art Theatre. (Knopf, 1917, 1925)
A review of the art theatres of Europe and America. The later edition brings the record up to 1925.

CARTER, HUNTLY. The New Spirit in Drama and Art. (Kennerley, 1913)
Rather general, and out of date, but still interesting.

CARTER, HUNTLY. The Theatre of Max Reinhardt. (Kennerley, 1913)
An excellent account of Reinhardt's earlier work.

SAYLER, OLIVER. Max Reinhardt and His Theatre. (Brentano's, 1924)
A compilation of articles by various authors.

SAYLER, OLIVER. The Russian Theatre (Brentano's, 1922)
A full account of the modern theatre in Russia, including the Moscow Art Theatre.

STANISLAVSKY, CONSTANTIN. My Life in Art. (Little, Brown, 1924)
An autobiography, but also a history of the Moscow Art Theatre.

BAKSHY, ALEXANDER. The Path of the Modern Russian Stage. (Luce, 1918)
A more general account, including a discussion of the Russian ballet.

GRANVILLE-BARKER, HARLEY. The Exemplary Theatre. (Little, Brown, 1922)
A stimulating philosophical discussion of the modern theatre.

ISAACS, EDITH J. R. (Editor) Theatre. (Little, Brown, 1927)
A compilation of leading articles from the files of *Theatre Arts*.

ZUCKER, ADOLPH E. The Chinese Theatre. (Little, Brown, 1925)
The best general account of the world's oldest theatrical tradition.

KINCAID, ZOË. Kabuki, the Popular Stage of Japan. (Macmillan, 1925)
Not a complete account of the Japanese theatre, but the most useful available book in the field.

GAMBLE, WILLIAM BURT. The Development of Scenic Art and Stage
Machinery. A list of references in the New York Public
Library. (N. Y. P. L., 1928)
A new and revised edition of the most complete bibliography of the
theatre in existence. Includes articles in periodicals and technical mag-
azines as well as books.

STAGECRAFT

PICHEL, IRVING. Modern Theatres. (Harcourt, Brace, 1925)
The best book on theatre design and construction.

KROWS, ARTHUR EDWIN. Play Production in America. (Holt, 1916)
A complete account of the back-stage methods of the commercial
theatre.

SMITH, ANDRE. The Scenewright. (Macmillan, 1926)
An interesting handbook on the design and construction of stage models
and model scenery.

GRIMBALL, ELIZABETH B., and WELLS, RHEA. Costuming a Play.
(Century, 1925)
The most practical and best illustrated of the smaller books on costume.

SAGE, ELIZABETH. A Study of Costume. (Scribner, 1926)
A somewhat fuller historical account. Good illustrations and short
bibliography.

CHALMERS, HELENA. The Art of Make-Up. (Appleton, 1925)
Probably the best readily available book on this topic.

McCANDLESS, STANLEY R. Glossary of Stage Lighting. (Theatre
Arts, 1927)
A descriptive dictionary of lighting equipment.

LUCKIESH, M. The Lighting Art. (McGraw, Hill, 1917)
By a technical expert in lighting. Includes stage lighting.

(See also the chapters on stagecraft in the various works on play
production listed above.)

VOICE AND DICTION

MURDOCH, JAMES E. The Technique of the Speaking Voice. (Ste-
phens, 1915)
Based on Rush's *Philosophy of the Human Voice*. An old book, but
a good one, by an actor whose own voice was one of the greatest.

CURRY, S. S. Mind and Voice. (Expression Co., 1910)
The safest of the comprehensive books on voice.

BIBLIOGRAPHY

FOWLER, H. W. Modern English Usage. (Oxford, 1926)
A dictionary of disputed points in our language, scholarly, but not pedantic, and intensely readable. A useful supplement to a regular dictionary.

JONES, DANIEL. An English Pronouncing Dictionary. (Dent, 1922)
The strictest of standards for those who wish to follow southern England.

KRAPP, GEORGE PHILIP. Pronunciation of Standard English in America. (Oxford, 1919)
A study of American standards.

(Among ordinary dictionaries the most complete and authoritative is the *Oxford English Dictionary;* but the American *Webster,* in the unabridged form, is entirely trustworthy. The *Standard* presents disputed pronunciations in a separate section, with the votes of other dictionaries, as well as those of its own editors, tabulated for comparison, and this is much more helpful than a single opinion. The phonograph recordings of famous actors and speakers are very helpful in the study of pronunciation and enunciation, especially the ones marketed by Windsor P. Daggett; some of the latter, however, are based on the southern English standard. The student of pronunciation should familiarize himself with the work of the International Phonetic Association, and especially with its alphabet.)

PLAY LISTS

(Play lists are such temporary things that the only practical plan is to renew them frequently by writing to the various publishers. Two books, however, should be mentioned.)

JOHNSON, GERTRUDE E. Choosing a Play. (Century, 1920)
The actual lists are partly out of date, but there are valuable suggestions and items of information.

SHAY, FRANK. One Thousand and One Plays for the Little Theatre. (Stewart Kidd, 1923)
Indispensable, and should be brought up to date. Contains a bibliography of books on the theatre, lists of published plays and collections of plays, and lists of publishers and brokers.

(The catalogues of the principal play publishers—Samuel French, New York, Penn Publishing Co., Philadelphia, Dramatic Publishing Co., Chicago, Walter H. Baker, Boston, Brentano's, New York, and Stewart Kidd, Cincinnati—are readily obtainable. Excellent lists of plays are prepared from time to time by the Drama League and its various centers, by the *Theatre Arts Monthly,* the *Drama,* the *Quarterly Journal of Speech,* and the *English Journal.* Many of the best plays of recent years are held in manuscript, but are obtainable for amateur production on a royalty basis. Lists of plays so held may be had from the American Play Co., New York, Sanger and Jordan, New York, or the Charles Frohman Play Bureau, New York. Longmans, Green, and Co. publish a series of plays with special prompt copies arranged for amateur production. Among the most voluminous publishers of plays and collections of plays in book form are Little, Brown, and Co., Bobbs Merrill Co., Mitchell Kennerley, and Stewart Kidd, in addition to those already mentioned. The *Theatre Arts Monthly* publishes a handy folder containing a list of play brokers, publishers, costumers, scene builders, stage lighting companies, and the like.)

PERIODICALS

The Theatre Arts Monthly. New York.

A magazine of the art theatre, with much attention to scenic investiture. Profusely illustrated. The best magazine for the student.

The Theatre Magazine. New York.

More concerned with the commercial theatre. The only theatrical magazine to be had on the regular news stands.

The Mask. Florence, Italy. (Obtainable through Brentano's)

A quarterly, somewhat like *Theatre Arts*. Founded by Gordon Craig.

The Drama. Chicago.

Official organ of the Drama League of America.

The Quarterly Journal of Speech. Champaign, Ill.

Official organ of the National Association of Teachers of Speech. Devotes considerable space to school and college dramatics.

(Interesting articles on the theatre also appear from time to time in the popular magazines, especially the *Ladies' Home Journal,* the *Woman's Home Companion,* and the *Saturday Evening Post;* also in such technical magazines as the *Architectural Review,* the *American Architect,* the *Builder,* the *Scientific American, Engineering,* the *Engineer,* and the *International Studio.* To keep up to date in theatrical discussion the student should refer constantly to the *Reader's Guide to Periodical Literature,* as well as to one or more of the regular theatrical magazines.)

INDEX

INDEX

INDEX

461

INDEX

465